ALICE *in* BISHOUNEN-LAND

1

Story: **Yushi Kawata** Art: **Yukito**

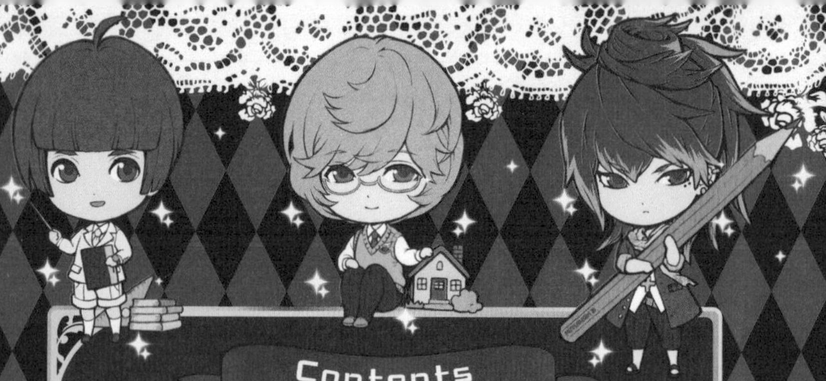

Contents

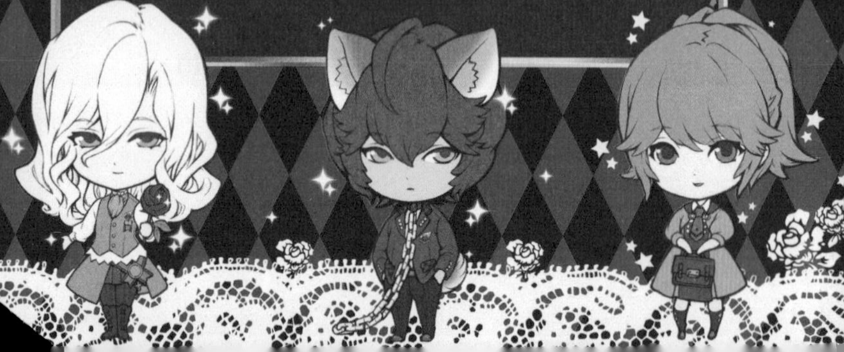

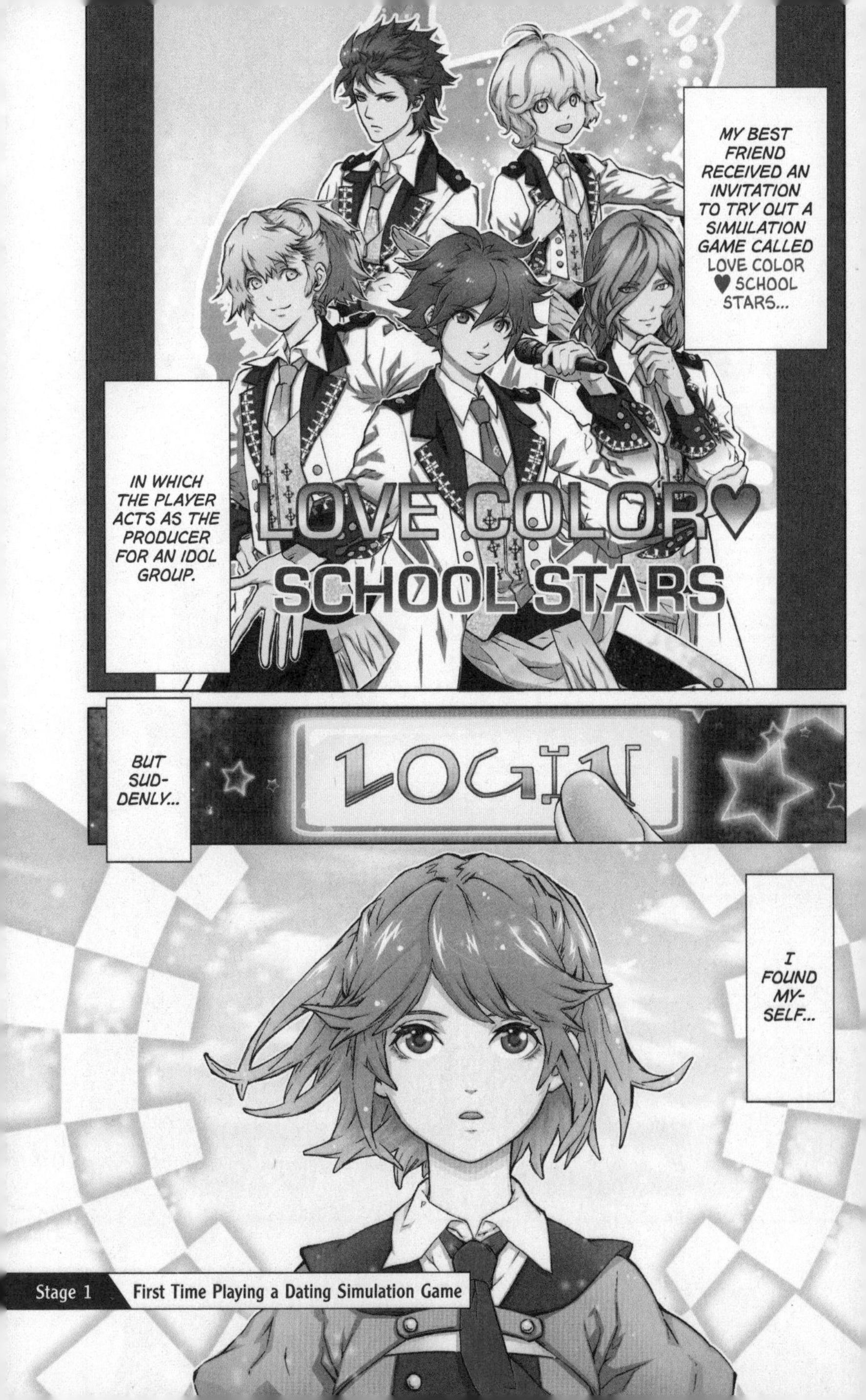
MY BEST FRIEND RECEIVED AN INVITATION TO TRY OUT A SIMULATION GAME CALLED LOVE COLOR ♥ SCHOOL STARS...
LOVE COLOR ♥ SCHOOL STARS
IN WHICH THE PLAYER ACTS AS THE PRODUCER FOR AN IDOL GROUP.
LOGIN
BUT SUD-DENLY...
I FOUND MY-SELF...
Stage 1
First Time Playing a Dating Simulation Game

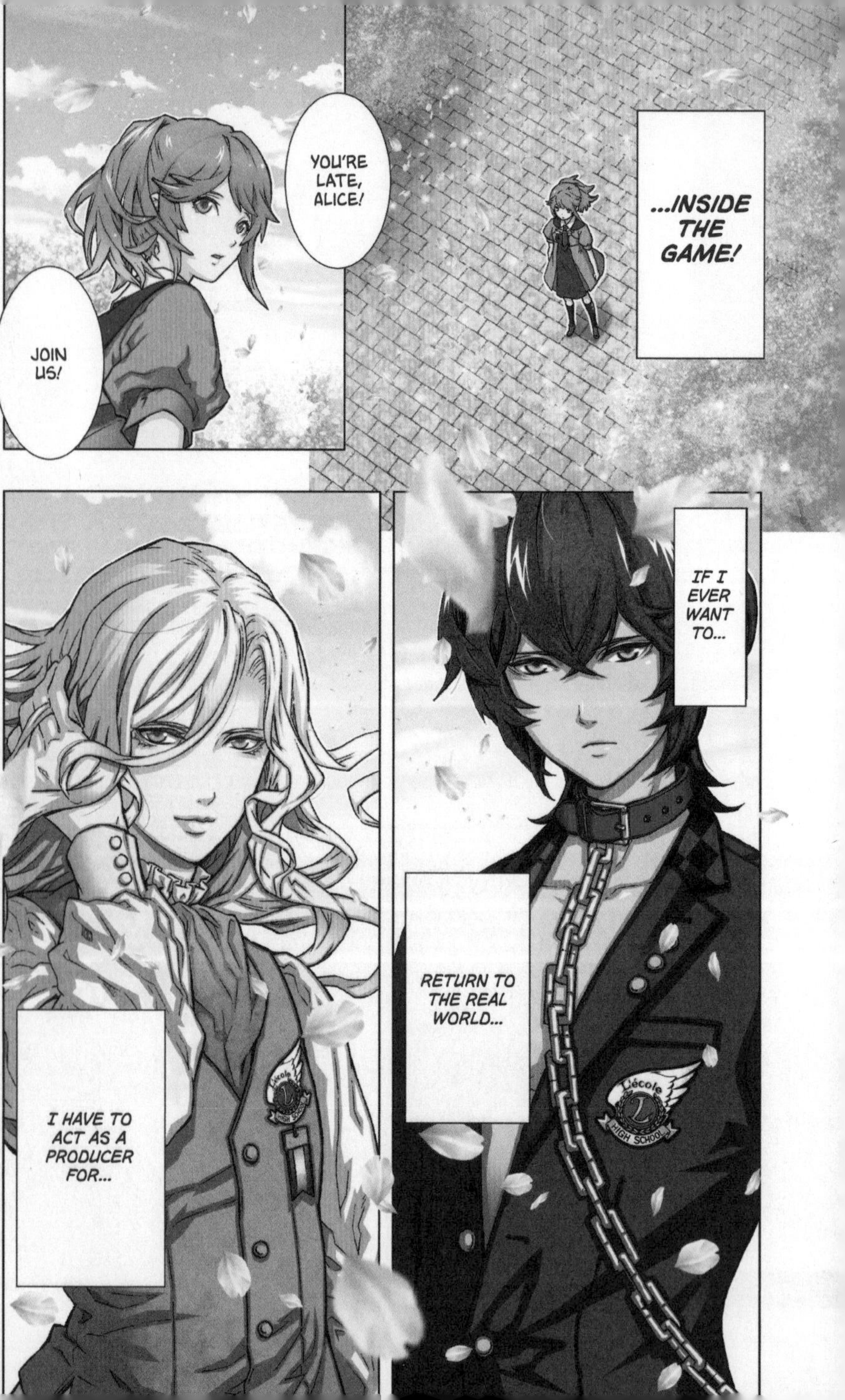
...INSIDE THE GAME!
YOU'RE LATE, ALICE!
JOIN US!
IF I EVER WANT TO...
RETURN TO THE REAL WORLD...
I HAVE TO ACT AS A PRODUCER FOR...

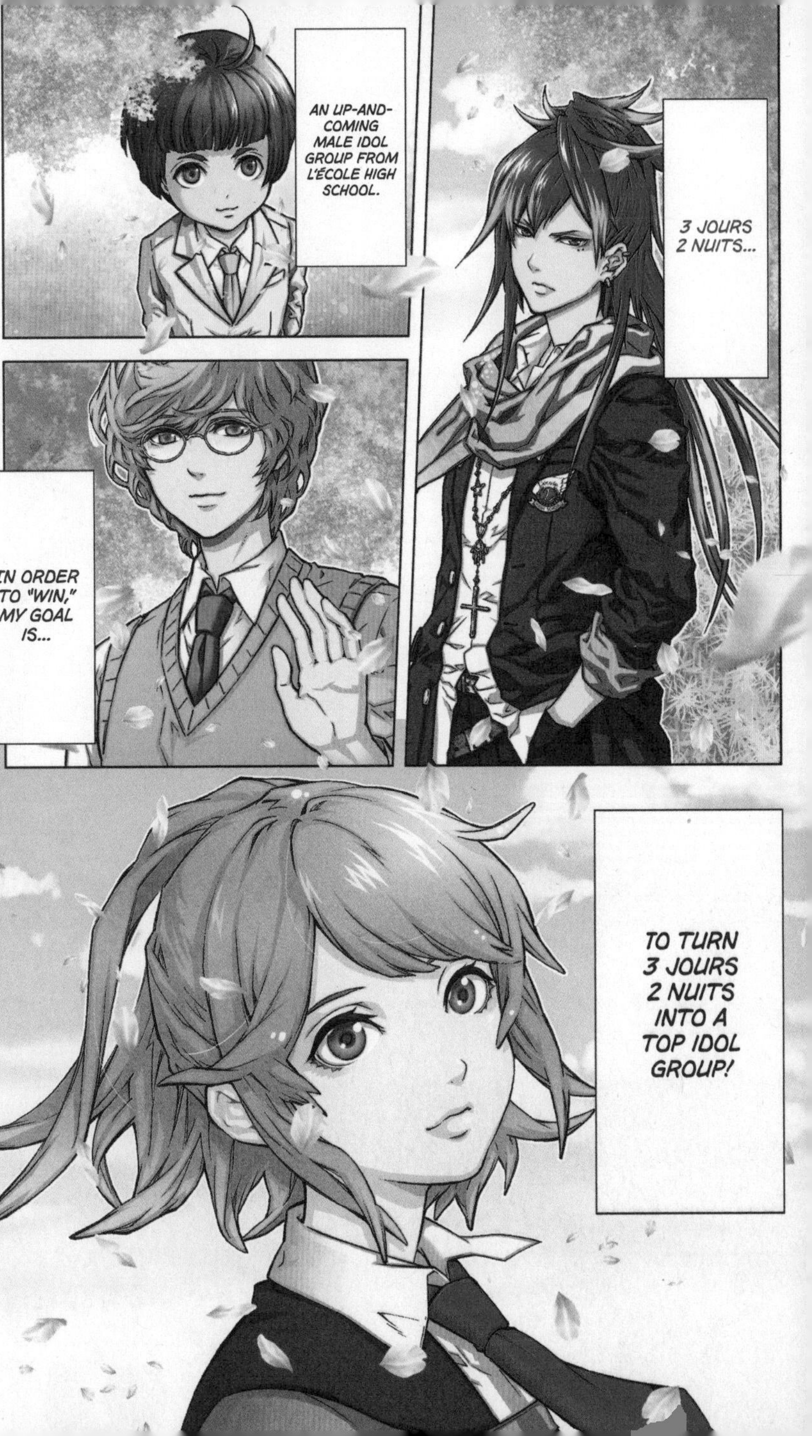
3 JOURS 2 NUITS...
AN UP-AND-COMING MALE IDOL GROUP FROM L'ÉCOLE HIGH SCHOOL.
IN ORDER TO "WIN," MY GOAL IS...
TO TURN 3 JOURS 2 NUITS INTO A TOP IDOL GROUP!

Stage 1

First Time Playing a Dating Simulation Game

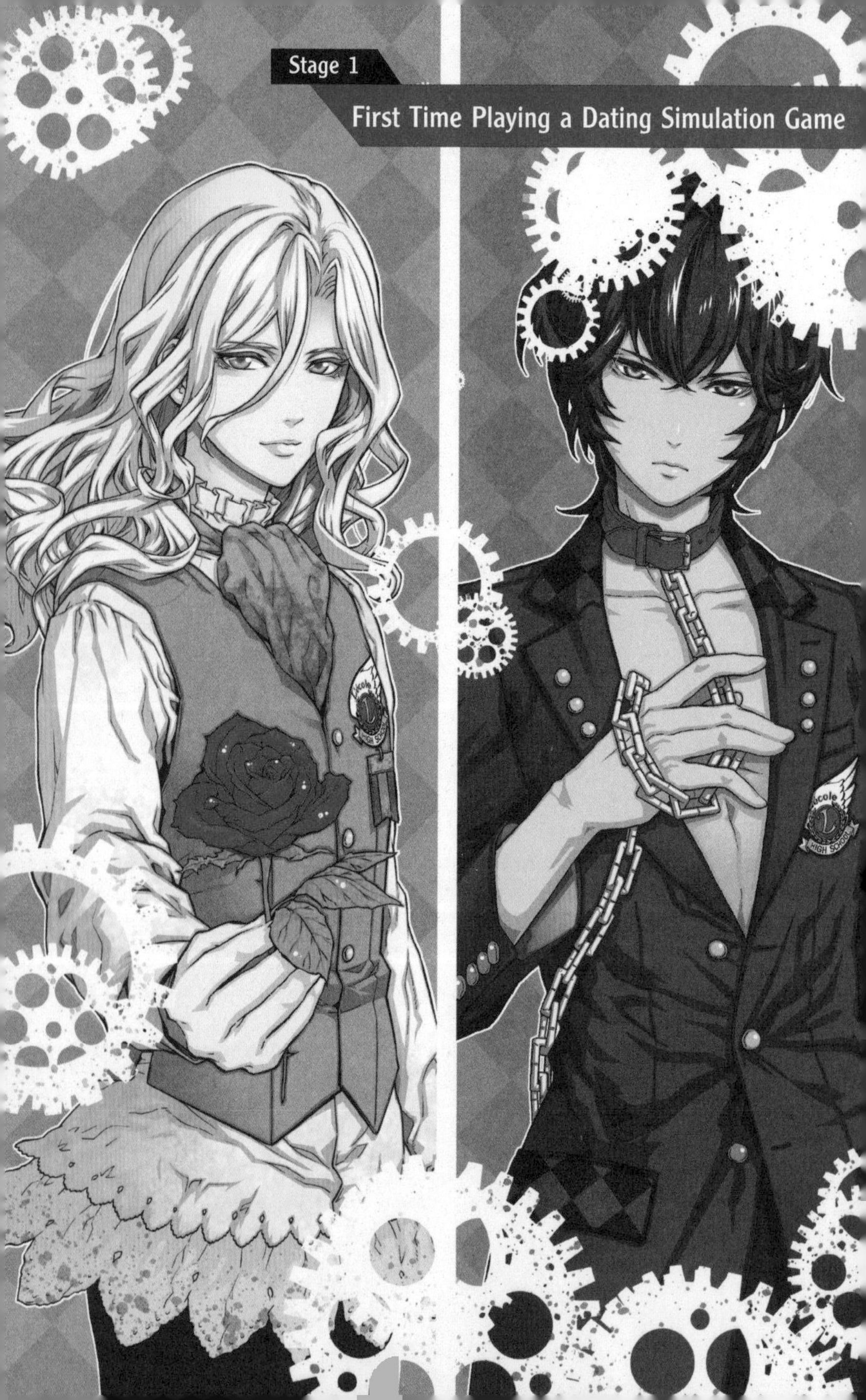

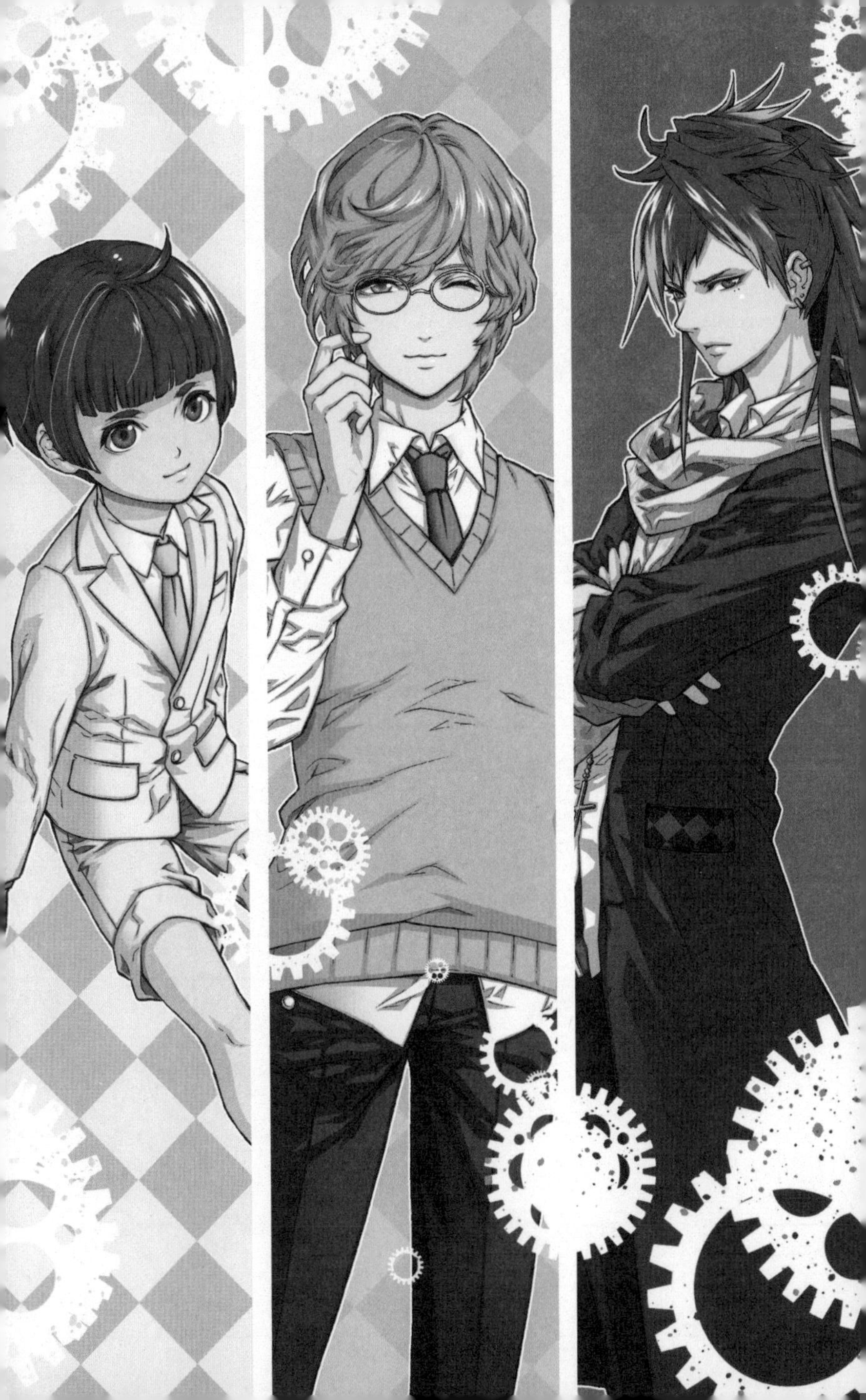

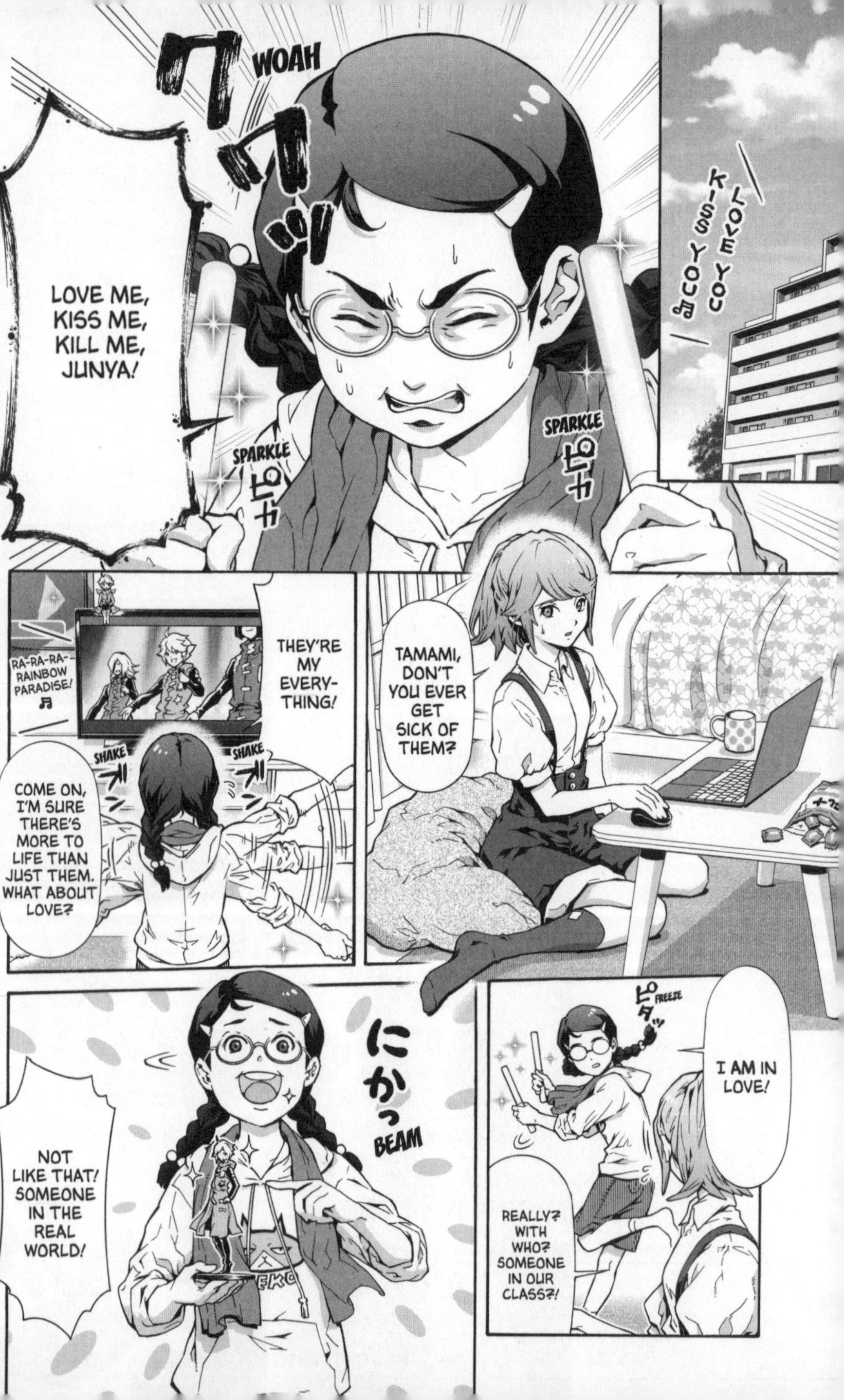
LOVE YOU KISS YOU ♫
WOAH
LOVE ME, KISS ME, KILL ME, JUNYA!
SPARKLE
ピカ
SPARKLE
ピカ
TAMAMI, DON'T YOU EVER GET SICK OF THEM?
THEY'RE MY EVERY-THING!
RA-RA-RA-RAINBOW PARADISE! ♫
SHAKE
SHAKE
COME ON, I'M SURE THERE'S MORE TO LIFE THAN JUST THEM. WHAT ABOUT LOVE?
ピタッ FREEZE
I AM IN LOVE!
REALLY? WITH WHO? SOMEONE IN OUR CLASS?!
にかっ BEAM
NOT LIKE THAT! SOMEONE IN THE REAL WORLD!

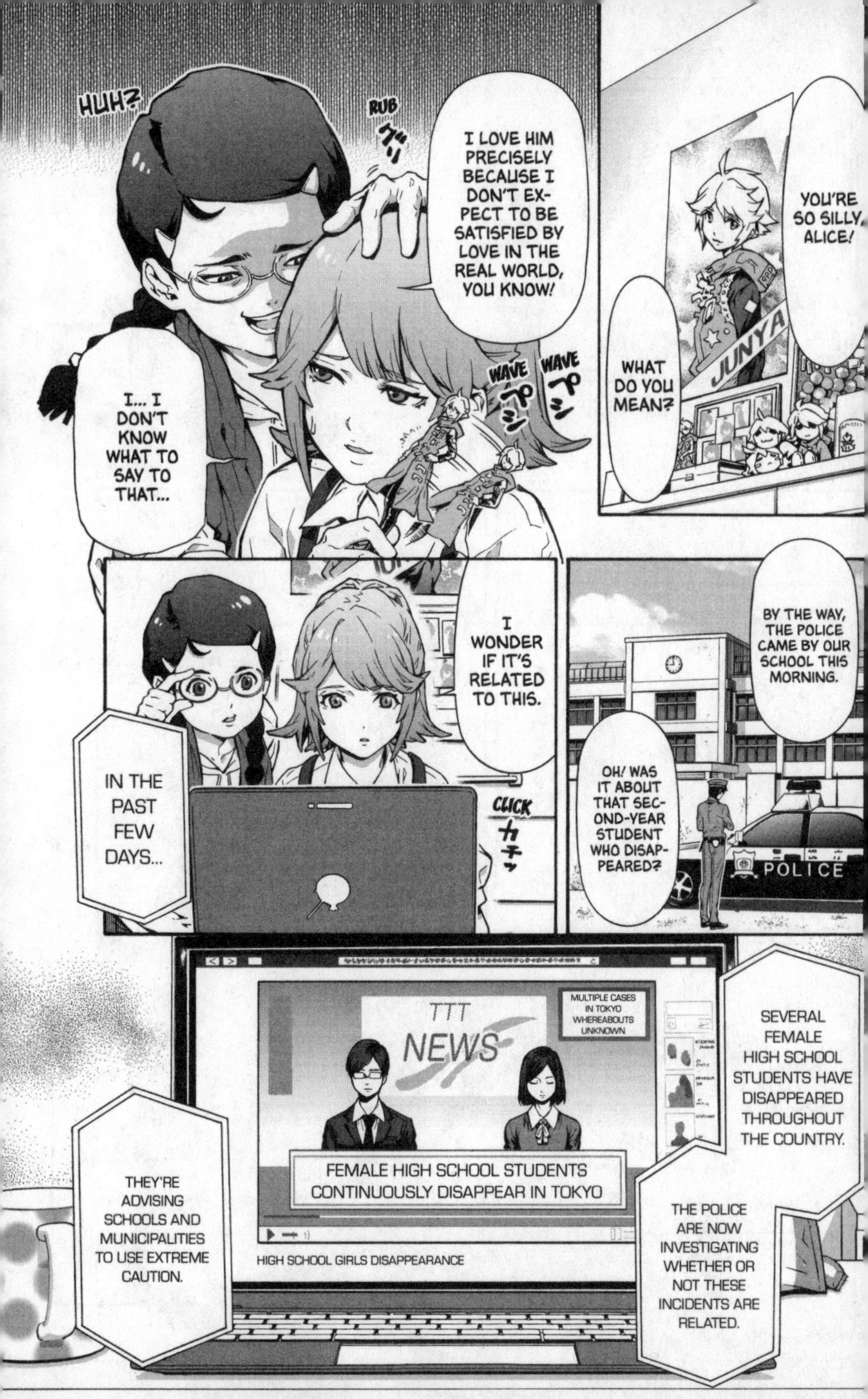

YOU'RE SO SILLY, ALICE!
JUNYA
WHAT DO YOU MEAN?
I LOVE HIM PRECISELY BECAUSE I DON'T EX-PECT TO BE SATISFIED BY LOVE IN THE REAL WORLD, YOU KNOW!
RUB
HUH?
WAVE
WAVE
I... I DON'T KNOW WHAT TO SAY TO THAT...
BY THE WAY, THE POLICE CAME BY OUR SCHOOL THIS MORNING.
OH! WAS IT ABOUT THAT SEC-OND-YEAR STUDENT WHO DISAP-PEARED?
POLICE
I WONDER IF IT'S RELATED TO THIS.
CLICK
IN THE PAST FEW DAYS...
SEVERAL FEMALE HIGH SCHOOL STUDENTS HAVE DISAPPEARED THROUGHOUT THE COUNTRY.
MULTIPLE CASES IN TOKYO WHEREABOUTS UNKNOWN
TTT NEWS
FEMALE HIGH SCHOOL STUDENTS CONTINUOUSLY DISAPPEAR IN TOKYO
HIGH SCHOOL GIRLS DISAPPEARANCE
THE POLICE ARE NOW INVESTIGATING WHETHER OR NOT THESE INCIDENTS ARE RELATED.
THEY'RE ADVISING SCHOOLS AND MUNICIPALITIES TO USE EXTREME CAUTION.

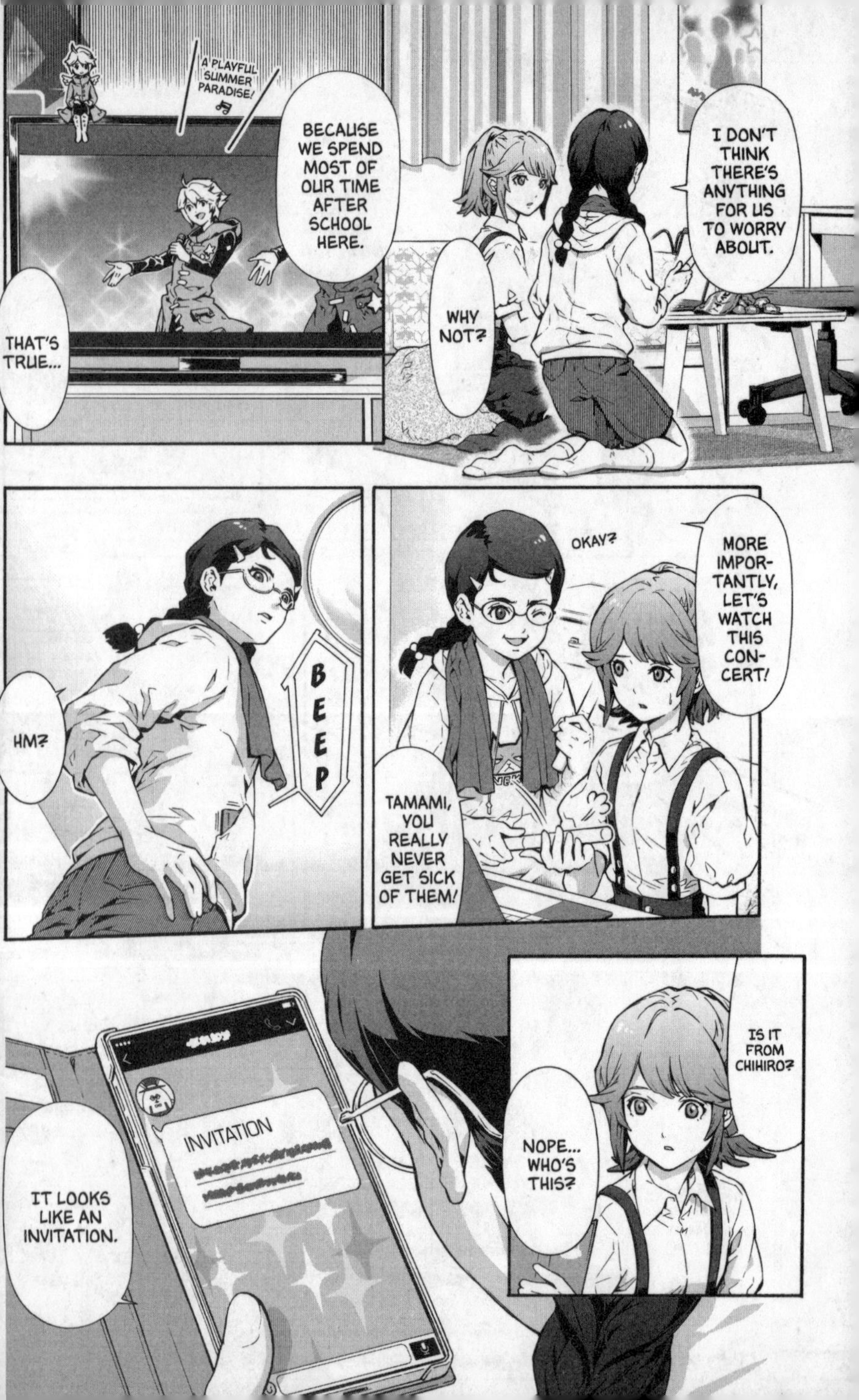
I DON'T THINK THERE'S ANYTHING FOR US TO WORRY ABOUT.
WHY NOT?
A PLAYFUL SUMMER PARADISE!
BECAUSE WE SPEND MOST OF OUR TIME AFTER SCHOOL HERE.
THAT'S TRUE...
MORE IMPORTANTLY, LET'S WATCH THIS CONCERT!
OKAY?
TAMAMI, YOU REALLY NEVER GET SICK OF THEM!
BEEP
HM?
IS IT FROM CHIHIRO?
NOPE... WHO'S THIS?
INVITATION
IT LOOKS LIKE AN INVITATION.

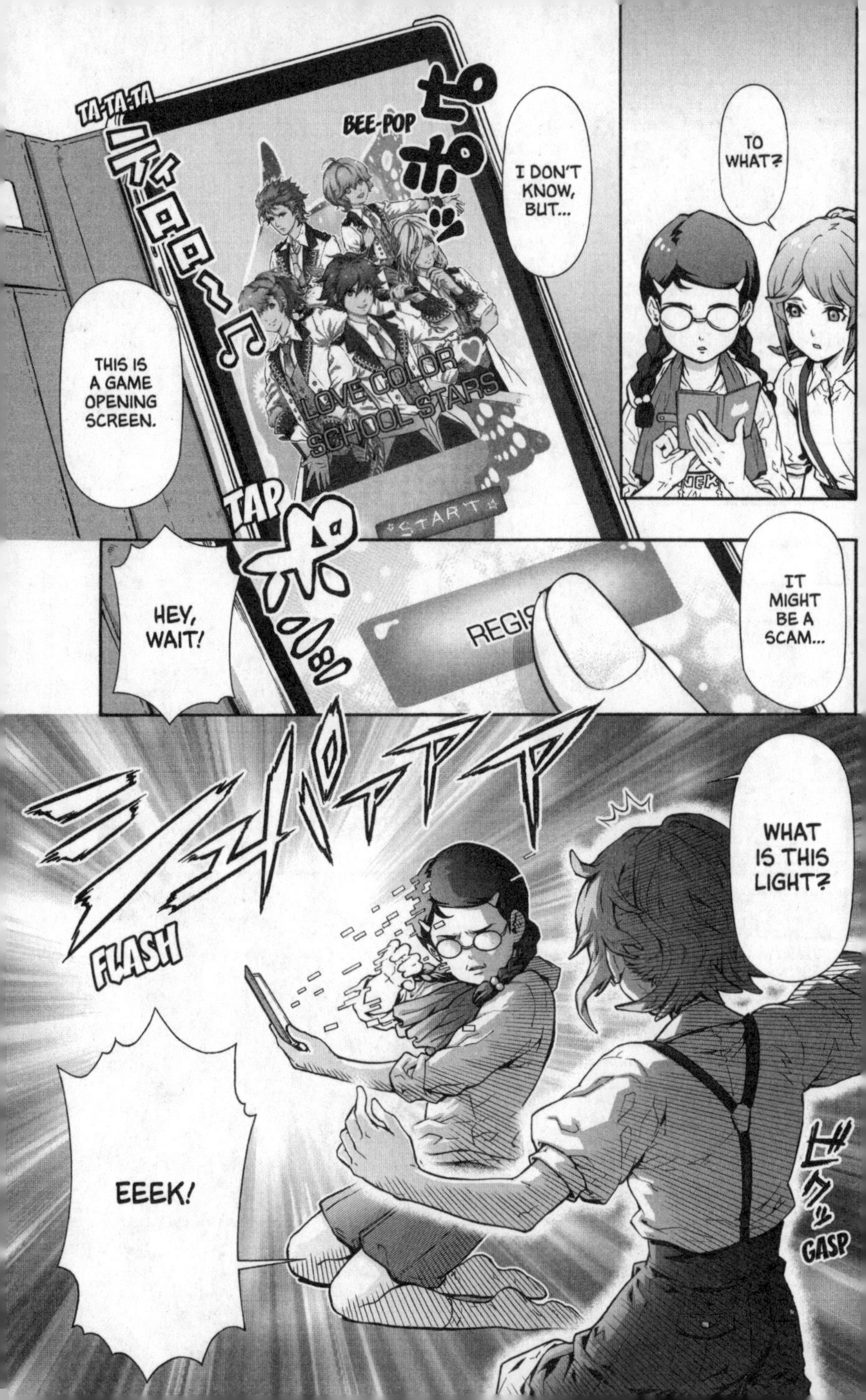
TO WHAT?
I DON'T KNOW, BUT...
BEE-POP
TA-TA-TA
THIS IS A GAME OPENING SCREEN.
LOVE COLOR SCHOOL STARS
START
TAP
IT MIGHT BE A SCAM...
REGIS
HEY, WAIT!
WHAT IS THIS LIGHT?
GASP
FLASH
EEEK!

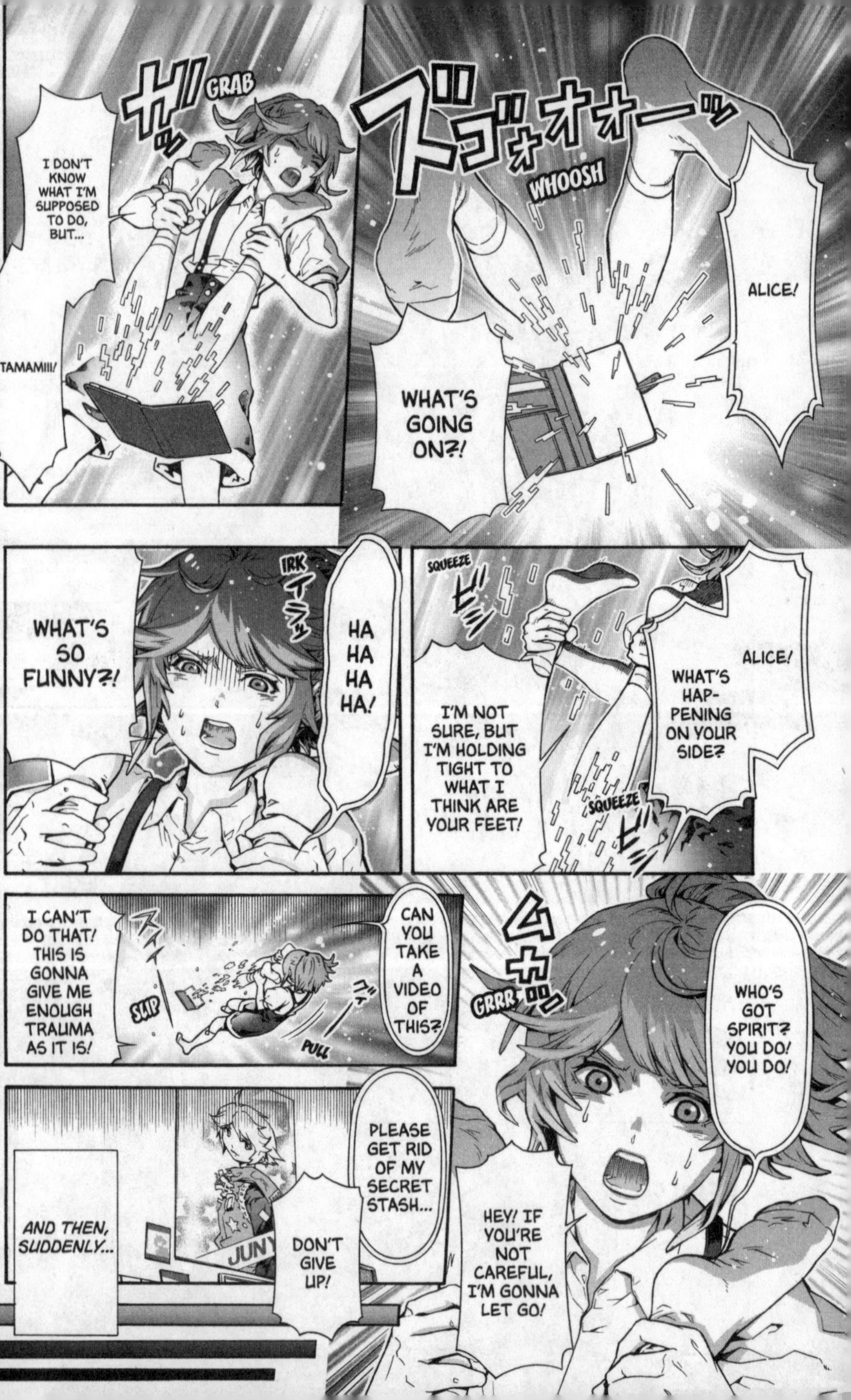
WHOOSH
ALICE!
WHAT'S GOING ON?!
GRAB
I DON'T KNOW WHAT I'M SUPPOSED TO DO, BUT...
TAMAMIII!
SQUEEZE
ALICE! WHAT'S HAP-PENING ON YOUR SIDE?
I'M NOT SURE, BUT I'M HOLDING TIGHT TO WHAT I THINK ARE YOUR FEET!
SQUEEZE
HA HA HA HA!
IRK
WHAT'S SO FUNNY?!
GRRR
WHO'S GOT SPIRIT? YOU DO! YOU DO!
HEY! IF YOU'RE NOT CAREFUL, I'M GONNA LET GO!
CAN YOU TAKE A VIDEO OF THIS?
PULL
SLIP
I CAN'T DO THAT! THIS IS GONNA GIVE ME ENOUGH TRAUMA AS IT IS!
PLEASE GET RID OF MY SECRET STASH...
DON'T GIVE UP!
AND THEN, SUDDENLY...

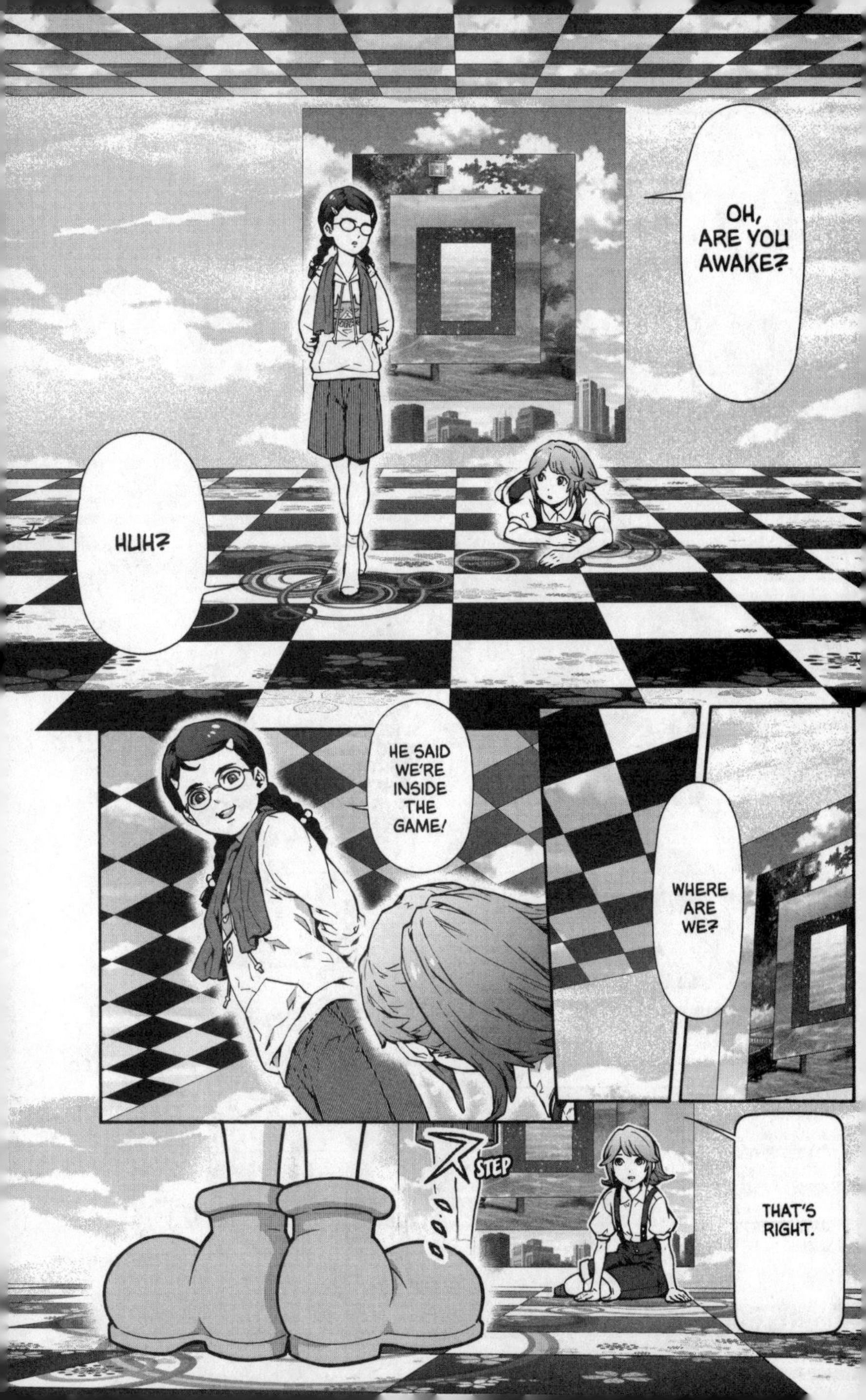
OH, ARE YOU AWAKE?
HUH?
WHERE ARE WE?
HE SAID WE'RE INSIDE THE GAME!
THAT'S RIGHT.
STEP

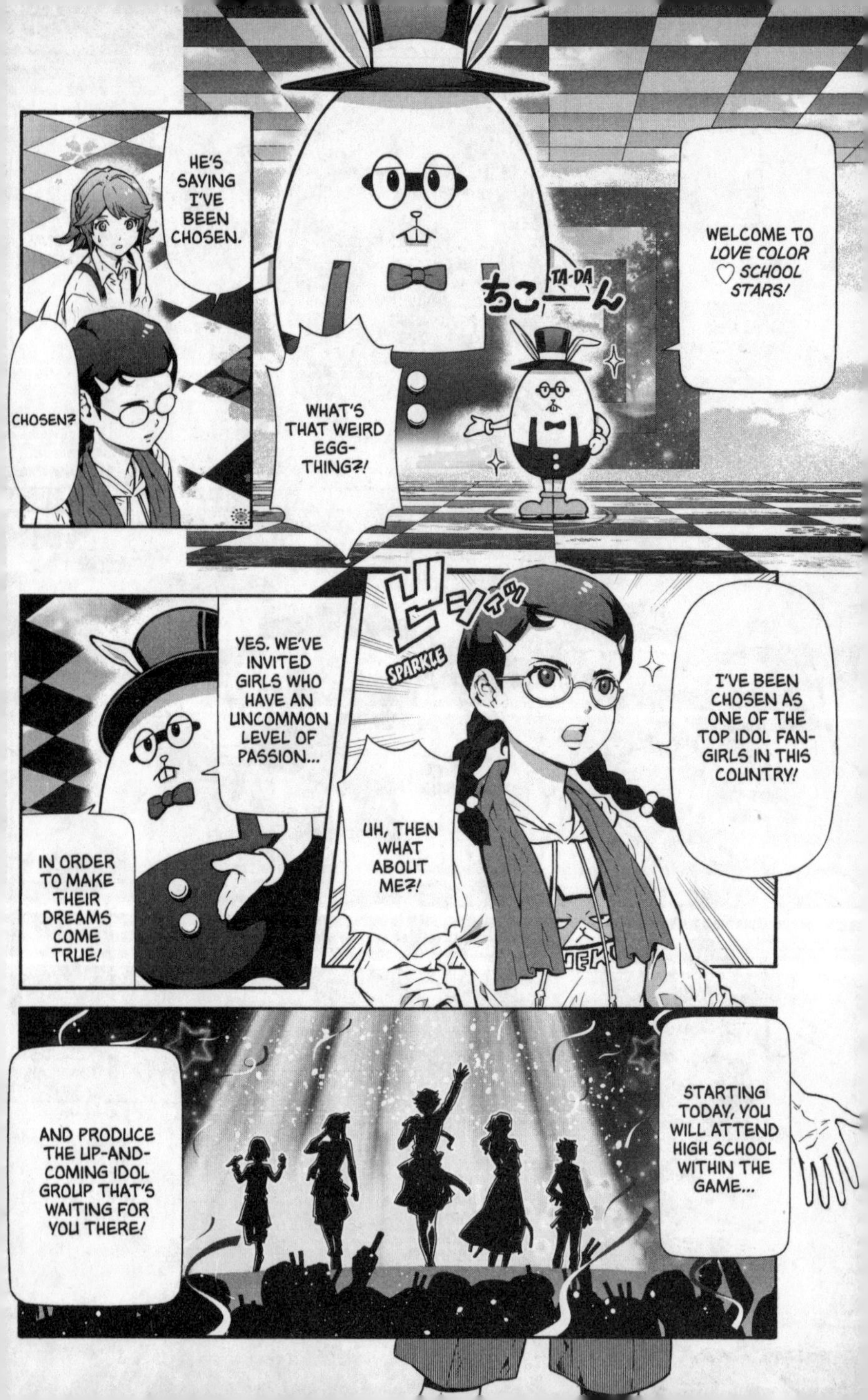

WELCOME TO LOVE COLOR ♡ SCHOOL STARS!
ちこーん
TA-DA
WHAT'S THAT WEIRD EGG-THING?!
HE'S SAYING I'VE BEEN CHOSEN.
CHOSEN?
ビシィッ
SPARKLE
I'VE BEEN CHOSEN AS ONE OF THE TOP IDOL FAN-GIRLS IN THIS COUNTRY!
UH, THEN WHAT ABOUT ME?!
YES. WE'VE INVITED GIRLS WHO HAVE AN UNCOMMON LEVEL OF PASSION...
IN ORDER TO MAKE THEIR DREAMS COME TRUE!
STARTING TODAY, YOU WILL ATTEND HIGH SCHOOL WITHIN THE GAME...
AND PRODUCE THE UP-AND-COMING IDOL GROUP THAT'S WAITING FOR YOU THERE!

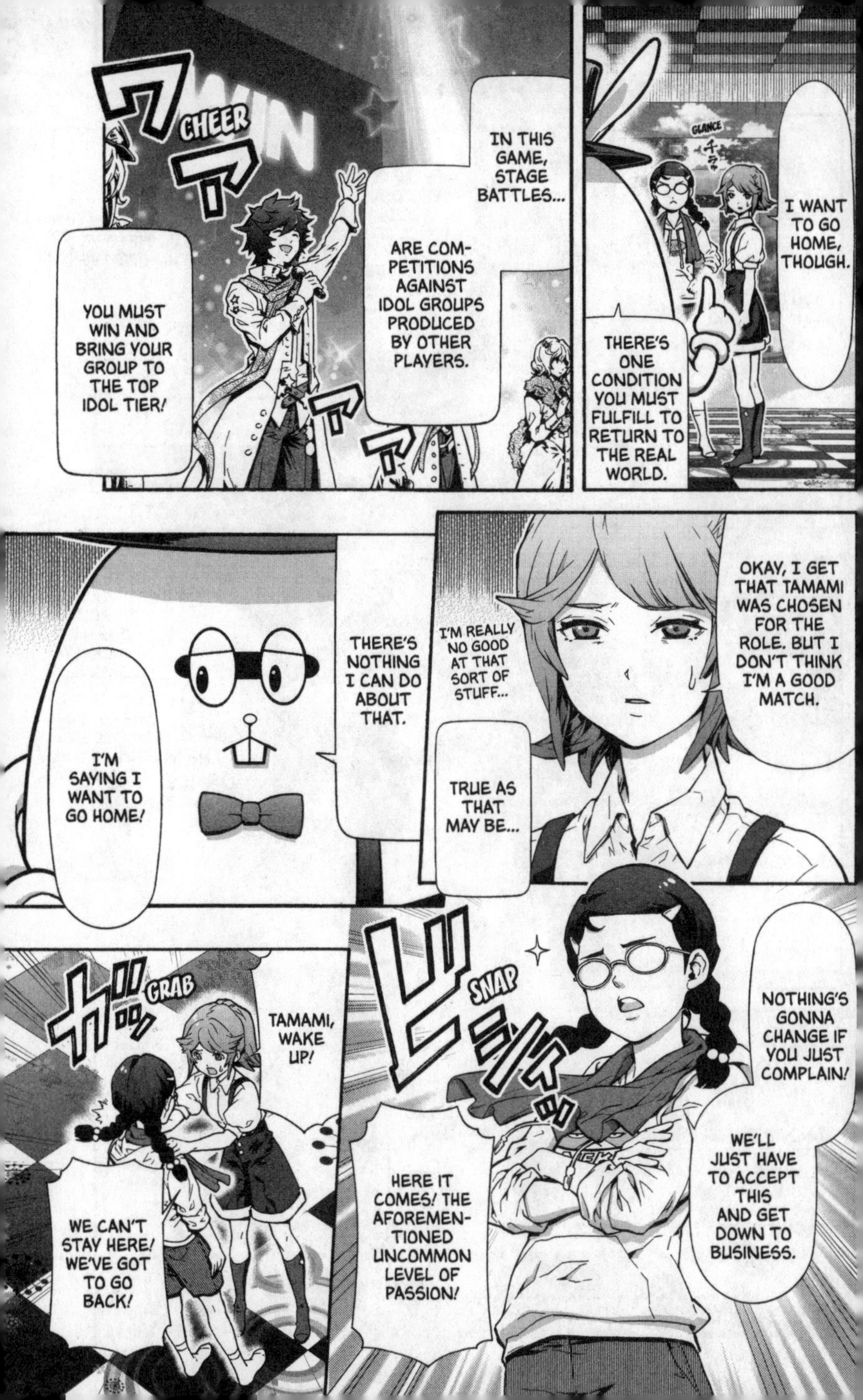
I WANT TO GO HOME, THOUGH.
GLANCE
THERE'S ONE CONDITION YOU MUST FULFILL TO RETURN TO THE REAL WORLD.
IN THIS GAME, STAGE BATTLES...
ARE COMPETITIONS AGAINST IDOL GROUPS PRODUCED BY OTHER PLAYERS.
CHEER
YOU MUST WIN AND BRING YOUR GROUP TO THE TOP IDOL TIER!
OKAY, I GET THAT TAMAMI WAS CHOSEN FOR THE ROLE. BUT I DON'T THINK I'M A GOOD MATCH.
I'M REALLY NO GOOD AT THAT SORT OF STUFF...
TRUE AS THAT MAY BE...
THERE'S NOTHING I CAN DO ABOUT THAT.
I'M SAYING I WANT TO GO HOME!
NOTHING'S GONNA CHANGE IF YOU JUST COMPLAIN!
WE'LL JUST HAVE TO ACCEPT THIS AND GET DOWN TO BUSINESS.
SNAP
HERE IT COMES! THE AFOREMENTIONED UNCOMMON LEVEL OF PASSION!
GRAB
TAMAMI, WAKE UP!
WE CAN'T STAY HERE! WE'VE GOT TO GO BACK!

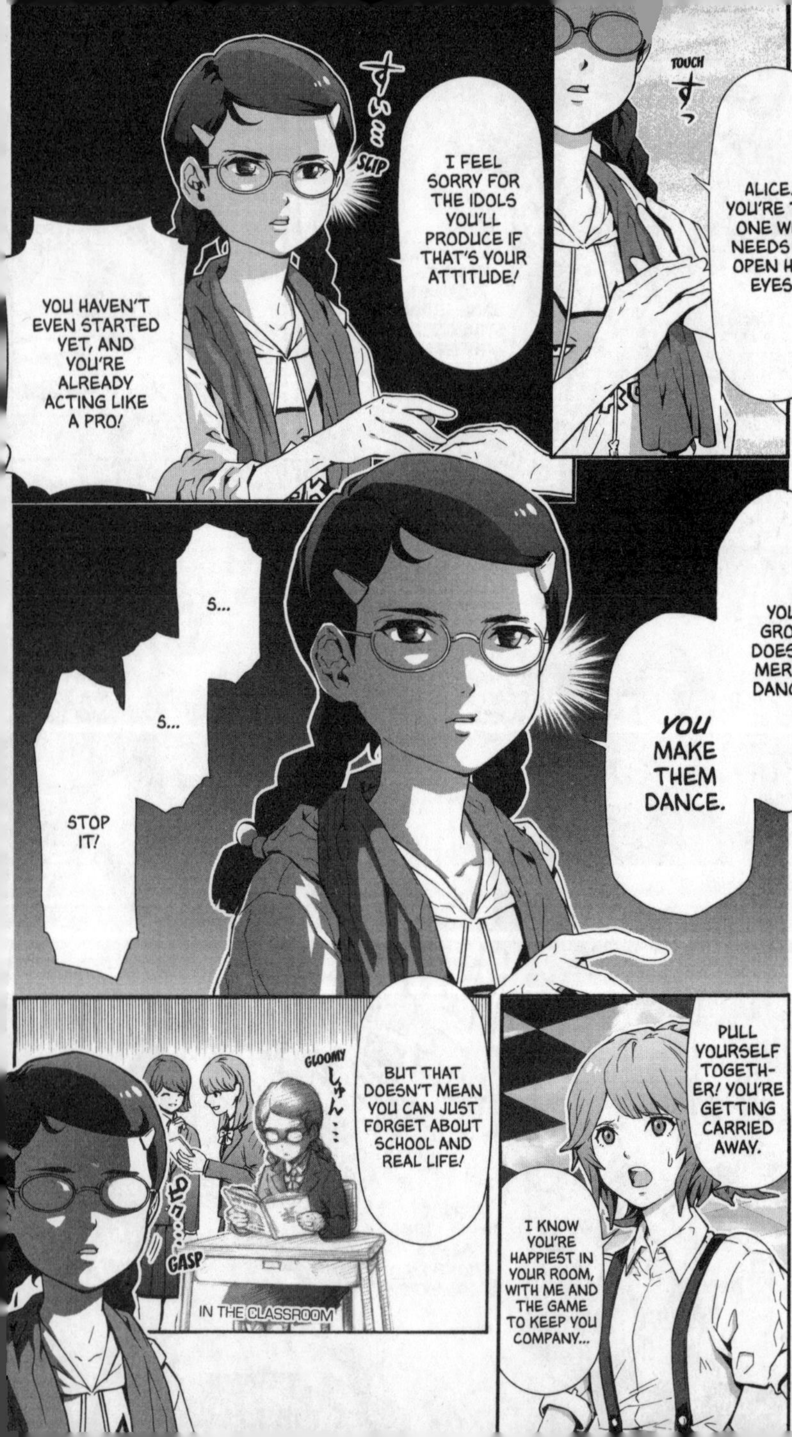
TOUCH
すっ
ALICE... YOU'RE THE ONE WHO NEEDS TO OPEN HER EYES!
SLIP
I FEEL SORRY FOR THE IDOLS YOU'LL PRODUCE IF THAT'S YOUR ATTITUDE!
YOU HAVEN'T EVEN STARTED YET, AND YOU'RE ALREADY ACTING LIKE A PRO!
YOUR GROUP DOESN'T MERELY DANCE...
YOU MAKE THEM DANCE.
S...
S...
STOP IT!
PULL YOURSELF TOGETH-ER! YOU'RE GETTING CARRIED AWAY.
I KNOW YOU'RE HAPPIEST IN YOUR ROOM, WITH ME AND THE GAME TO KEEP YOU COMPANY...
BUT THAT DOESN'T MEAN YOU CAN JUST FORGET ABOUT SCHOOL AND REAL LIFE!
GLOOMY
しゅん…
GASP
IN THE CLASSROOM

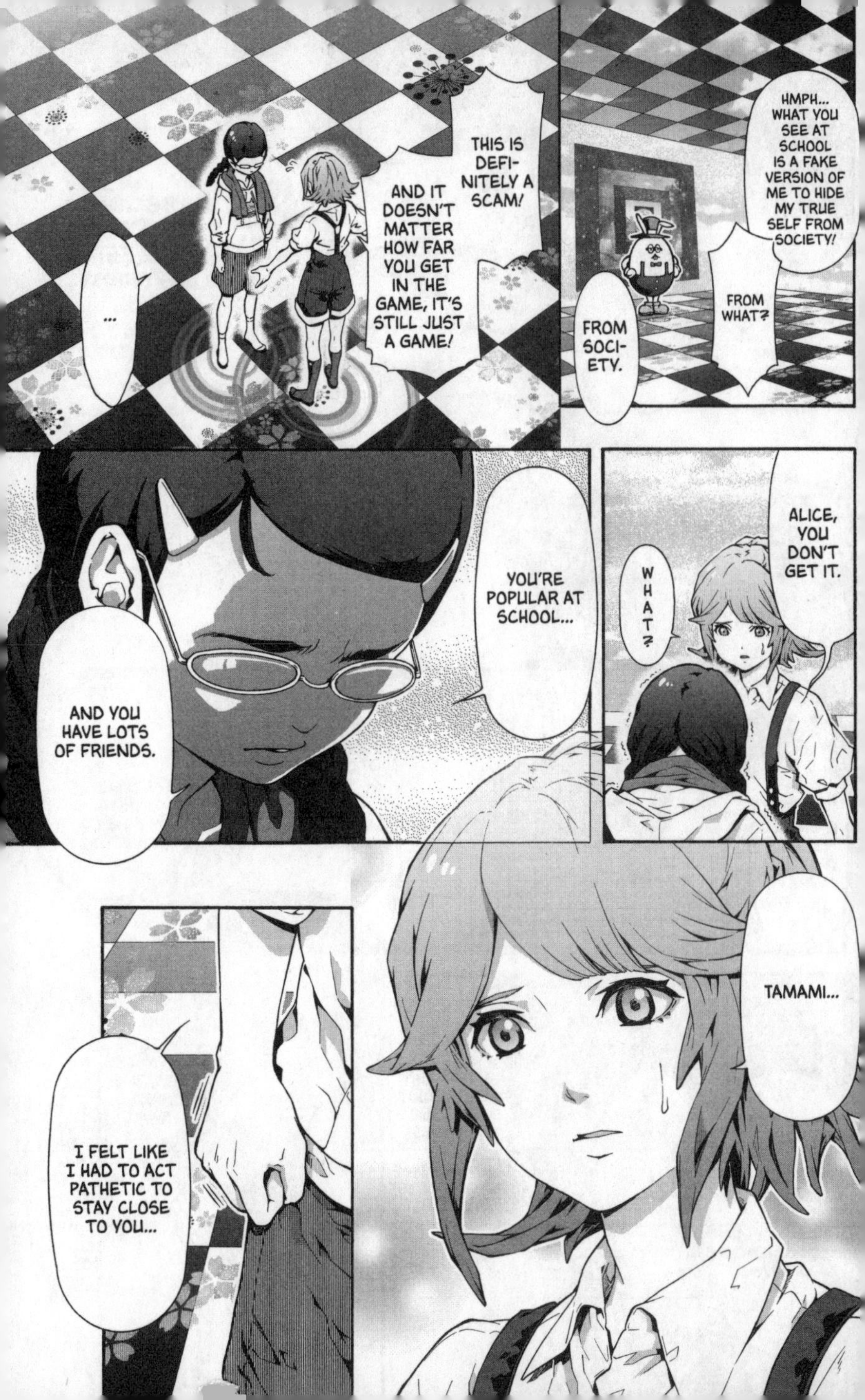
HMPH... WHAT YOU SEE AT SCHOOL IS A FAKE VERSION OF ME TO HIDE MY TRUE SELF FROM SOCIETY!
FROM WHAT?
FROM SOCIETY.
THIS IS DEFINITELY A SCAM!
AND IT DOESN'T MATTER HOW FAR YOU GET IN THE GAME, IT'S STILL JUST A GAME!
...
ALICE, YOU DON'T GET IT.
WHAT?
YOU'RE POPULAR AT SCHOOL...
AND YOU HAVE LOTS OF FRIENDS.
TAMAMI...
I FELT LIKE I HAD TO ACT PATHETIC TO STAY CLOSE TO YOU...

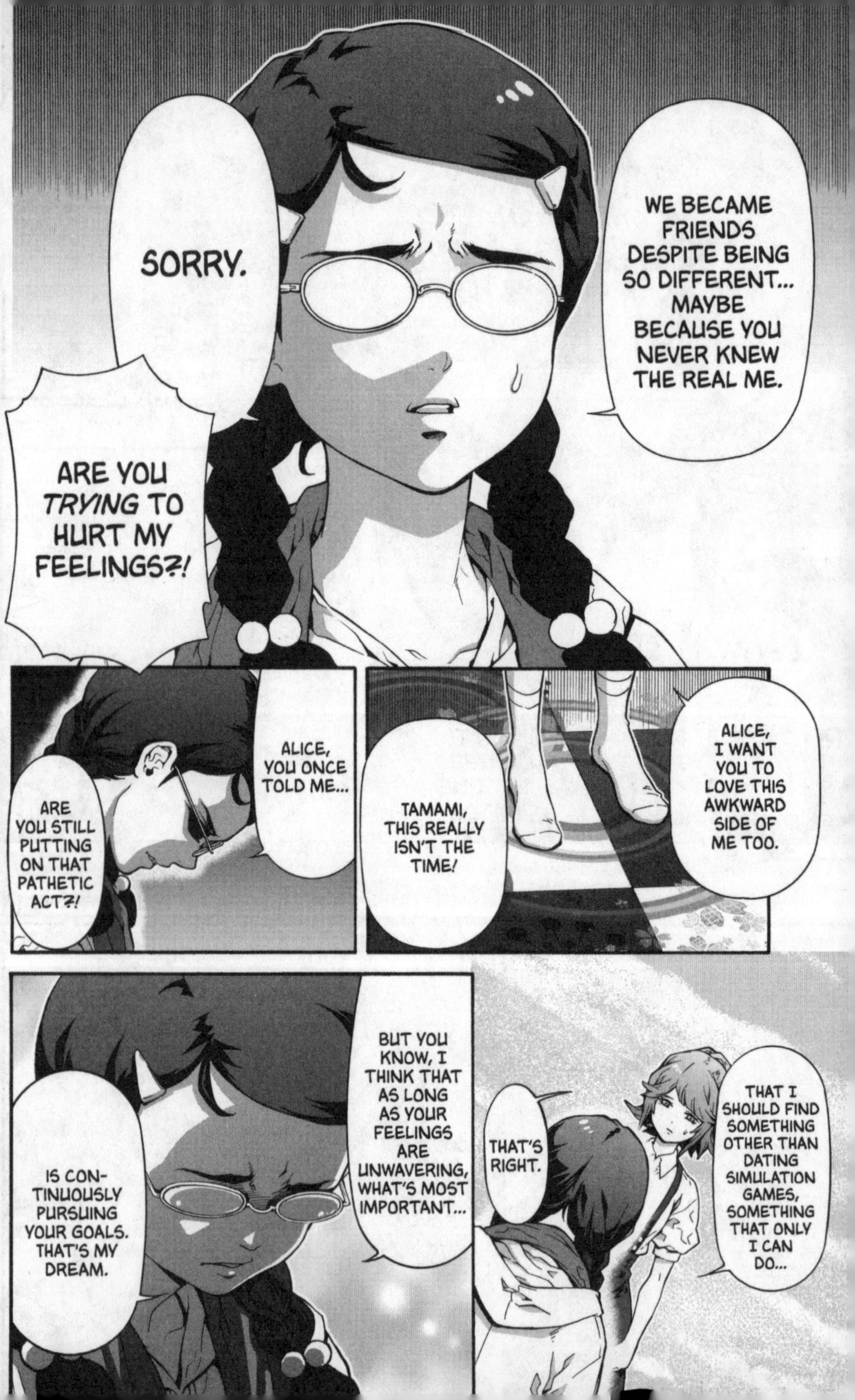
WE BECAME FRIENDS DESPITE BEING SO DIFFERENT... MAYBE BECAUSE YOU NEVER KNEW THE REAL ME.
SORRY.
ARE YOU *TRYING* TO HURT MY FEELINGS?!
ALICE, I WANT YOU TO LOVE THIS AWKWARD SIDE OF ME TOO.
TAMAMI, THIS REALLY ISN'T THE TIME!
ALICE, YOU ONCE TOLD ME...
ARE YOU STILL PUTTING ON THAT PATHETIC ACT?!
THAT I SHOULD FIND SOMETHING OTHER THAN DATING SIMULATION GAMES, SOMETHING THAT ONLY I CAN DO...
THAT'S RIGHT.
BUT YOU KNOW, I THINK THAT AS LONG AS YOUR FEELINGS ARE UNWAVERING, WHAT'S MOST IMPORTANT...
IS CON-TINUOUSLY PURSUING YOUR GOALS. THAT'S MY DREAM.

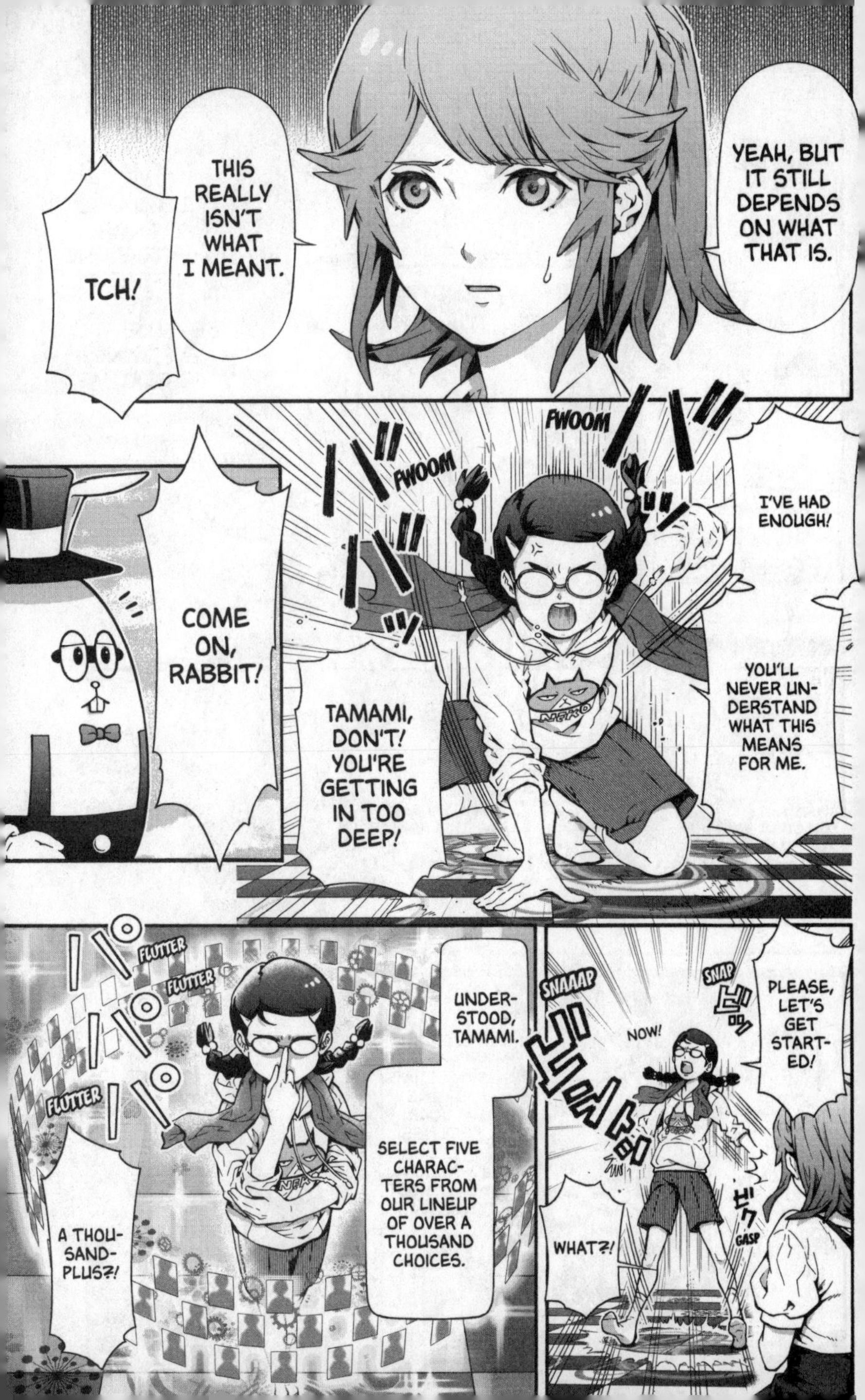
YEAH, BUT IT STILL DEPENDS ON WHAT THAT IS.
THIS REALLY ISN'T WHAT I MEANT.
TCH!
FWOOM
FWOOM
I'VE HAD ENOUGH!
YOU'LL NEVER UNDERSTAND WHAT THIS MEANS FOR ME.
TAMAMI, DON'T! YOU'RE GETTING IN TOO DEEP!
COME ON, RABBIT!
SNAP
PLEASE, LET'S GET STARTED!
NOW!
SNAAAP
GASP
WHAT?!
UNDERSTOOD, TAMAMI.
SELECT FIVE CHARACTERS FROM OUR LINEUP OF OVER A THOUSAND CHOICES.
FLUTTER
FLUTTER
FLUTTER
A THOUSAND-PLUS?!

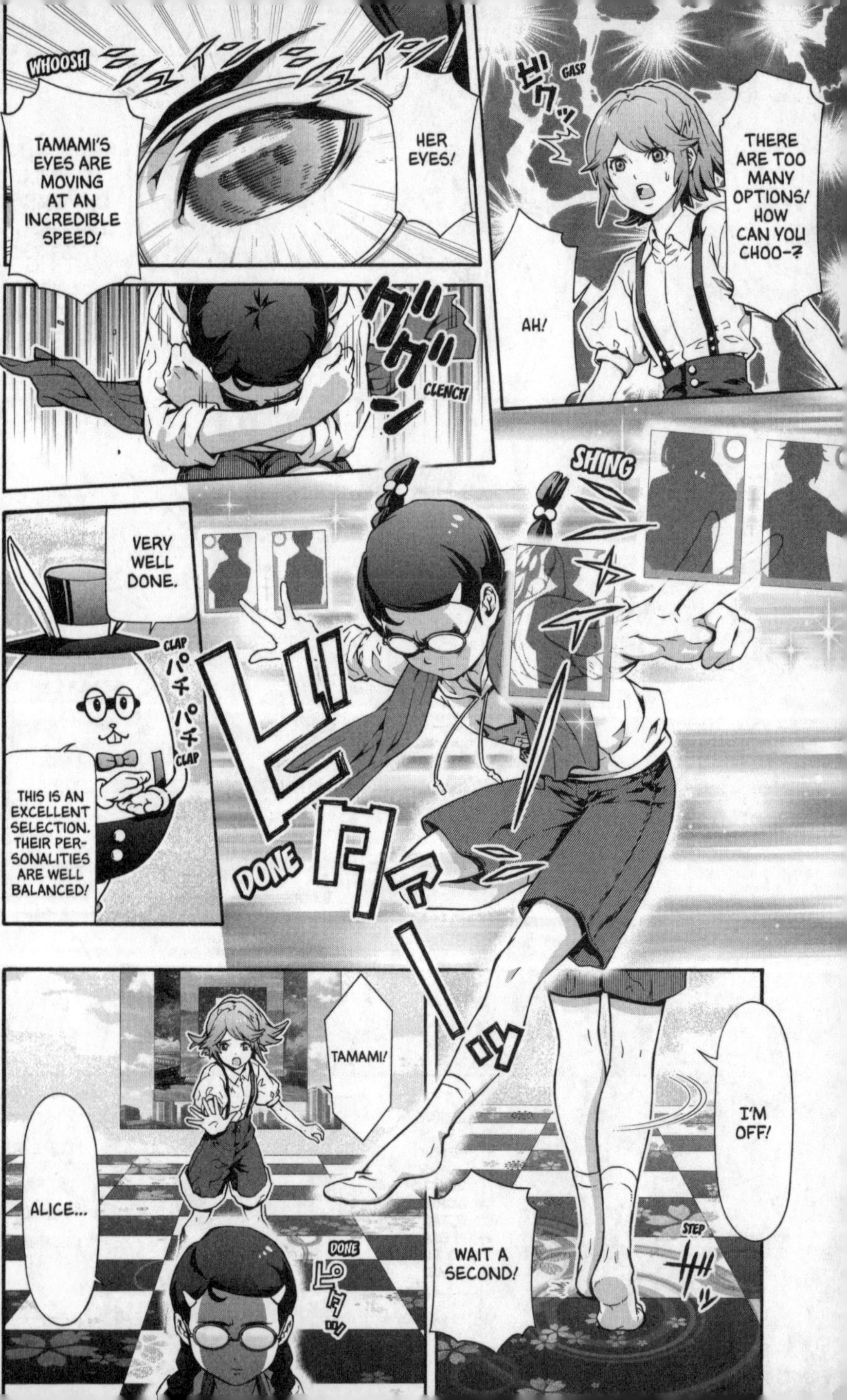
GASP
THERE ARE TOO MANY OPTIONS! HOW CAN YOU CHOO-?
AH!
WHOOSH
HER EYES!
TAMAMI'S EYES ARE MOVING AT AN INCREDIBLE SPEED!
CLENCH
SHING
DONE
VERY WELL DONE.
CLAP
CLAP
THIS IS AN EXCELLENT SELECTION. THEIR PERSONALITIES ARE WELL BALANCED!
I'M OFF!
STEP
WAIT A SECOND!
TAMAMI!
DONE
ALICE...

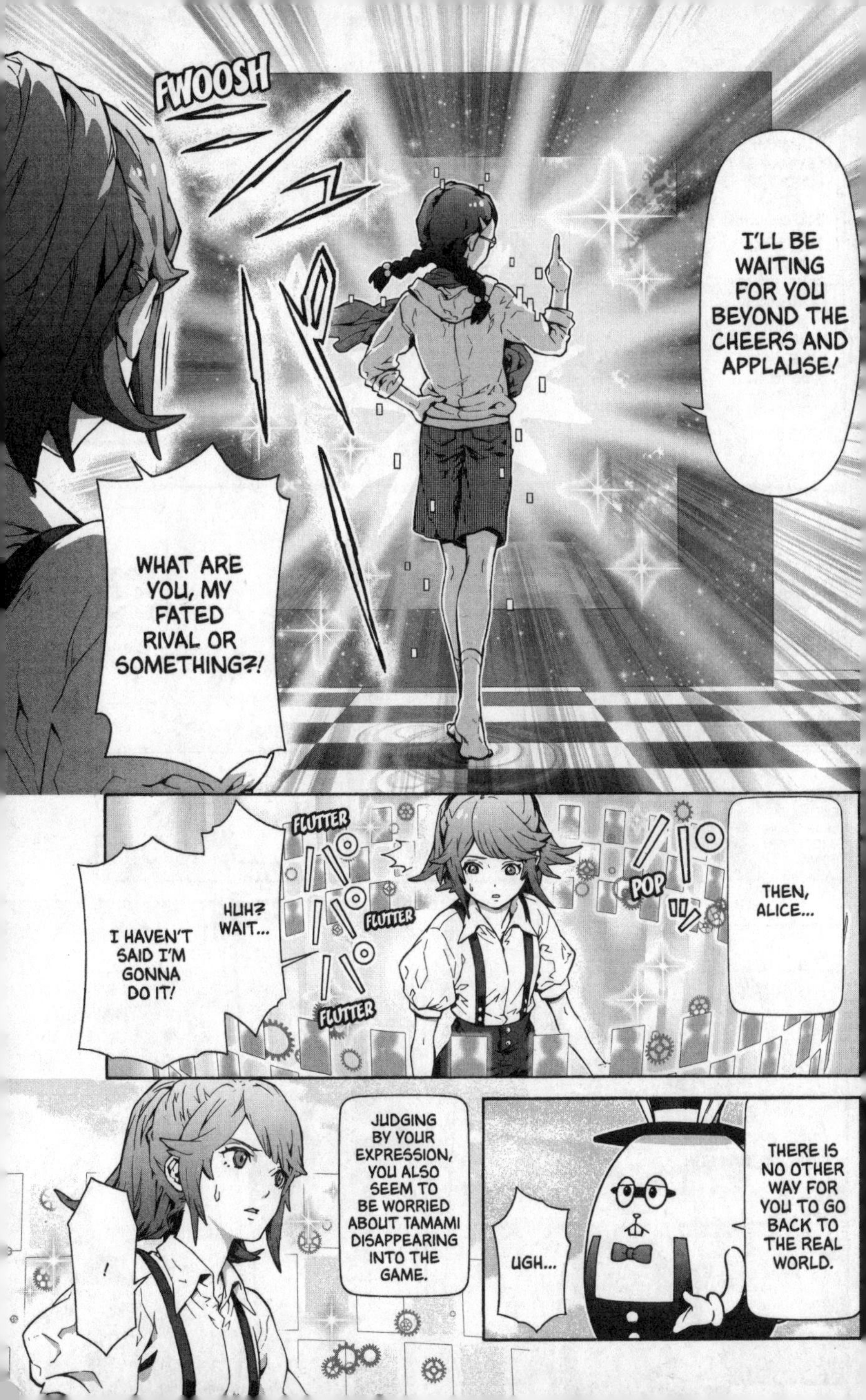
I'LL BE WAITING FOR YOU BEYOND THE CHEERS AND APPLAUSE!
FWOOSH
WHAT ARE YOU, MY FATED RIVAL OR SOMETHING?!
THEN, ALICE...
POP
FLUTTER
FLUTTER
FLUTTER
HUH? WAIT...
I HAVEN'T SAID I'M GONNA DO IT!
THERE IS NO OTHER WAY FOR YOU TO GO BACK TO THE REAL WORLD.
UGH...
JUDGING BY YOUR EXPRESSION, YOU ALSO SEEM TO BE WORRIED ABOUT TAMAMI DISAPPEARING INTO THE GAME.
!

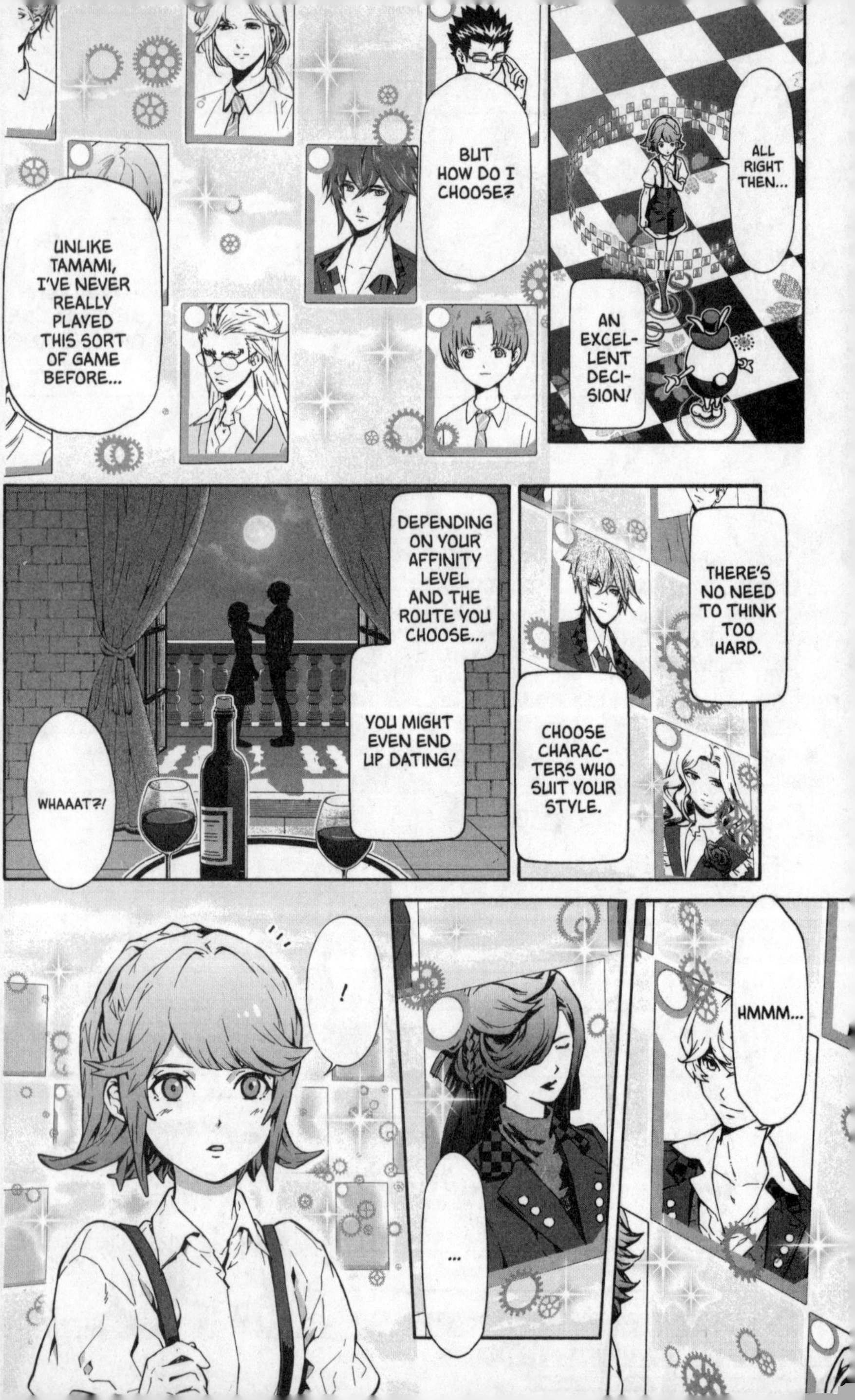
ALL RIGHT THEN...
AN EXCEL-LENT DECI-SION!
BUT HOW DO I CHOOSE?
UNLIKE TAMAMI, I'VE NEVER REALLY PLAYED THIS SORT OF GAME BEFORE...
THERE'S NO NEED TO THINK TOO HARD.
CHOOSE CHARAC-TERS WHO SUIT YOUR STYLE.
DEPENDING ON YOUR AFFINITY LEVEL AND THE ROUTE YOU CHOOSE...
YOU MIGHT EVEN END UP DATING!
WHAAAT?!
HMMM...
...
!

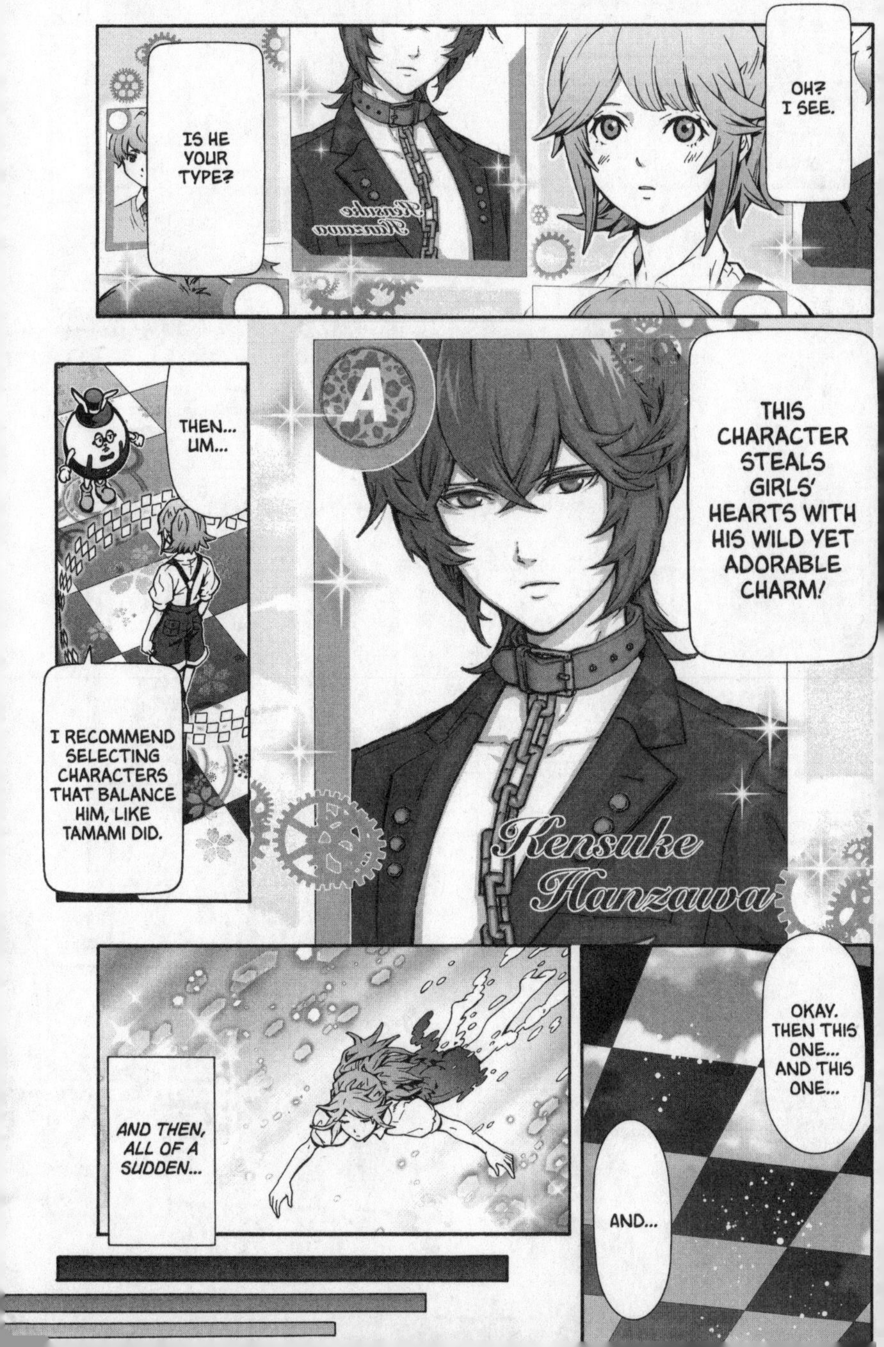
OH? I SEE.
IS HE YOUR TYPE?
THIS CHARACTER STEALS GIRLS' HEARTS WITH HIS WILD YET ADORABLE CHARM!
A
Kensuke Hanzawa
THEN... UM...
I RECOMMEND SELECTING CHARACTERS THAT BALANCE HIM, LIKE TAMAMI DID.
OKAY. THEN THIS ONE... AND THIS ONE...
AND...
AND THEN, ALL OF A SUDDEN...

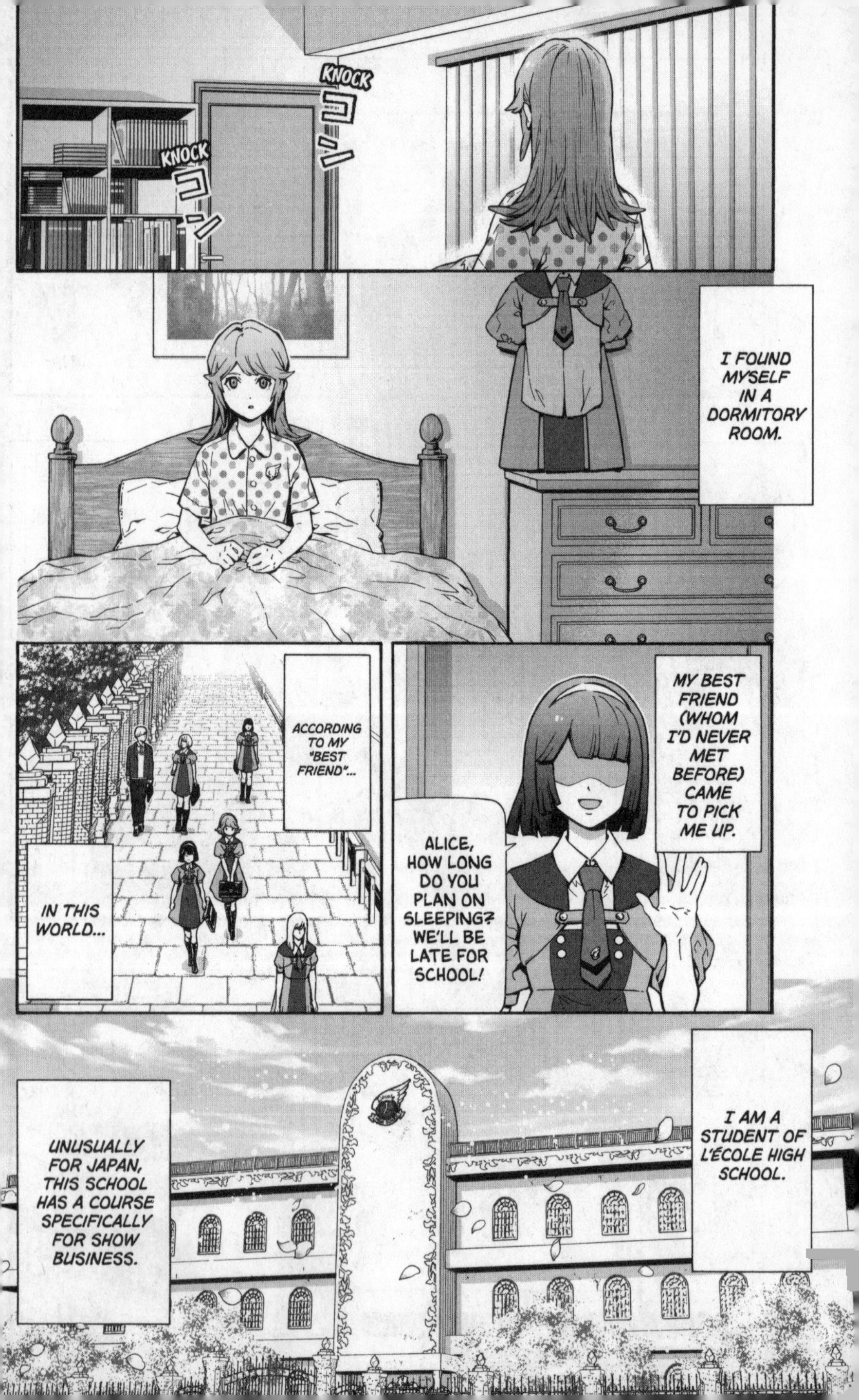
KNOCK
コン
KNOCK
コン
I FOUND MYSELF IN A DORMITORY ROOM.
MY BEST FRIEND (WHOM I'D NEVER MET BEFORE) CAME TO PICK ME UP.
ALICE, HOW LONG DO YOU PLAN ON SLEEPING? WE'LL BE LATE FOR SCHOOL!
ACCORDING TO MY "BEST FRIEND"...
IN THIS WORLD...
I AM A STUDENT OF L'ÉCOLE HIGH SCHOOL.
UNUSUALLY FOR JAPAN, THIS SCHOOL HAS A COURSE SPECIFICALLY FOR SHOW BUSINESS.

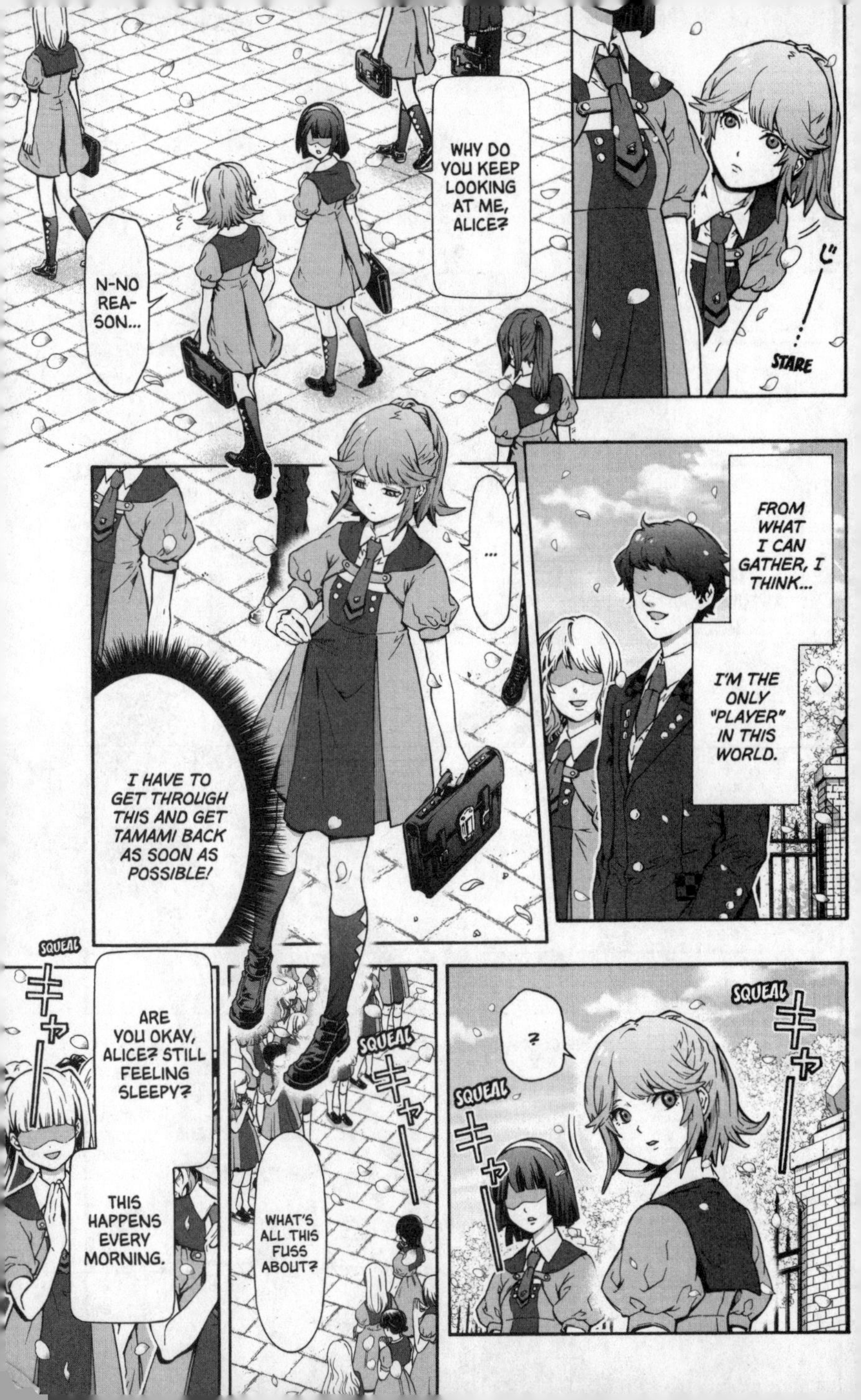
じ
STARE
WHY DO YOU KEEP LOOKING AT ME, ALICE?
N-NO REA-SON...
FROM WHAT I CAN GATHER, I THINK...
I'M THE ONLY "PLAYER" IN THIS WORLD.
...
I HAVE TO GET THROUGH THIS AND GET TAMAMI BACK AS SOON AS POSSIBLE!
SQUEAL
キャー
SQUEAL
キャー
?
SQUEAL
キャー
WHAT'S ALL THIS FUSS ABOUT?
SQUEAL
キャー
ARE YOU OKAY, ALICE? STILL FEELING SLEEPY?
THIS HAPPENS EVERY MORNING.

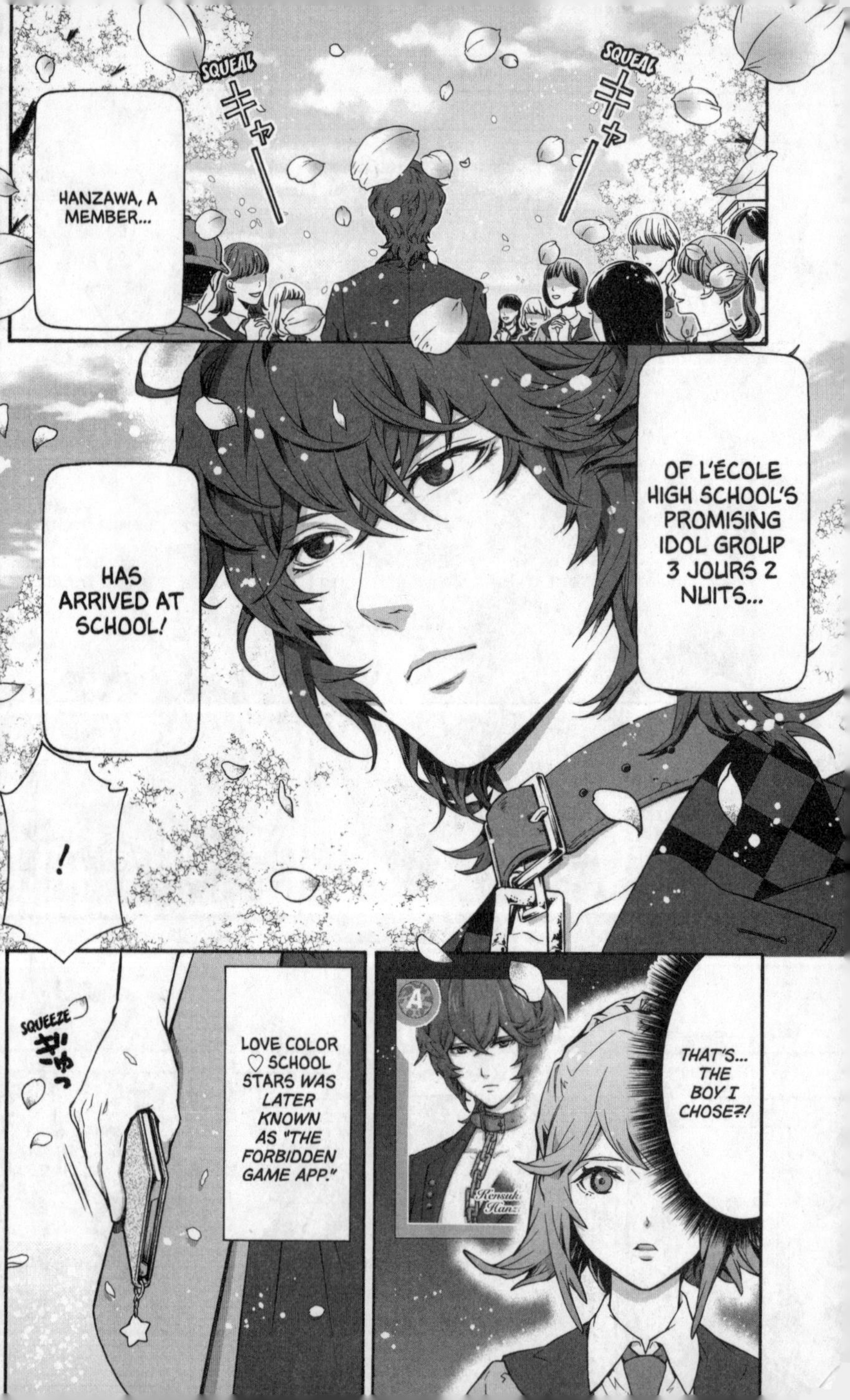
SQUEAL
キャー
SQUEAL
キャー
HANZAWA, A MEMBER...
OF L'ÉCOLE HIGH SCHOOL'S PROMISING IDOL GROUP 3 JOURS 2 NUITS...
HAS ARRIVED AT SCHOOL!
!
THAT'S... THE BOY I CHOSE?!
LOVE COLOR ♡ SCHOOL STARS WAS LATER KNOWN AS "THE FORBIDDEN GAME APP."
SQUEEZE
ぎゅっ

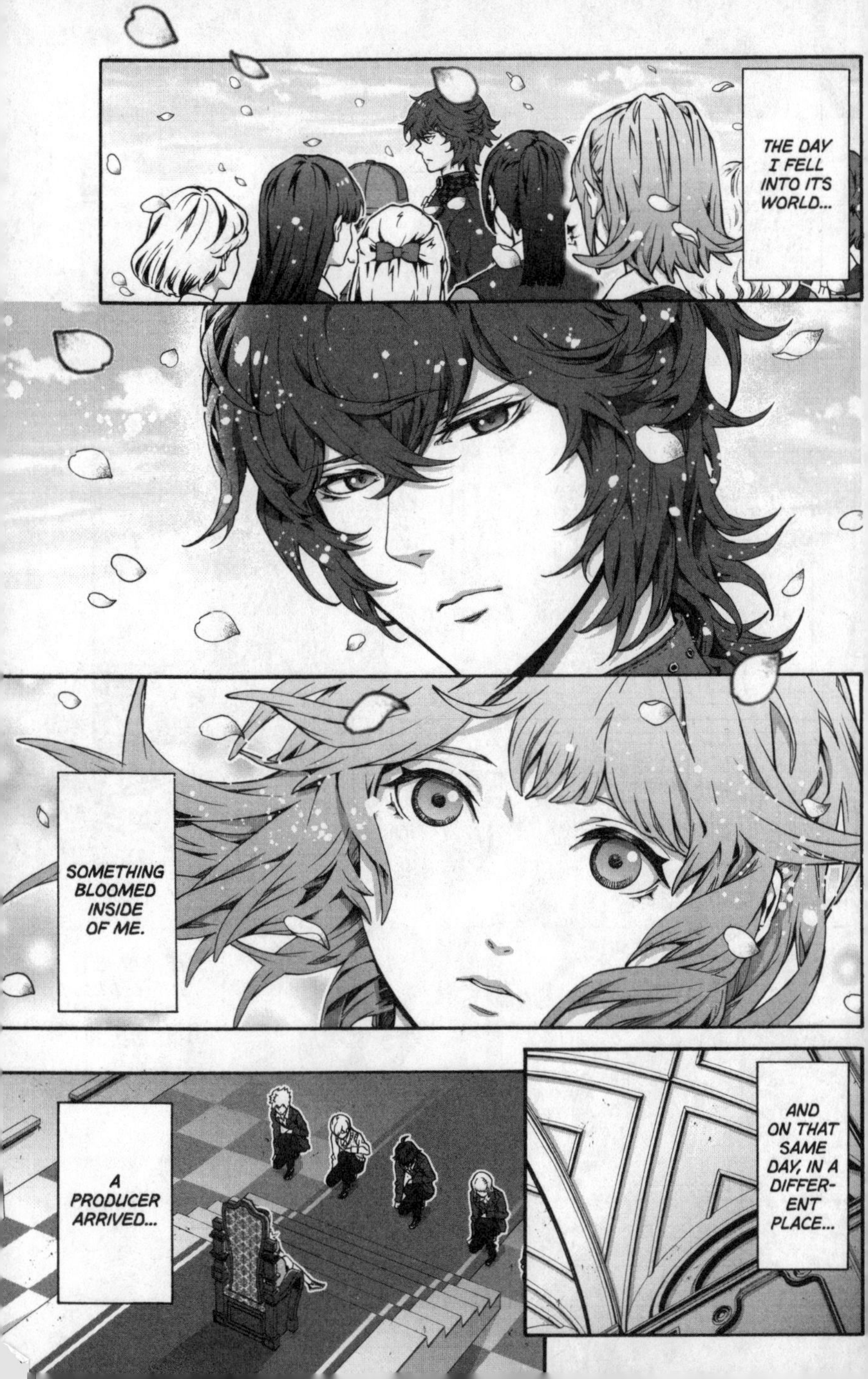
THE DAY I FELL INTO ITS WORLD...
SOMETHING BLOOMED INSIDE OF ME.
AND ON THAT SAME DAY, IN A DIFFER-ENT PLACE...
A PRODUCER ARRIVED...

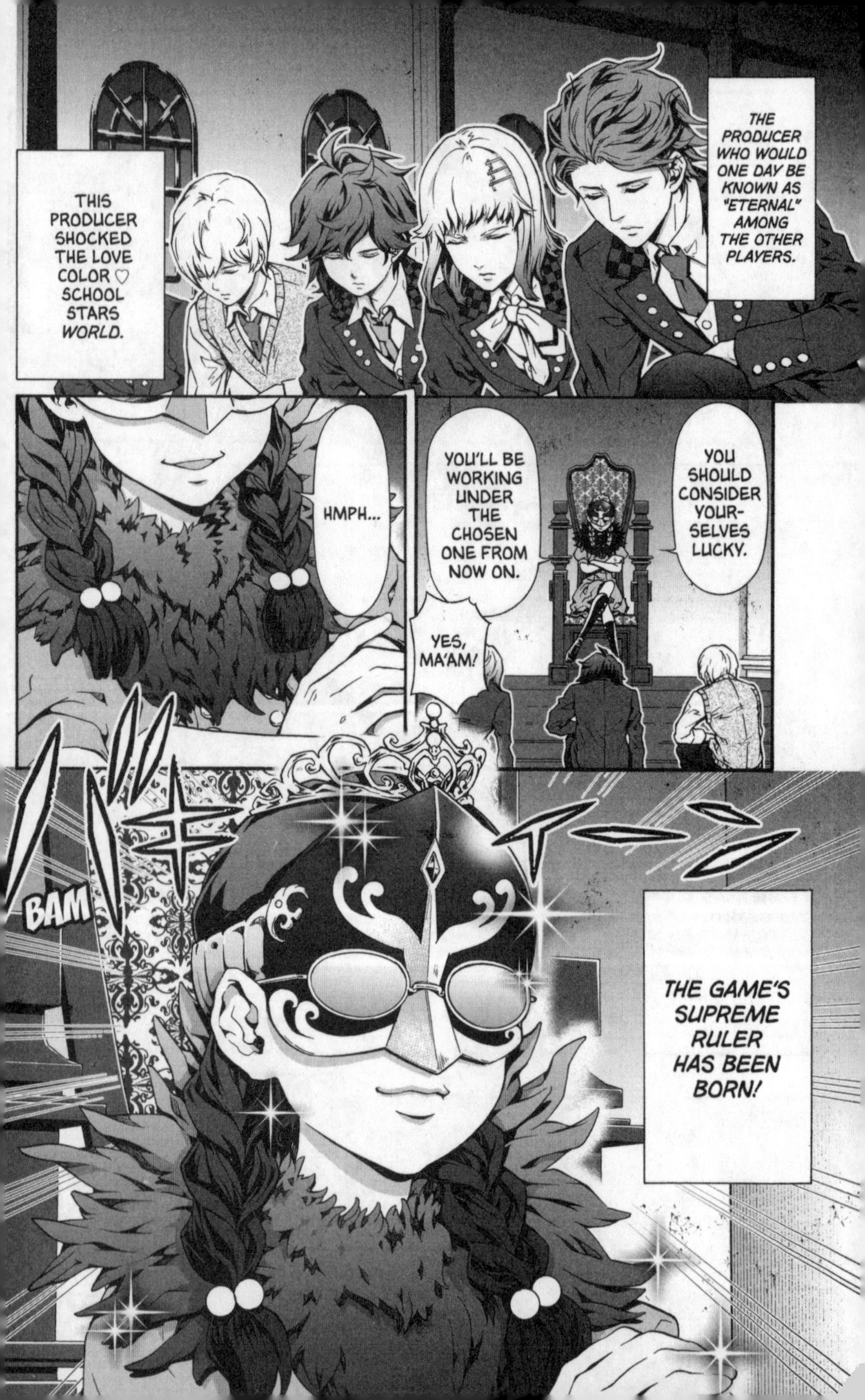
THE PRODUCER WHO WOULD ONE DAY BE KNOWN AS "ETERNAL" AMONG THE OTHER PLAYERS.
THIS PRODUCER SHOCKED THE LOVE COLOR ♡ SCHOOL STARS *WORLD.*
YOU SHOULD CONSIDER YOURSELVES LUCKY.
YOU'LL BE WORKING UNDER THE CHOSEN ONE FROM NOW ON.
YES, MA'AM!
HMPH...
THE GAME'S SUPREME RULER HAS BEEN BORN!
BAM

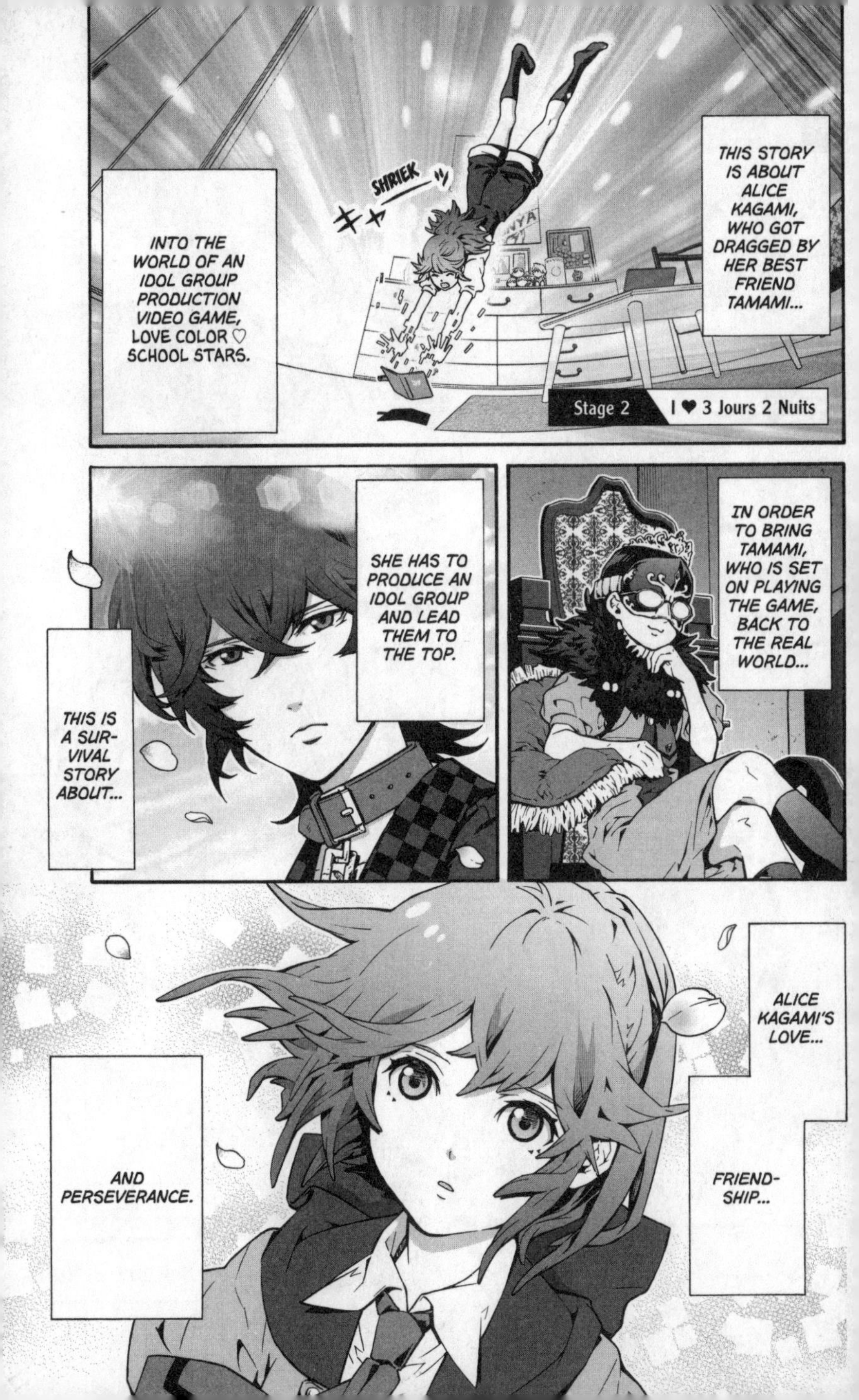
THIS STORY IS ABOUT ALICE KAGAMI, WHO GOT DRAGGED BY HER BEST FRIEND TAMAMI...
SHRIEK
キャ
INTO THE WORLD OF AN IDOL GROUP PRODUCTION VIDEO GAME, LOVE COLOR ♡ SCHOOL STARS.
Stage 2 I ♥ 3 Jours 2 Nuits
IN ORDER TO BRING TAMAMI, WHO IS SET ON PLAYING THE GAME, BACK TO THE REAL WORLD...
SHE HAS TO PRODUCE AN IDOL GROUP AND LEAD THEM TO THE TOP.
THIS IS A SUR-VIVAL STORY ABOUT...
ALICE KAGAMI'S LOVE...
FRIEND-SHIP...
AND PERSEVERANCE.

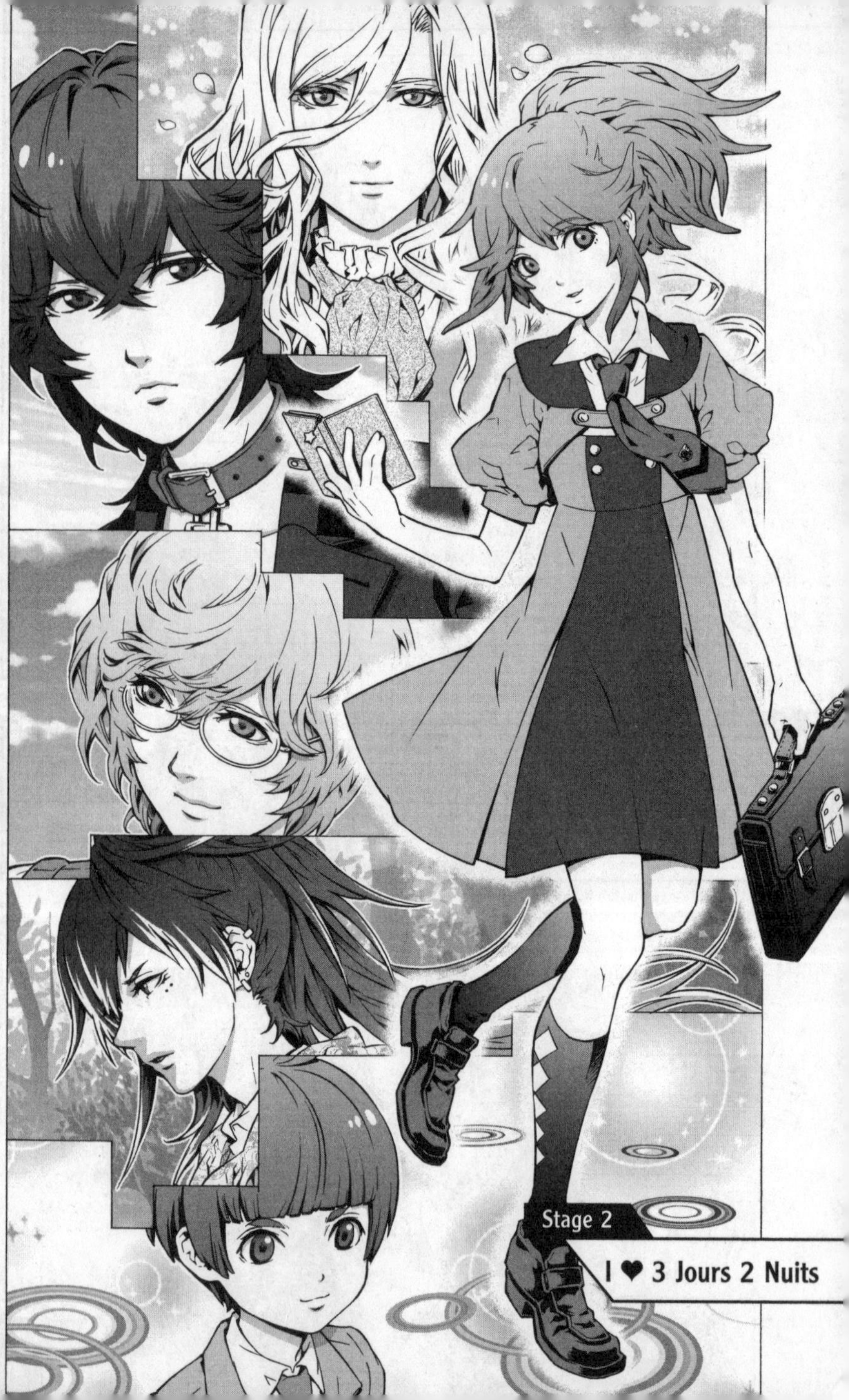
Stage 2
I ❤ 3 Jours 2 Nuits

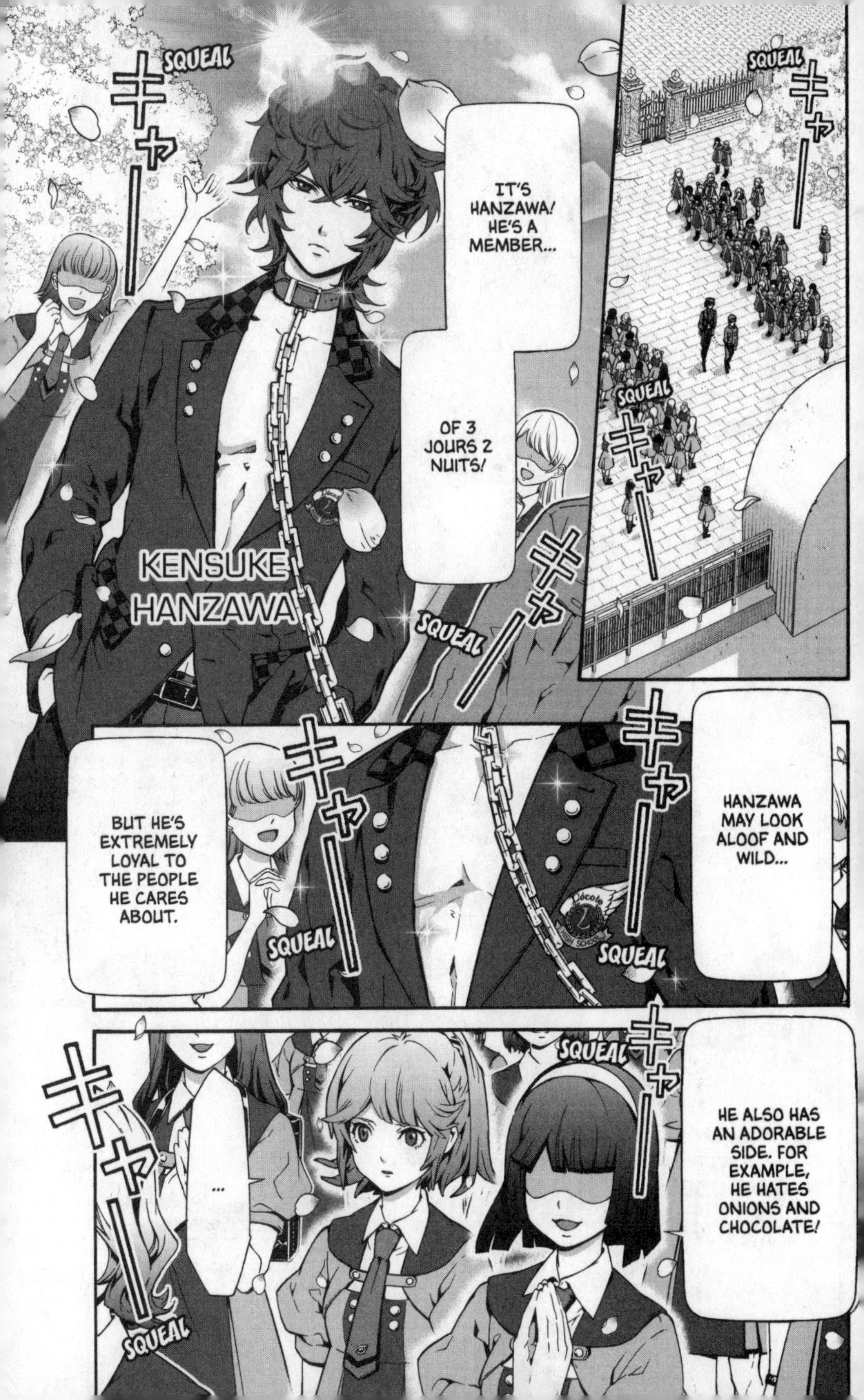

SQUEAL
キャー
SQUEAL
キャー
SQUEAL
キャー
IT'S HANZAWA! HE'S A MEMBER...
OF 3 JOURS 2 NUITS!
KENSUKE HANZAWA
SQUEAL
キャー
HANZAWA MAY LOOK ALOOF AND WILD...
SQUEAL
キャー
BUT HE'S EXTREMELY LOYAL TO THE PEOPLE HE CARES ABOUT.
SQUEAL
キャー
HE ALSO HAS AN ADORABLE SIDE. FOR EXAMPLE, HE HATES ONIONS AND CHOCOLATE!
SQUEAL
キャー
...
SQUEAL
キャー

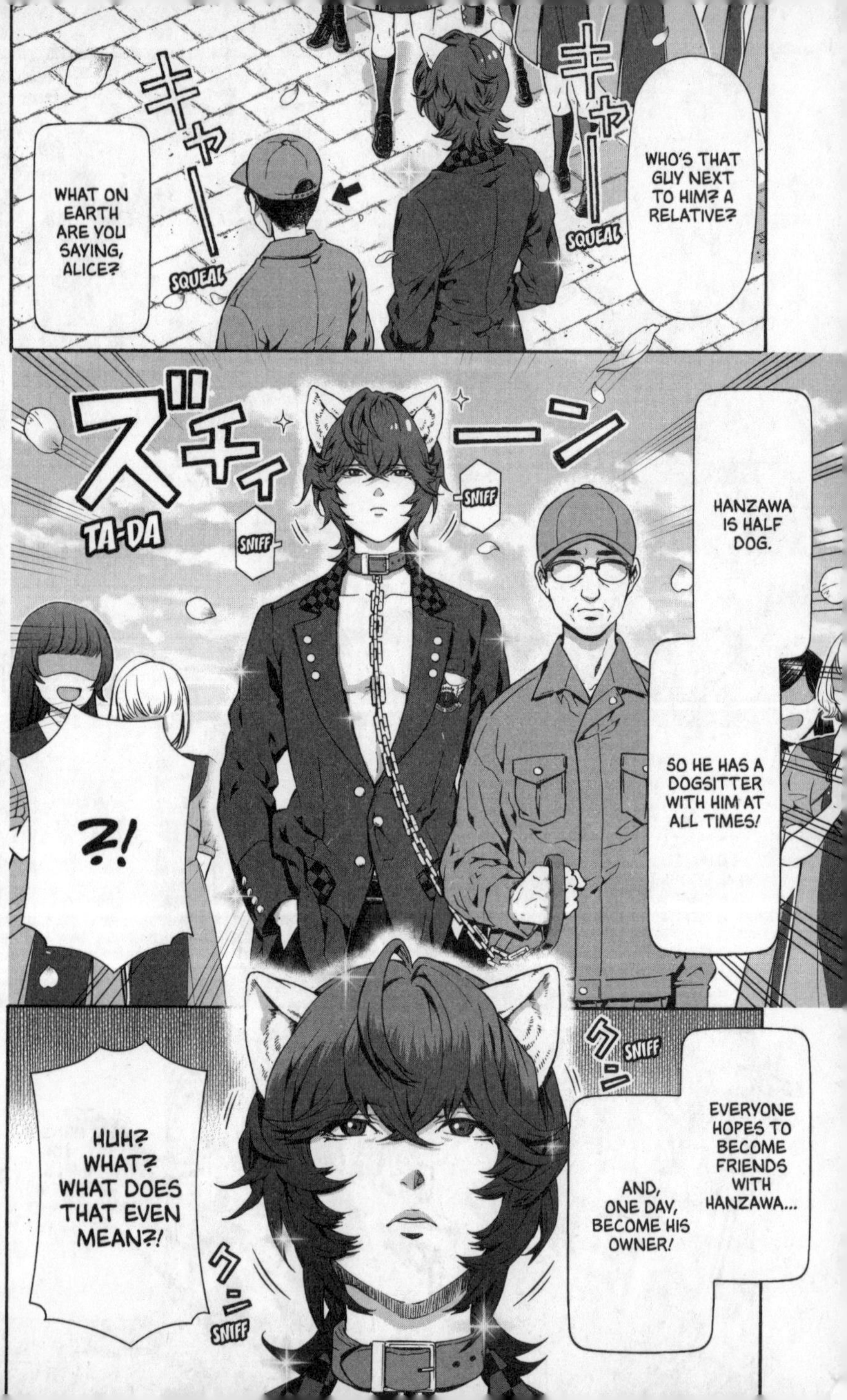
キャー
SQUEAL
WHO'S THAT GUY NEXT TO HIM? A RELATIVE?
キャー
SQUEAL
WHAT ON EARTH ARE YOU SAYING, ALICE?
HANZAWA IS HALF DOG.
SO HE HAS A DOGSITTER WITH HIM AT ALL TIMES!
ズチィーン
TA-DA
SNIFF
SNIFF
?!
EVERYONE HOPES TO BECOME FRIENDS WITH HANZAWA...
AND, ONE DAY, BECOME HIS OWNER!
SNIFF
HUH? WHAT? WHAT DOES THAT EVEN MEAN?!
SNIFF

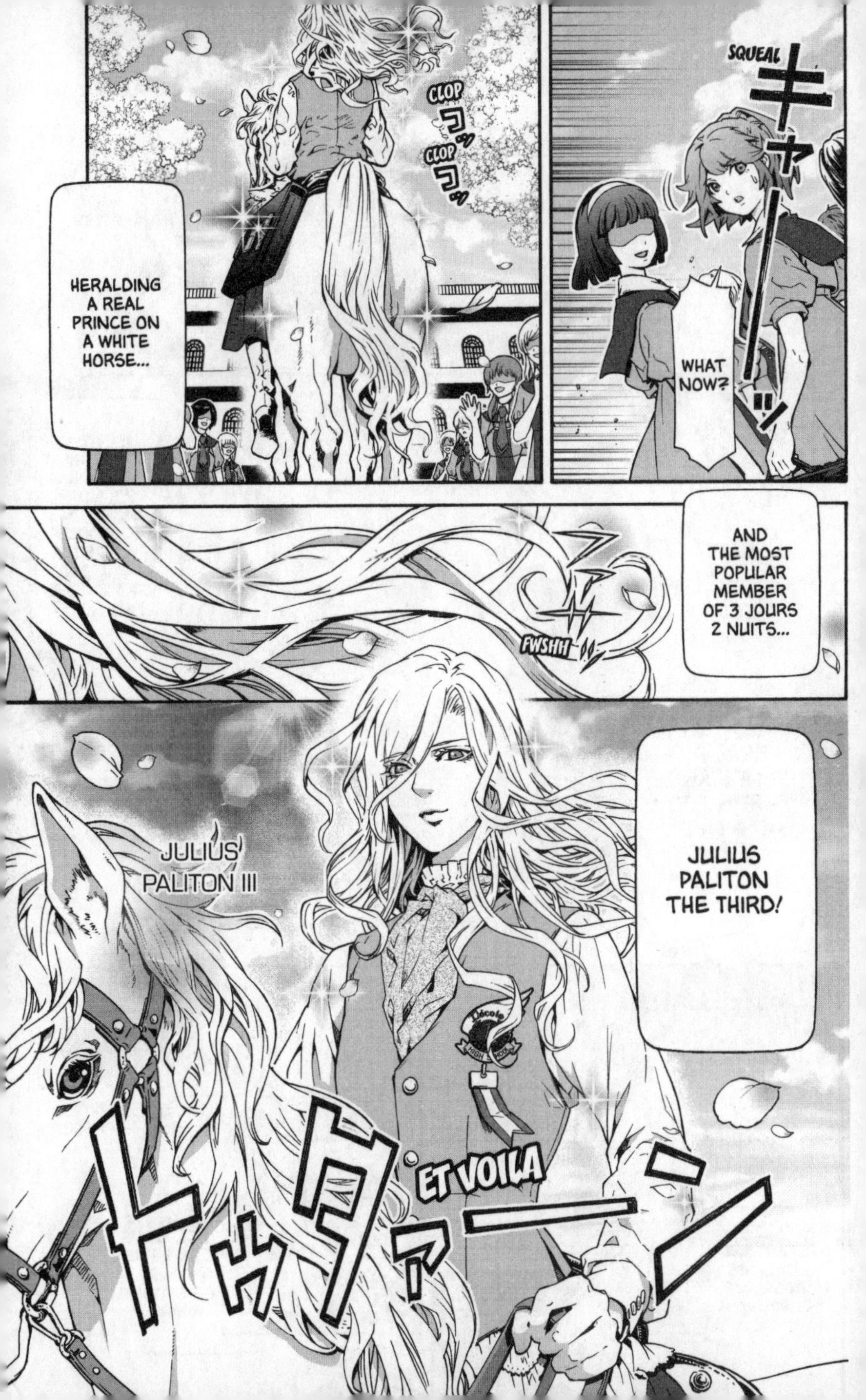
SQUEAL
WHAT NOW?
CLOP
CLOP
HERALDING A REAL PRINCE ON A WHITE HORSE...
AND THE MOST POPULAR MEMBER OF 3 JOURS 2 NUITS...
FWSHH
JULIUS PALITON THE THIRD!
JULIUS PALITON III
ET VOILA

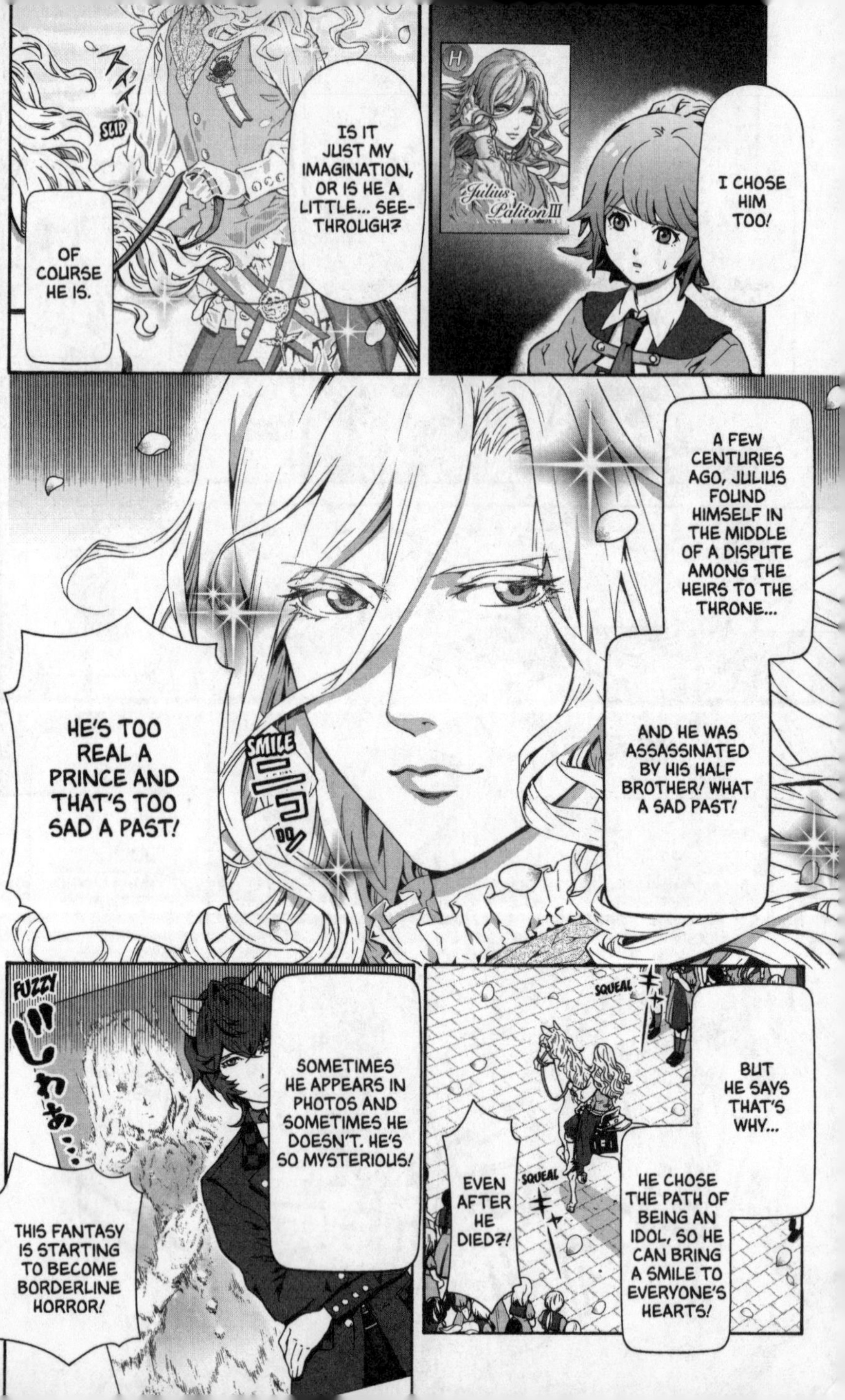
H
Julius Paliton III
I CHOSE HIM TOO!
IS IT JUST MY IMAGINATION, OR IS HE A LITTLE... SEE-THROUGH?
SLIP
OF COURSE HE IS.
A FEW CENTURIES AGO, JULIUS FOUND HIMSELF IN THE MIDDLE OF A DISPUTE AMONG THE HEIRS TO THE THRONE...
AND HE WAS ASSASSINATED BY HIS HALF BROTHER! WHAT A SAD PAST!
SMILE
HE'S TOO REAL A PRINCE AND THAT'S TOO SAD A PAST!
SQUEAL
BUT HE SAYS THAT'S WHY...
HE CHOSE THE PATH OF BEING AN IDOL, SO HE CAN BRING A SMILE TO EVERYONE'S HEARTS!
SQUEAL
EVEN AFTER HE DIED?!
SOMETIMES HE APPEARS IN PHOTOS AND SOMETIMES HE DOESN'T. HE'S SO MYSTERIOUS!
FUZZY
THIS FANTASY IS STARTING TO BECOME BORDERLINE HORROR!

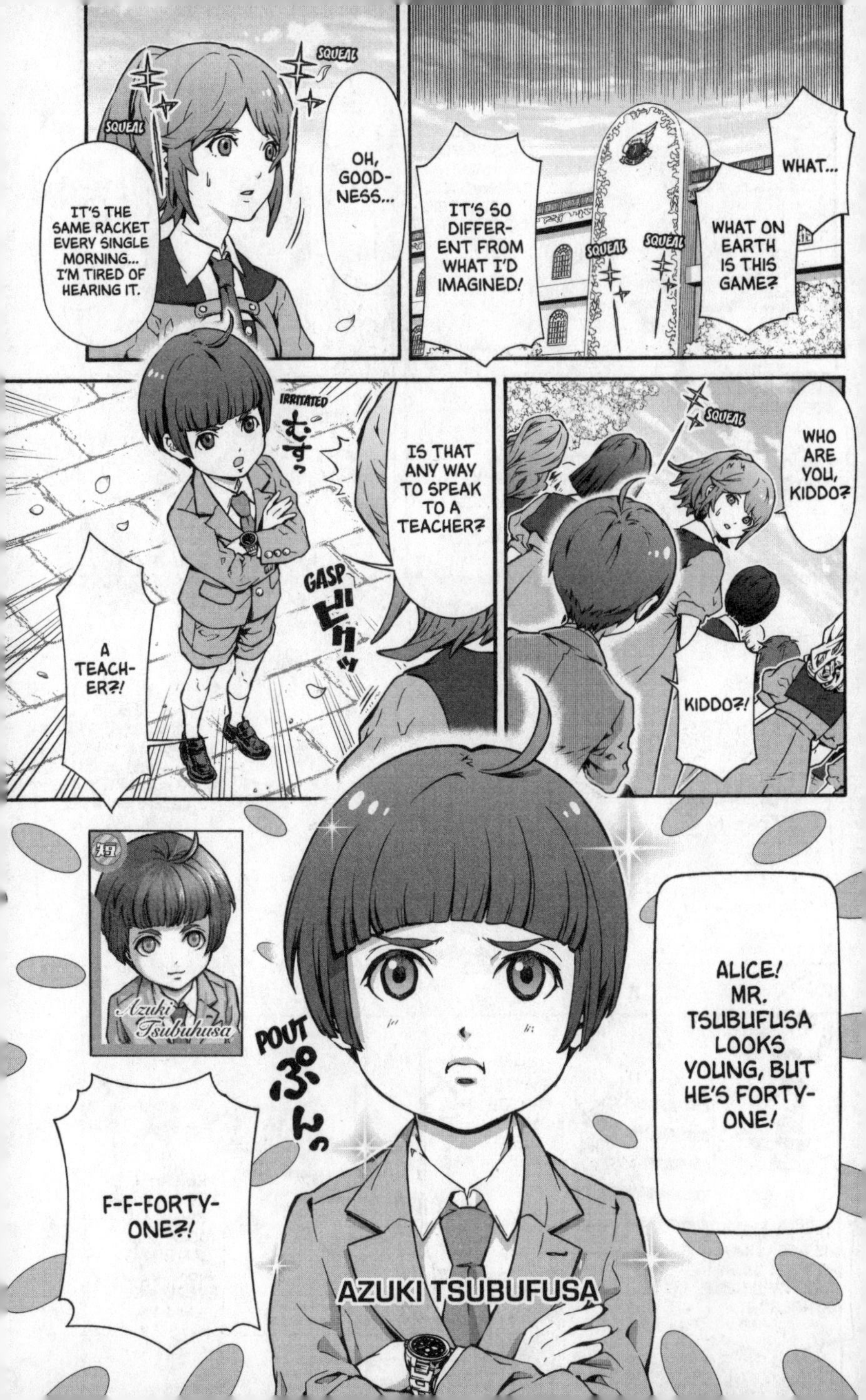
WHAT...
WHAT ON EARTH IS THIS GAME?
SQUEAL
SQUEAL
IT'S SO DIFFERENT FROM WHAT I'D IMAGINED!
SQUEAL
OH, GOODNESS...
SQUEAL
IT'S THE SAME RACKET EVERY SINGLE MORNING... I'M TIRED OF HEARING IT.
SQUEAL
WHO ARE YOU, KIDDO?
KIDDO?!
IS THAT ANY WAY TO SPEAK TO A TEACHER?
IRRITATED むすっ
GASP ビクッ
A TEACHER?!
ALICE! MR. TSUBUFUSA LOOKS YOUNG, BUT HE'S FORTY-ONE!
POUT ぷんっ
F-F-FORTY-ONE?!
Azuki Tsubuhusa
AZUKI TSUBUFUSA

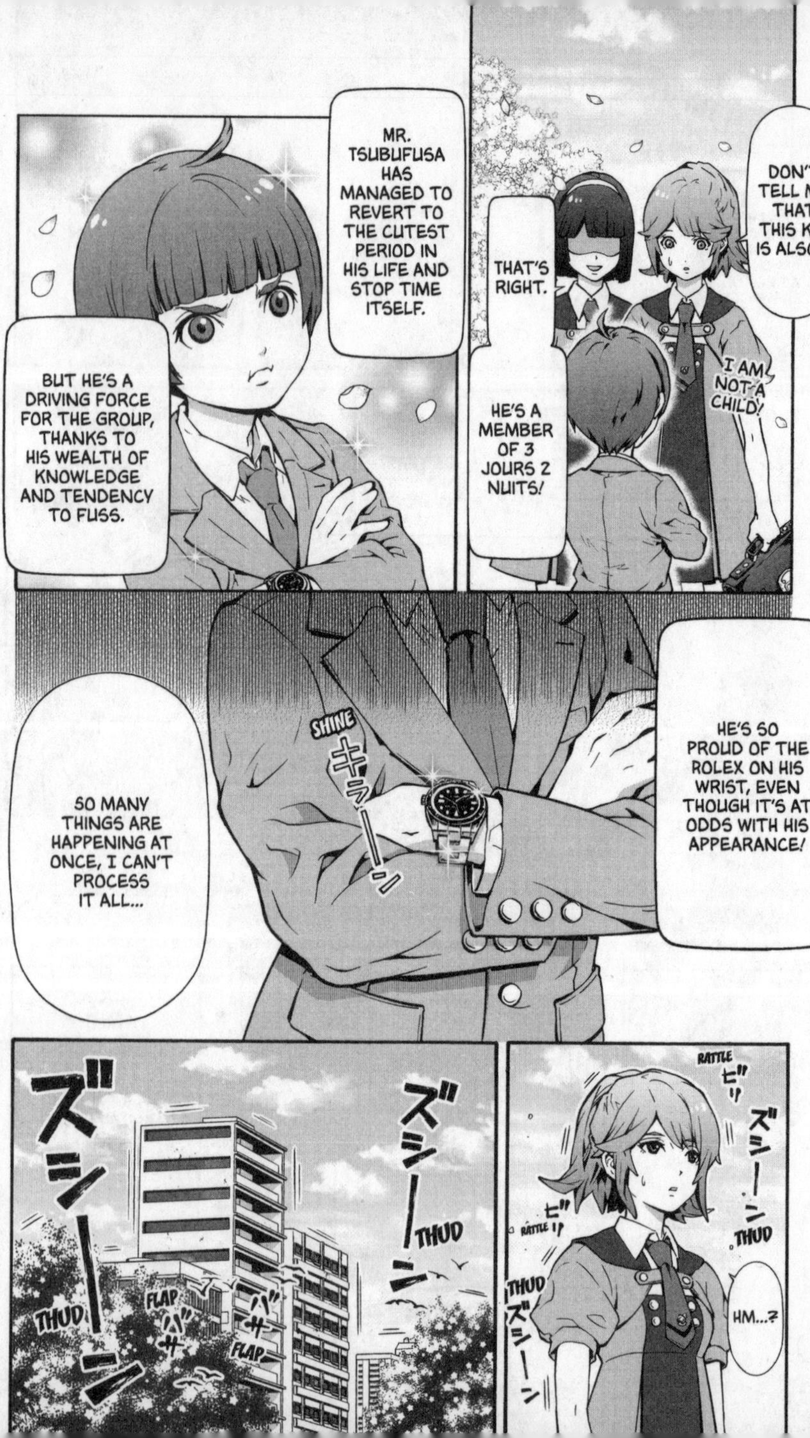
DON'T TELL ME THAT THIS KID IS ALSO...
THAT'S RIGHT.
HE'S A MEMBER OF 3 JOURS 2 NUITS!
I AM NOT A CHILD!
MR. TSUBUFUSA HAS MANAGED TO REVERT TO THE CUTEST PERIOD IN HIS LIFE AND STOP TIME ITSELF.
BUT HE'S A DRIVING FORCE FOR THE GROUP, THANKS TO HIS WEALTH OF KNOWLEDGE AND TENDENCY TO FUSS.
HE'S SO PROUD OF THE ROLEX ON HIS WRIST, EVEN THOUGH IT'S AT ODDS WITH HIS APPEARANCE!
SHINE
キラーン
SO MANY THINGS ARE HAPPENING AT ONCE, I CAN'T PROCESS IT ALL...
RATTLE
ビリ
ズシーン
THUD
RATTLE
ビリ
THUD
ズシーン
HM...?
ズシーン
THUD
FLAP
バサ
FLAP
バサ
ズシーン
THUD

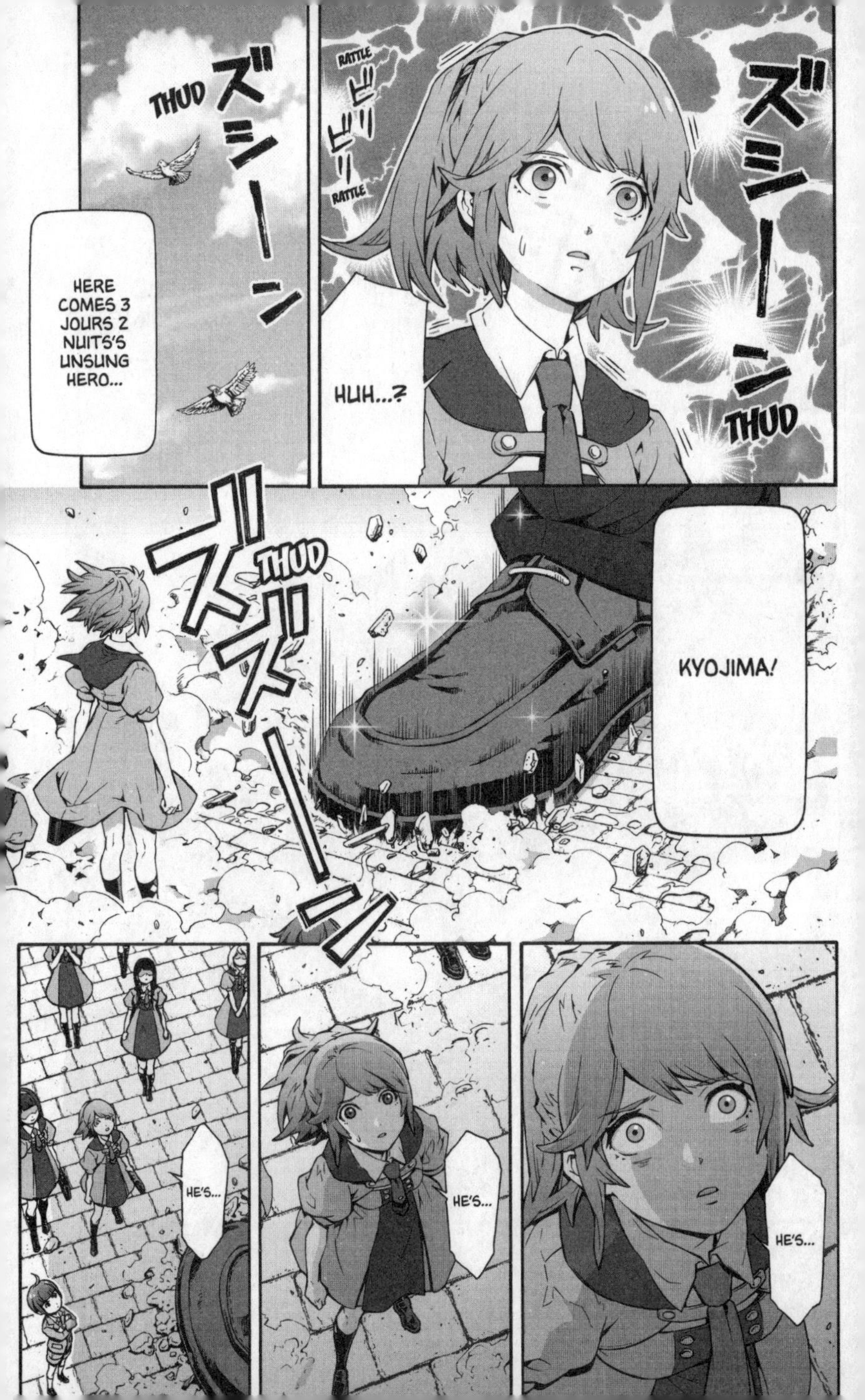
ズシーーン
THUD
RATTLE
ビリビリ
RATTLE
HUH...?
ズシーン
THUD
HERE COMES 3 JOURS 2 NUITS'S UNSUNG HERO...
KYOJIMA!
ズズズーン
THUD
HE'S...
HE'S...
HE'S...

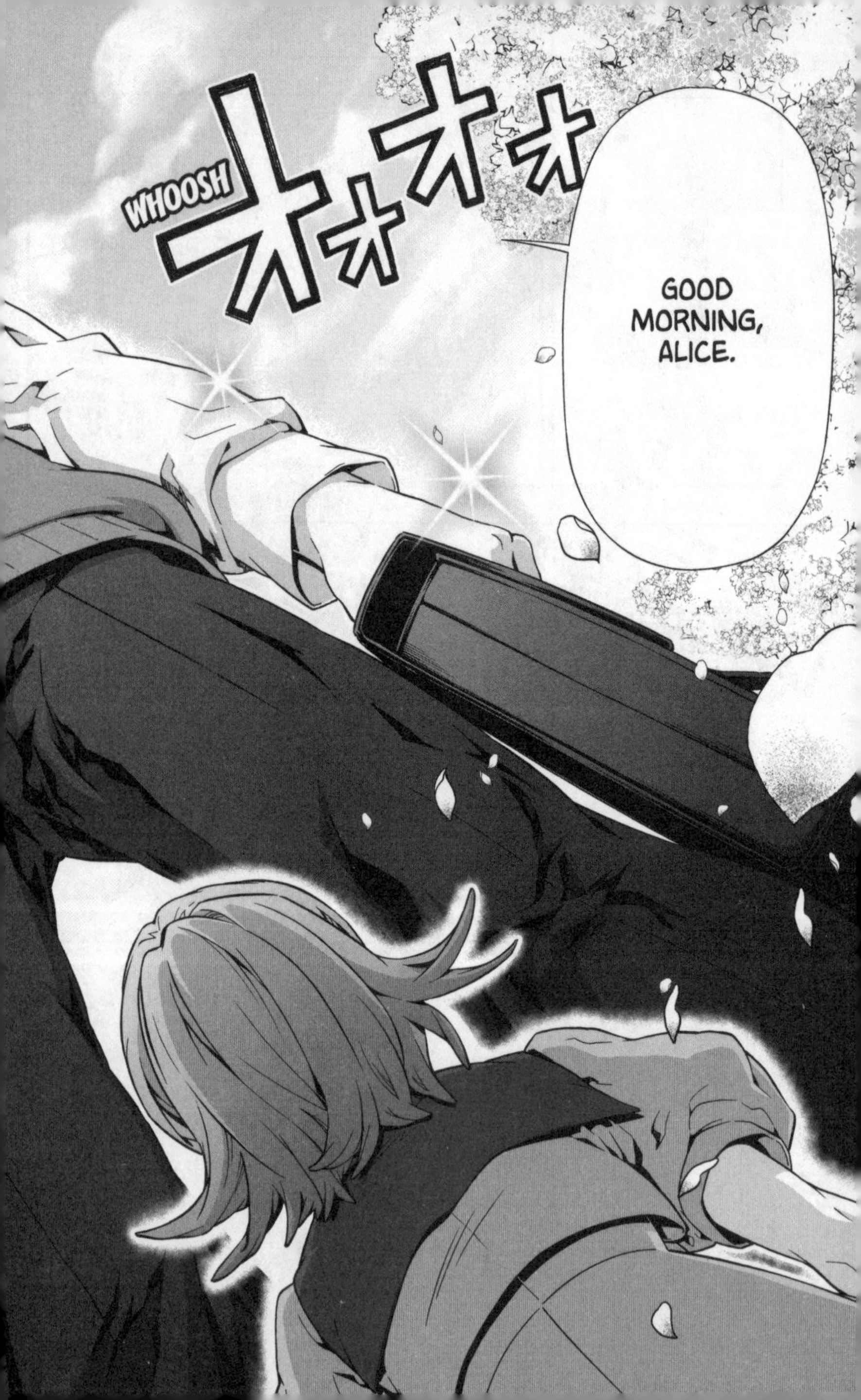

WHOOSH
オォオォ
GOOD MORNING, ALICE.

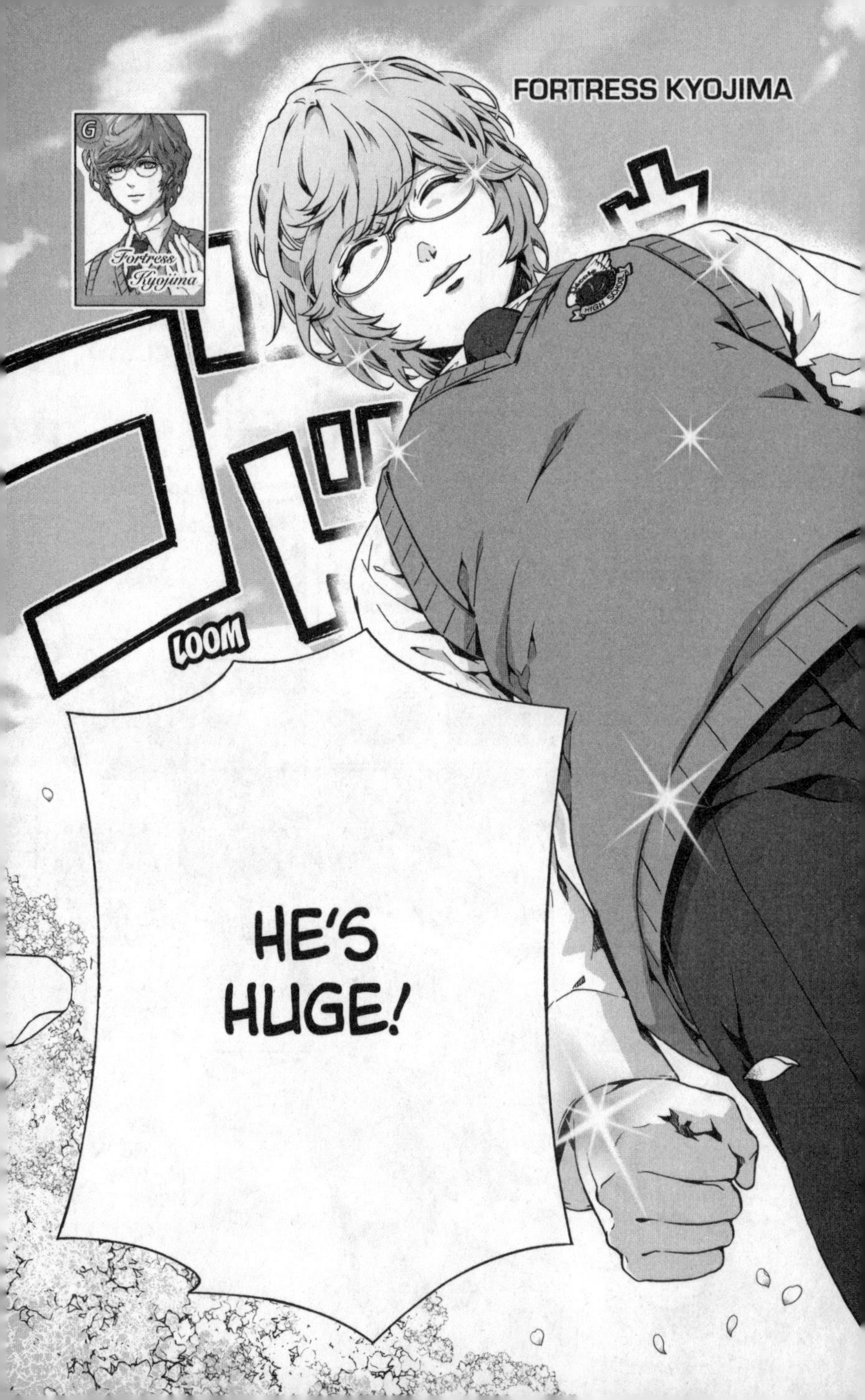
FORTRESS KYOJIMA
Fortress Kyojima
LOOM
HE'S HUGE!

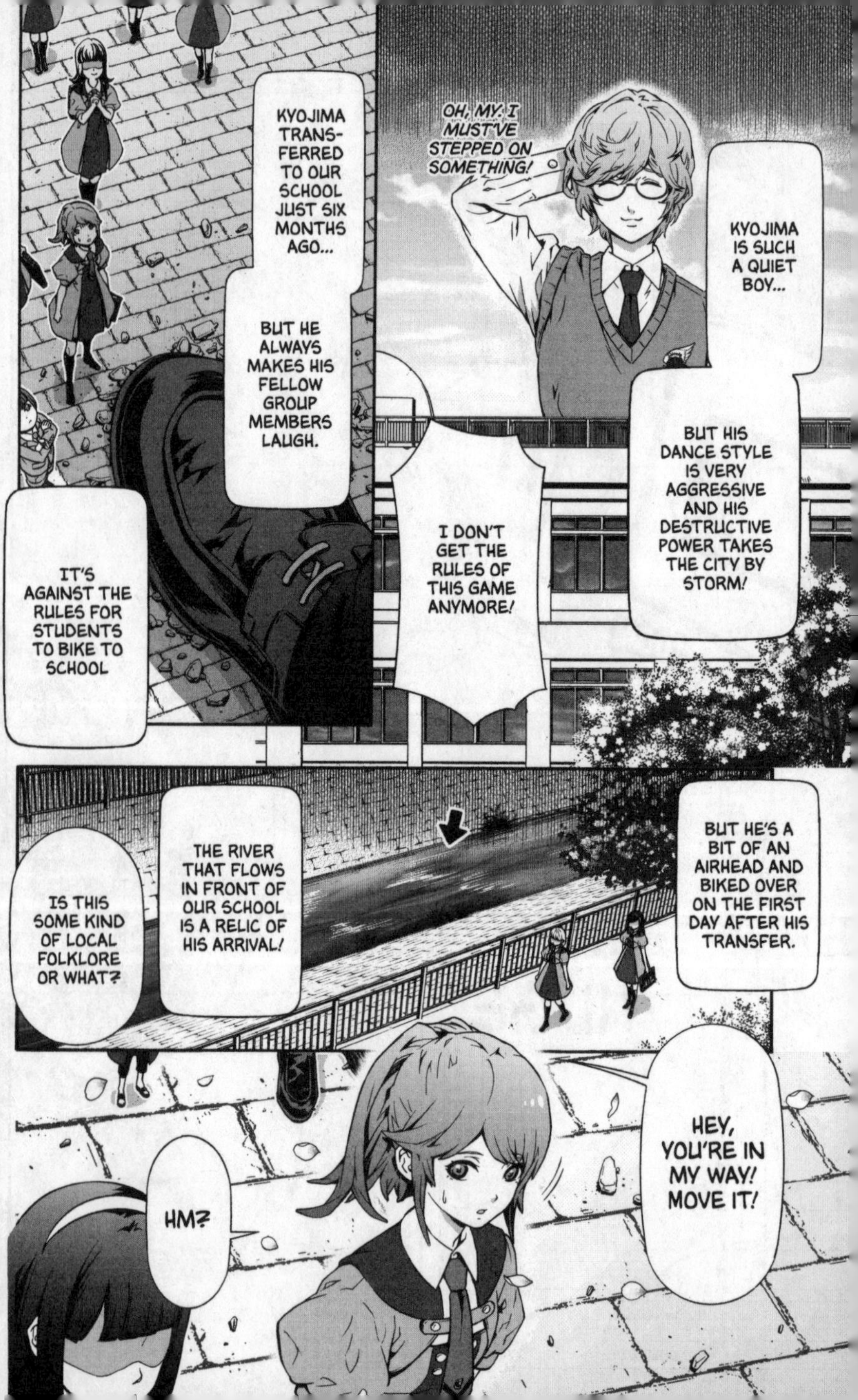

OH, MY. I MUST'VE STEPPED ON SOMETHING!
KYOJIMA IS SUCH A QUIET BOY...
BUT HIS DANCE STYLE IS VERY AGGRESSIVE AND HIS DESTRUCTIVE POWER TAKES THE CITY BY STORM!
I DON'T GET THE RULES OF THIS GAME ANYMORE!
KYOJIMA TRANS-FERRED TO OUR SCHOOL JUST SIX MONTHS AGO...
BUT HE ALWAYS MAKES HIS FELLOW GROUP MEMBERS LAUGH.
IT'S AGAINST THE RULES FOR STUDENTS TO BIKE TO SCHOOL
BUT HE'S A BIT OF AN AIRHEAD AND BIKED OVER ON THE FIRST DAY AFTER HIS TRANSFER.
THE RIVER THAT FLOWS IN FRONT OF OUR SCHOOL IS A RELIC OF HIS ARRIVAL!
IS THIS SOME KIND OF LOCAL FOLKLORE OR WHAT?
HEY, YOU'RE IN MY WAY! MOVE IT!
HM?

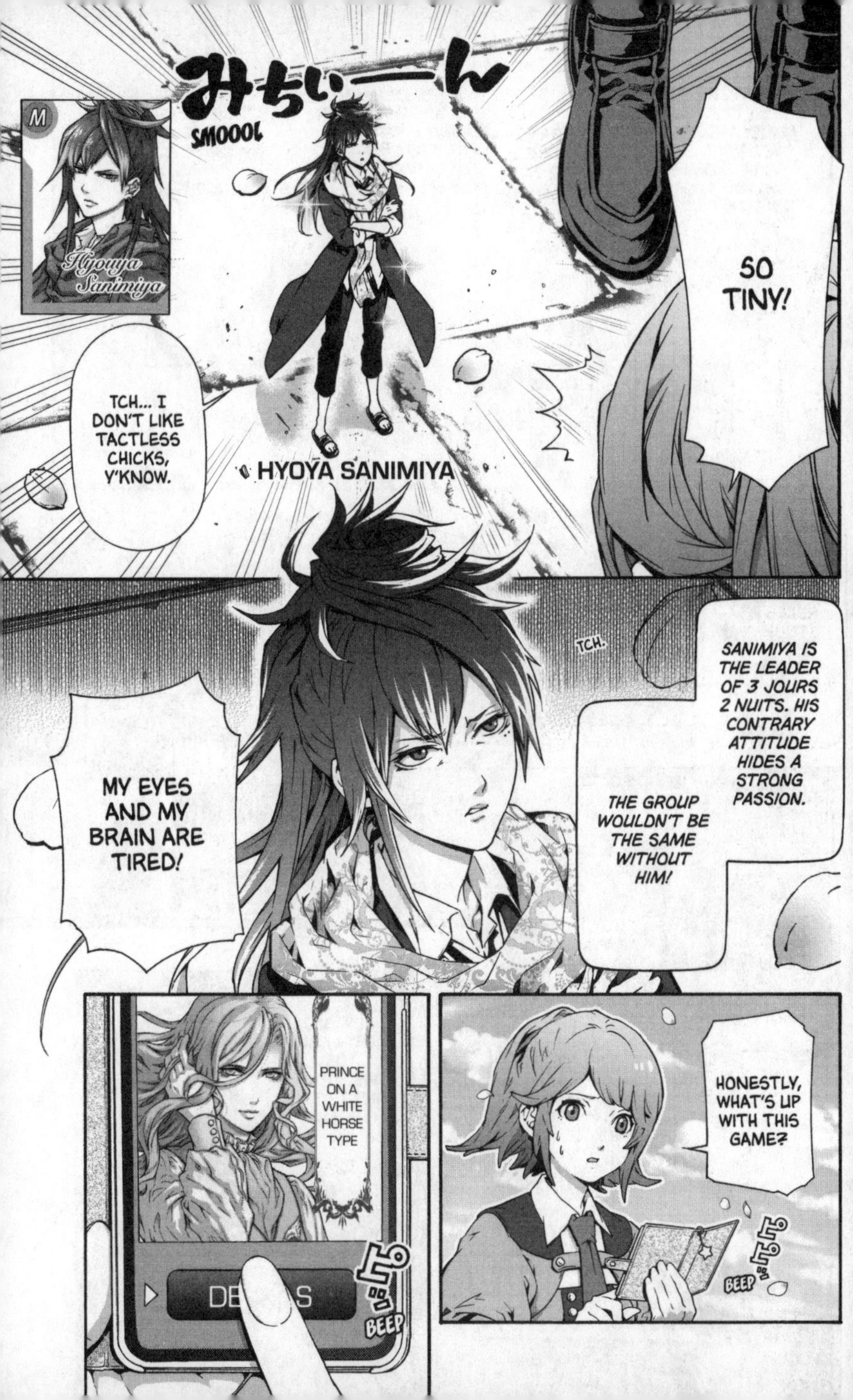
SO TINY!
みちぃーーん
SMOOOL
M
Hyouya Sanimiya
HYOYA SANIMIYA
TCH... I DON'T LIKE TACTLESS CHICKS, Y'KNOW.
TCH.
SANIMIYA IS THE LEADER OF 3 JOURS 2 NUITS. HIS CONTRARY ATTITUDE HIDES A STRONG PASSION.
THE GROUP WOULDN'T BE THE SAME WITHOUT HIM!
MY EYES AND MY BRAIN ARE TIRED!
HONESTLY, WHAT'S UP WITH THIS GAME?
BEEP
PRINCE ON A WHITE HORSE TYPE
BEEP

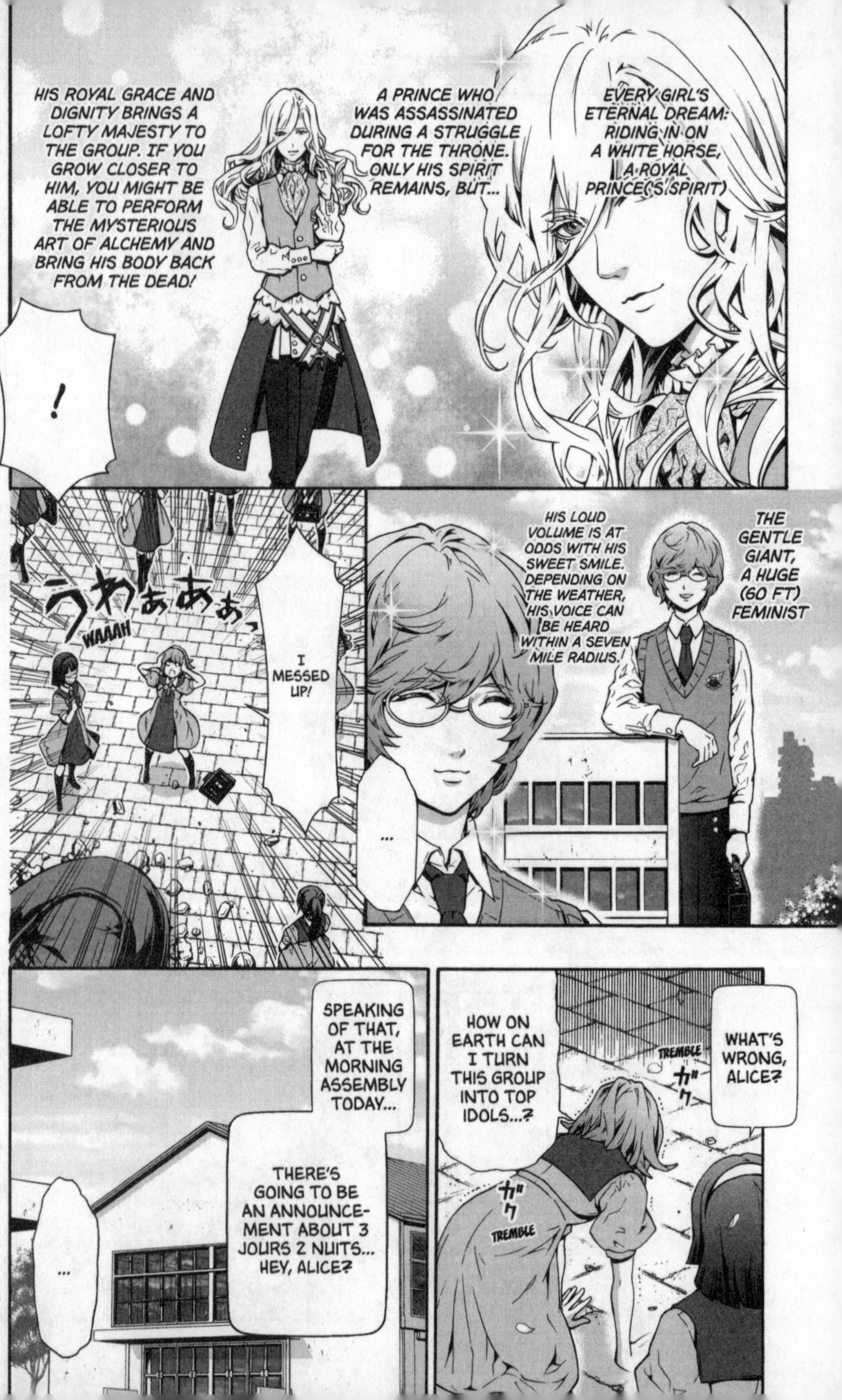
EVERY GIRL'S ETERNAL DREAM: RIDING IN ON A WHITE HORSE, A ROYAL PRINCE('S SPIRIT)
A PRINCE WHO WAS ASSASSINATED DURING A STRUGGLE FOR THE THRONE. ONLY HIS SPIRIT REMAINS, BUT...
HIS ROYAL GRACE AND DIGNITY BRINGS A LOFTY MAJESTY TO THE GROUP. IF YOU GROW CLOSER TO HIM, YOU MIGHT BE ABLE TO PERFORM THE MYSTERIOUS ART OF ALCHEMY AND BRING HIS BODY BACK FROM THE DEAD!
!
THE GENTLE GIANT, A HUGE (60 FT) FEMINIST
HIS LOUD VOLUME IS AT ODDS WITH HIS SWEET SMILE. DEPENDING ON THE WEATHER, HIS VOICE CAN BE HEARD WITHIN A SEVEN MILE RADIUS!
...
うわぁぁぁぁ
WAAAH
I MESSED UP!
WHAT'S WRONG, ALICE?
TREMBLE
HOW ON EARTH CAN I TURN THIS GROUP INTO TOP IDOLS...?
TREMBLE
SPEAKING OF THAT, AT THE MORNING ASSEMBLY TODAY...
THERE'S GOING TO BE AN ANNOUNCE-MENT ABOUT 3 JOURS 2 NUITS... HEY, ALICE?
...

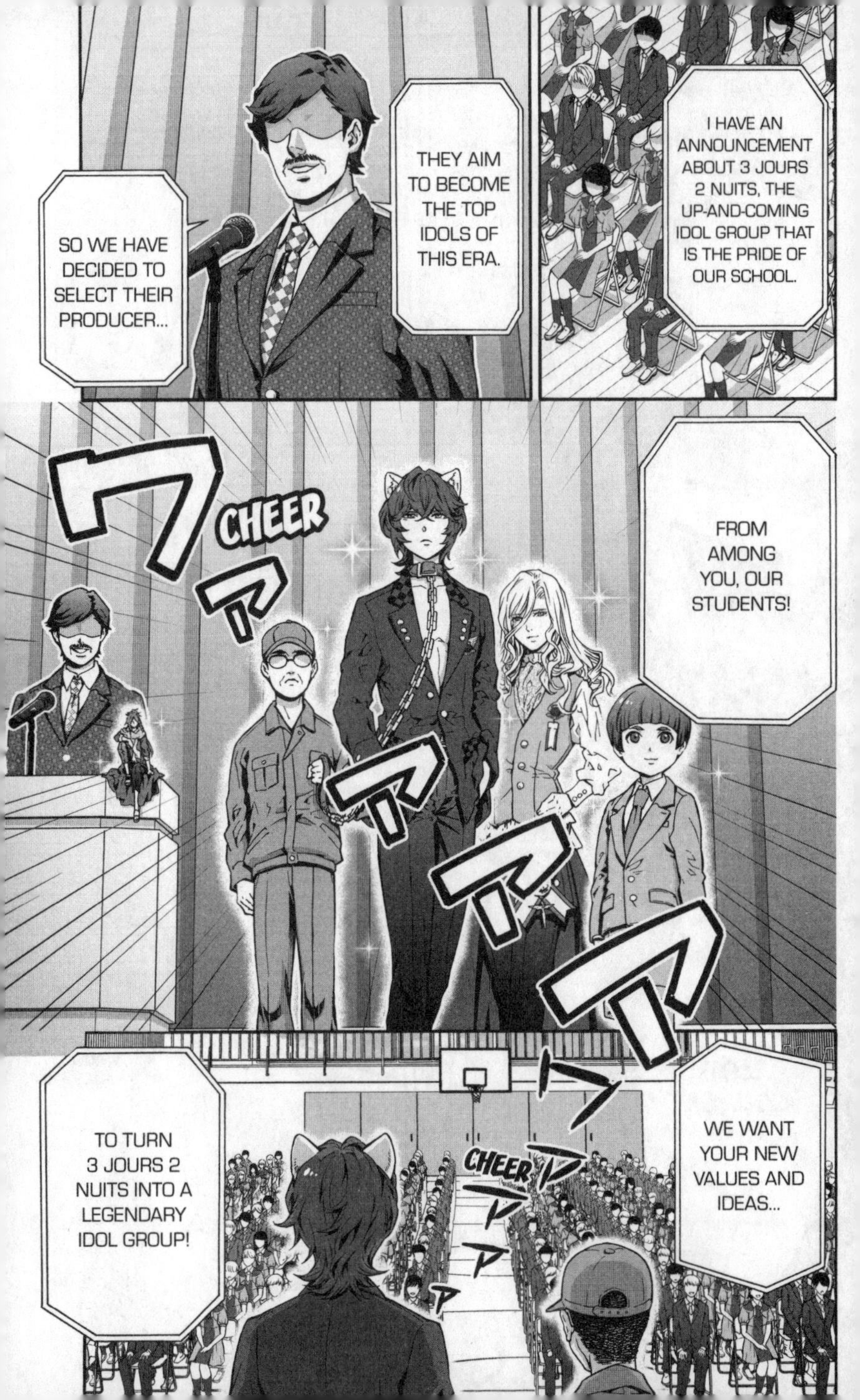
I HAVE AN ANNOUNCEMENT ABOUT 3 JOURS 2 NUITS, THE UP-AND-COMING IDOL GROUP THAT IS THE PRIDE OF OUR SCHOOL.
THEY AIM TO BECOME THE TOP IDOLS OF THIS ERA.
SO WE HAVE DECIDED TO SELECT THEIR PRODUCER...
FROM AMONG YOU, OUR STUDENTS!
CHEER
WE WANT YOUR NEW VALUES AND IDEAS...
TO TURN 3 JOURS 2 NUITS INTO A LEGENDARY IDOL GROUP!
CHEER

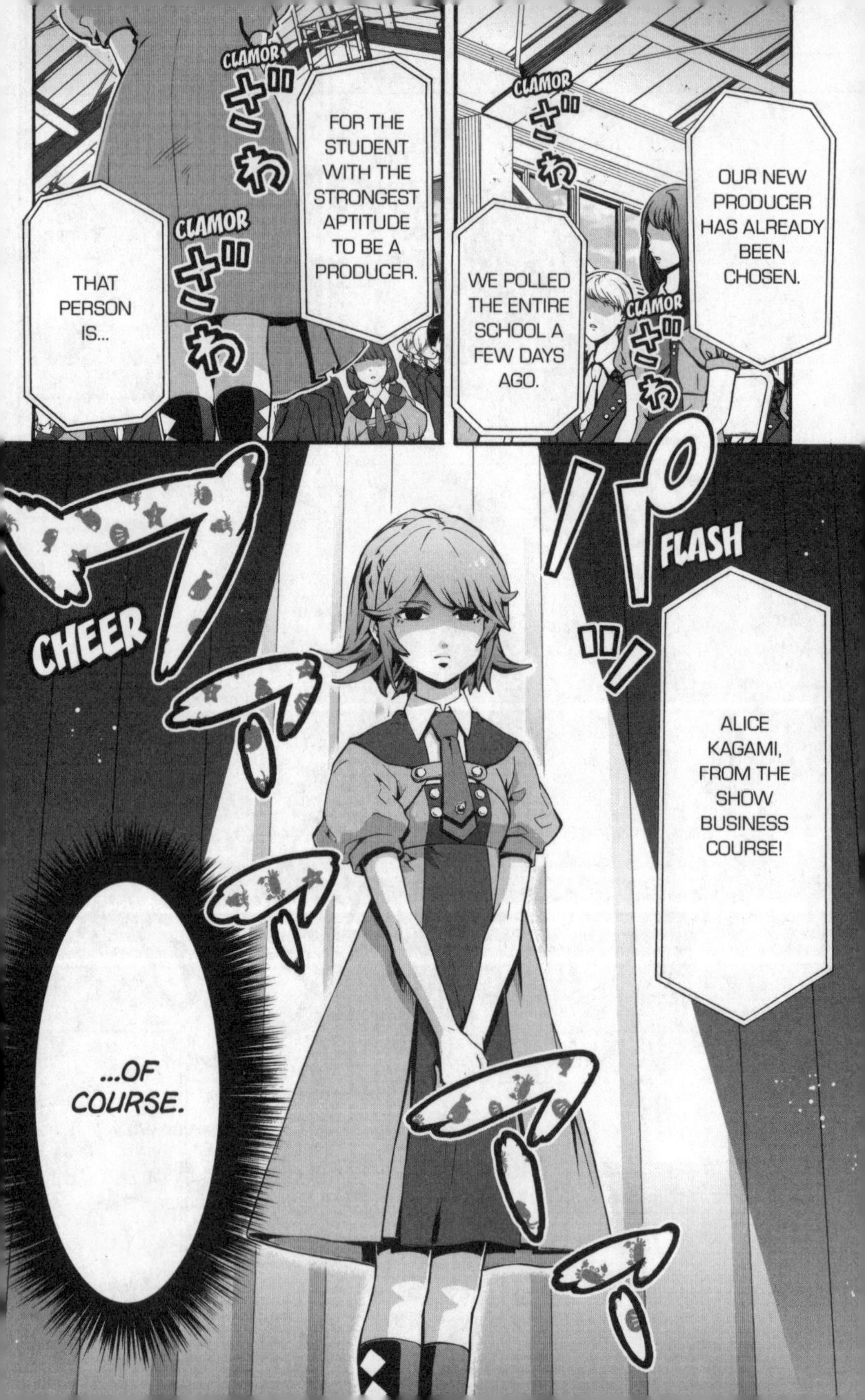
OUR NEW PRODUCER HAS ALREADY BEEN CHOSEN.
CLAMOR
ざわ
CLAMOR
ざわ
WE POLLED THE ENTIRE SCHOOL A FEW DAYS AGO.
FOR THE STUDENT WITH THE STRONGEST APTITUDE TO BE A PRODUCER.
CLAMOR
ざわ
CLAMOR
ざわ
THAT PERSON IS...
FLASH
パッ
ALICE KAGAMI, FROM THE SHOW BUSINESS COURSE!
CHEER
ワ
...OF COURSE.

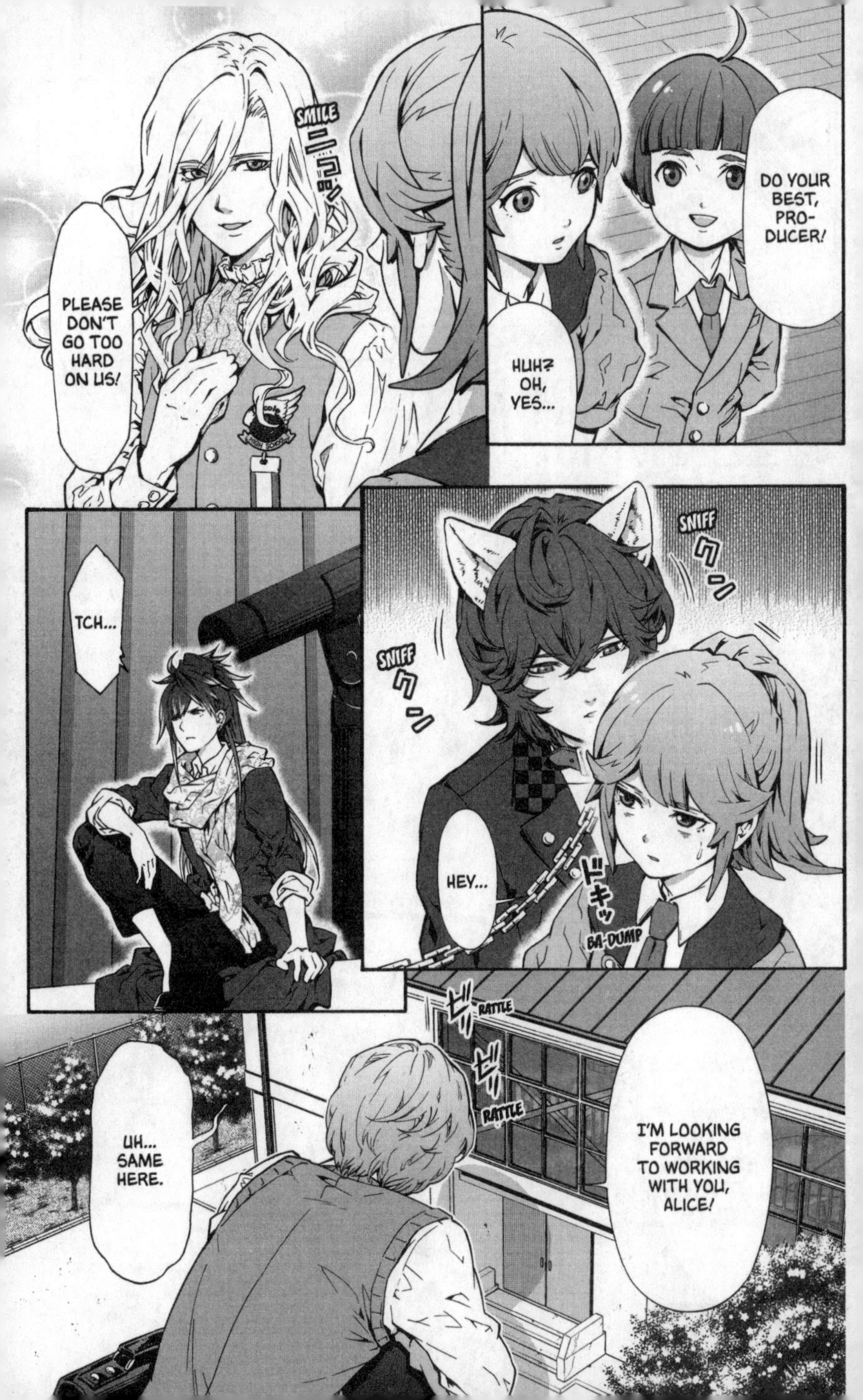
DO YOUR BEST, PRO-DUCER!
HUH? OH, YES...
SMILE
PLEASE DON'T GO TOO HARD ON US!
SNIFF
SNIFF
HEY...
BA-DUMP
TCH...
RATTLE
RATTLE
I'M LOOKING FORWARD TO WORKING WITH YOU, ALICE!
UH... SAME HERE.

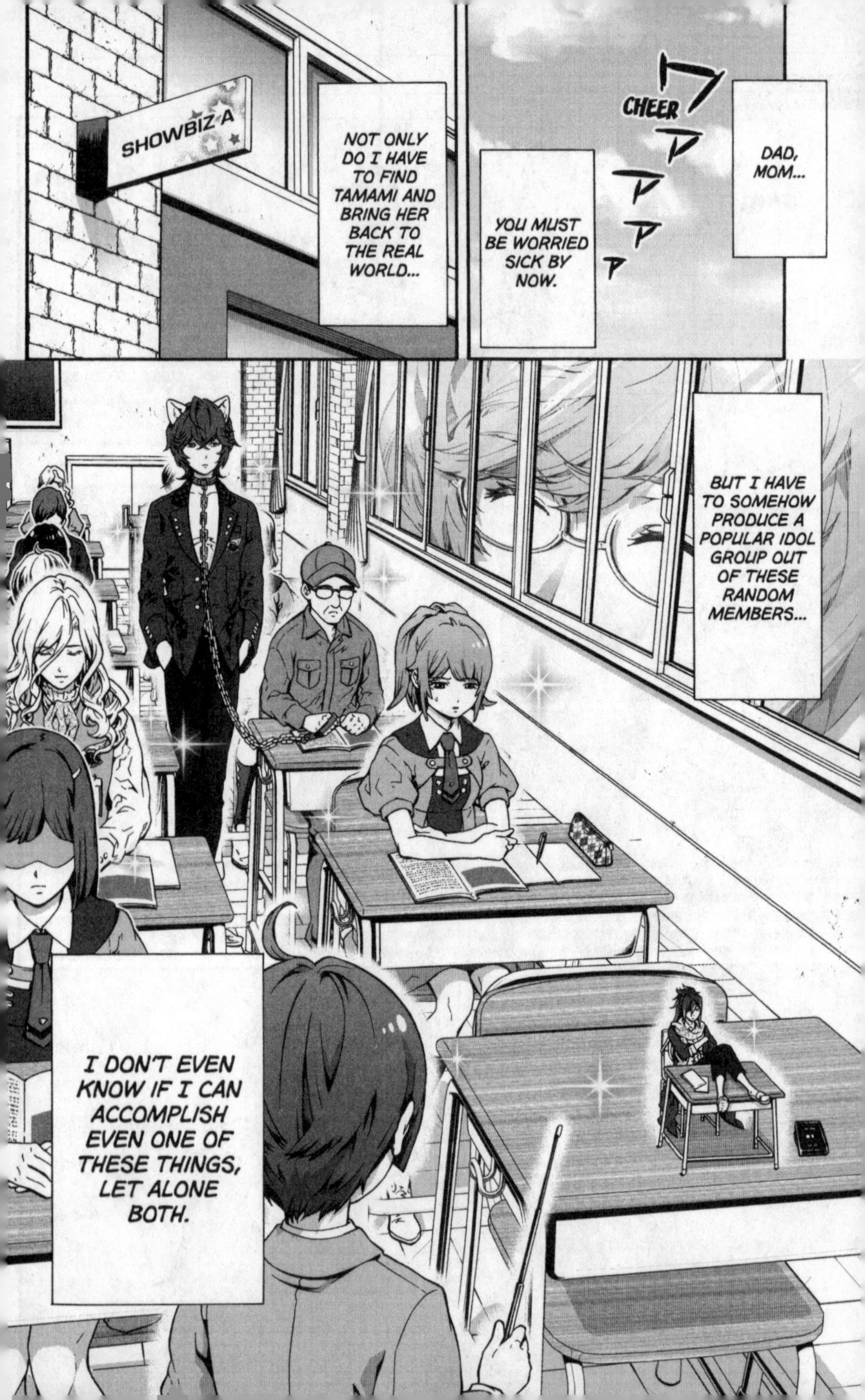
DAD, MOM...
CHEER
YOU MUST BE WORRIED SICK BY NOW.
SHOWBIZ A
NOT ONLY DO I HAVE TO FIND TAMAMI AND BRING HER BACK TO THE REAL WORLD...
BUT I HAVE TO SOMEHOW PRODUCE A POPULAR IDOL GROUP OUT OF THESE RANDOM MEMBERS...
I DON'T EVEN KNOW IF I CAN ACCOMPLISH EVEN ONE OF THESE THINGS, LET ALONE BOTH.

Stage 3 3 Jours 2 Nuits, Reborn

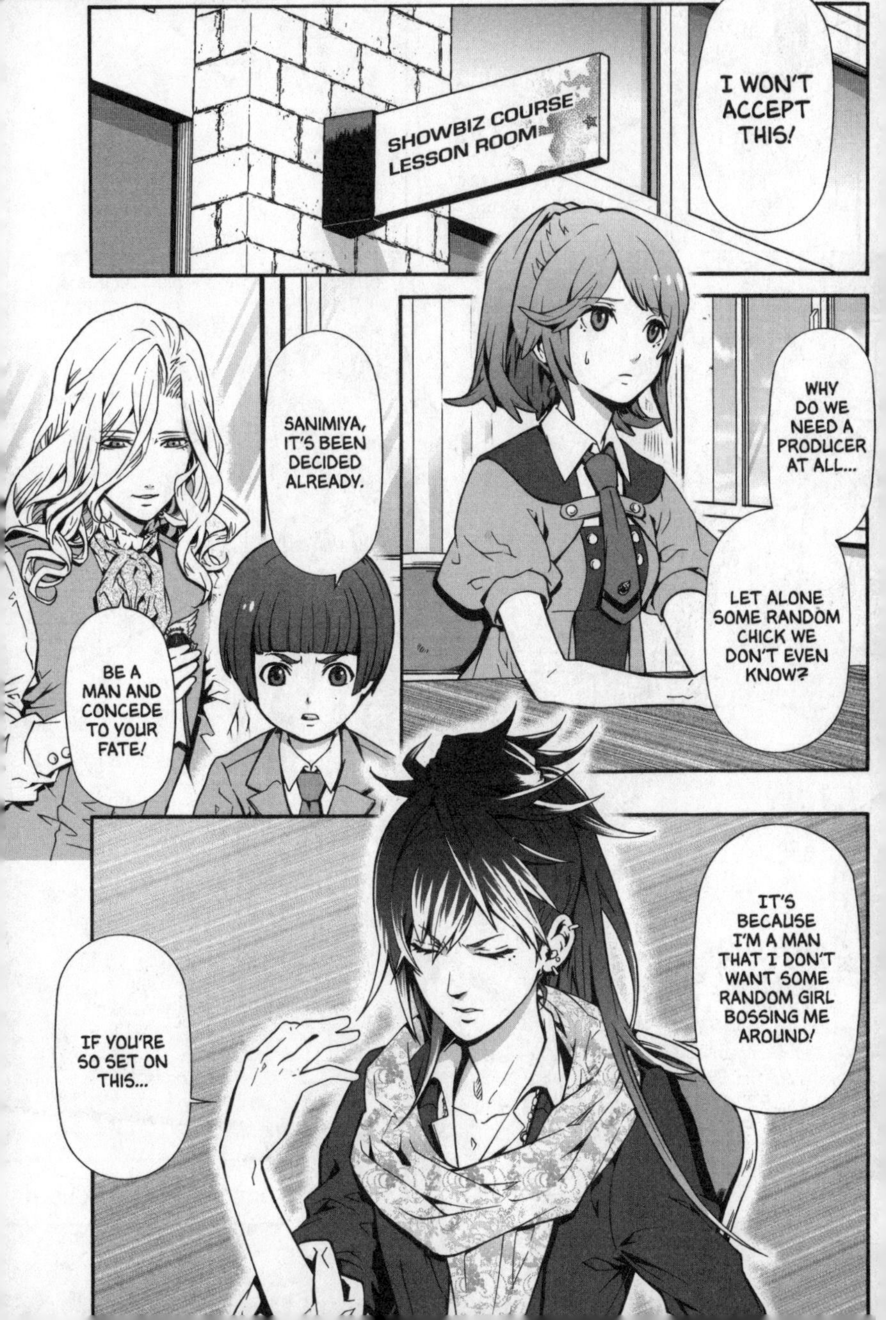
I WON'T ACCEPT THIS!
SHOWBIZ COURSE LESSON ROOM
WHY DO WE NEED A PRODUCER AT ALL...
LET ALONE SOME RANDOM CHICK WE DON'T EVEN KNOW?
SANIMIYA, IT'S BEEN DECIDED ALREADY.
BE A MAN AND CONCEDE TO YOUR FATE!
IT'S BECAUSE I'M A MAN THAT I DON'T WANT SOME RANDOM GIRL BOSSING ME AROUND!
IF YOU'RE SO SET ON THIS...

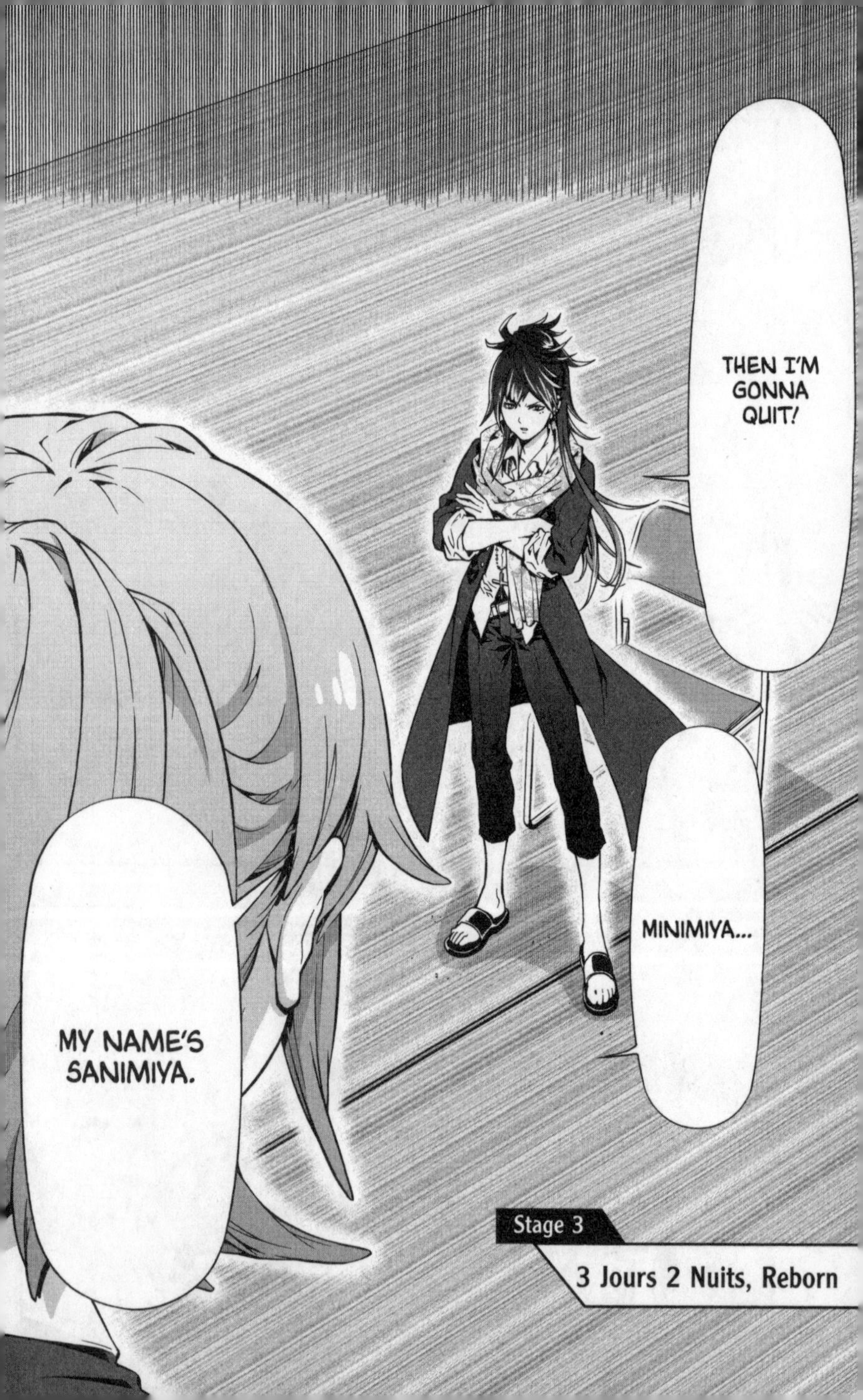
THEN I'M GONNA QUIT!
MINIMIYA...
MY NAME'S SANIMIYA.
Stage 3
3 Jours 2 Nuits, Reborn

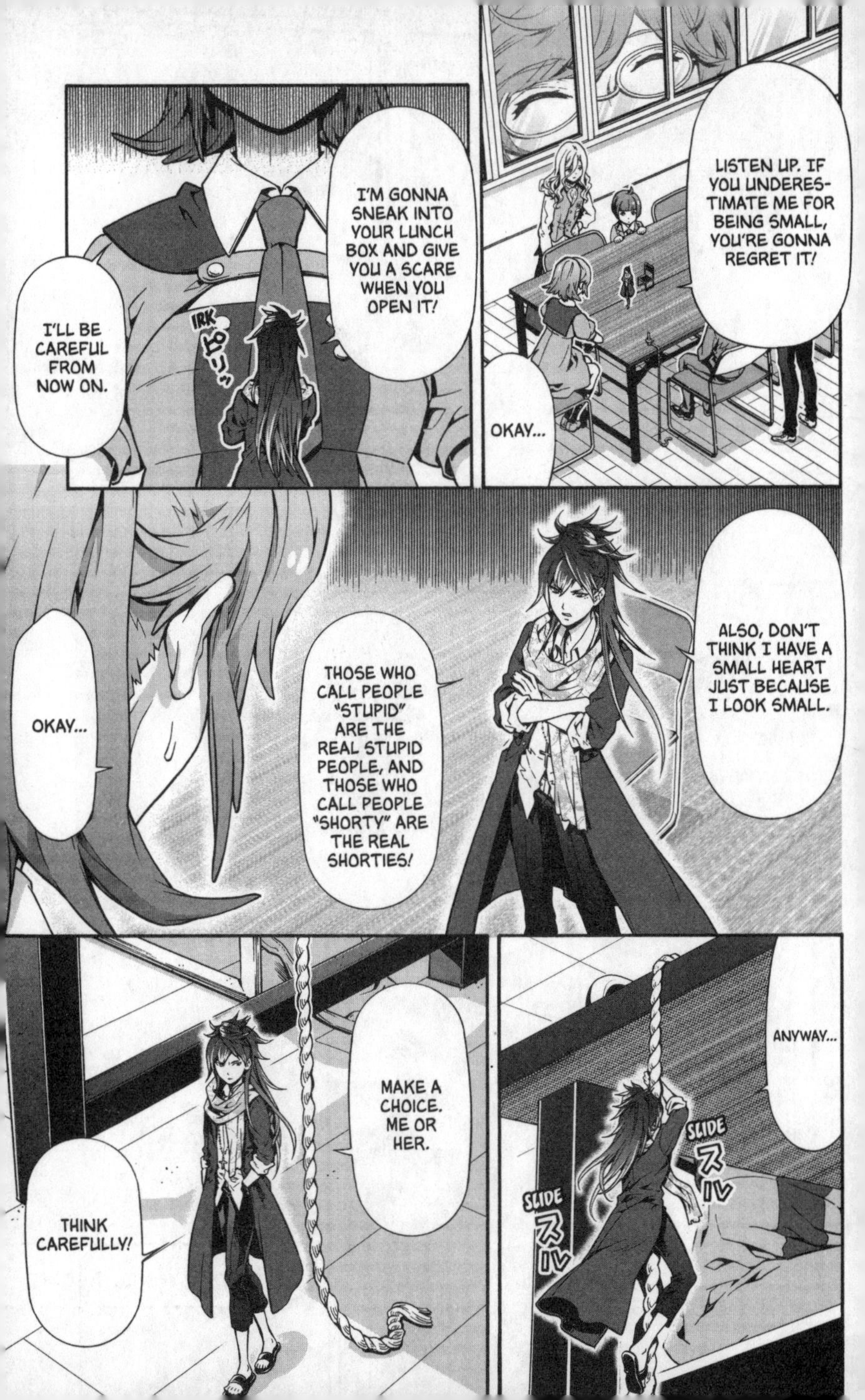
LISTEN UP. IF YOU UNDERES-TIMATE ME FOR BEING SMALL, YOU'RE GONNA REGRET IT!
OKAY...
I'M GONNA SNEAK INTO YOUR LUNCH BOX AND GIVE YOU A SCARE WHEN YOU OPEN IT!
IRK
ピリッ
I'LL BE CAREFUL FROM NOW ON.
ALSO, DON'T THINK I HAVE A SMALL HEART JUST BECAUSE I LOOK SMALL.
THOSE WHO CALL PEOPLE "STUPID" ARE THE REAL STUPID PEOPLE, AND THOSE WHO CALL PEOPLE "SHORTY" ARE THE REAL SHORTIES!
OKAY...
ANYWAY...
SLIDE
スル
SLIDE
スル
MAKE A CHOICE. ME OR HER.
THINK CAREFULLY!

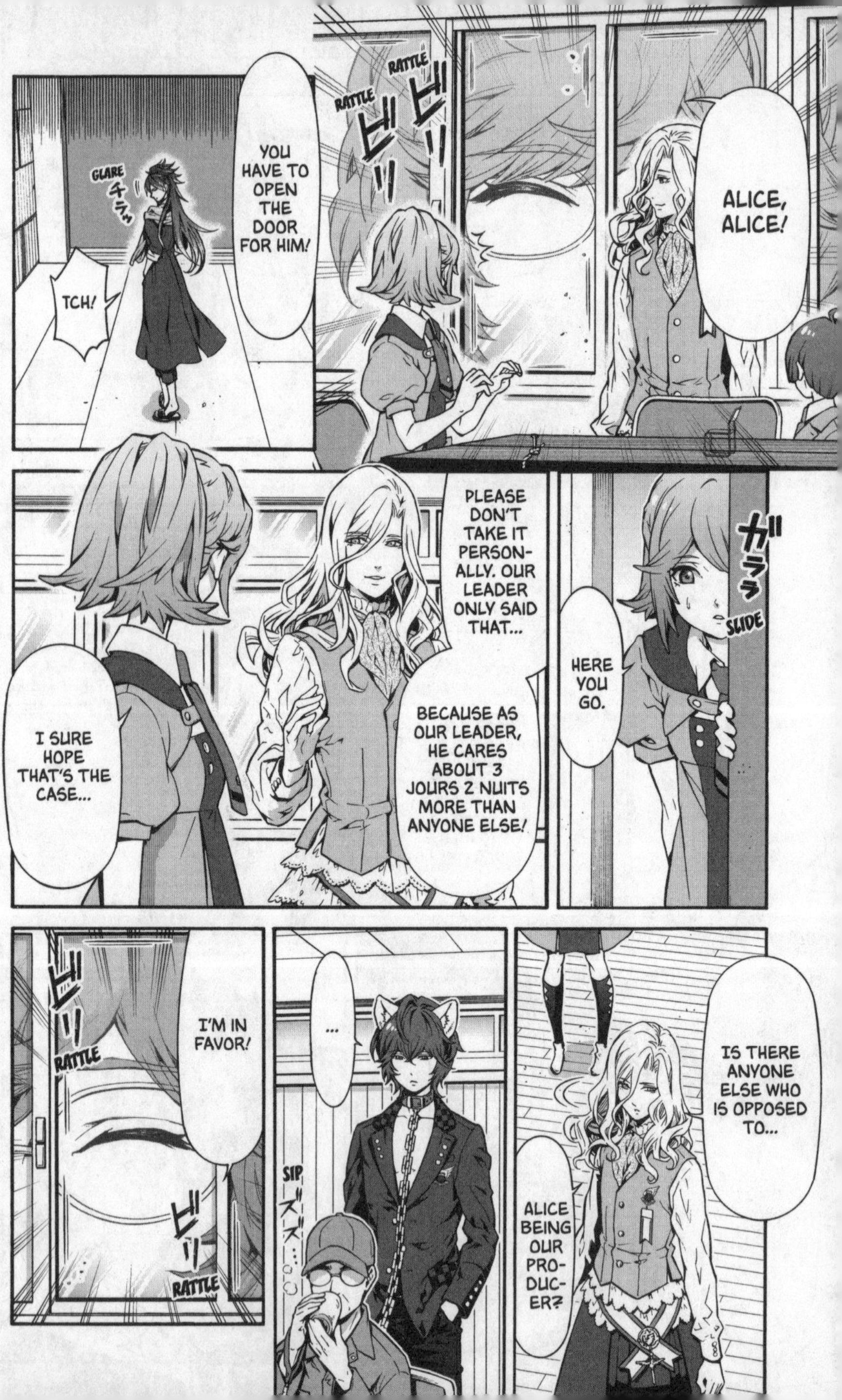
ALICE, ALICE!
RATTLE
RATTLE
YOU HAVE TO OPEN THE DOOR FOR HIM!
GLARE
チラッ
TCH!
ガララ
SLIDE
HERE YOU GO.
PLEASE DON'T TAKE IT PERSON-ALLY. OUR LEADER ONLY SAID THAT...
BECAUSE AS OUR LEADER, HE CARES ABOUT 3 JOURS 2 NUITS MORE THAN ANYONE ELSE!
I SURE HOPE THAT'S THE CASE...
IS THERE ANYONE ELSE WHO IS OPPOSED TO...
ALICE BEING OUR PRO-DUC-ER?
...
SIP
RATTLE
I'M IN FAVOR!
RATTLE

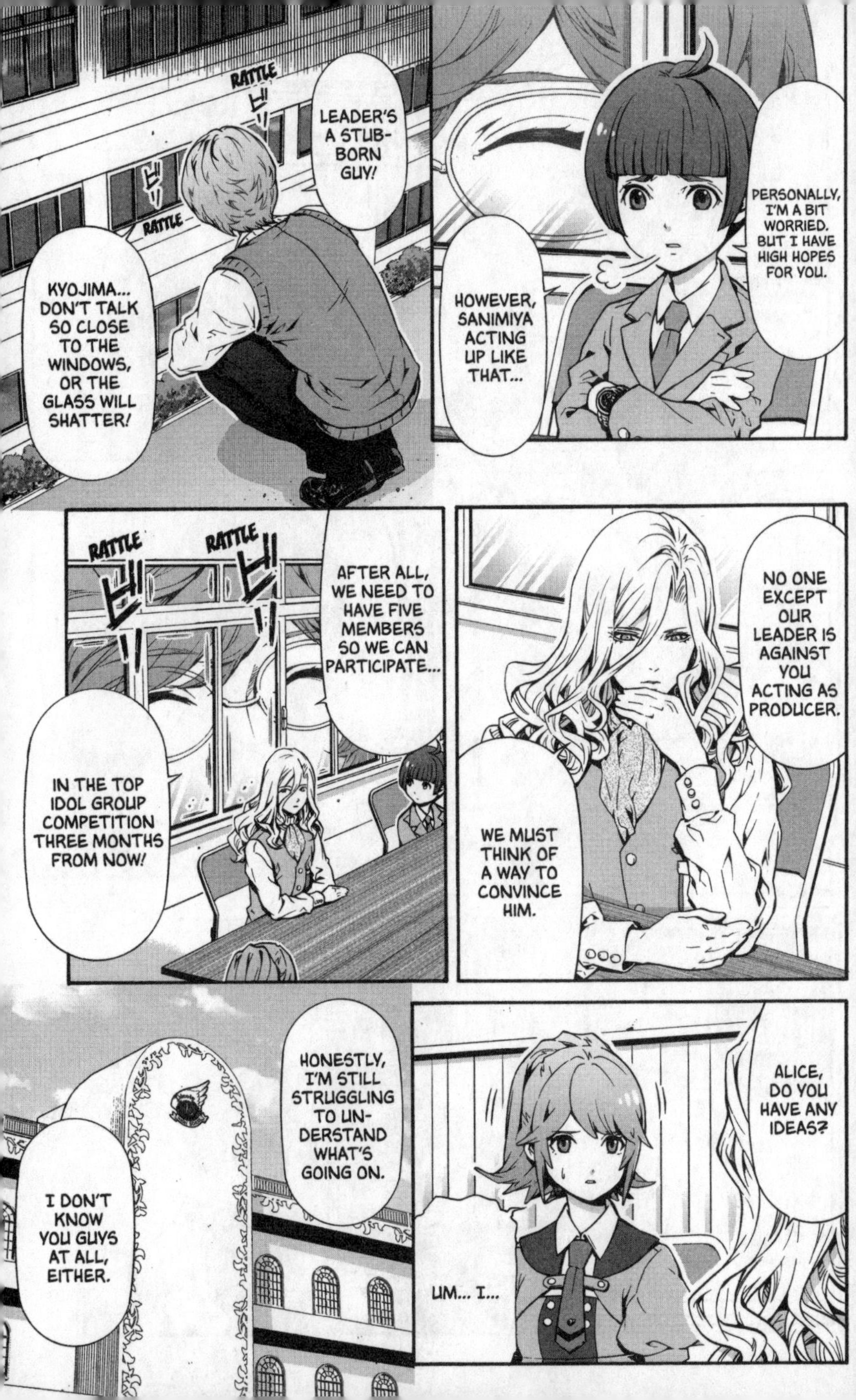
PERSONALLY, I'M A BIT WORRIED. BUT I HAVE HIGH HOPES FOR YOU.
HOWEVER, SANIMIYA ACTING UP LIKE THAT...
RATTLE
RATTLE
LEADER'S A STUB-BORN GUY!
KYOJIMA... DON'T TALK SO CLOSE TO THE WINDOWS, OR THE GLASS WILL SHATTER!
NO ONE EXCEPT OUR LEADER IS AGAINST YOU ACTING AS PRODUCER.
WE MUST THINK OF A WAY TO CONVINCE HIM.
RATTLE
RATTLE
AFTER ALL, WE NEED TO HAVE FIVE MEMBERS SO WE CAN PARTICIPATE...
IN THE TOP IDOL GROUP COMPETITION THREE MONTHS FROM NOW!
ALICE, DO YOU HAVE ANY IDEAS?
UM... I...
HONESTLY, I'M STILL STRUGGLING TO UN-DERSTAND WHAT'S GOING ON.
I DON'T KNOW YOU GUYS AT ALL, EITHER.

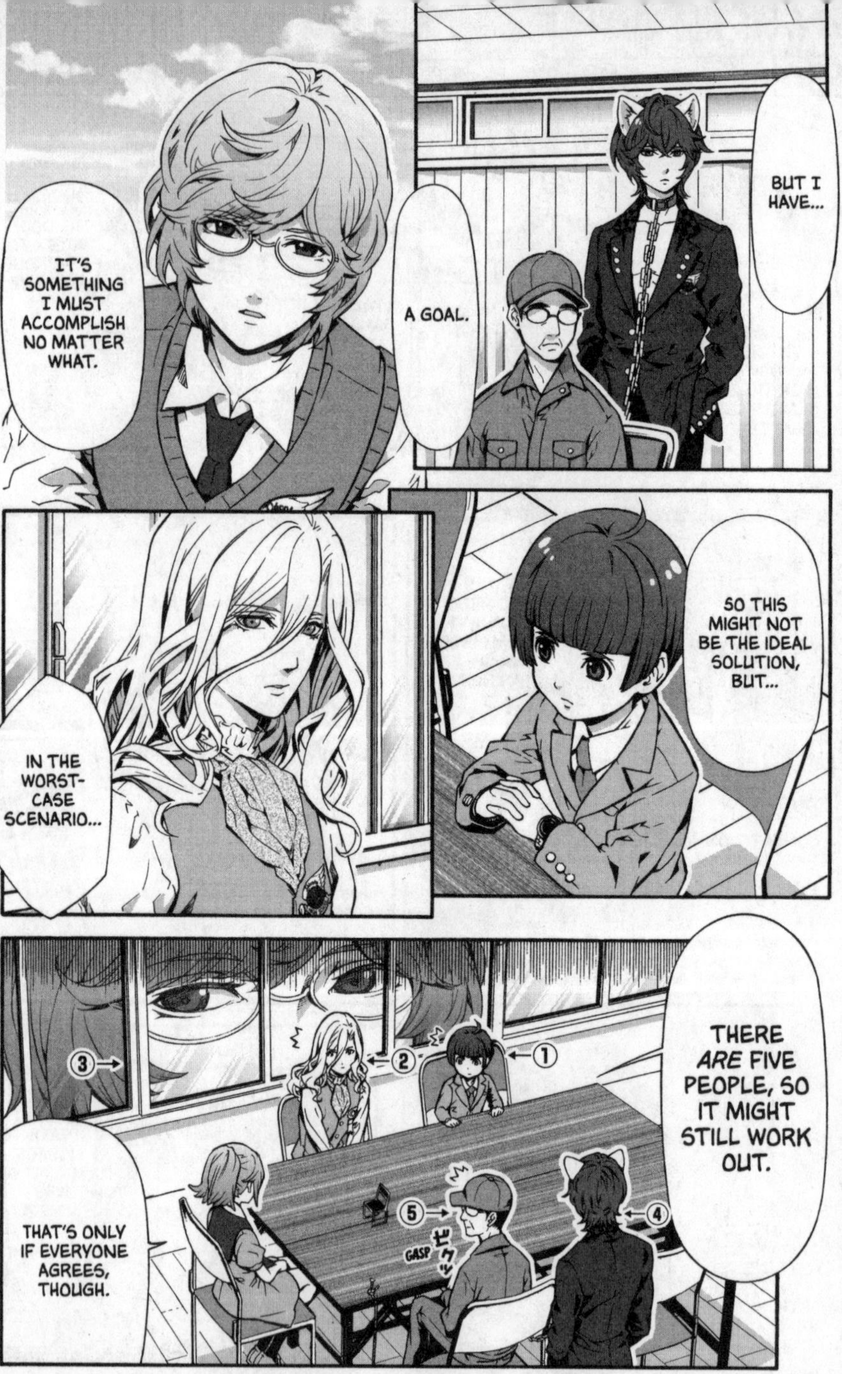
BUT I HAVE...
A GOAL.
IT'S SOMETHING I MUST ACCOMPLISH NO MATTER WHAT.
SO THIS MIGHT NOT BE THE IDEAL SOLUTION, BUT...
IN THE WORST-CASE SCENARIO...
THERE *ARE* FIVE PEOPLE, SO IT MIGHT STILL WORK OUT.
1
2
3
4
5
GASP ビクッ
THAT'S ONLY IF EVERYONE AGREES, THOUGH.

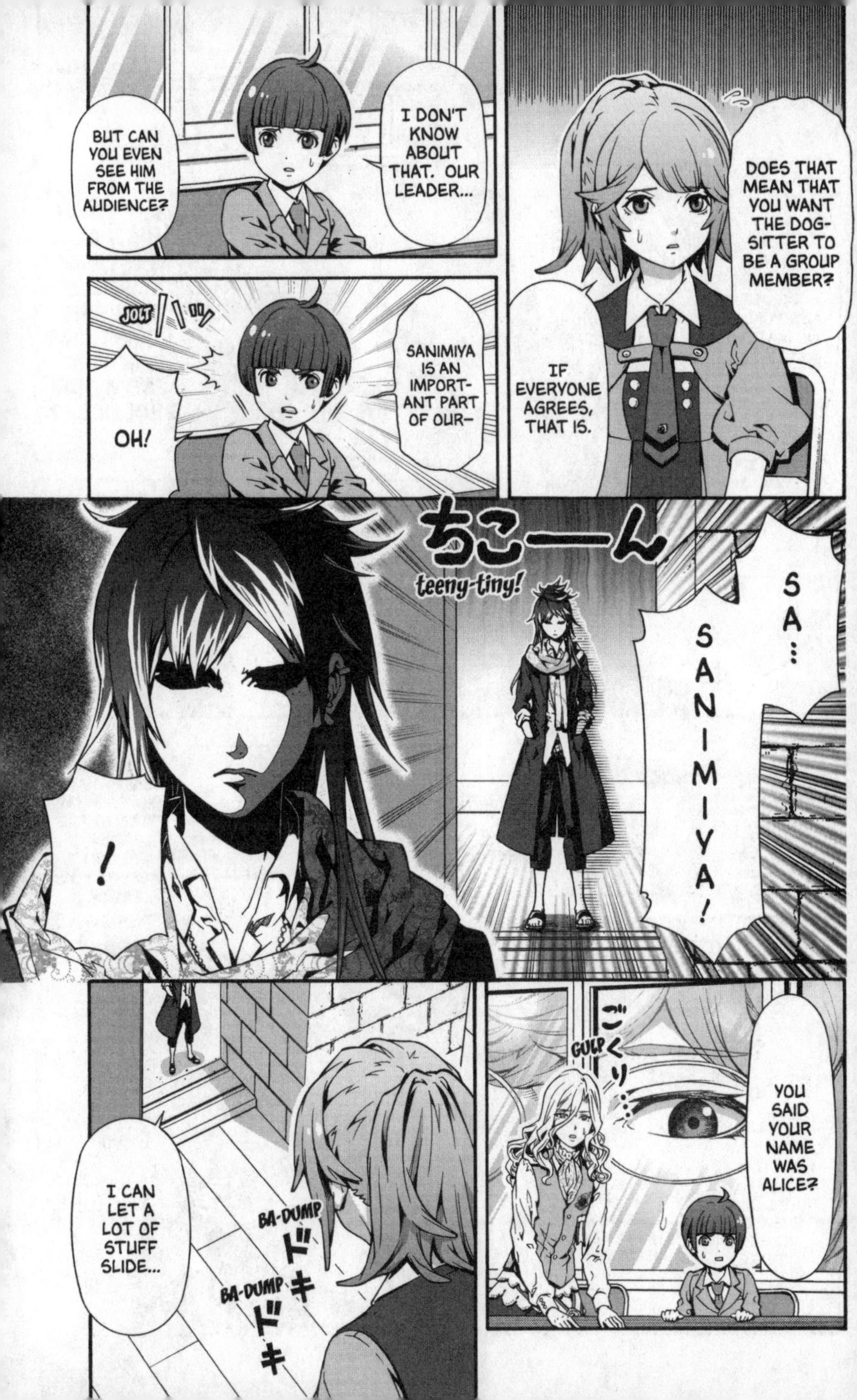
DOES THAT MEAN THAT YOU WANT THE DOG-SITTER TO BE A GROUP MEMBER?
IF EVERYONE AGREES, THAT IS.
I DON'T KNOW ABOUT THAT. OUR LEADER...
BUT CAN YOU EVEN SEE HIM FROM THE AUDIENCE?
SANIMIYA IS AN IMPORTANT PART OF OUR–
JOLT
OH!
SA... SANIMIYA!
ちこーん
teeny-tiny!
!
YOU SAID YOUR NAME WAS ALICE?
ごくり
GULP
I CAN LET A LOT OF STUFF SLIDE...
BA-DUMP ドキ
BA-DUMP ドキ

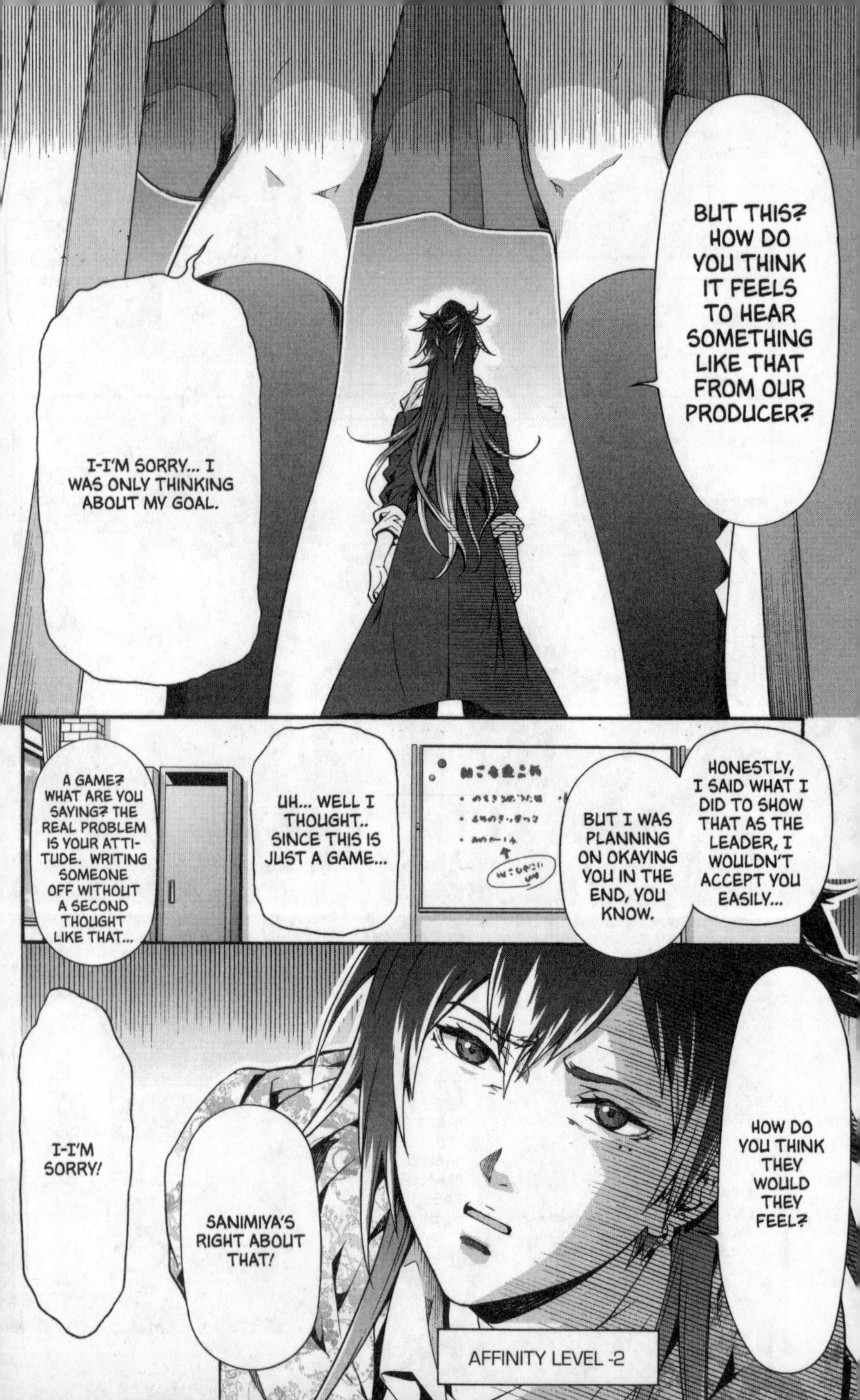
BUT THIS? HOW DO YOU THINK IT FEELS TO HEAR SOMETHING LIKE THAT FROM OUR PRODUCER?
I-I'M SORRY... I WAS ONLY THINKING ABOUT MY GOAL.
HONESTLY, I SAID WHAT I DID TO SHOW THAT AS THE LEADER, I WOULDN'T ACCEPT YOU EASILY...
BUT I WAS PLANNING ON OKAYING YOU IN THE END, YOU KNOW.
UH... WELL I THOUGHT.. SINCE THIS IS JUST A GAME...
A GAME? WHAT ARE YOU SAYING? THE REAL PROBLEM IS YOUR ATTI-TUDE. WRITING SOMEONE OFF WITHOUT A SECOND THOUGHT LIKE THAT...
HOW DO YOU THINK THEY WOULD THEY FEEL?
SANIMIYA'S RIGHT ABOUT THAT!
I-I'M SORRY!
AFFINITY LEVEL -2

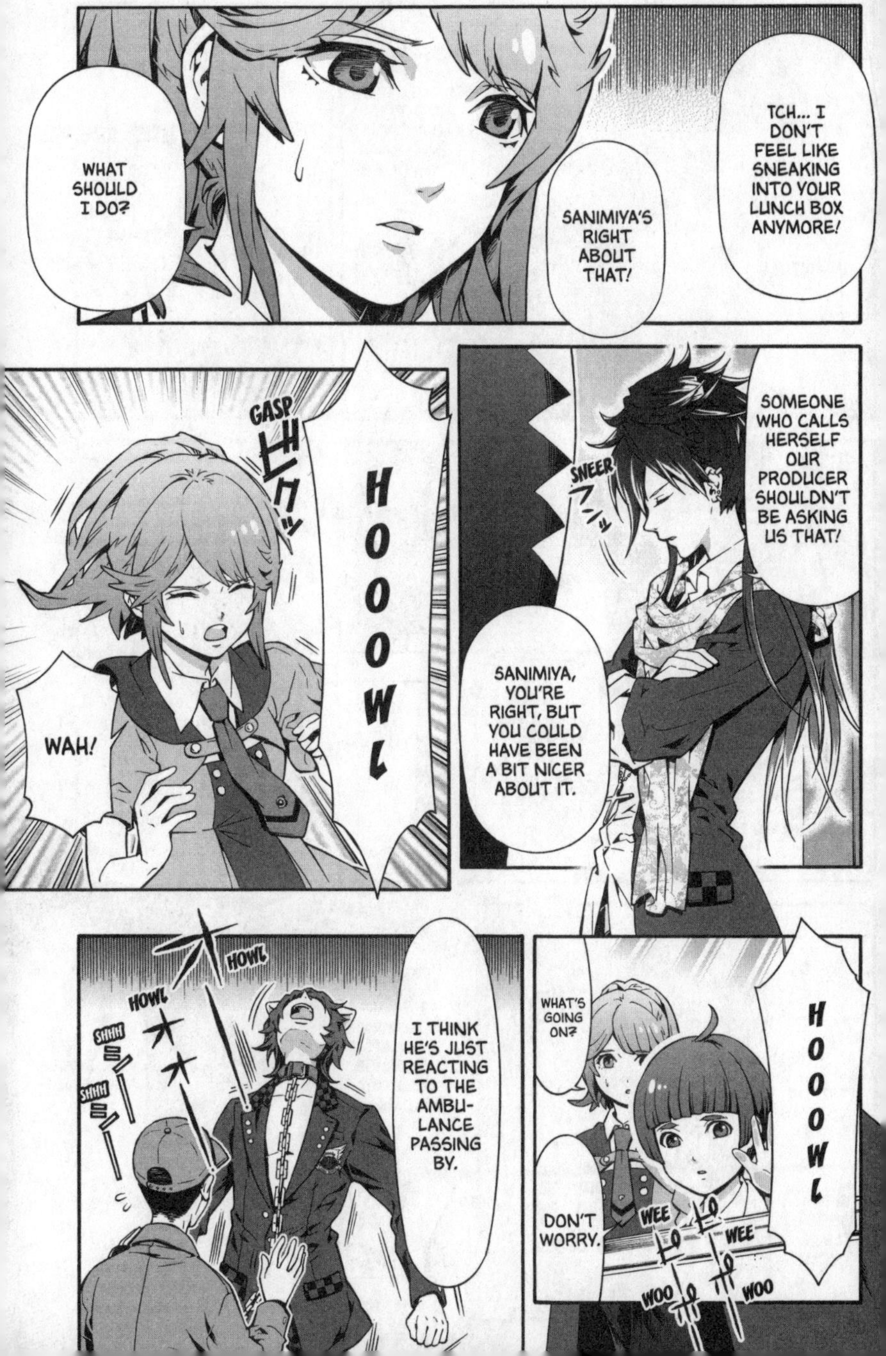
TCH... I DON'T FEEL LIKE SNEAKING INTO YOUR LUNCH BOX ANYMORE!
SANIMIYA'S RIGHT ABOUT THAT!
WHAT SHOULD I DO?
SOMEONE WHO CALLS HERSELF OUR PRODUCER SHOULDN'T BE ASKING US THAT!
SNEER
SANIMIYA, YOU'RE RIGHT, BUT YOU COULD HAVE BEEN A BIT NICER ABOUT IT.
HOOOWL
GASP
WAH!
HOOOWL
WHAT'S GOING ON?
WEE
WEE
WOO
WOO
DON'T WORRY.
I THINK HE'S JUST REACTING TO THE AMBULANCE PASSING BY.
HOWL
HOWL
SHHH
SHHH

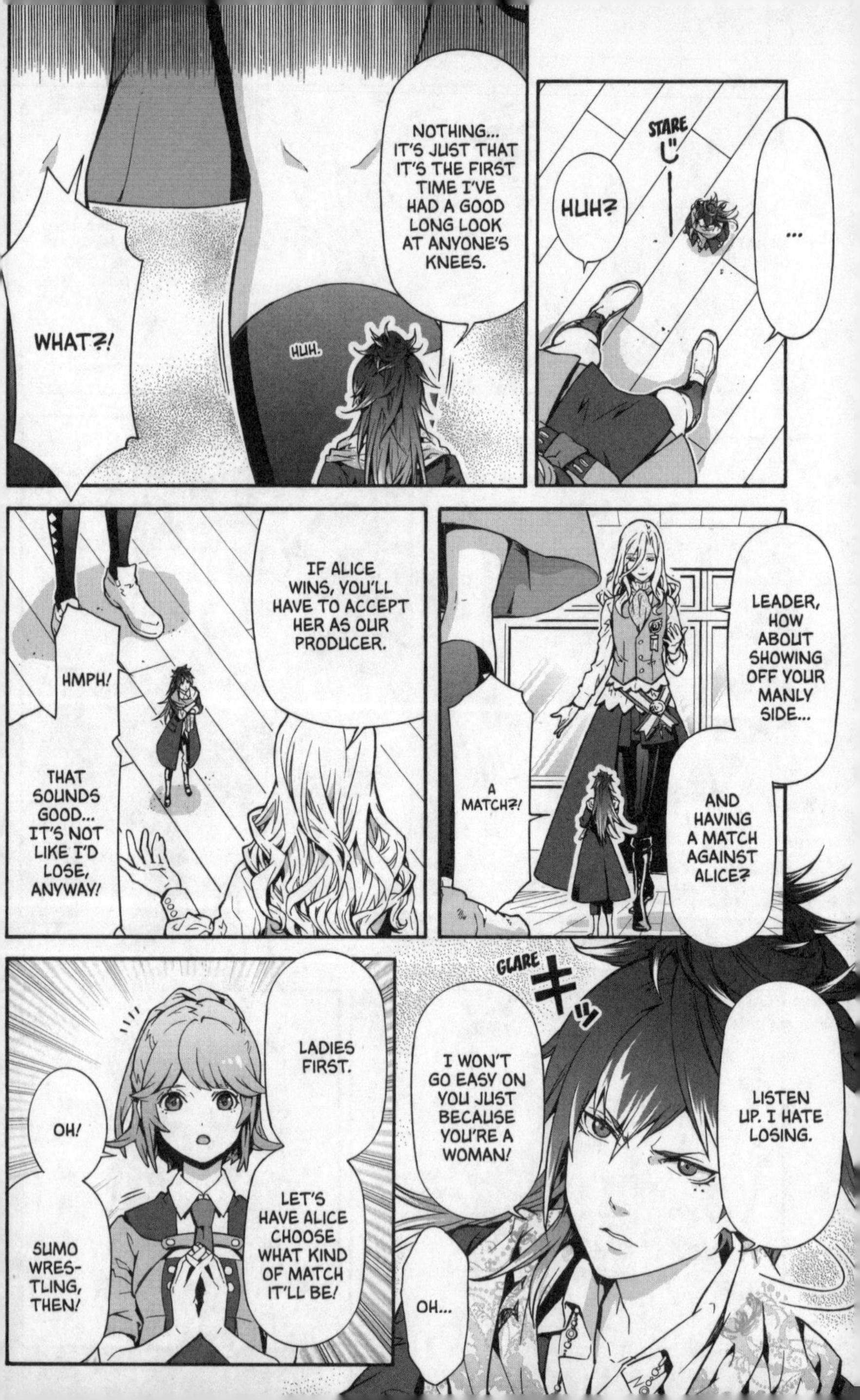
...
STARE
HUH?
NOTHING... IT'S JUST THAT IT'S THE FIRST TIME I'VE HAD A GOOD LONG LOOK AT ANYONE'S KNEES.
HUH.
WHAT?!
LEADER, HOW ABOUT SHOWING OFF YOUR MANLY SIDE...
AND HAVING A MATCH AGAINST ALICE?
A MATCH?!
IF ALICE WINS, YOU'LL HAVE TO ACCEPT HER AS OUR PRODUCER.
HMPH!
THAT SOUNDS GOOD... IT'S NOT LIKE I'D LOSE, ANYWAY!
GLARE
LISTEN UP. I HATE LOSING.
I WON'T GO EASY ON YOU JUST BECAUSE YOU'RE A WOMAN!
OH...
LADIES FIRST.
LET'S HAVE ALICE CHOOSE WHAT KIND OF MATCH IT'LL BE!
OH!
SUMO WRES-TLING, THEN!

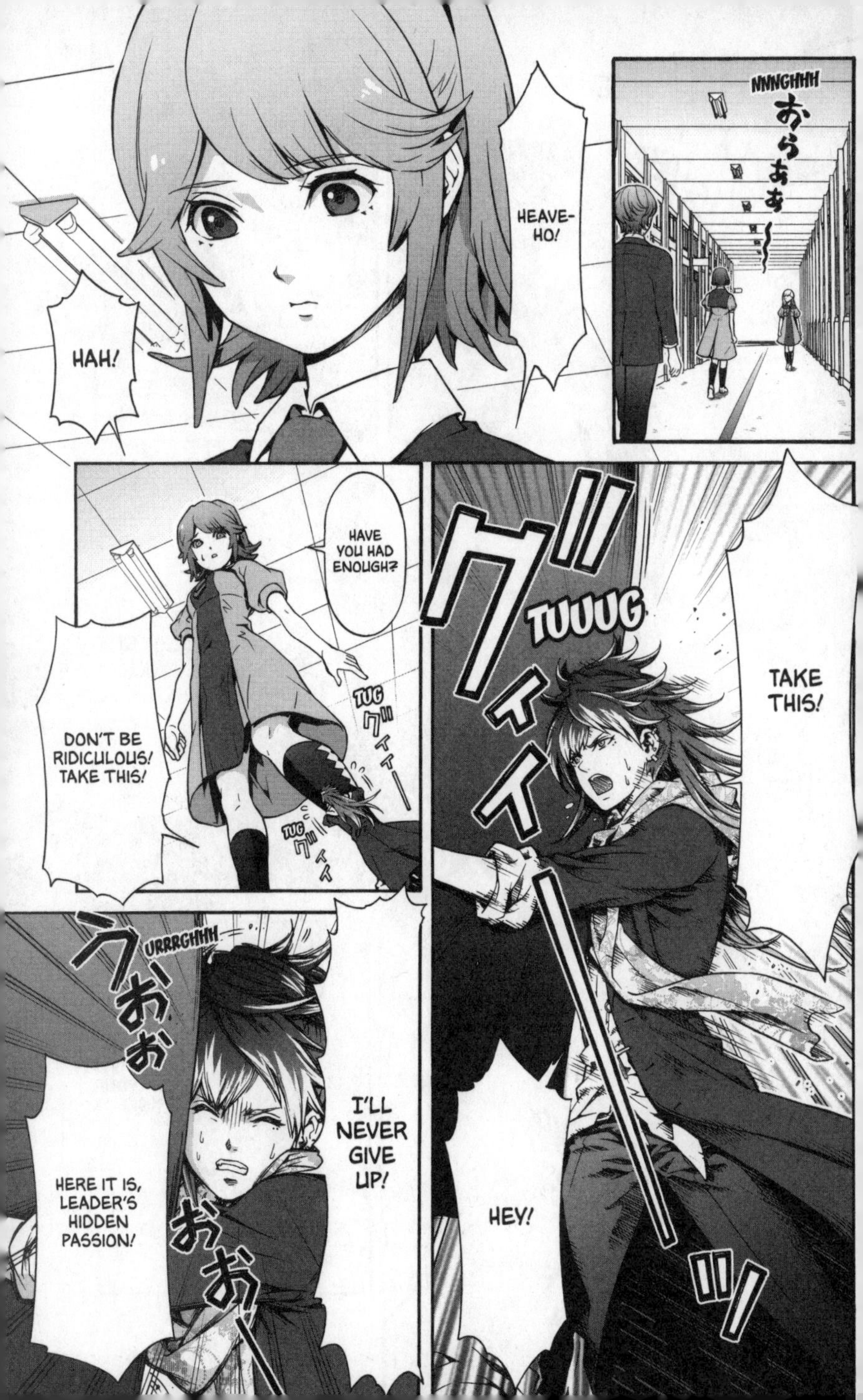
NNNGHHH
おらあぁ~~
HEAVE-HO!
HAH!
TAKE THIS!
グィィーッ
TUUUG
HEY!
HAVE YOU HAD ENOUGH?
DON'T BE RIDICULOUS! TAKE THIS!
TUG
グィィー
TUG
グィイ
URRRGHHH
うおぉおぉ
I'LL NEVER GIVE UP!
HERE IT IS, LEADER'S HIDDEN PASSION!

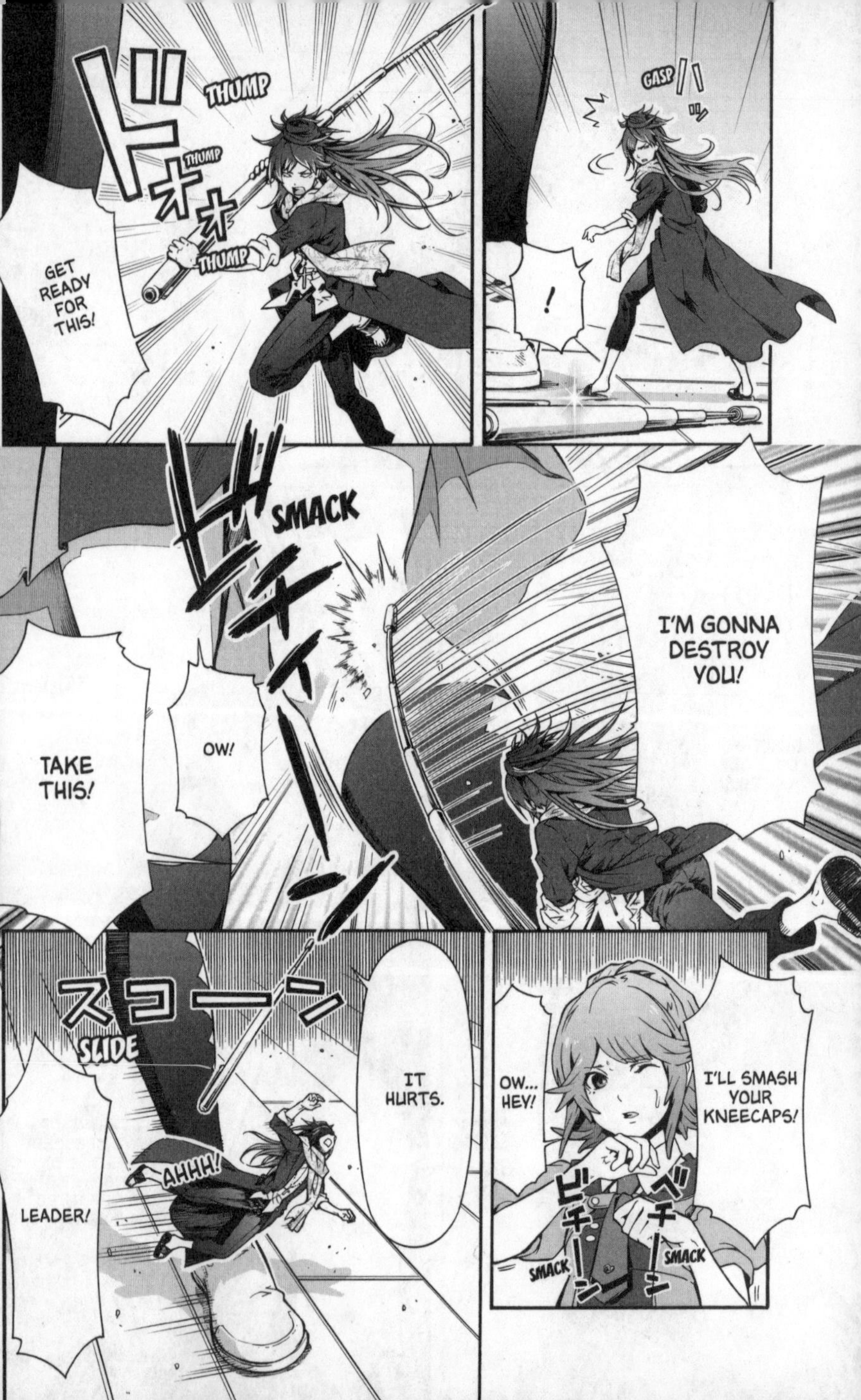
GASP
!
THUMP
THUMP
THUMP
GET READY FOR THIS!
I'M GONNA DESTROY YOU!
SMACK
OW!
TAKE THIS!
I'LL SMASH YOUR KNEECAPS!
OW... HEY!
SMACK
SMACK
IT HURTS.
SLIDE
AHHH!
LEADER!

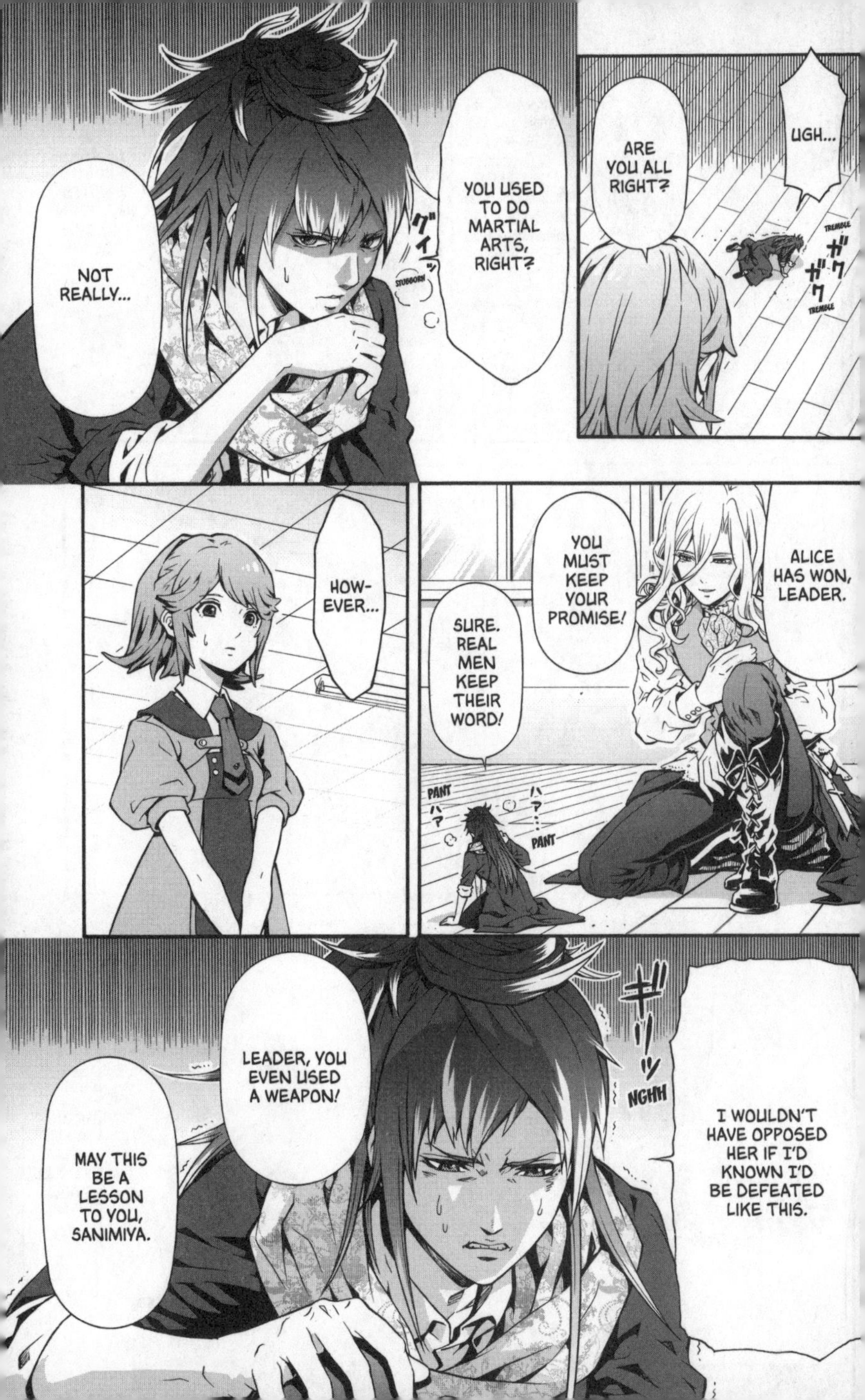
UGH...
TREMBLE
TREMBLE
ARE YOU ALL RIGHT?
YOU USED TO DO MARTIAL ARTS, RIGHT?
STUBBORN
NOT REALLY...
ALICE HAS WON, LEADER.
YOU MUST KEEP YOUR PROMISE!
SURE. REAL MEN KEEP THEIR WORD!
PANT
PANT
HOW-EVER...
I WOULDN'T HAVE OPPOSED HER IF I'D KNOWN I'D BE DEFEATED LIKE THIS.
NGHH
LEADER, YOU EVEN USED A WEAPON!
MAY THIS BE A LESSON TO YOU, SANIMIYA.

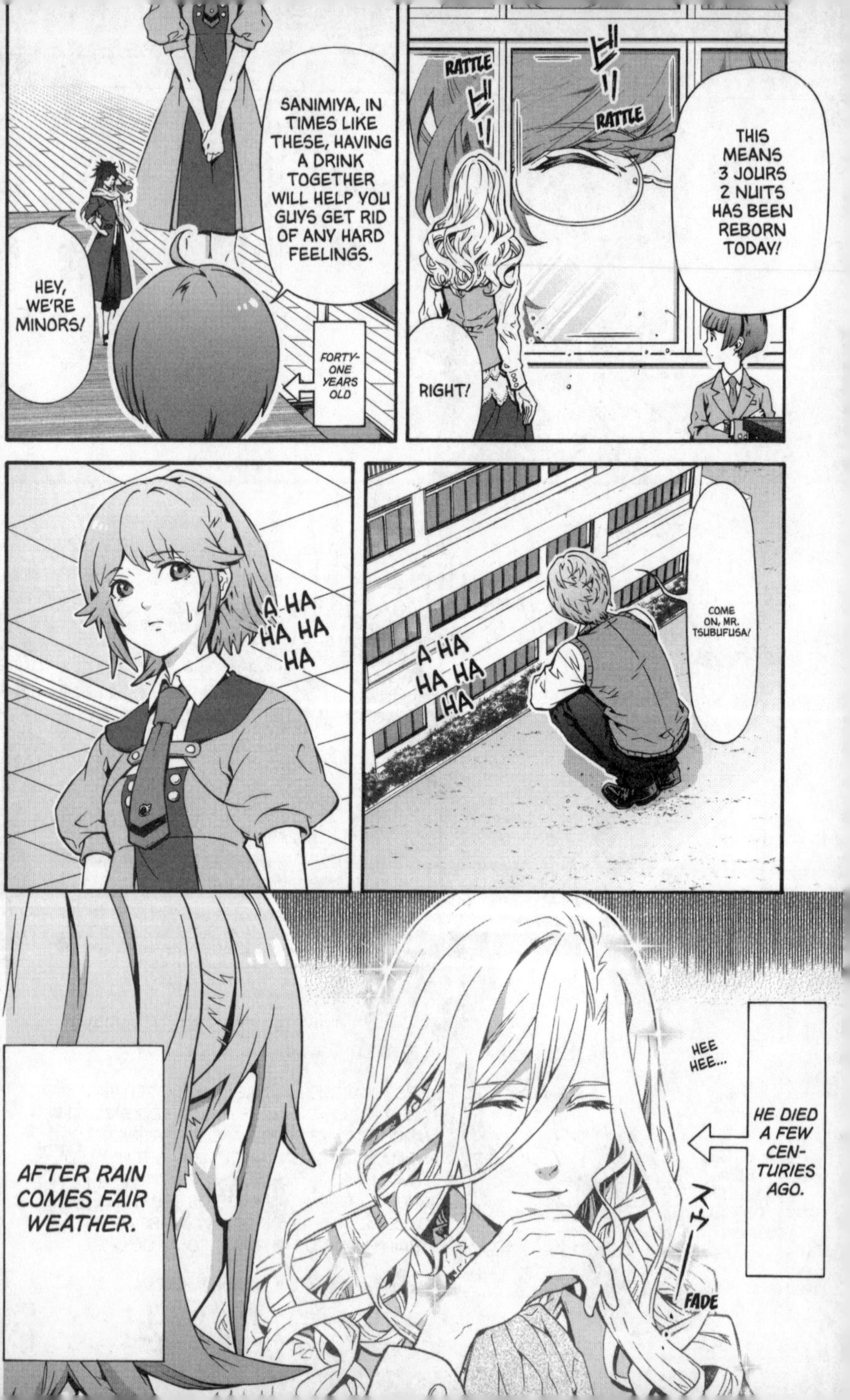
RATTLE
RATTLE
THIS MEANS 3 JOURS 2 NUITS HAS BEEN REBORN TODAY!
RIGHT!
SANIMIYA, IN TIMES LIKE THESE, HAVING A DRINK TOGETHER WILL HELP YOU GUYS GET RID OF ANY HARD FEELINGS.
HEY, WE'RE MINORS!
FORTY-ONE YEARS OLD
COME ON, MR. TSUBUFUSA!
A-HA HA HA HA
A-HA HA HA HA
HEE HEE...
HE DIED A FEW CEN-TURIES AGO.
FADE
AFTER RAIN COMES FAIR WEATHER.

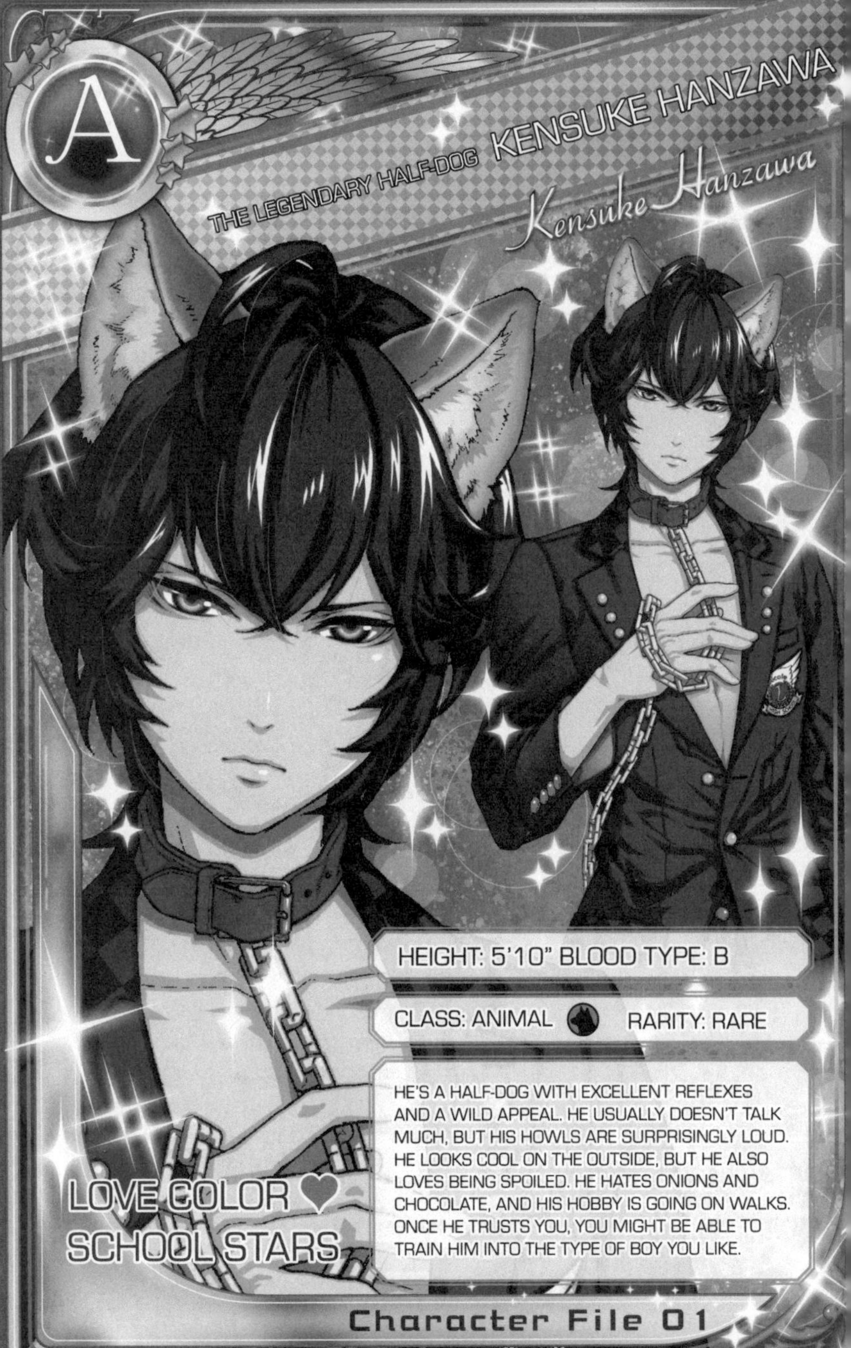
A
THE LEGENDARY HALF-DOG KENSUKE HANZAWA
Kensuke Hanzawa
HEIGHT: 5'10" BLOOD TYPE: B
CLASS: ANIMAL
RARITY: RARE
HE'S A HALF-DOG WITH EXCELLENT REFLEXES AND A WILD APPEAL. HE USUALLY DOESN'T TALK MUCH, BUT HIS HOWLS ARE SURPRISINGLY LOUD. HE LOOKS COOL ON THE OUTSIDE, BUT HE ALSO LOVES BEING SPOILED. HE HATES ONIONS AND CHOCOLATE, AND HIS HOBBY IS GOING ON WALKS. ONCE HE TRUSTS YOU, YOU MIGHT BE ABLE TO TRAIN HIM INTO THE TYPE OF BOY YOU LIKE.
LOVE COLOR ♥ SCHOOL STARS
Character File 01

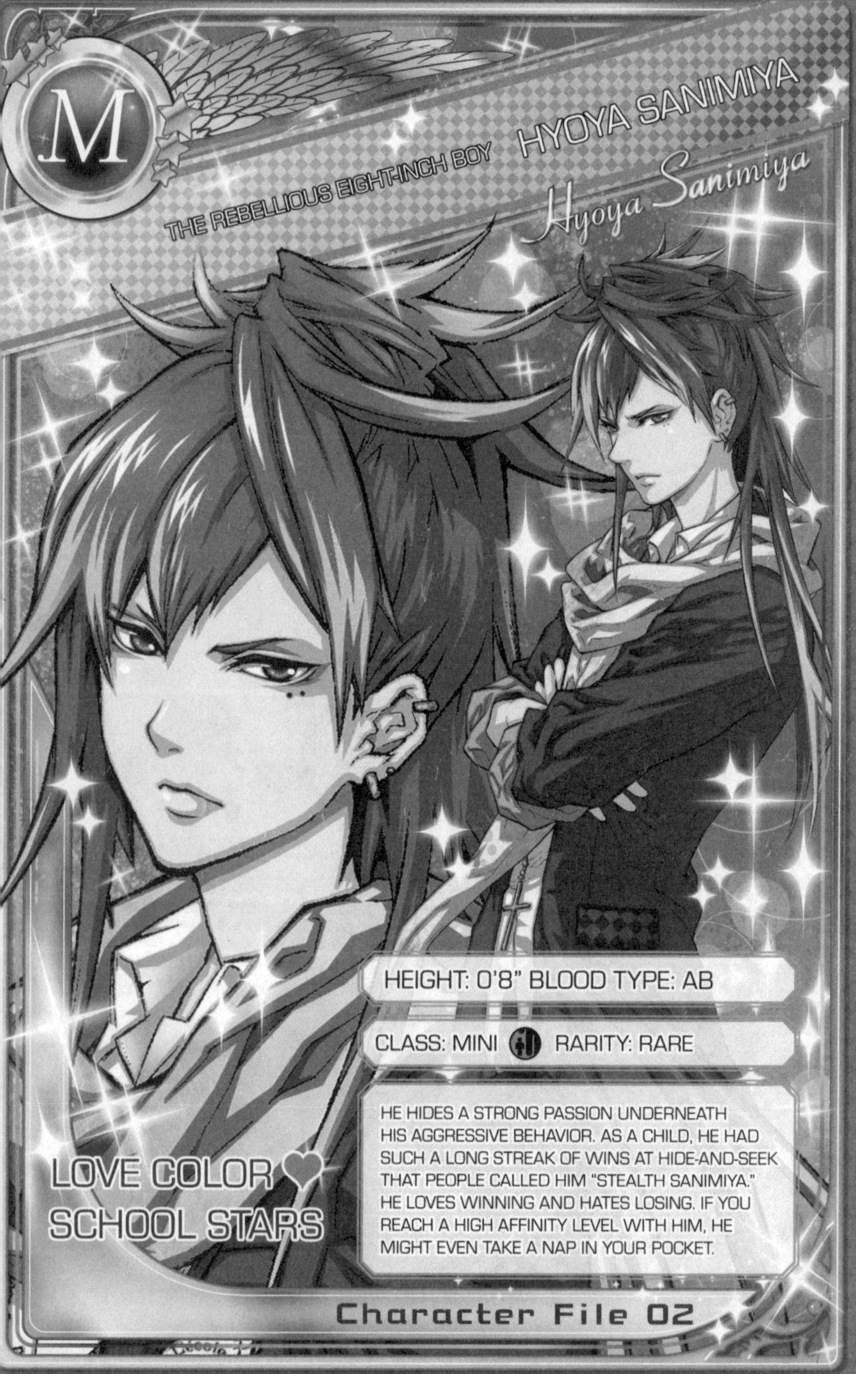
M
THE REBELLIOUS EIGHT-INCH BOY
HYOYA SANIMIYA
Hyoya Sanimiya
HEIGHT: 0'8" BLOOD TYPE: AB
CLASS: MINI RARITY: RARE
HE HIDES A STRONG PASSION UNDERNEATH HIS AGGRESSIVE BEHAVIOR. AS A CHILD, HE HAD SUCH A LONG STREAK OF WINS AT HIDE-AND-SEEK THAT PEOPLE CALLED HIM "STEALTH SANIMIYA." HE LOVES WINNING AND HATES LOSING. IF YOU REACH A HIGH AFFINITY LEVEL WITH HIM, HE MIGHT EVEN TAKE A NAP IN YOUR POCKET.
LOVE COLOR ♥ SCHOOL STARS
Character File 02

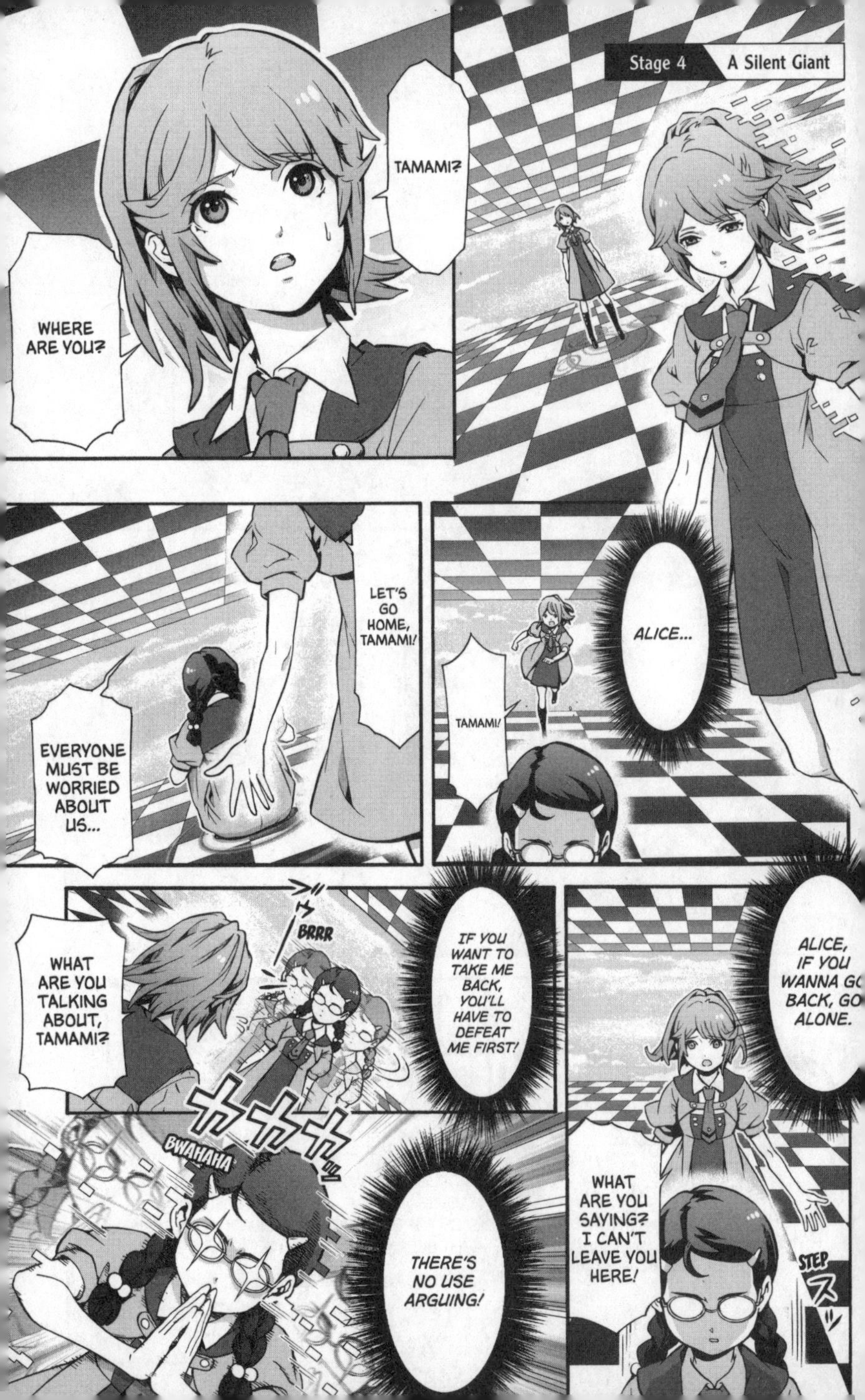
Stage 4 A Silent Giant
TAMAMI?
WHERE ARE YOU?
ALICE...
TAMAMI!
LET'S GO HOME, TAMAMI!
EVERYONE MUST BE WORRIED ABOUT US...
ALICE, IF YOU WANNA GO BACK, GO ALONE.
WHAT ARE YOU SAYING? I CAN'T LEAVE YOU HERE!
STEP
IF YOU WANT TO TAKE ME BACK, YOU'LL HAVE TO DEFEAT ME FIRST!
BRRR
WHAT ARE YOU TALKING ABOUT, TAMAMI?
BWAHAHA
THERE'S NO USE ARGUING!

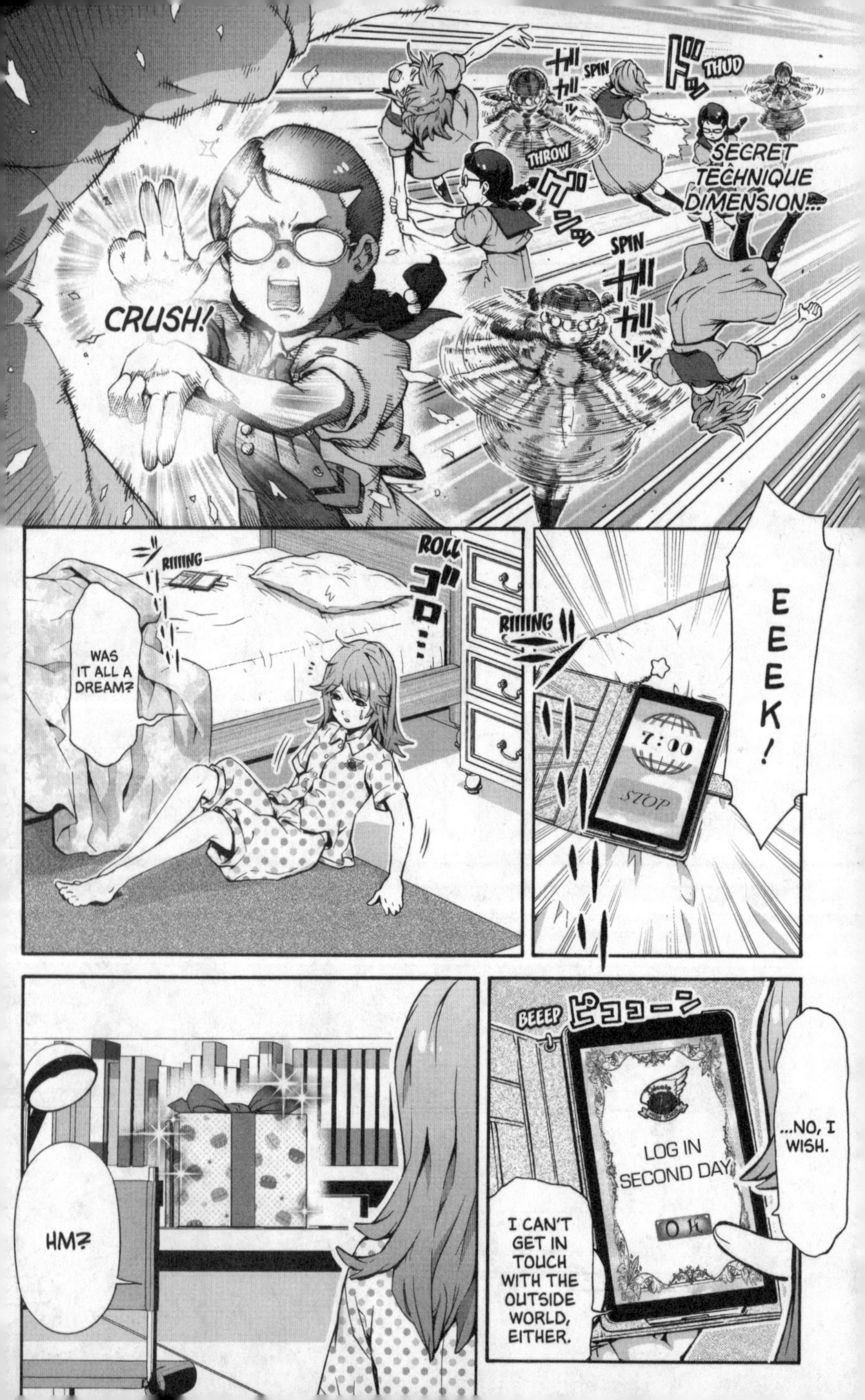
THUD
SPIN
SECRET TECHNIQUE DIMENSION...
THROW
SPIN
CRUSH!
EEEK!
7:00
STOP
ROLL
RIIIING
RIIIING
WAS IT ALL A DREAM?
BEEEP
LOG IN SECOND DAY
OK
...NO, I WISH.
I CAN'T GET IN TOUCH WITH THE OUTSIDE WORLD, EITHER.
HM?

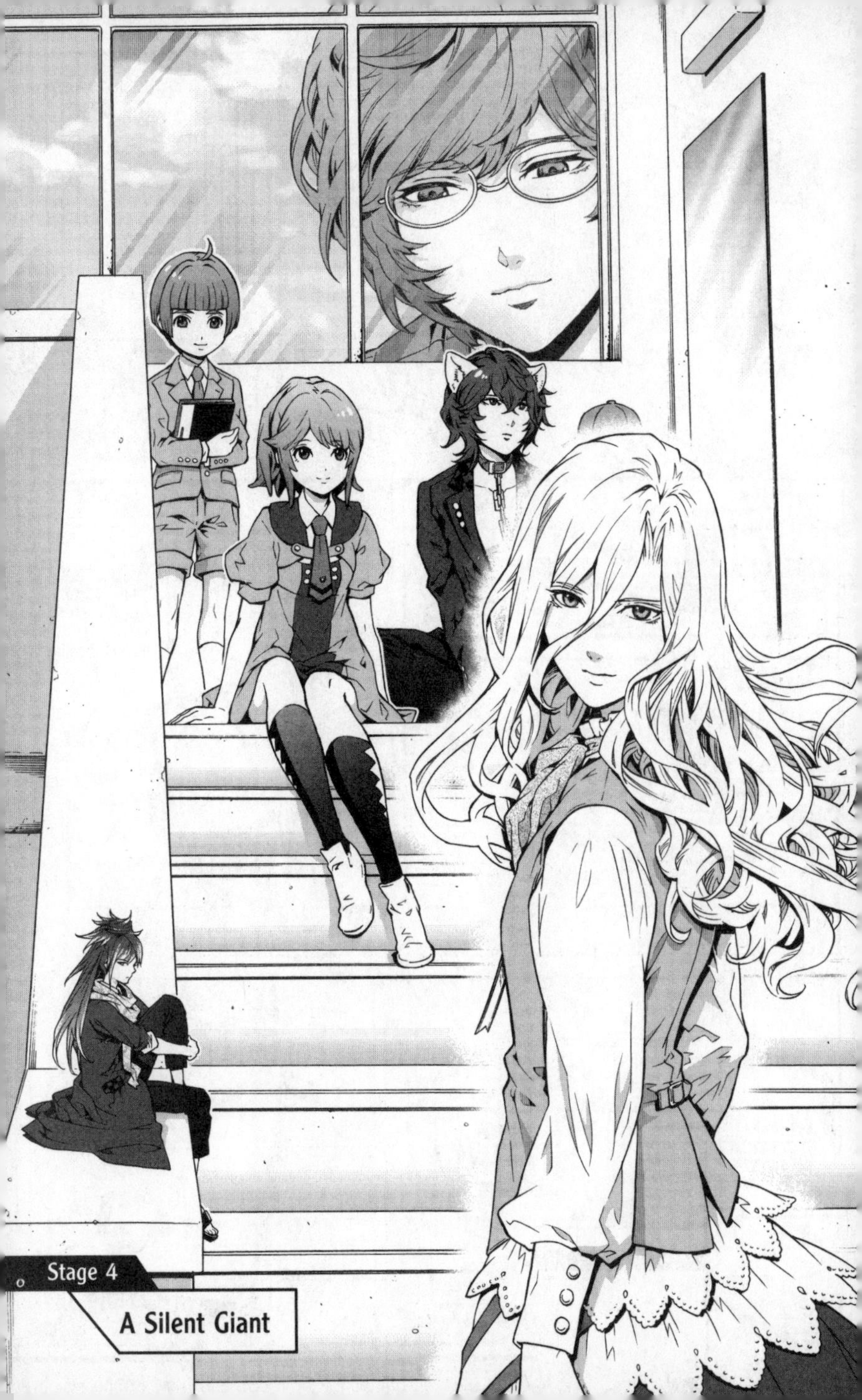
Stage 4
A Silent Giant

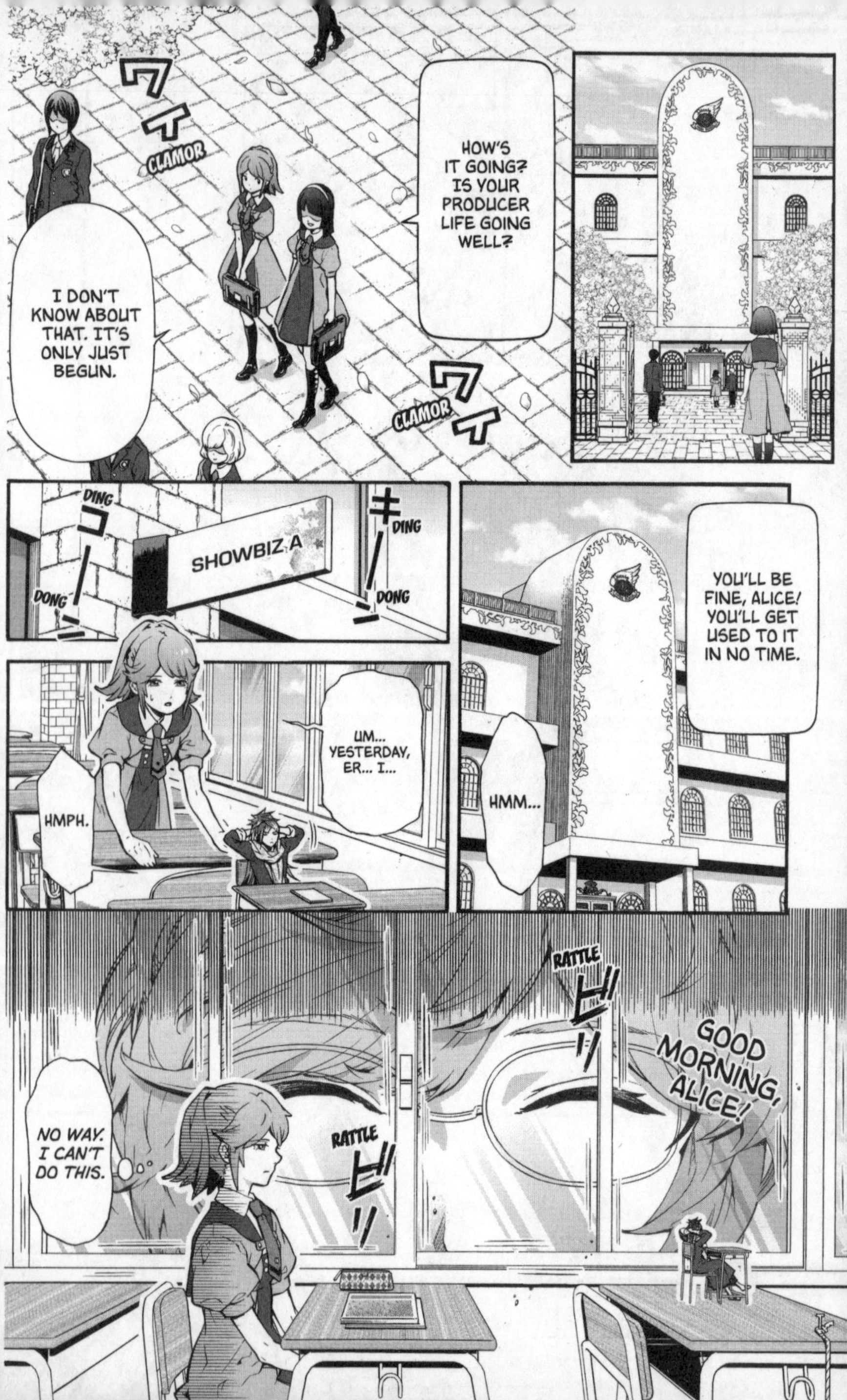
HOW'S IT GOING? IS YOUR PRODUCER LIFE GOING WELL?
CLAMOR
I DON'T KNOW ABOUT THAT. IT'S ONLY JUST BEGUN.
CLAMOR
YOU'LL BE FINE, ALICE! YOU'LL GET USED TO IT IN NO TIME.
HMM...
DING
DONG
SHOWBIZ A
DING
DONG
UM... YESTERDAY, ER... I...
HMPH.
GOOD MORNING, ALICE!
RATTLE
RATTLE
NO WAY. I CAN'T DO THIS.

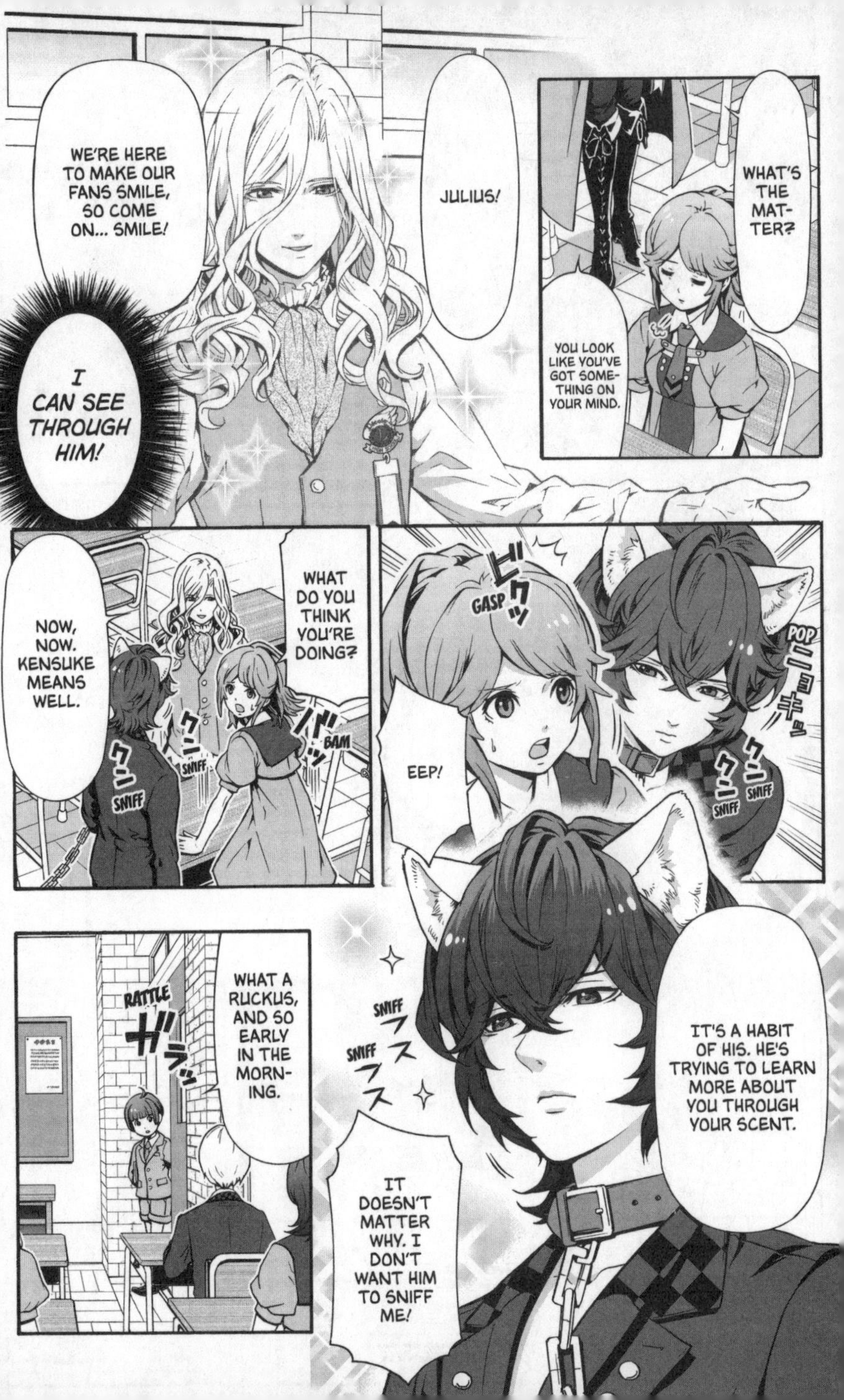
WHAT'S THE MATTER?
YOU LOOK LIKE YOU'VE GOT SOMETHING ON YOUR MIND.
JULIUS!
WE'RE HERE TO MAKE OUR FANS SMILE, SO COME ON... SMILE!
I CAN SEE THROUGH HIM!
GASP
EEP!
POP
SNIFF
SNIFF
WHAT DO YOU THINK YOU'RE DOING?
BAM
SNIFF
SNIFF
NOW, NOW. KENSUKE MEANS WELL.
IT'S A HABIT OF HIS. HE'S TRYING TO LEARN MORE ABOUT YOU THROUGH YOUR SCENT.
SNIFF
SNIFF
IT DOESN'T MATTER WHY. I DON'T WANT HIM TO SNIFF ME!
WHAT A RUCKUS, AND SO EARLY IN THE MORNING.
RATTLE

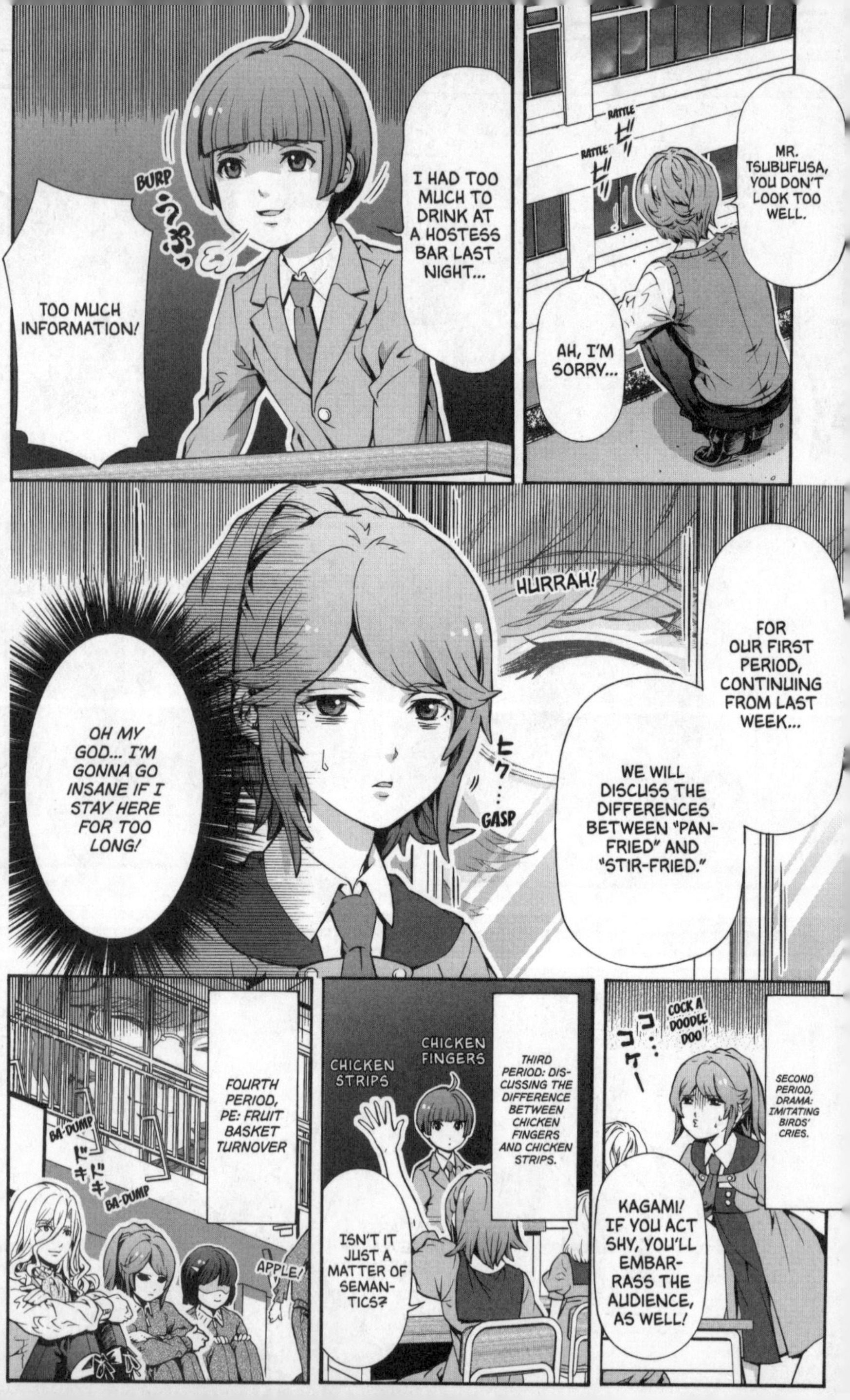
MR. TSUBUFUSA, YOU DON'T LOOK TOO WELL.
RATTLE
RATTLE
AH, I'M SORRY...
I HAD TOO MUCH TO DRINK AT A HOSTESS BAR LAST NIGHT...
BURP
TOO MUCH INFORMATION!
FOR OUR FIRST PERIOD, CONTINUING FROM LAST WEEK...
WE WILL DISCUSS THE DIFFERENCES BETWEEN "PAN-FRIED" AND "STIR-FRIED."
HURRAH!
GASP
OH MY GOD... I'M GONNA GO INSANE IF I STAY HERE FOR TOO LONG!
SECOND PERIOD, DRAMA: IMITATING BIRDS' CRIES.
COCK A DOODLE DOO
KAGAMI! IF YOU ACT SHY, YOU'LL EMBARRASS THE AUDIENCE, AS WELL!
THIRD PERIOD: DISCUSSING THE DIFFERENCE BETWEEN CHICKEN FINGERS AND CHICKEN STRIPS.
CHICKEN FINGERS
CHICKEN STRIPS
ISN'T IT JUST A MATTER OF SEMANTICS?
FOURTH PERIOD, PE: FRUIT BASKET TURNOVER
BA-DUMP
BA-DUMP
APPLE!

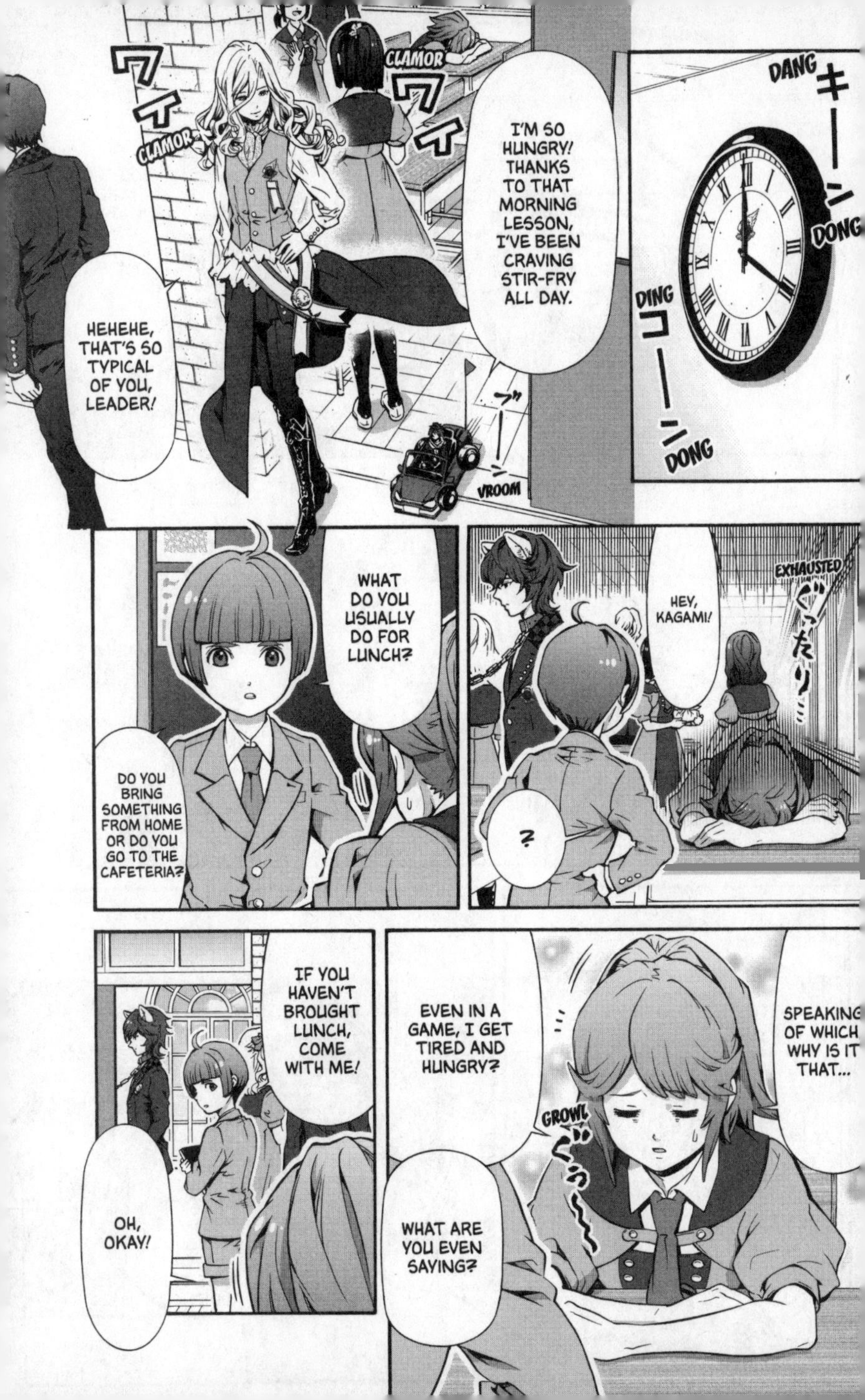

DANG
キーン
DONG
DING
コーン
DONG
CLAMOR
ワイワイ
I'M SO HUNGRY! THANKS TO THAT MORNING LESSON, I'VE BEEN CRAVING STIR-FRY ALL DAY.
CLAMOR
HEHEHE, THAT'S SO TYPICAL OF YOU, LEADER!
VROOM
EXHAUSTED
HEY, KAGAMI!
?
WHAT DO YOU USUALLY DO FOR LUNCH?
DO YOU BRING SOMETHING FROM HOME OR DO YOU GO TO THE CAFETERIA?
SPEAKING OF WHICH WHY IS IT THAT...
EVEN IN A GAME, I GET TIRED AND HUNGRY?
GROWL
WHAT ARE YOU EVEN SAYING?
IF YOU HAVEN'T BROUGHT LUNCH, COME WITH ME!
OH, OKAY!

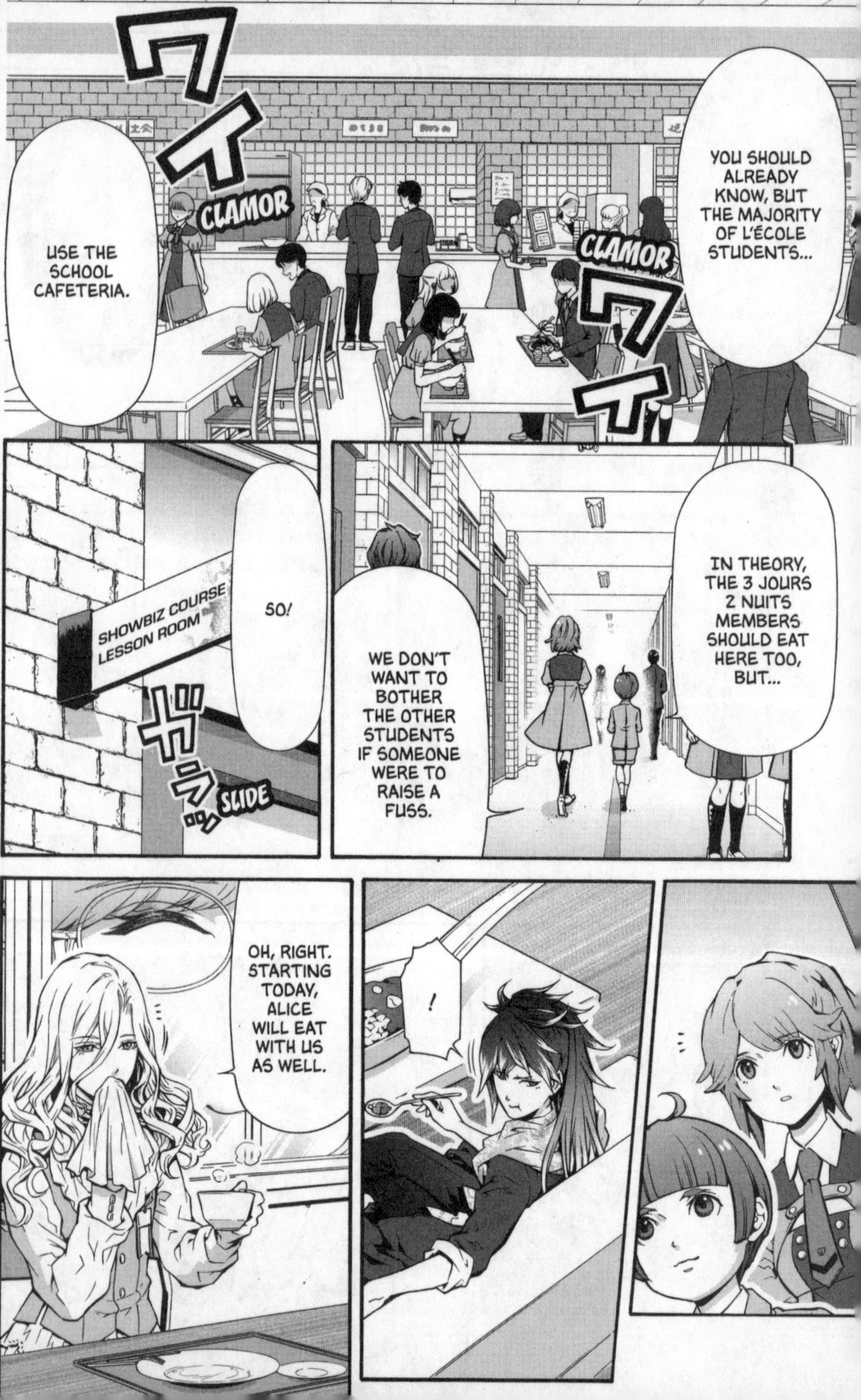
YOU SHOULD ALREADY KNOW, BUT THE MAJORITY OF L'ÉCOLE STUDENTS...
CLAMOR
ワイ
CLAMOR
ワイ
USE THE SCHOOL CAFETERIA.
IN THEORY, THE 3 JOURS 2 NUITS MEMBERS SHOULD EAT HERE TOO, BUT...
WE DON'T WANT TO BOTHER THE OTHER STUDENTS IF SOMEONE WERE TO RAISE A FUSS.
SO!
SHOWBIZ COURSE LESSON ROOM
ガラッ
SLIDE
!
OH, RIGHT. STARTING TODAY, ALICE WILL EAT WITH US AS WELL.

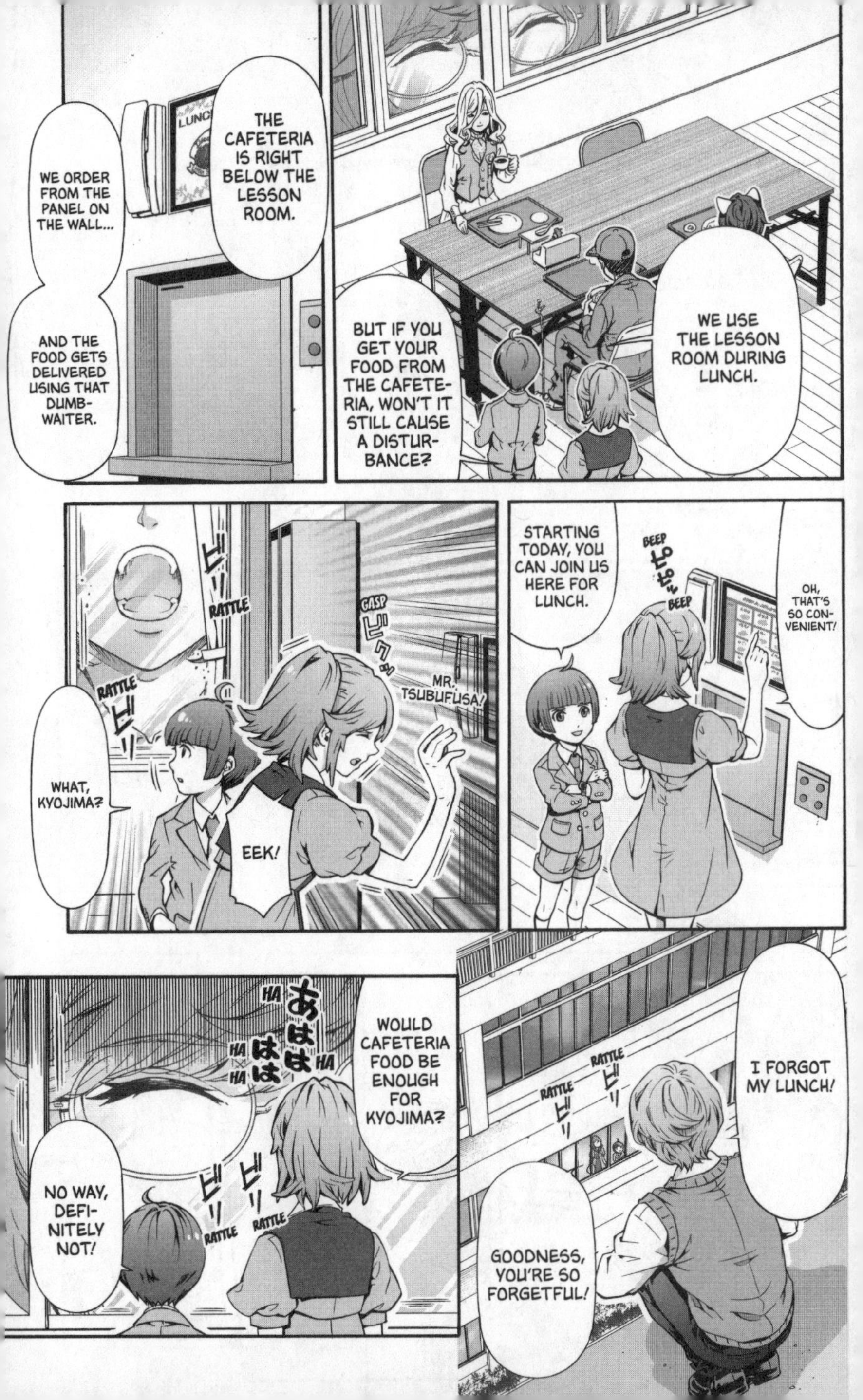
WE USE THE LESSON ROOM DURING LUNCH.
BUT IF YOU GET YOUR FOOD FROM THE CAFETERIA, WON'T IT STILL CAUSE A DISTURBANCE?
THE CAFETERIA IS RIGHT BELOW THE LESSON ROOM.
WE ORDER FROM THE PANEL ON THE WALL...
AND THE FOOD GETS DELIVERED USING THAT DUMBWAITER.
OH, THAT'S SO CONVENIENT!
BEEP
BEEP
STARTING TODAY, YOU CAN JOIN US HERE FOR LUNCH.
MR. TSUBUFUSA!
GASP
RATTLE
RATTLE
EEK!
WHAT, KYOJIMA?
I FORGOT MY LUNCH!
RATTLE
RATTLE
GOODNESS, YOU'RE SO FORGETFUL!
HA HA
HA HA
WOULD CAFETERIA FOOD BE ENOUGH FOR KYOJIMA?
RATTLE
RATTLE
NO WAY, DEFINITELY NOT!

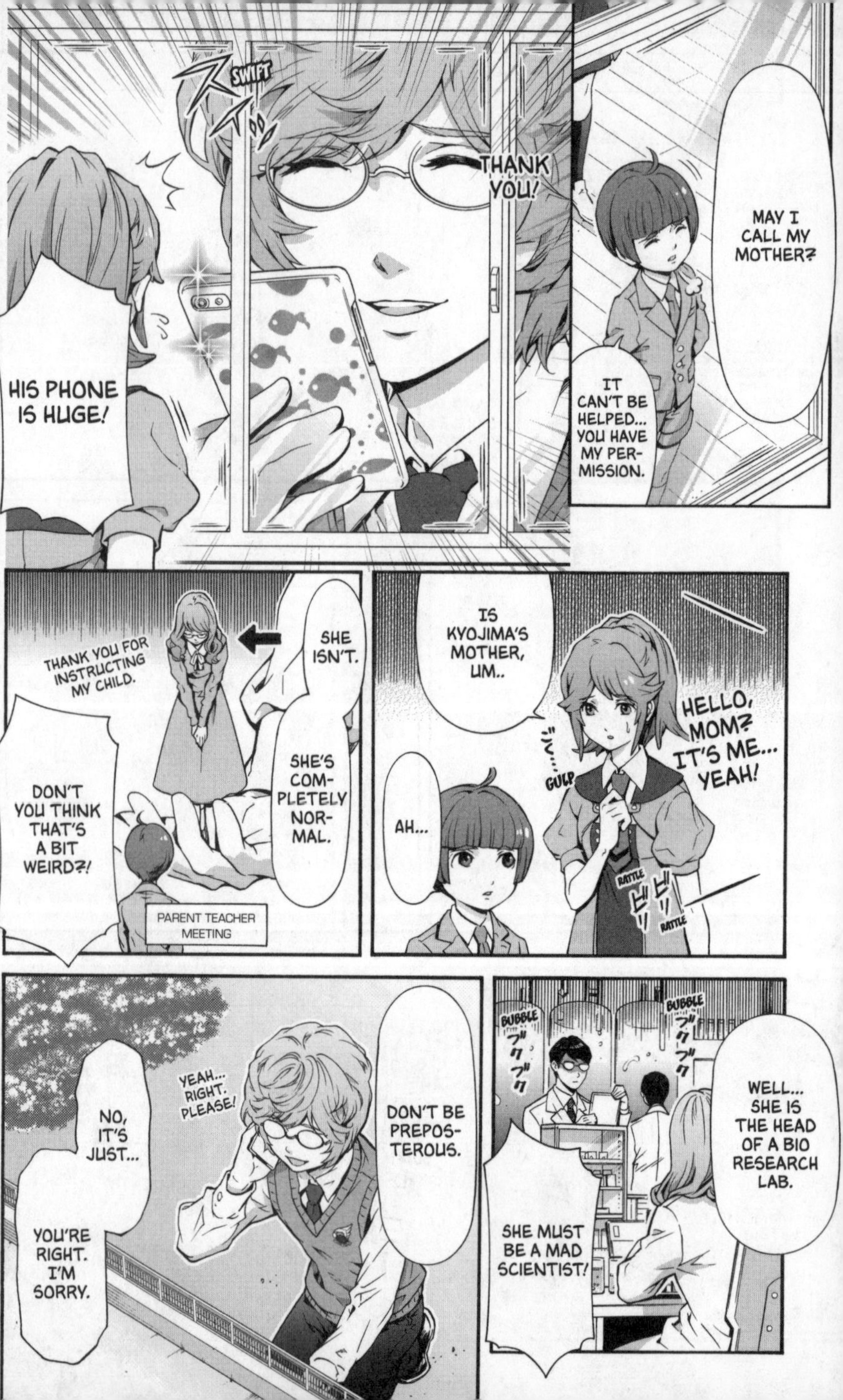
MAY I CALL MY MOTHER?
IT CAN'T BE HELPED... YOU HAVE MY PERMISSION.
SWIFT
THANK YOU!
HIS PHONE IS HUGE!
IS KYOJIMA'S MOTHER, UM..
HELLO, MOM? IT'S ME... YEAH!
GULP
AH...
RATTLE
RATTLE
SHE ISN'T.
THANK YOU FOR INSTRUCTING MY CHILD.
SHE'S COMPLETELY NORMAL.
DON'T YOU THINK THAT'S A BIT WEIRD?!
PARENT TEACHER MEETING
WELL... SHE IS THE HEAD OF A BIO RESEARCH LAB.
BUBBLE
BUBBLE
SHE MUST BE A MAD SCIENTIST!
DON'T BE PREPOSTEROUS.
YEAH... RIGHT. PLEASE!
NO, IT'S JUST...
YOU'RE RIGHT. I'M SORRY.

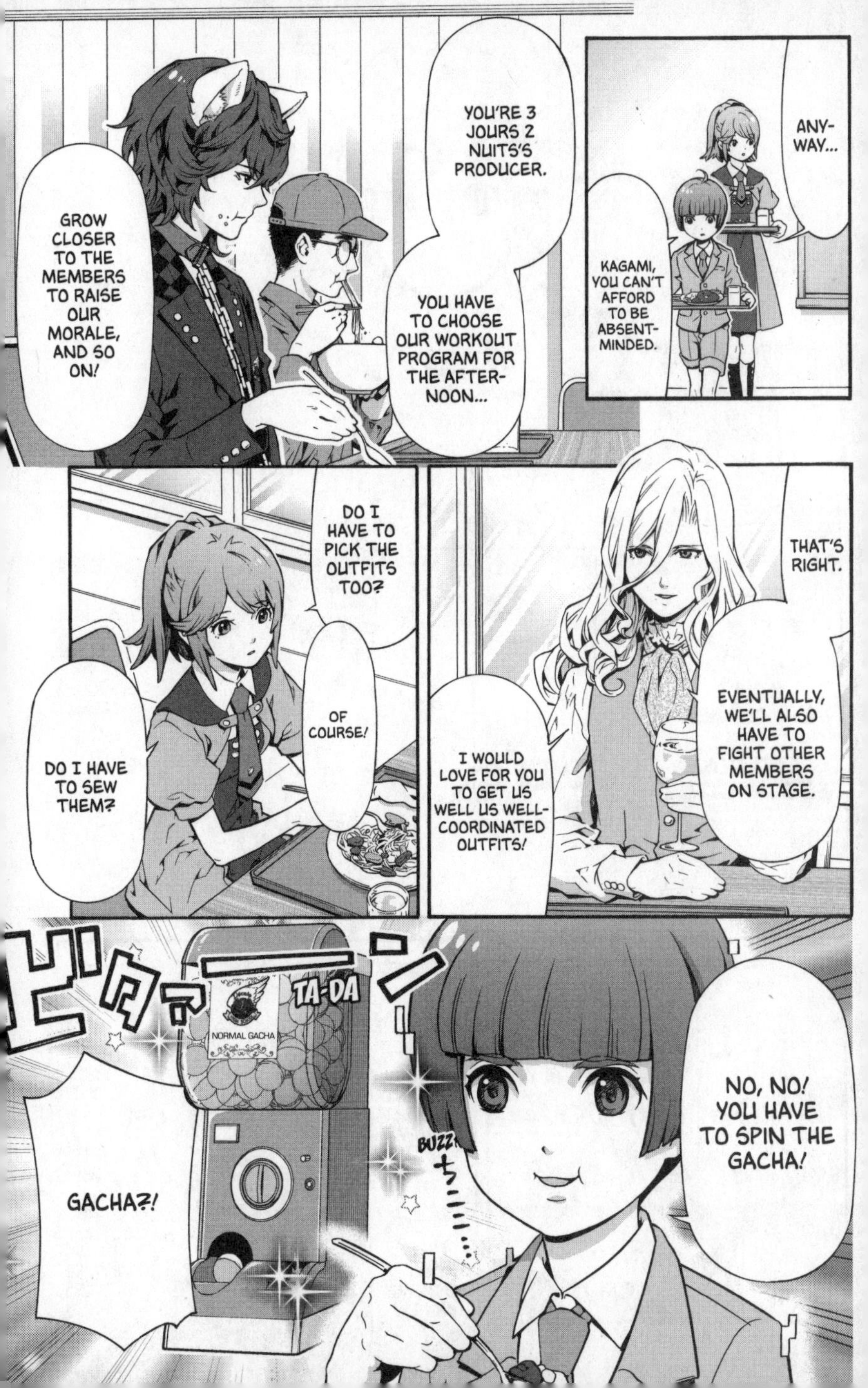
ANY-WAY...
KAGAMI, YOU CAN'T AFFORD TO BE ABSENT-MINDED.
YOU'RE 3 JOURS 2 NUITS'S PRODUCER.
YOU HAVE TO CHOOSE OUR WORKOUT PROGRAM FOR THE AFTER-NOON...
GROW CLOSER TO THE MEMBERS TO RAISE OUR MORALE, AND SO ON!
THAT'S RIGHT.
EVENTUALLY, WE'LL ALSO HAVE TO FIGHT OTHER MEMBERS ON STAGE.
I WOULD LOVE FOR YOU TO GET US WELL US WELL-COORDINATED OUTFITS!
DO I HAVE TO PICK THE OUTFITS TOO?
OF COURSE!
DO I HAVE TO SEW THEM?
NO, NO! YOU HAVE TO SPIN THE GACHA!
BUZZ
TA-DA
NORMAL GACHA
GACHA?!

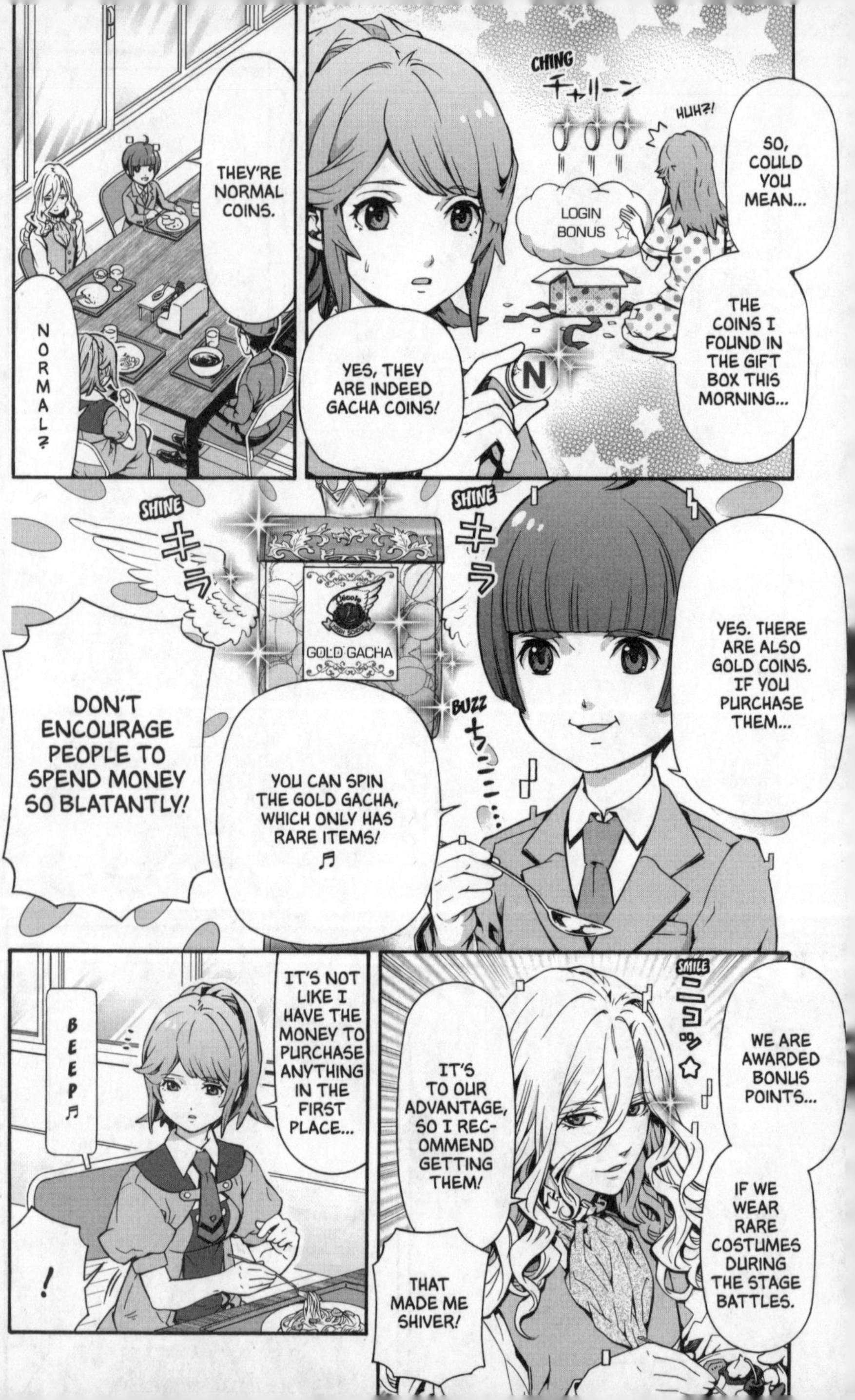
CHING
チャリーン
HUH?!
SO, COULD YOU MEAN...
LOGIN BONUS
THE COINS I FOUND IN THE GIFT BOX THIS MORNING...
YES, THEY ARE INDEED GACHA COINS!
N
THEY'RE NORMAL COINS.
NORMAL?
SHINE
キラ
YES. THERE ARE ALSO GOLD COINS. IF YOU PURCHASE THEM...
BUZZ
YOU CAN SPIN THE GOLD GACHA, WHICH ONLY HAS RARE ITEMS! ♪
SHINE
キラ
GOLD GACHA
DON'T ENCOURAGE PEOPLE TO SPEND MONEY SO BLATANTLY!
SMILE
ニコッ☆
WE ARE AWARDED BONUS POINTS...
IF WE WEAR RARE COSTUMES DURING THE STAGE BATTLES.
IT'S TO OUR ADVANTAGE, SO I RECOMMEND GETTING THEM!
THAT MADE ME SHIVER!
IT'S NOT LIKE I HAVE THE MONEY TO PURCHASE ANYTHING IN THE FIRST PLACE...
BEEP♪
!

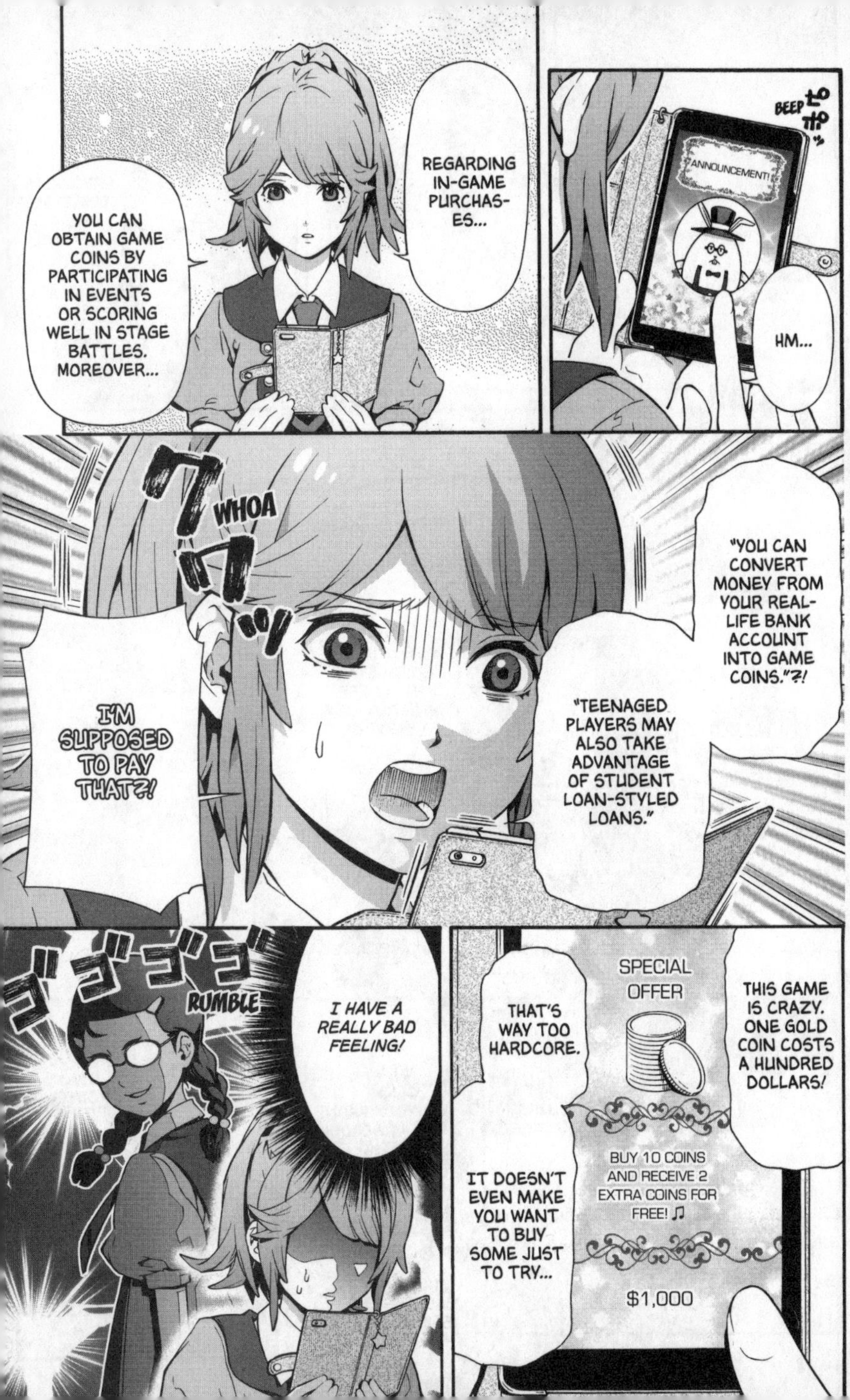
BEEP
ANNOUNCEMENT!
HM...
REGARDING IN-GAME PURCHASES...
YOU CAN OBTAIN GAME COINS BY PARTICIPATING IN EVENTS OR SCORING WELL IN STAGE BATTLES. MOREOVER...
"YOU CAN CONVERT MONEY FROM YOUR REAL-LIFE BANK ACCOUNT INTO GAME COINS."?!
"TEENAGED PLAYERS MAY ALSO TAKE ADVANTAGE OF STUDENT LOAN-STYLED LOANS."
WHOA
I'M SUPPOSED TO PAY THAT?!
THIS GAME IS CRAZY. ONE GOLD COIN COSTS A HUNDRED DOLLARS!
SPECIAL OFFER
BUY 10 COINS AND RECEIVE 2 EXTRA COINS FOR FREE! ♫
$1,000
THAT'S WAY TOO HARDCORE.
IT DOESN'T EVEN MAKE YOU WANT TO BUY SOME JUST TO TRY...
I HAVE A REALLY BAD FEELING!
RUMBLE

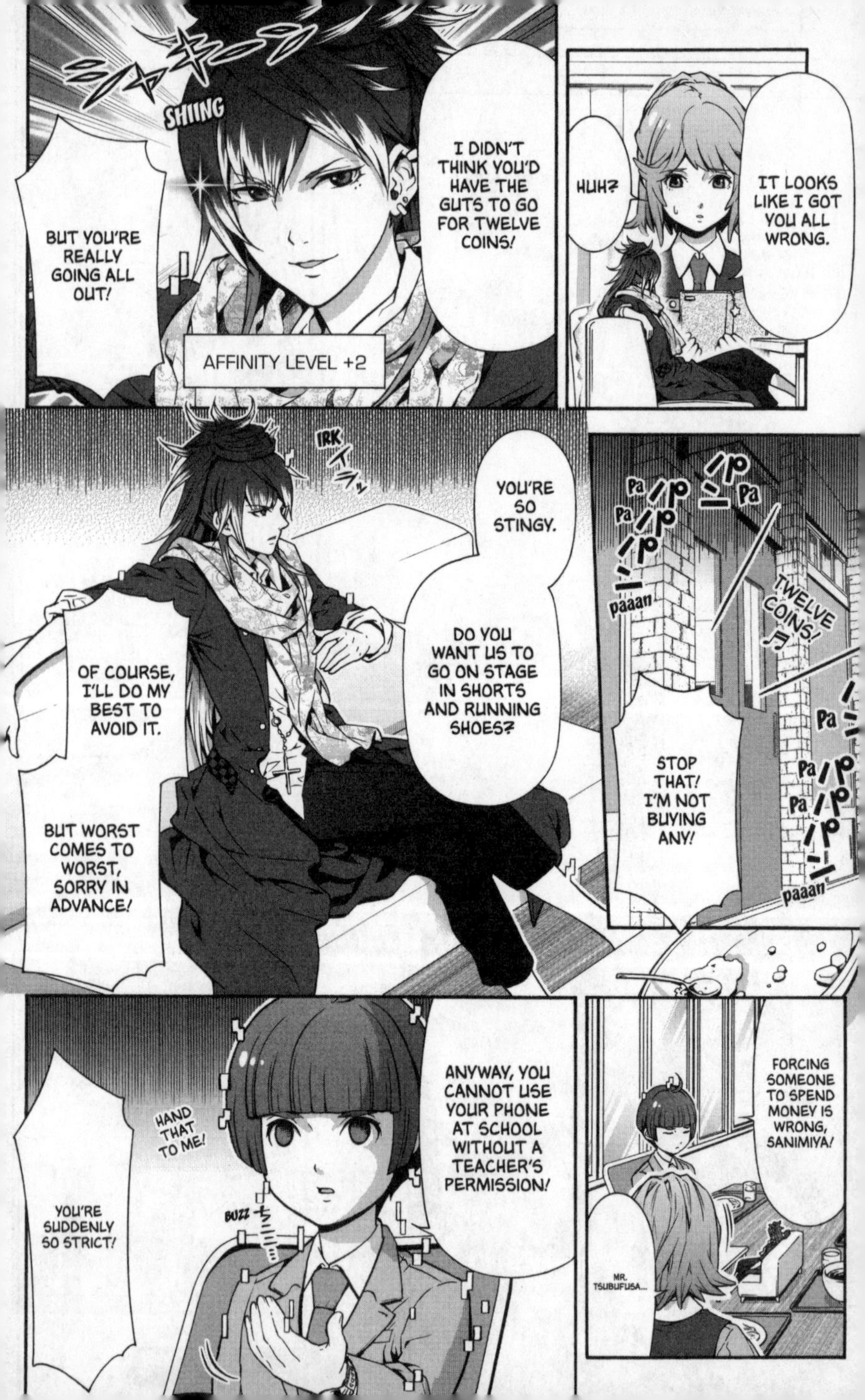
IT LOOKS LIKE I GOT YOU ALL WRONG.
HUH?
SHIING
I DIDN'T THINK YOU'D HAVE THE GUTS TO GO FOR TWELVE COINS!
BUT YOU'RE REALLY GOING ALL OUT!
AFFINITY LEVEL +2
Pa Pa Pa Pa paaan
TWELVE COINS! ♪
STOP THAT! I'M NOT BUYING ANY!
Pa Pa Pa paaan
IRK
YOU'RE SO STINGY.
DO YOU WANT US TO GO ON STAGE IN SHORTS AND RUNNING SHOES?
OF COURSE, I'LL DO MY BEST TO AVOID IT.
BUT WORST COMES TO WORST, SORRY IN ADVANCE!
FORCING SOMEONE TO SPEND MONEY IS WRONG, SANIMIYA!
MR. TSUBUFUSA...
ANYWAY, YOU CANNOT USE YOUR PHONE AT SCHOOL WITHOUT A TEACHER'S PERMISSION!
HAND THAT TO ME!
BUZZ
YOU'RE SUDDENLY SO STRICT!

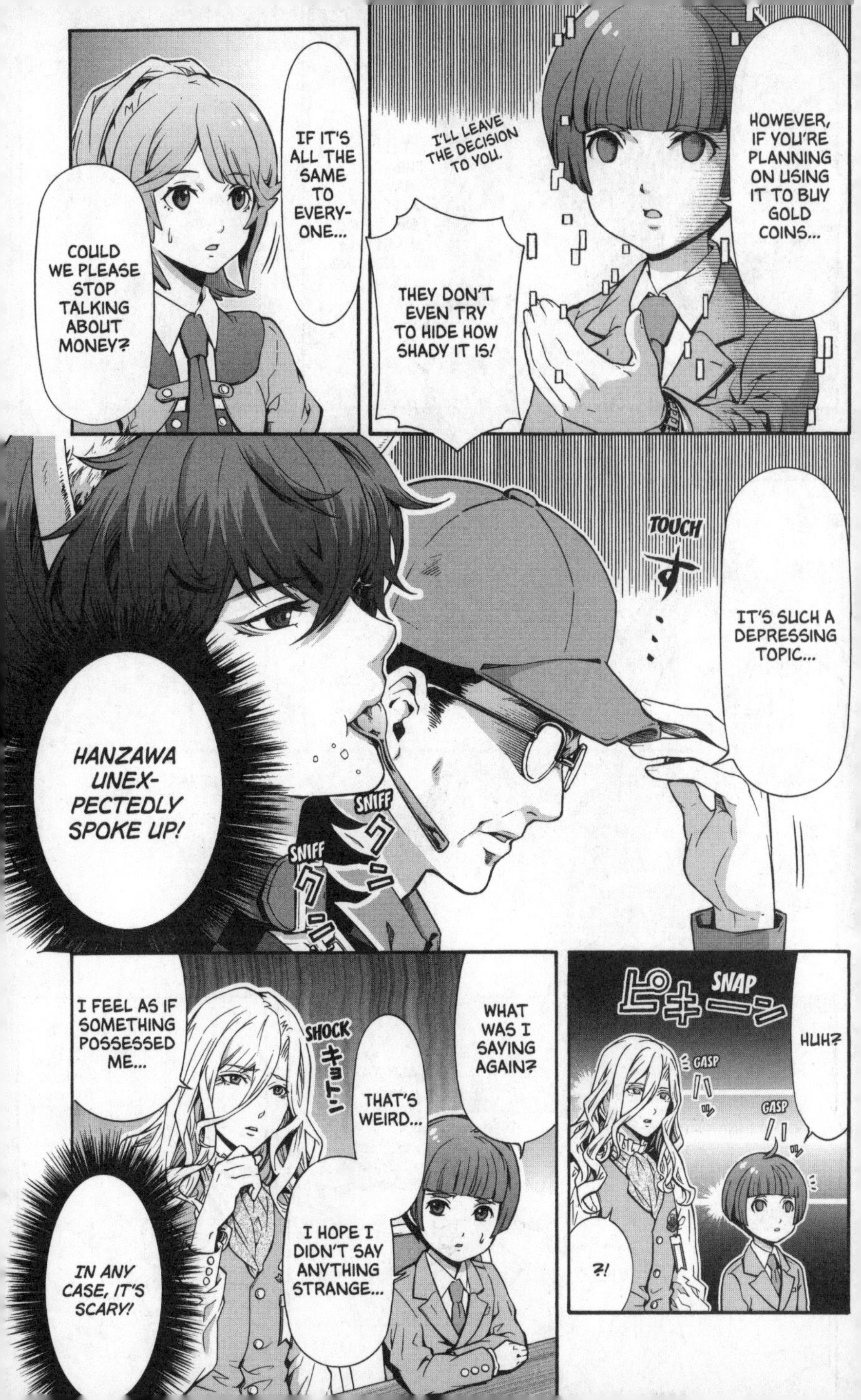
HOWEVER, IF YOU'RE PLANNING ON USING IT TO BUY GOLD COINS...
I'LL LEAVE THE DECISION TO YOU.
THEY DON'T EVEN TRY TO HIDE HOW SHADY IT IS!
IF IT'S ALL THE SAME TO EVERY-ONE...
COULD WE PLEASE STOP TALKING ABOUT MONEY?
TOUCH
IT'S SUCH A DEPRESSING TOPIC...
SNIFF
SNIFF
HANZAWA UNEX-PECTEDLY SPOKE UP!
SNAP
HUH?
GASP
GASP
?!
WHAT WAS I SAYING AGAIN?
I FEEL AS IF SOMETHING POSSESSED ME...
SHOCK
THAT'S WEIRD...
I HOPE I DIDN'T SAY ANYTHING STRANGE...
IN ANY CASE, IT'S SCARY!

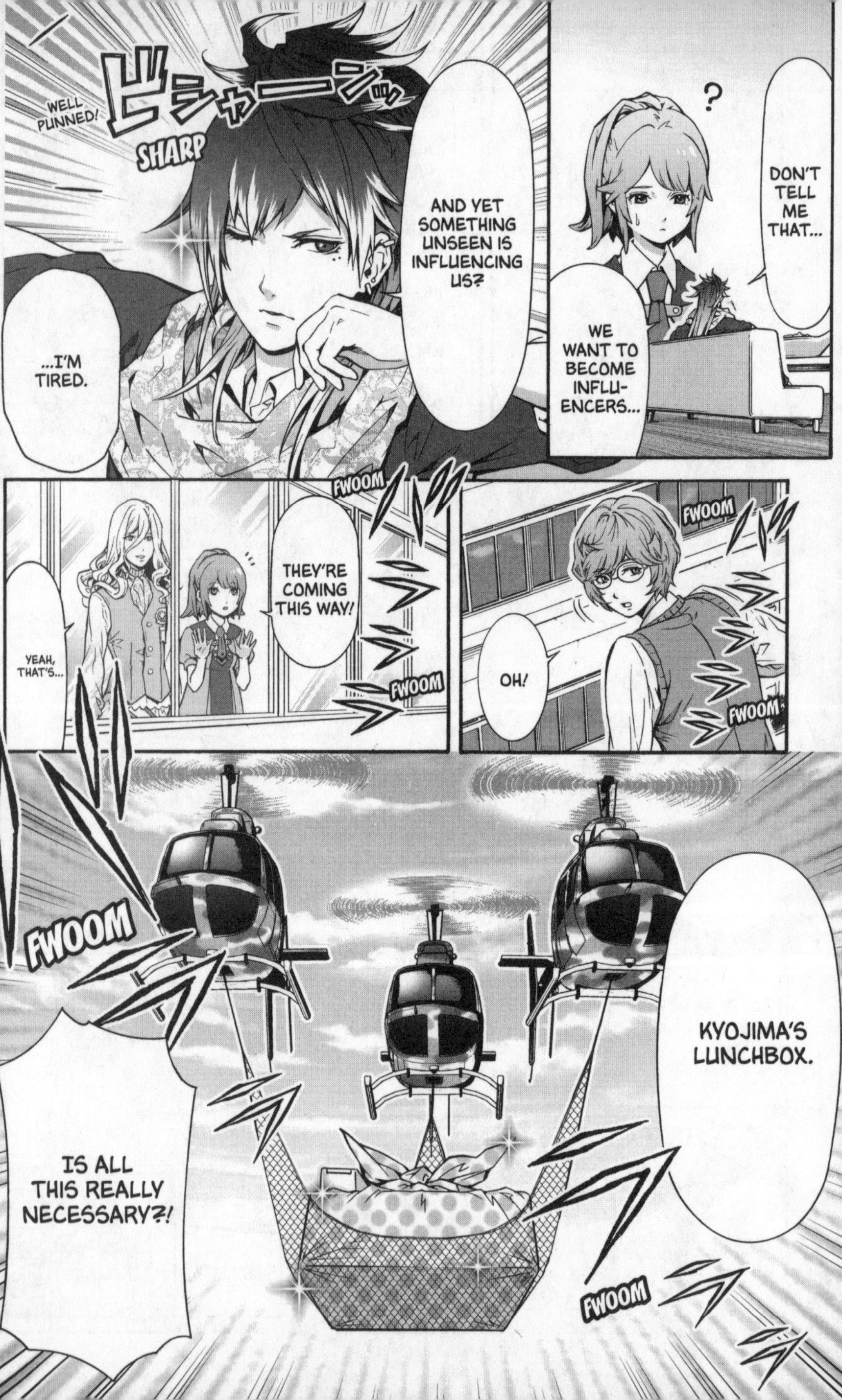
?
DON'T TELL ME THAT...
WE WANT TO BECOME INFLU-ENCERS...
ビシャーーン
WELL PUNNED!
SHARP
AND YET SOMETHING UNSEEN IS INFLUENCING US?
...I'M TIRED.
FWOOM
OH!
FWOOM
FWOOM
THEY'RE COMING THIS WAY!
FWOOM
YEAH, THAT'S...
KYOJIMA'S LUNCHBOX.
FWOOM
IS ALL THIS REALLY NECESSARY?!
FWOOM

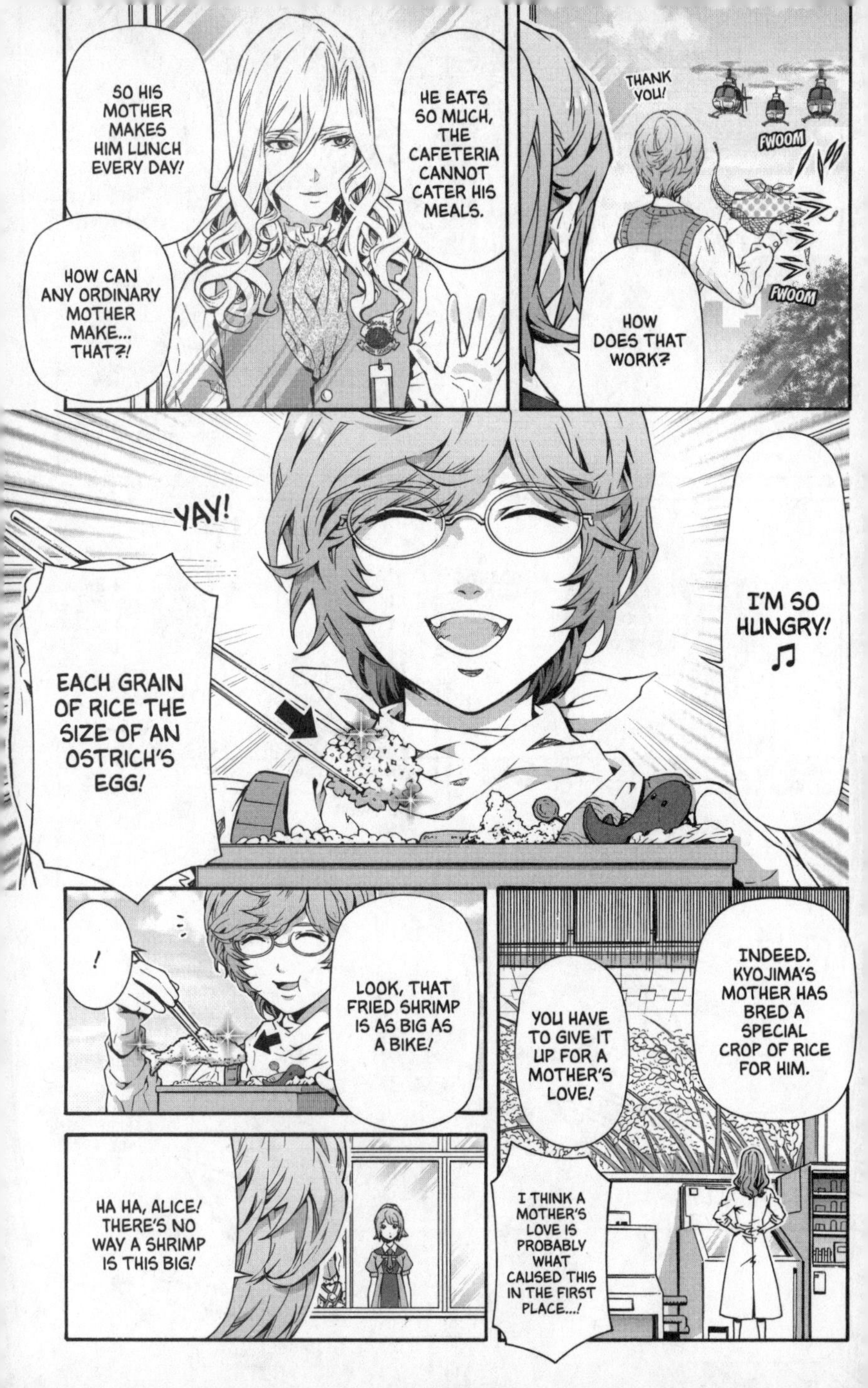
THANK YOU!
FWOOM
FWOOM
HOW DOES THAT WORK?
HE EATS SO MUCH, THE CAFETERIA CANNOT CATER HIS MEALS.
SO HIS MOTHER MAKES HIM LUNCH EVERY DAY!
HOW CAN ANY ORDINARY MOTHER MAKE... THAT?!
I'M SO HUNGRY! ♫
YAY!
EACH GRAIN OF RICE THE SIZE OF AN OSTRICH'S EGG!
INDEED. KYOJIMA'S MOTHER HAS BRED A SPECIAL CROP OF RICE FOR HIM.
YOU HAVE TO GIVE IT UP FOR A MOTHER'S LOVE!
I THINK A MOTHER'S LOVE IS PROBABLY WHAT CAUSED THIS IN THE FIRST PLACE...!
LOOK, THAT FRIED SHRIMP IS AS BIG AS A BIKE!
!
HA HA, ALICE! THERE'S NO WAY A SHRIMP IS THIS BIG!

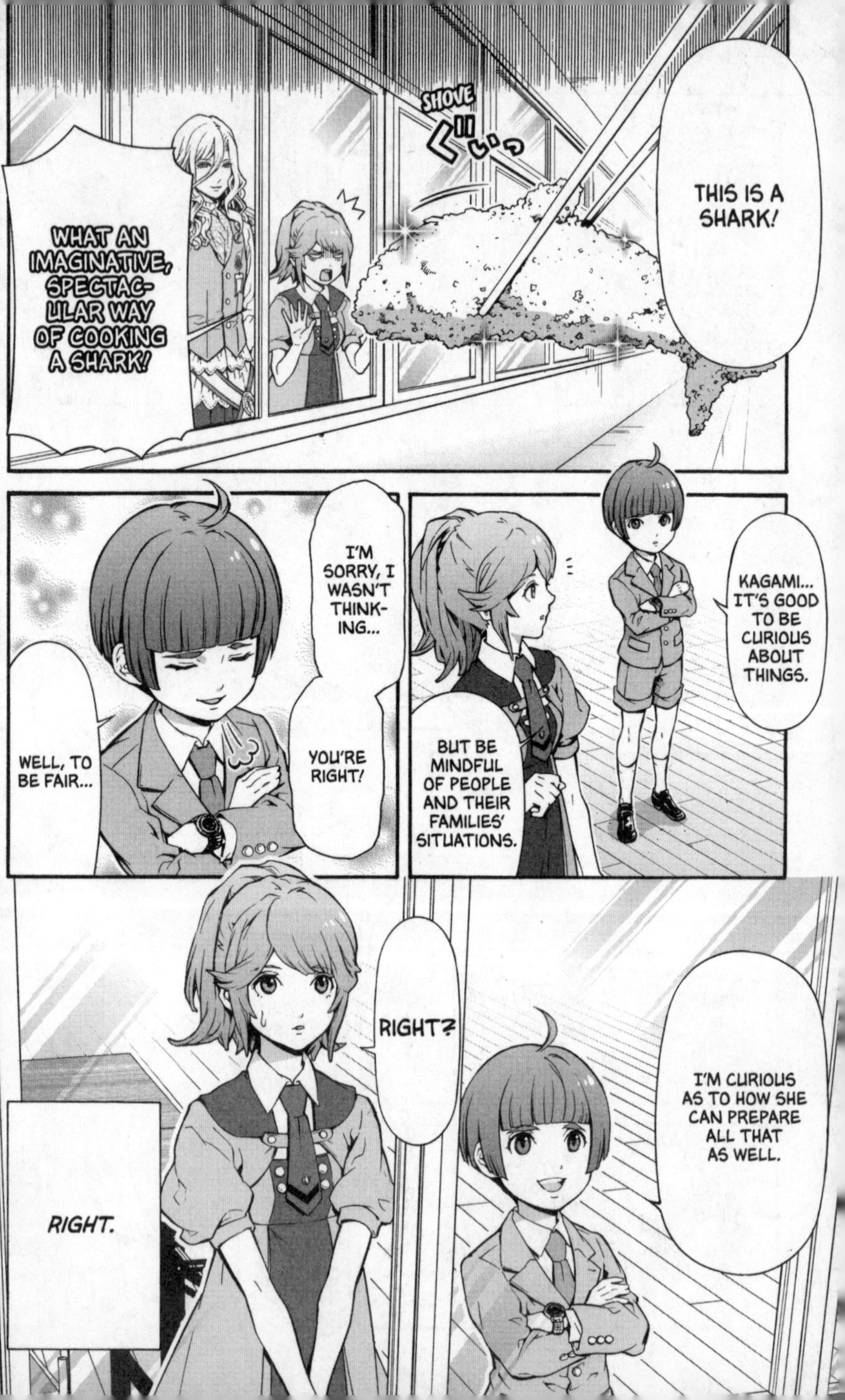
THIS IS A SHARK!
SHOVE
WHAT AN IMAGINATIVE, SPECTACULAR WAY OF COOKING A SHARK!
KAGAMI... IT'S GOOD TO BE CURIOUS ABOUT THINGS.
BUT BE MINDFUL OF PEOPLE AND THEIR FAMILIES' SITUATIONS.
I'M SORRY, I WASN'T THINKING...
YOU'RE RIGHT!
WELL, TO BE FAIR...
I'M CURIOUS AS TO HOW SHE CAN PREPARE ALL THAT AS WELL.
RIGHT?
RIGHT.

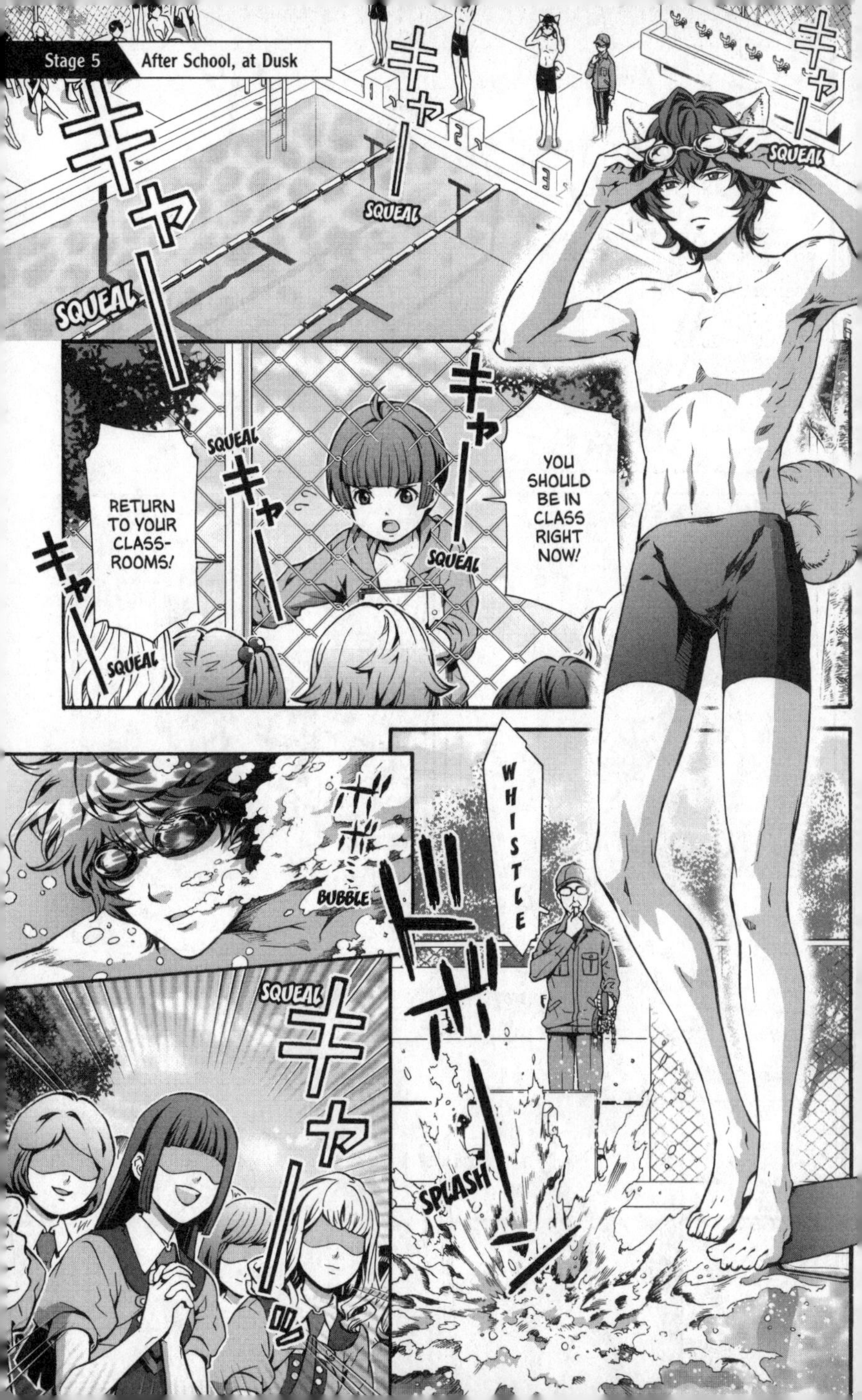
Stage 5
After School, at Dusk
キャー
SQUEAL
キャー
SQUEAL
キャー
SQUEAL
YOU SHOULD BE IN CLASS RIGHT NOW!
キャー
SQUEAL
キャー
SQUEAL
RETURN TO YOUR CLASS-ROOMS!
キャー
SQUEAL
WHISTLE
SPLASH
BUBBLE
SQUEAL
キャー

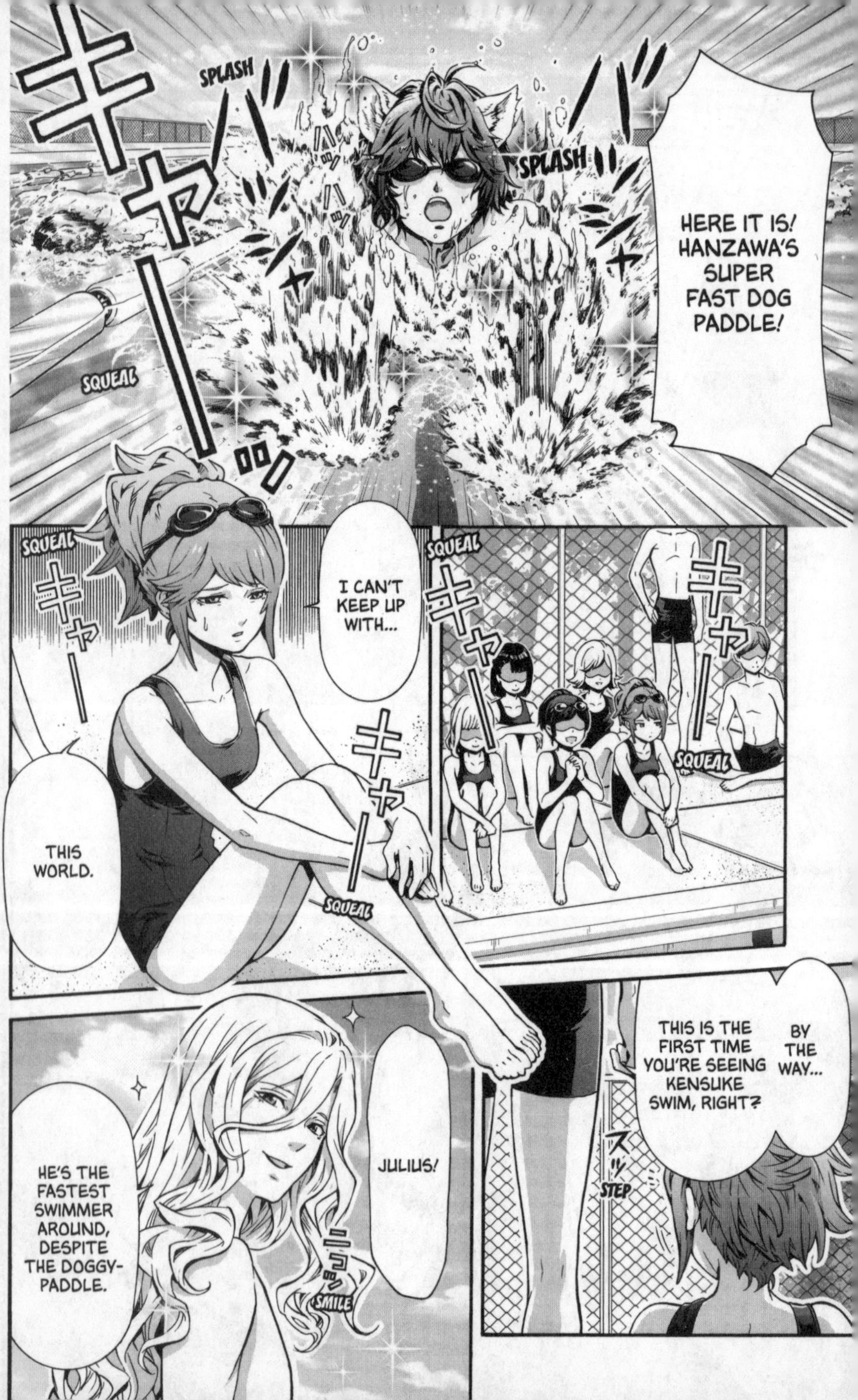
HERE IT IS! HANZAWA'S SUPER FAST DOG PADDLE!
SPLASH
SPLASH
SQUEAL
SQUEAL
SQUEAL
I CAN'T KEEP UP WITH...
THIS WORLD.
SQUEAL
SQUEAL
BY THE WAY...
THIS IS THE FIRST TIME YOU'RE SEEING KENSUKE SWIM, RIGHT?
STEP
JULIUS!
HE'S THE FASTEST SWIMMER AROUND, DESPITE THE DOGGY-PADDLE.
SMILE

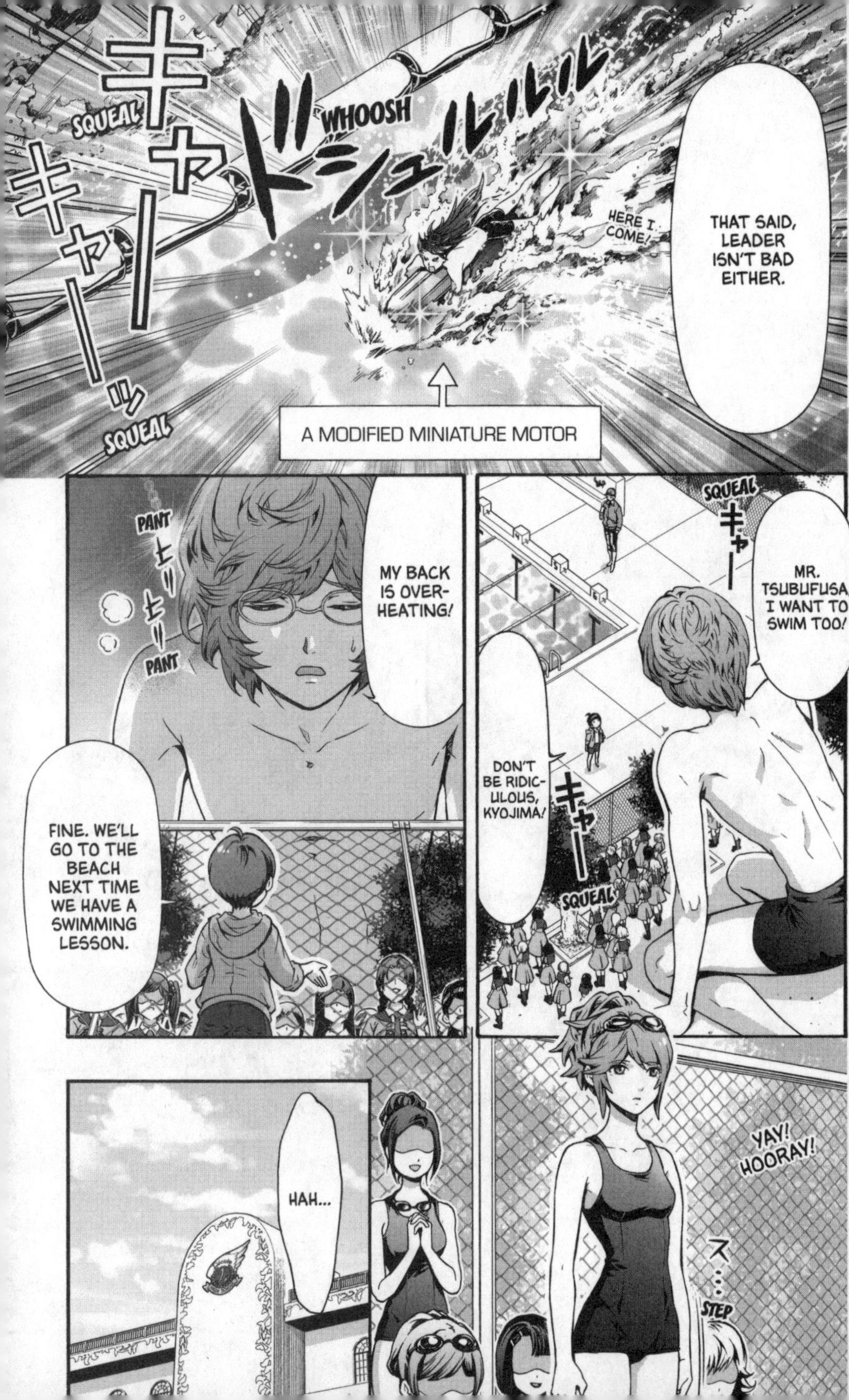
THAT SAID, LEADER ISN'T BAD EITHER.
HERE I COME!
WHOOSH
SQUEAL
SQUEAL
A MODIFIED MINIATURE MOTOR
SQUEAL
MR. TSUBUFUSA, I WANT TO SWIM TOO!
DON'T BE RIDICULOUS, KYOJIMA!
SQUEAL
MY BACK IS OVER-HEATING!
PANT
PANT
FINE. WE'LL GO TO THE BEACH NEXT TIME WE HAVE A SWIMMING LESSON.
YAY! HOORAY!
STEP
HAH...

Stage 5

After School, at Dusk

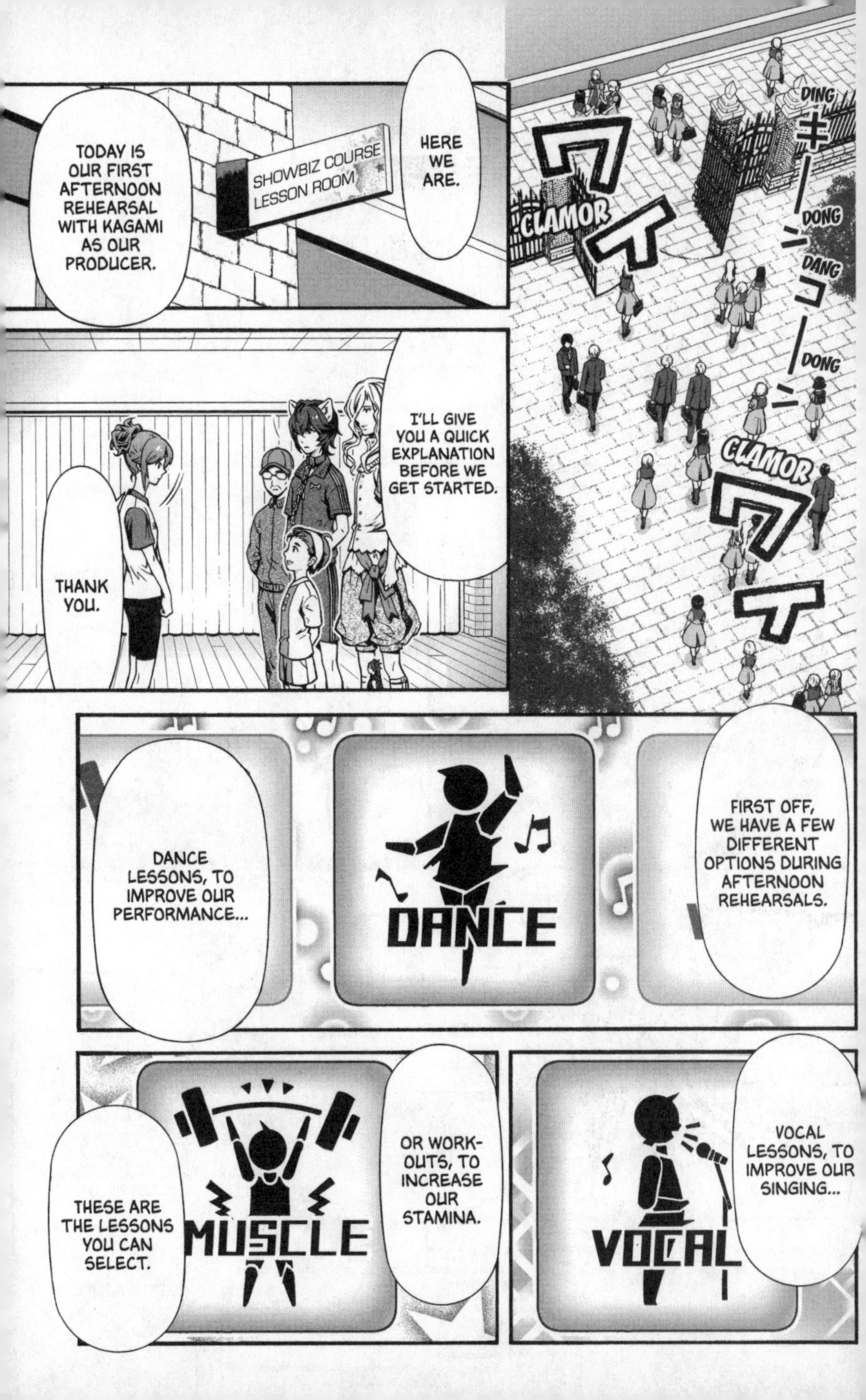
DING
キーン
DONG
DANG
コーン
DONG
ワイワイ
CLAMOR
ワイワイ
CLAMOR
HERE WE ARE.
SHOWBIZ COURSE LESSON ROOM
TODAY IS OUR FIRST AFTERNOON REHEARSAL WITH KAGAMI AS OUR PRODUCER.
I'LL GIVE YOU A QUICK EXPLANATION BEFORE WE GET STARTED.
THANK YOU.
FIRST OFF, WE HAVE A FEW DIFFERENT OPTIONS DURING AFTERNOON REHEARSALS.
DANCE
DANCE LESSONS, TO IMPROVE OUR PERFORMANCE...
VOCAL LESSONS, TO IMPROVE OUR SINGING...
VOCAL
OR WORK-OUTS, TO INCREASE OUR STAMINA.
MUSCLE
THESE ARE THE LESSONS YOU CAN SELECT.

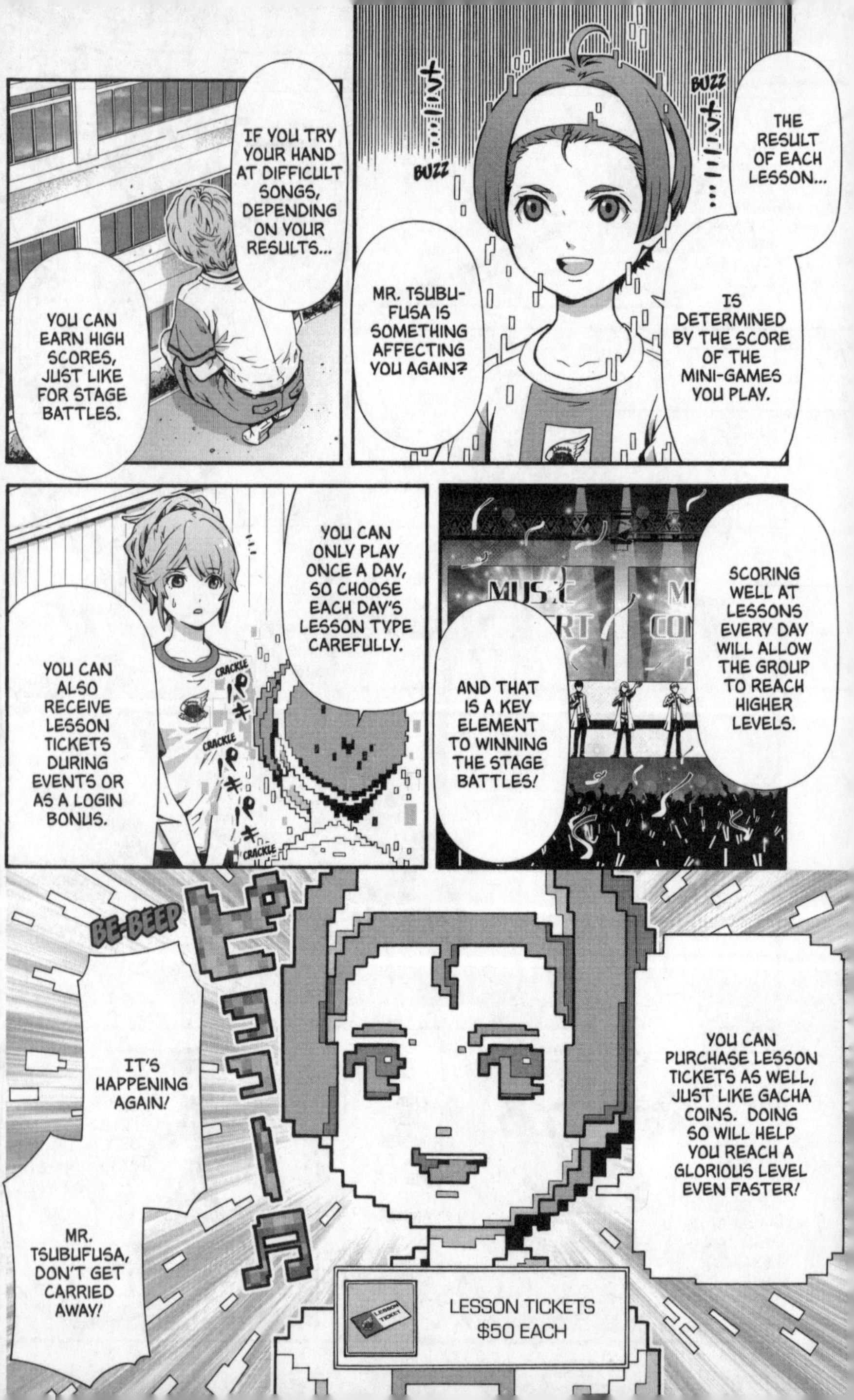
BUZZ
THE RESULT OF EACH LESSON...
IS DETERMINED BY THE SCORE OF THE MINI-GAMES YOU PLAY.
BUZZ
MR. TSUBUFUSA IS SOMETHING AFFECTING YOU AGAIN?
IF YOU TRY YOUR HAND AT DIFFICULT SONGS, DEPENDING ON YOUR RESULTS...
YOU CAN EARN HIGH SCORES, JUST LIKE FOR STAGE BATTLES.
SCORING WELL AT LESSONS EVERY DAY WILL ALLOW THE GROUP TO REACH HIGHER LEVELS.
AND THAT IS A KEY ELEMENT TO WINNING THE STAGE BATTLES!
YOU CAN ONLY PLAY ONCE A DAY, SO CHOOSE EACH DAY'S LESSON TYPE CAREFULLY.
CRACKLE
CRACKLE
CRACKLE
YOU CAN ALSO RECEIVE LESSON TICKETS DURING EVENTS OR AS A LOGIN BONUS.
YOU CAN PURCHASE LESSON TICKETS AS WELL, JUST LIKE GACHA COINS. DOING SO WILL HELP YOU REACH A GLORIOUS LEVEL EVEN FASTER!
LESSON TICKETS $50 EACH
BE-BEEP
IT'S HAPPENING AGAIN!
MR. TSUBUFUSA, DON'T GET CARRIED AWAY!

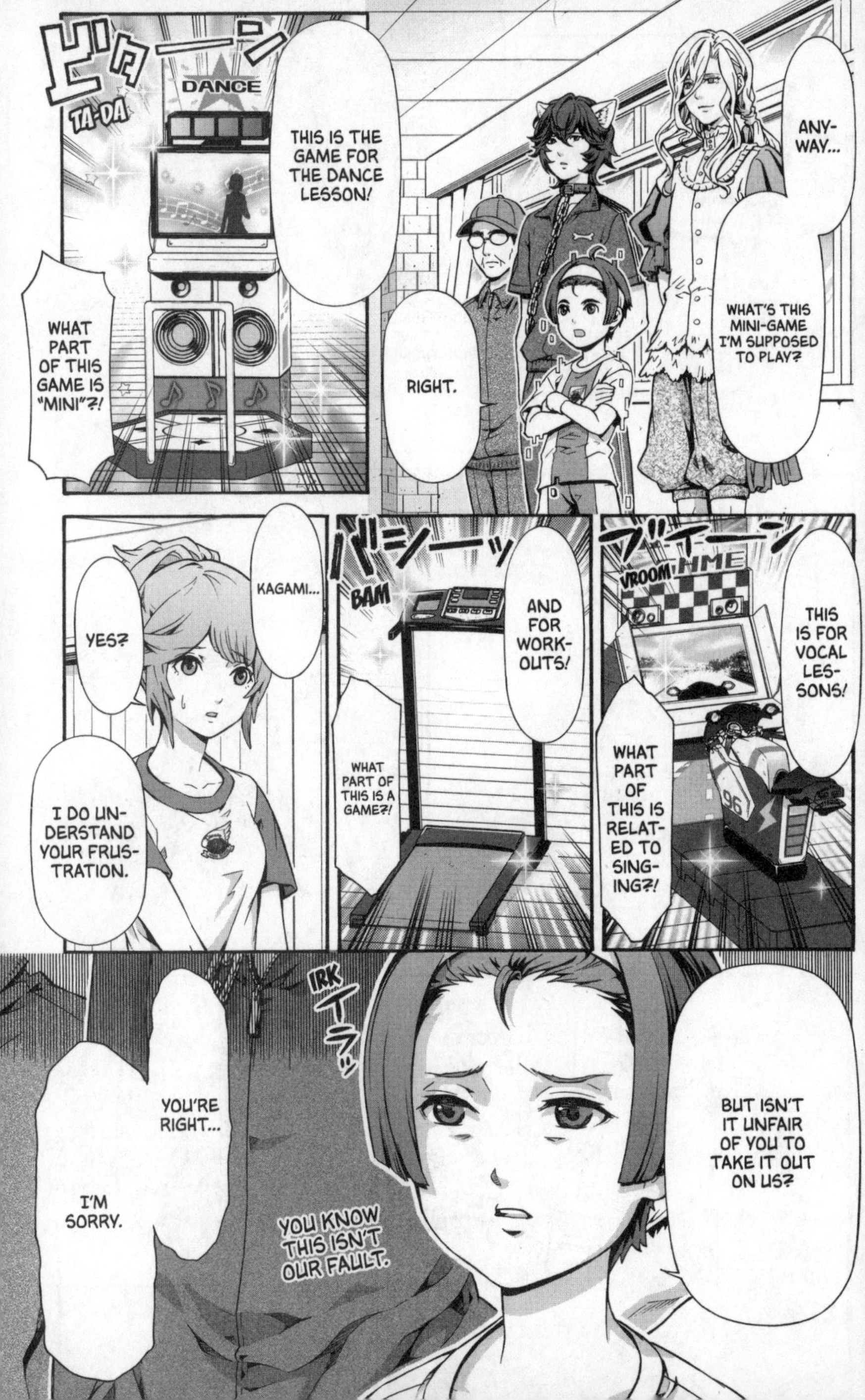
ANY-WAY...
WHAT'S THIS MINI-GAME I'M SUPPOSED TO PLAY?
RIGHT.
TA-DA
DANCE
THIS IS THE GAME FOR THE DANCE LESSON!
WHAT PART OF THIS GAME IS "MINI"?!
VROOM
THIS IS FOR VOCAL LESSONS!
WHAT PART OF THIS IS RELATED TO SINGING?!
BAM
AND FOR WORK-OUTS!
WHAT PART OF THIS IS A GAME?!
KAGAMI...
YES?
I DO UNDERSTAND YOUR FRUSTRATION.
IRK
BUT ISN'T IT UNFAIR OF YOU TO TAKE IT OUT ON US?
YOU KNOW THIS ISN'T OUR FAULT.
YOU'RE RIGHT...
I'M SORRY.

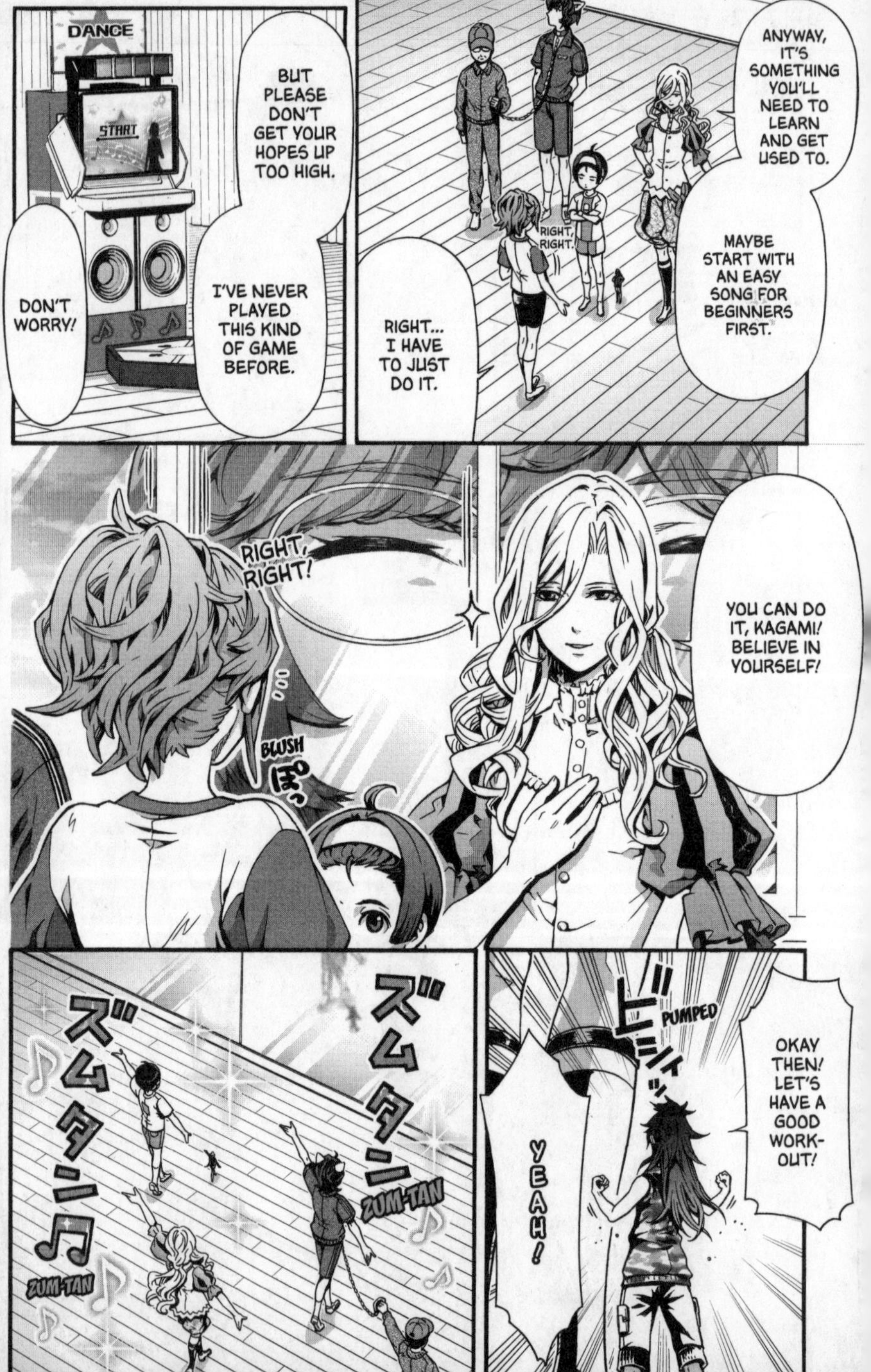
ANYWAY, IT'S SOMETHING YOU'LL NEED TO LEARN AND GET USED TO.
MAYBE START WITH AN EASY SONG FOR BEGINNERS FIRST.
RIGHT, RIGHT.
RIGHT... I HAVE TO JUST DO IT.
DANCE
START
BUT PLEASE DON'T GET YOUR HOPES UP TOO HIGH.
I'VE NEVER PLAYED THIS KIND OF GAME BEFORE.
DON'T WORRY!
YOU CAN DO IT, KAGAMI! BELIEVE IN YOURSELF!
RIGHT, RIGHT!
BLUSH
ぽっ
OKAY THEN! LET'S HAVE A GOOD WORK-OUT!
ビシッ
PUMPED
YEAH!
ズムタ〜ン
ZUM-TAN
ズムタ〜ン
ZUM-TAN

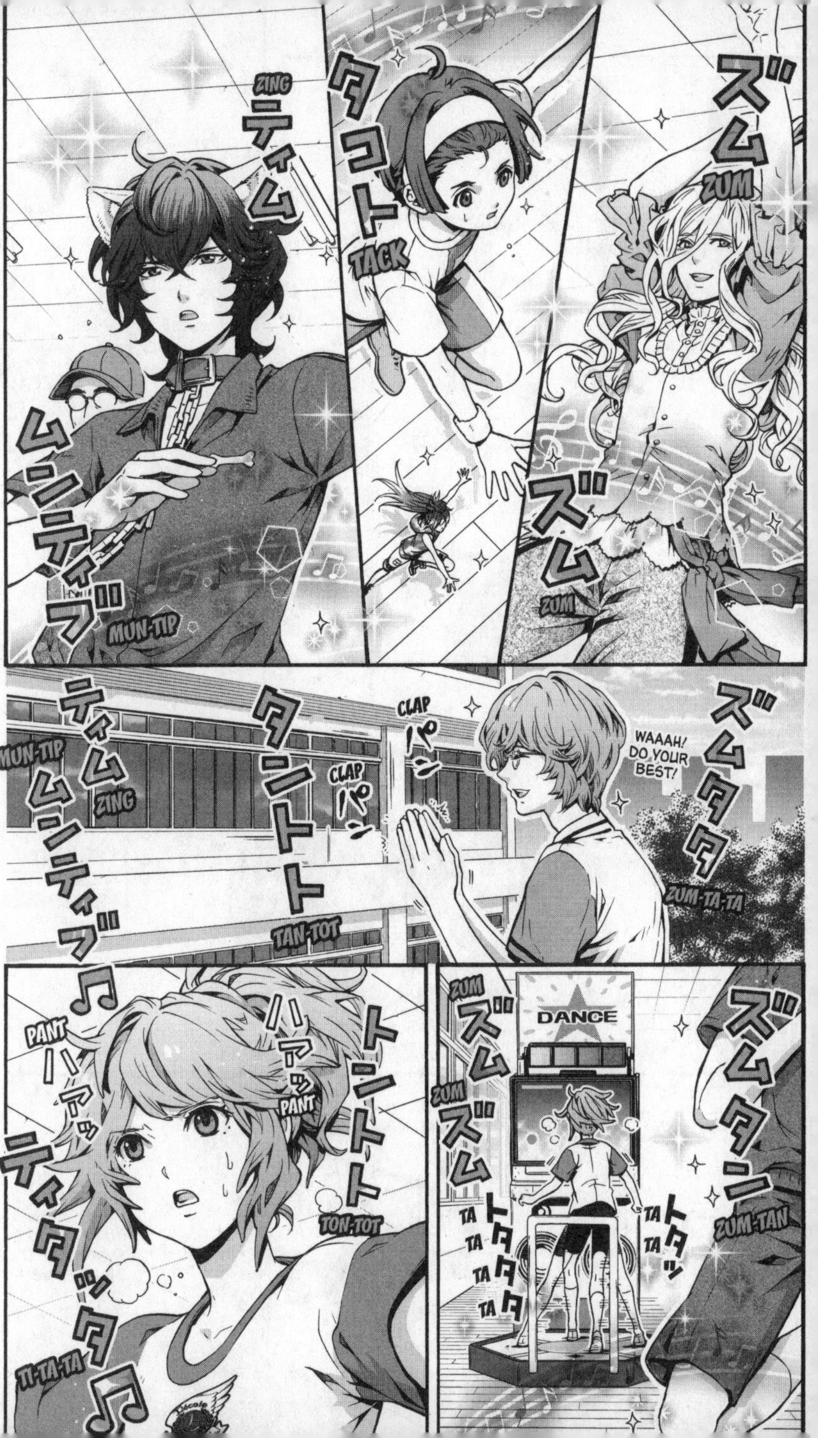
ズム
ZUM
ズム
ZUM
タコト
TACK
ティム
ZING
ムンティブ
MUN-TIP
ズムタタ
ZUM-TA-TA
WAAAH! DO YOUR BEST!
パン
CLAP
パン
CLAP
タントト
TAN-TOT
ティム
ZING
ムンティブ
MUN-TIP
ズムタン
ZUM-TAN
ズム
ZUM
ズム
ZUM
DANCE
トタッ
TA TA
トタタタ
TA TA TA TA
トントト
TON-TOT
ハァッ
PANT
ハァッ
PANT
ティタタ
TI-TA-TA

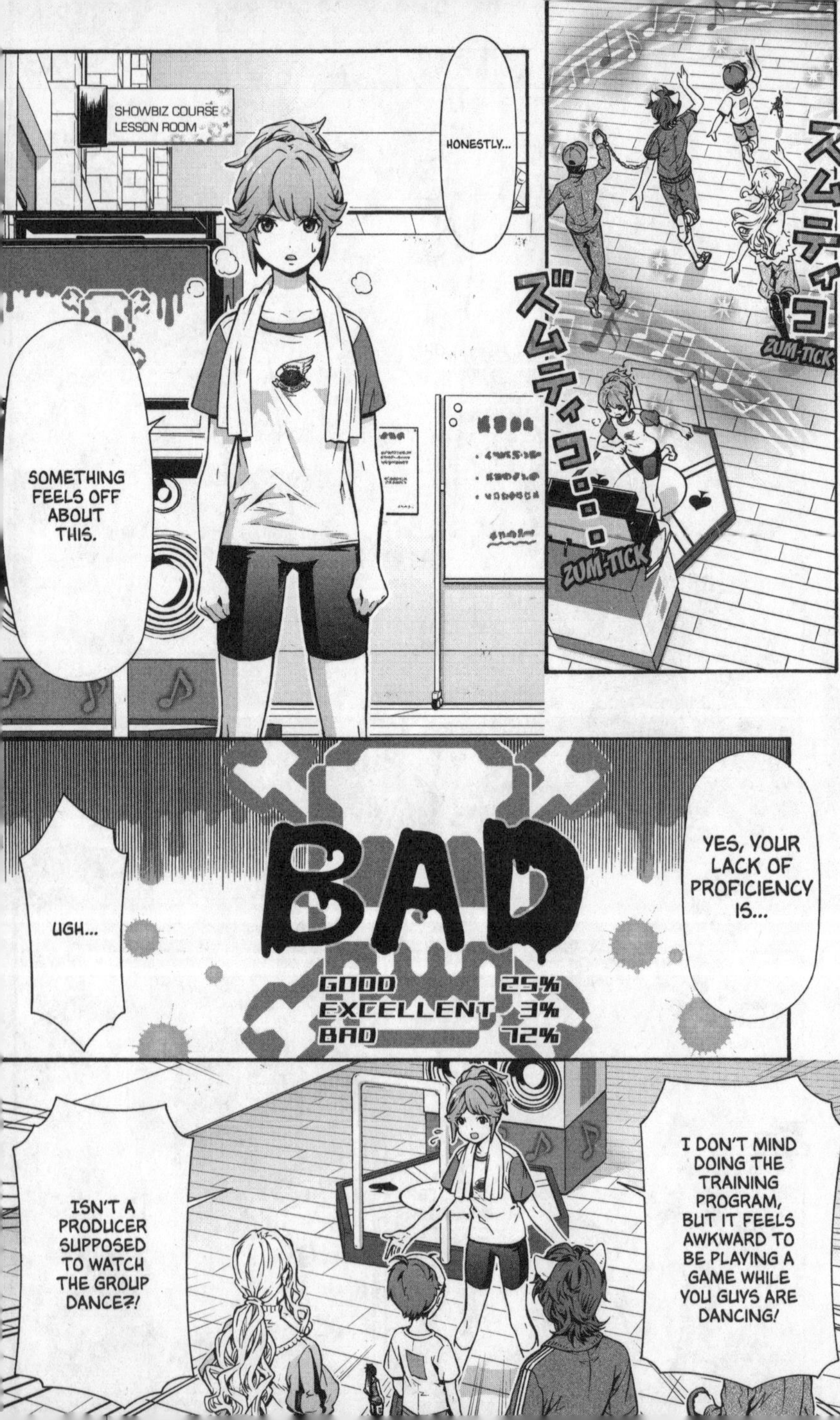
ズムティコ
ZUM-TICK
ズムティコ…
ZUM-TICK
SHOWBIZ COURSE LESSON ROOM
HONESTLY...
SOMETHING FEELS OFF ABOUT THIS.
YES, YOUR LACK OF PROFICIENCY IS...
BAD
GOOD 25%
EXCELLENT 3%
BAD 72%
UGH...
I DON'T MIND DOING THE TRAINING PROGRAM, BUT IT FEELS AWKWARD TO BE PLAYING A GAME WHILE YOU GUYS ARE DANCING!
ISN'T A PRODUCER SUPPOSED TO WATCH THE GROUP DANCE?!

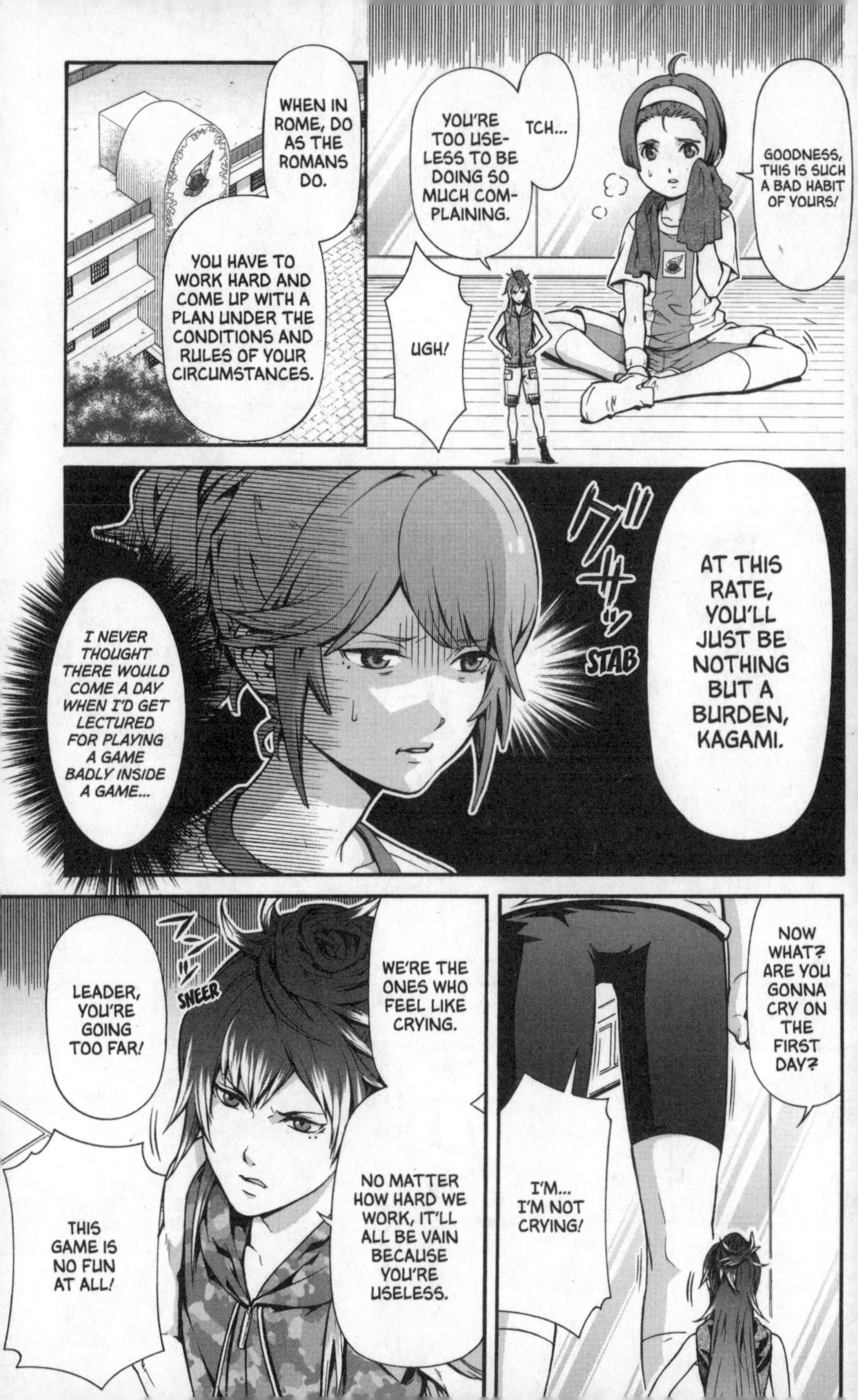
GOODNESS, THIS IS SUCH A BAD HABIT OF YOURS!
TCH...
YOU'RE TOO USE-LESS TO BE DOING SO MUCH COM-PLAINING.
UGH!
WHEN IN ROME, DO AS THE ROMANS DO.
YOU HAVE TO WORK HARD AND COME UP WITH A PLAN UNDER THE CONDITIONS AND RULES OF YOUR CIRCUMSTANCES.
AT THIS RATE, YOU'LL JUST BE NOTHING BUT A BURDEN, KAGAMI.
STAB
I NEVER THOUGHT THERE WOULD COME A DAY WHEN I'D GET LECTURED FOR PLAYING A GAME BADLY INSIDE A GAME...
NOW WHAT? ARE YOU GONNA CRY ON THE FIRST DAY?
I'M... I'M NOT CRYING!
WE'RE THE ONES WHO FEEL LIKE CRYING.
SNEER
LEADER, YOU'RE GOING TOO FAR!
NO MATTER HOW HARD WE WORK, IT'LL ALL BE VAIN BECAUSE YOU'RE USELESS.
THIS GAME IS NO FUN AT ALL!

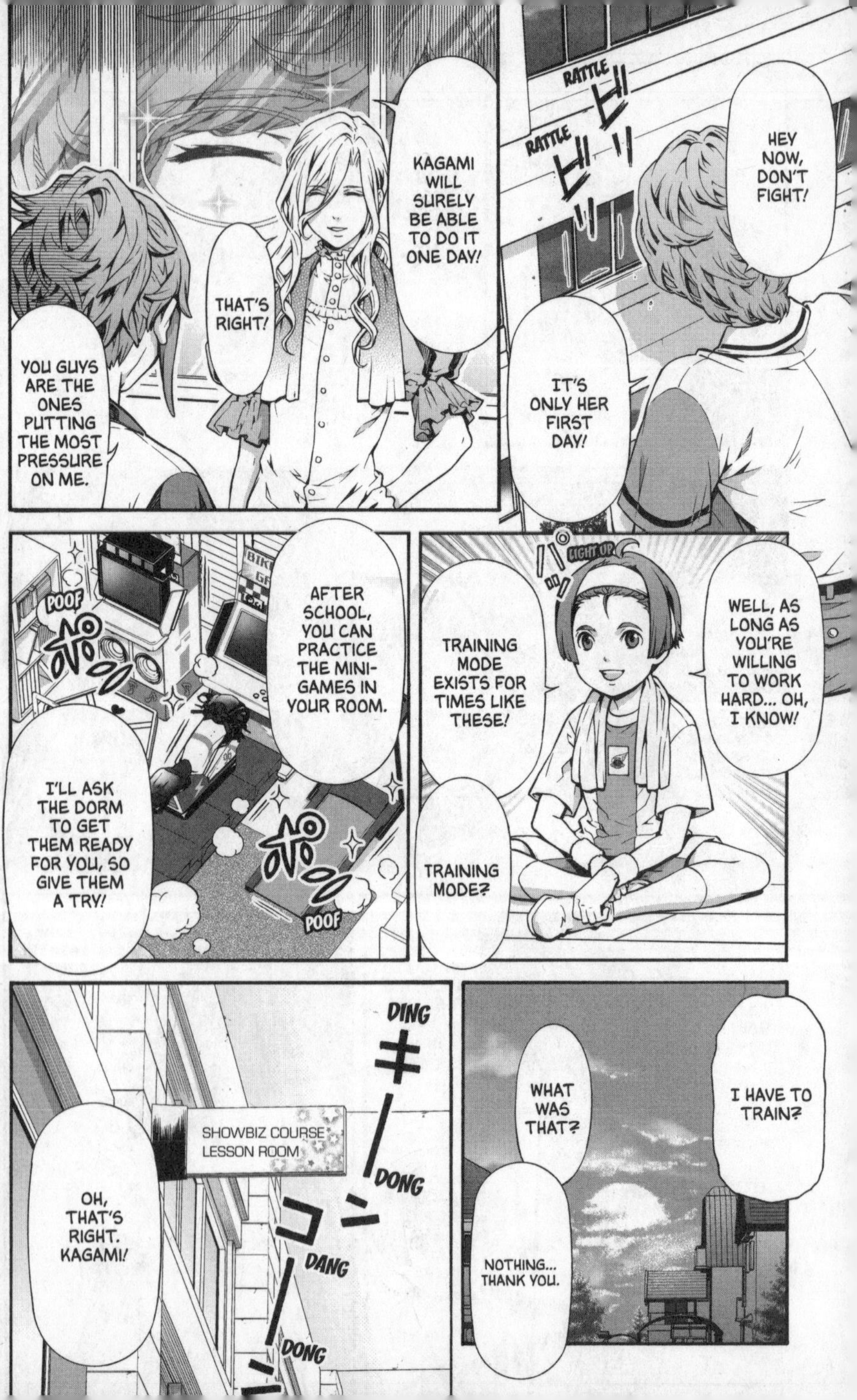
RATTLE
RATTLE
HEY NOW, DON'T FIGHT!
IT'S ONLY HER FIRST DAY!
KAGAMI WILL SURELY BE ABLE TO DO IT ONE DAY!
THAT'S RIGHT!
YOU GUYS ARE THE ONES PUTTING THE MOST PRESSURE ON ME.
LIGHT UP
WELL, AS LONG AS YOU'RE WILLING TO WORK HARD... OH, I KNOW!
TRAINING MODE EXISTS FOR TIMES LIKE THESE!
TRAINING MODE?
AFTER SCHOOL, YOU CAN PRACTICE THE MINI-GAMES IN YOUR ROOM.
POOF
I'LL ASK THE DORM TO GET THEM READY FOR YOU, SO GIVE THEM A TRY!
POOF
I HAVE TO TRAIN?
WHAT WAS THAT?
NOTHING... THANK YOU.
DING
SHOWBIZ COURSE
LESSON ROOM
DONG
OH, THAT'S RIGHT. KAGAMI!
DANG
DONG

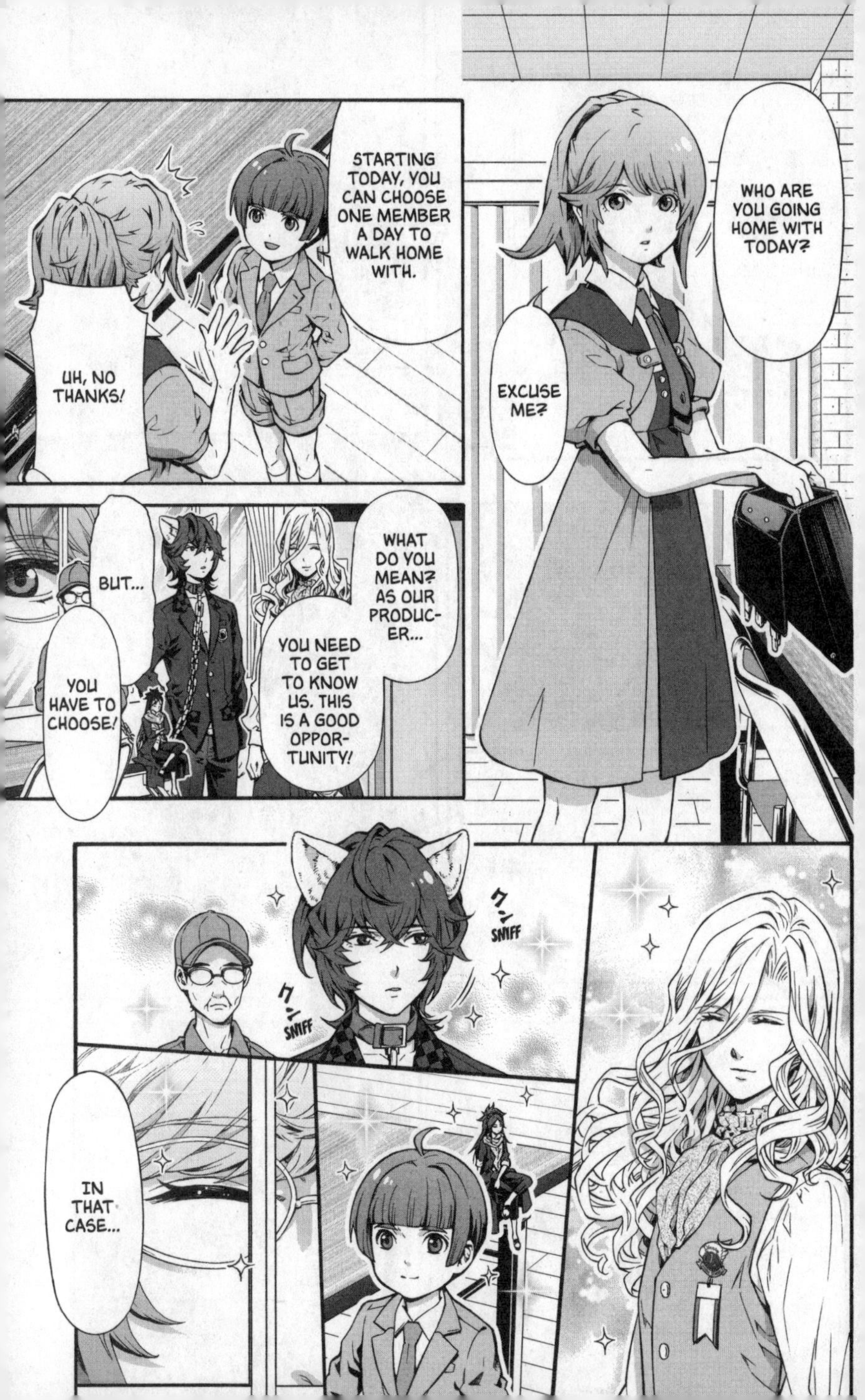
WHO ARE YOU GOING HOME WITH TODAY?
EXCUSE ME?
STARTING TODAY, YOU CAN CHOOSE ONE MEMBER A DAY TO WALK HOME WITH.
UH, NO THANKS!
WHAT DO YOU MEAN? AS OUR PRODUCER...
YOU NEED TO GET TO KNOW US. THIS IS A GOOD OPPORTUNITY!
BUT...
YOU HAVE TO CHOOSE!
クン SNIFF
クン SNIFF
IN THAT CASE...

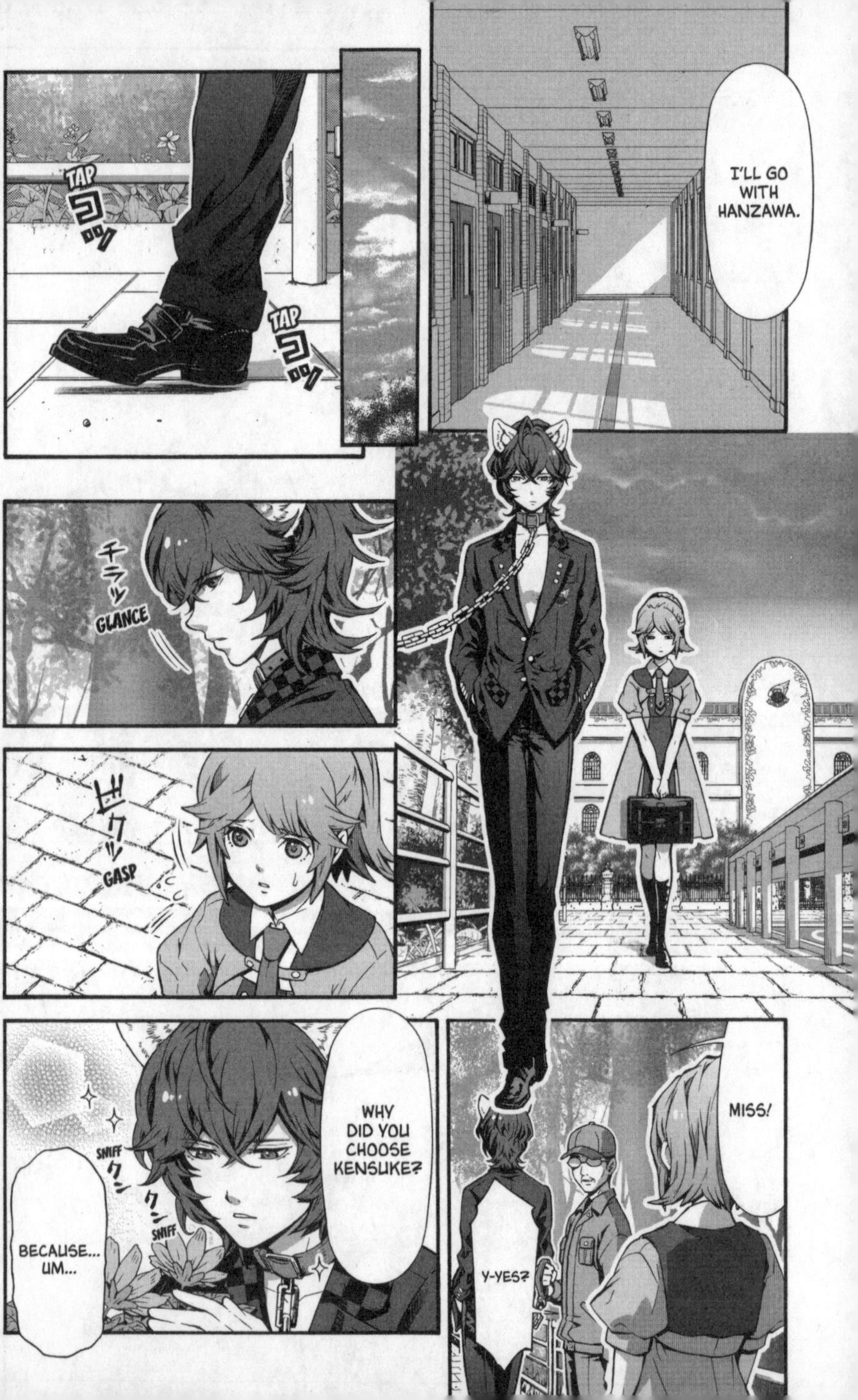
I'LL GO WITH HANZAWA.
TAP
TAP
チラッ
GLANCE
ビクッ
GASP
MISS!
Y-YES?
WHY DID YOU CHOOSE KENSUKE?
クン
SNIFF
クン
SNIFF
BECAUSE... UM...

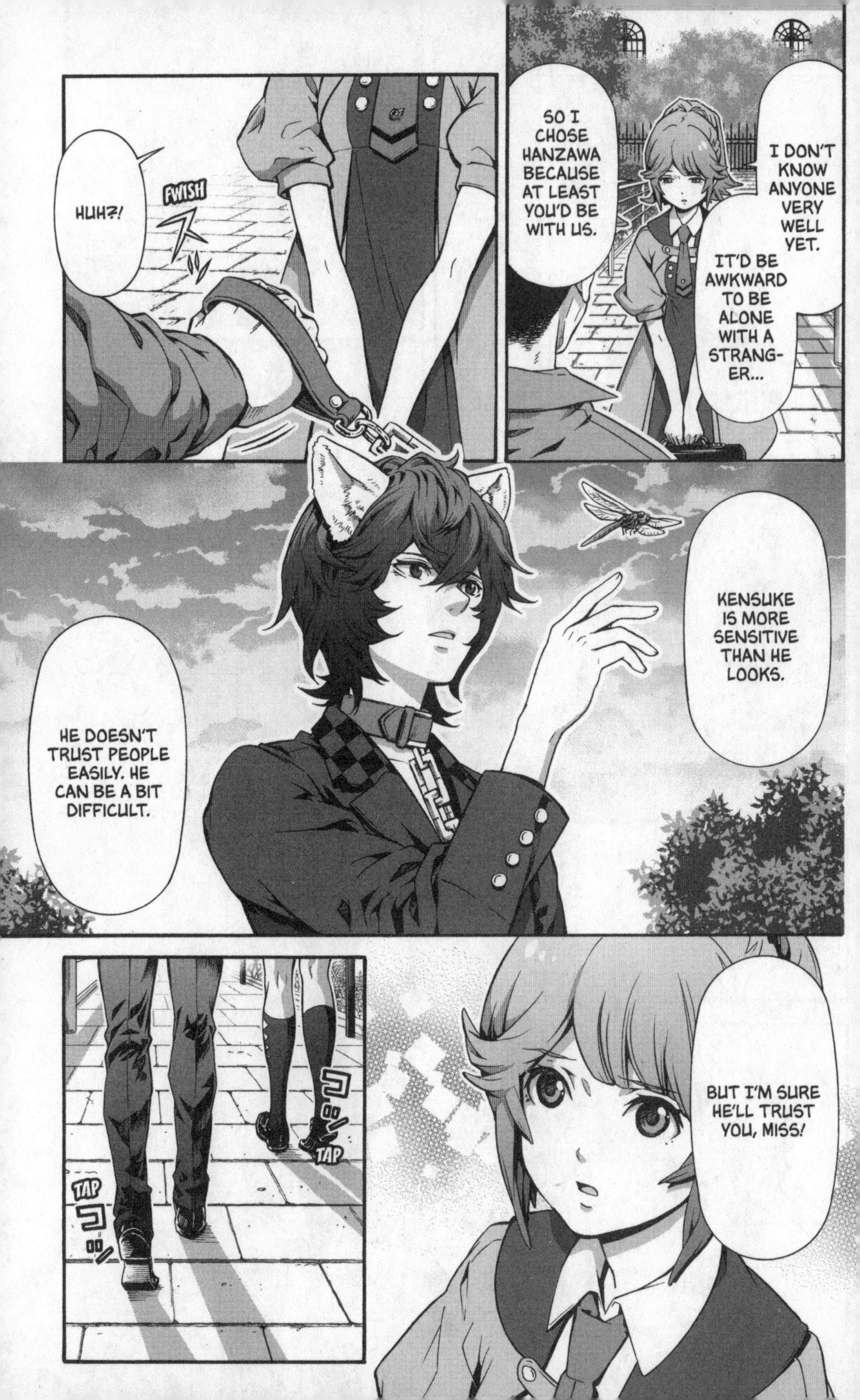
I DON'T KNOW ANYONE VERY WELL YET.
IT'D BE AWKWARD TO BE ALONE WITH A STRANG-ER...
SO I CHOSE HANZAWA BECAUSE AT LEAST YOU'D BE WITH US.
FWISH
HUH?!
KENSUKE IS MORE SENSITIVE THAN HE LOOKS.
HE DOESN'T TRUST PEOPLE EASILY. HE CAN BE A BIT DIFFICULT.
BUT I'M SURE HE'LL TRUST YOU, MISS!
TAP
TAP

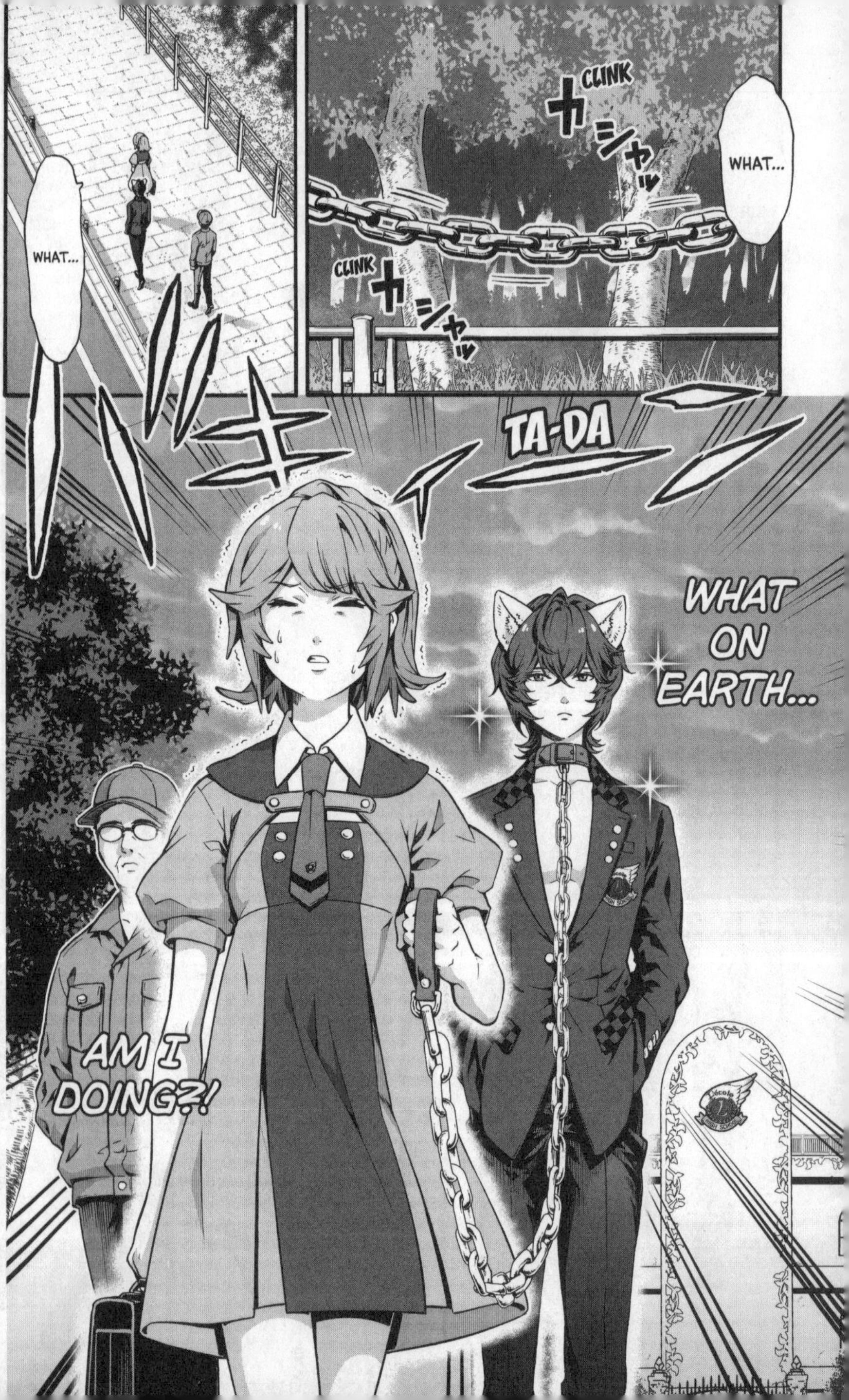
WHAT...
CLINK
カシャッ
CLINK
カシャッ
WHAT...
TA-DA
WHAT ON EARTH...
AM I DOING?!

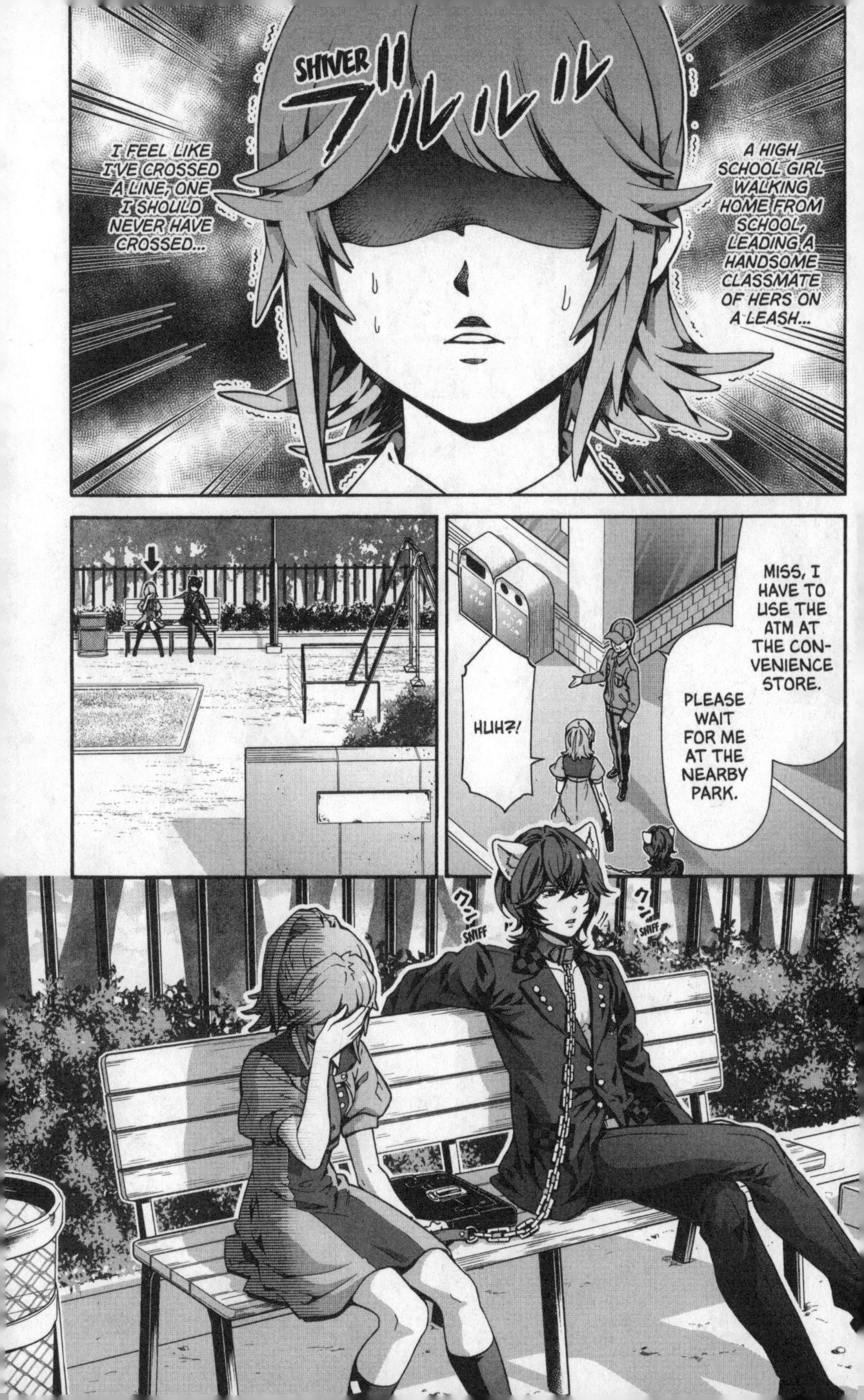
SHIVER
ブルルル
A HIGH SCHOOL GIRL WALKING HOME FROM SCHOOL, LEADING A HANDSOME CLASSMATE OF HERS ON A LEASH...
I FEEL LIKE I'VE CROSSED A LINE, ONE I SHOULD NEVER HAVE CROSSED...
MISS, I HAVE TO USE THE ATM AT THE CONVENIENCE STORE.
PLEASE WAIT FOR ME AT THE NEARBY PARK.
HUH?!
クン
SNIFF
クン
SNIFF

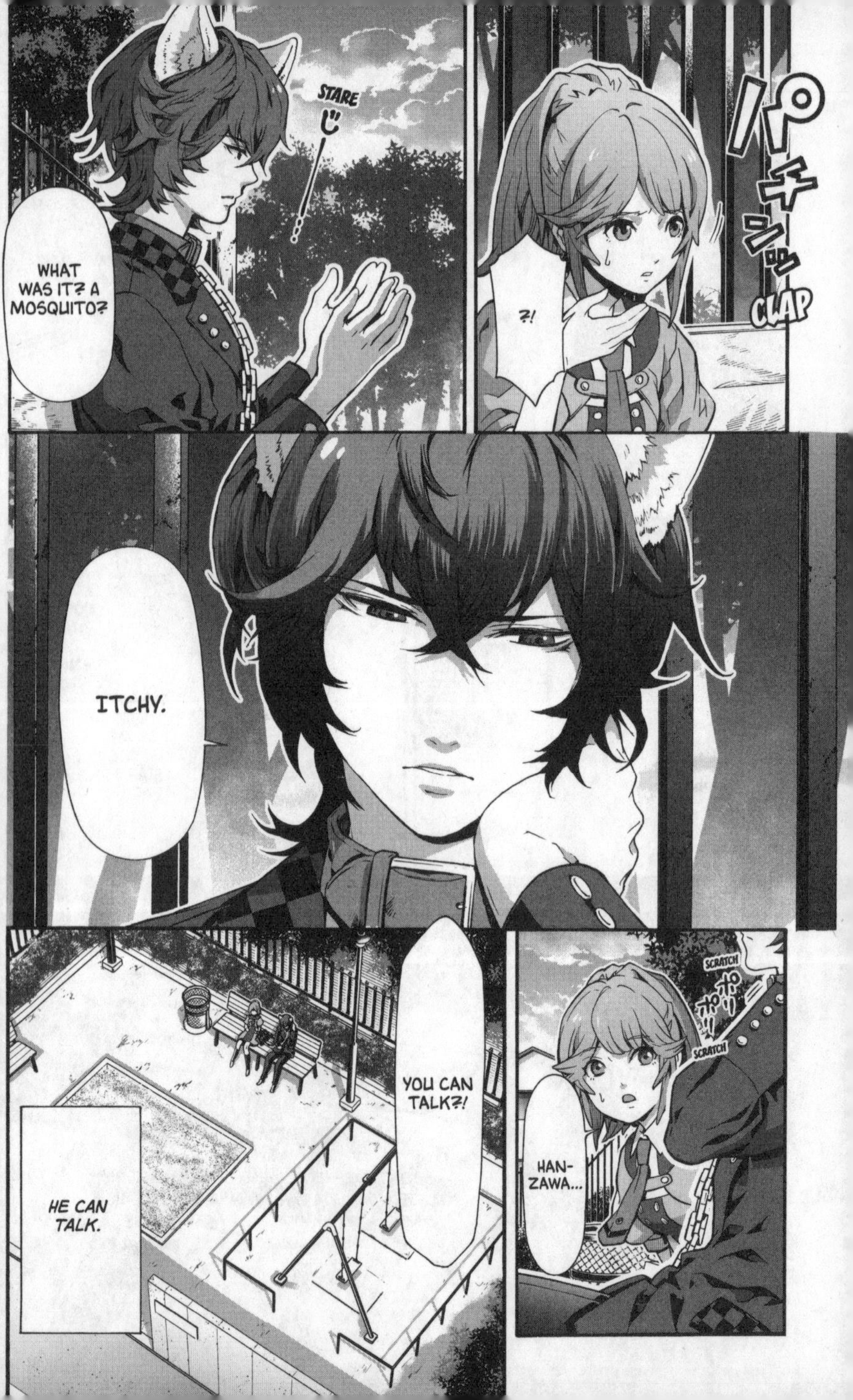
パチンッ
CLAP
?!
STARE
じ
WHAT WAS IT? A MOSQUITO?
ITCHY.
SCRATCH
ポリ
ポリ
SCRATCH
HAN-ZAWA...
YOU CAN TALK?!
HE CAN TALK.

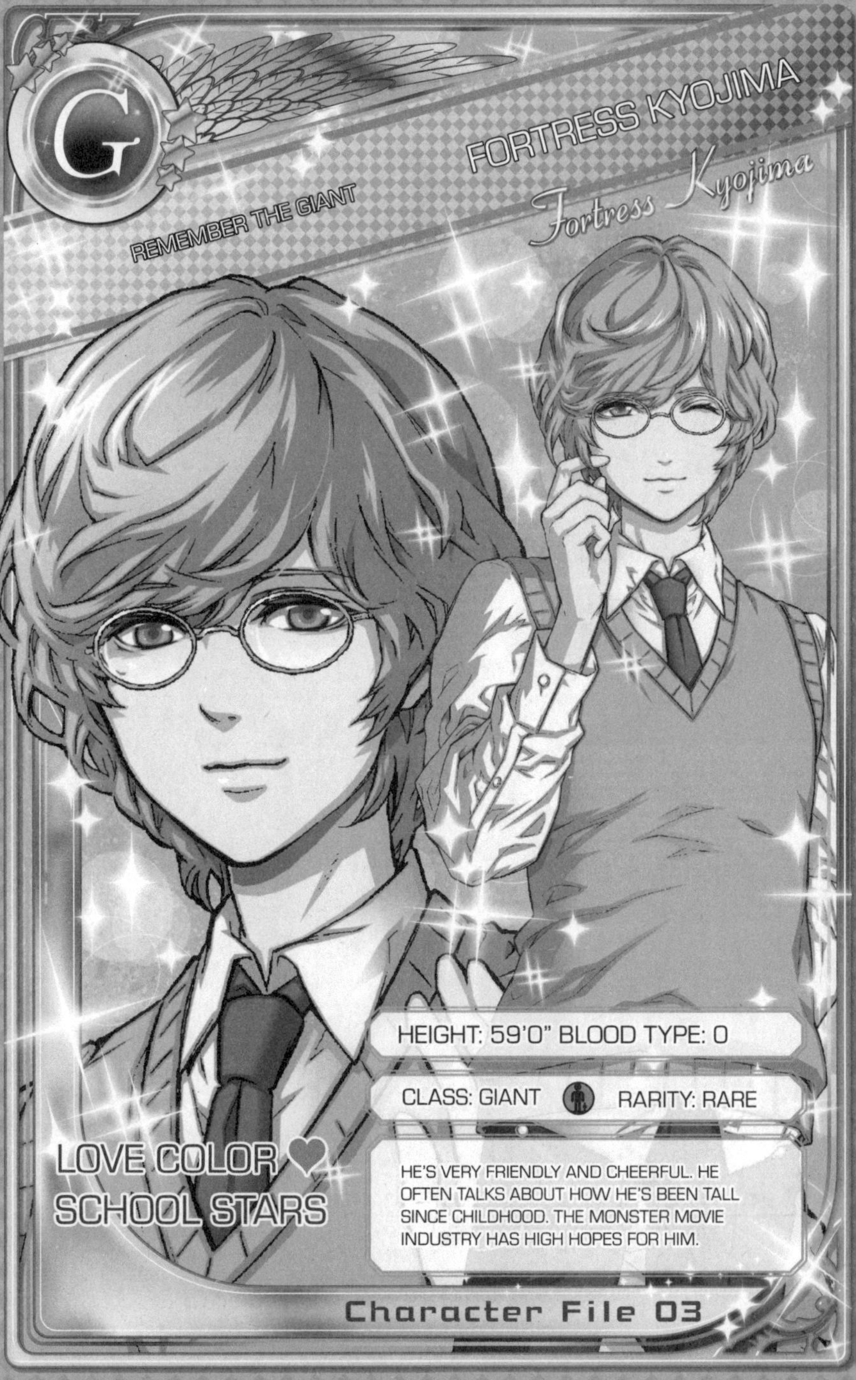
G
REMEMBER THE GIANT
FORTRESS KYOJIMA
Fortress Kyojima
HEIGHT: 59'0" BLOOD TYPE: O
CLASS: GIANT
RARITY: RARE
LOVE COLOR ♥ SCHOOL STARS
HE'S VERY FRIENDLY AND CHEERFUL. HE OFTEN TALKS ABOUT HOW HE'S BEEN TALL SINCE CHILDHOOD. THE MONSTER MOVIE INDUSTRY HAS HIGH HOPES FOR HIM.
Character File 03

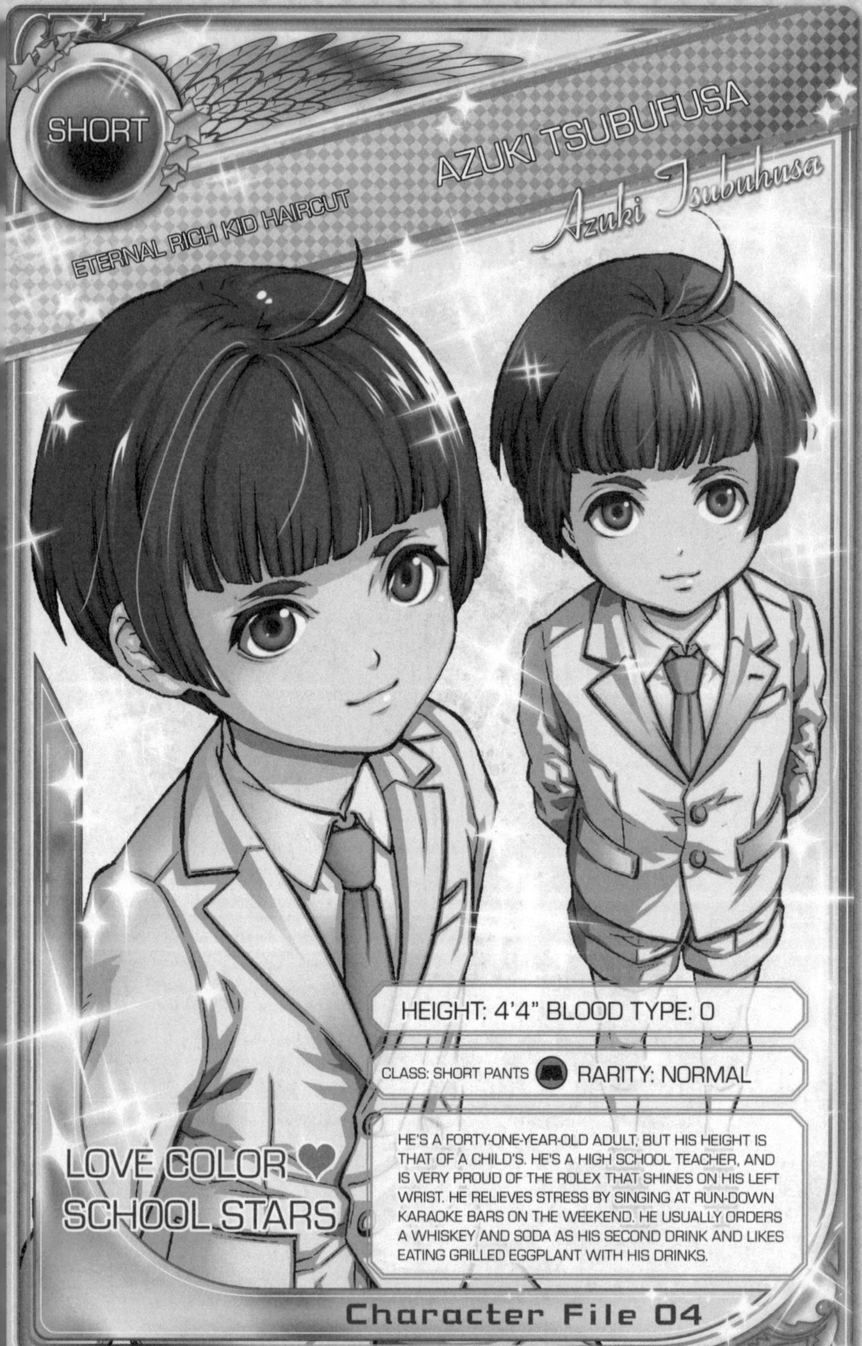
SHORT
AZUKI TSUBUFUSA
Azuki Tsubuhusa
ETERNAL RICH KID HAIRCUT
HEIGHT: 4'4" BLOOD TYPE: O
CLASS: SHORT PANTS
RARITY: NORMAL
LOVE COLOR ♥ SCHOOL STARS
HE'S A FORTY-ONE-YEAR-OLD ADULT, BUT HIS HEIGHT IS THAT OF A CHILD'S. HE'S A HIGH SCHOOL TEACHER, AND IS VERY PROUD OF THE ROLEX THAT SHINES ON HIS LEFT WRIST. HE RELIEVES STRESS BY SINGING AT RUN-DOWN KARAOKE BARS ON THE WEEKEND. HE USUALLY ORDERS A WHISKEY AND SODA AS HIS SECOND DRINK AND LIKES EATING GRILLED EGGPLANT WITH HIS DRINKS.
Character File 04

Stage 6 Fortress's Feelings

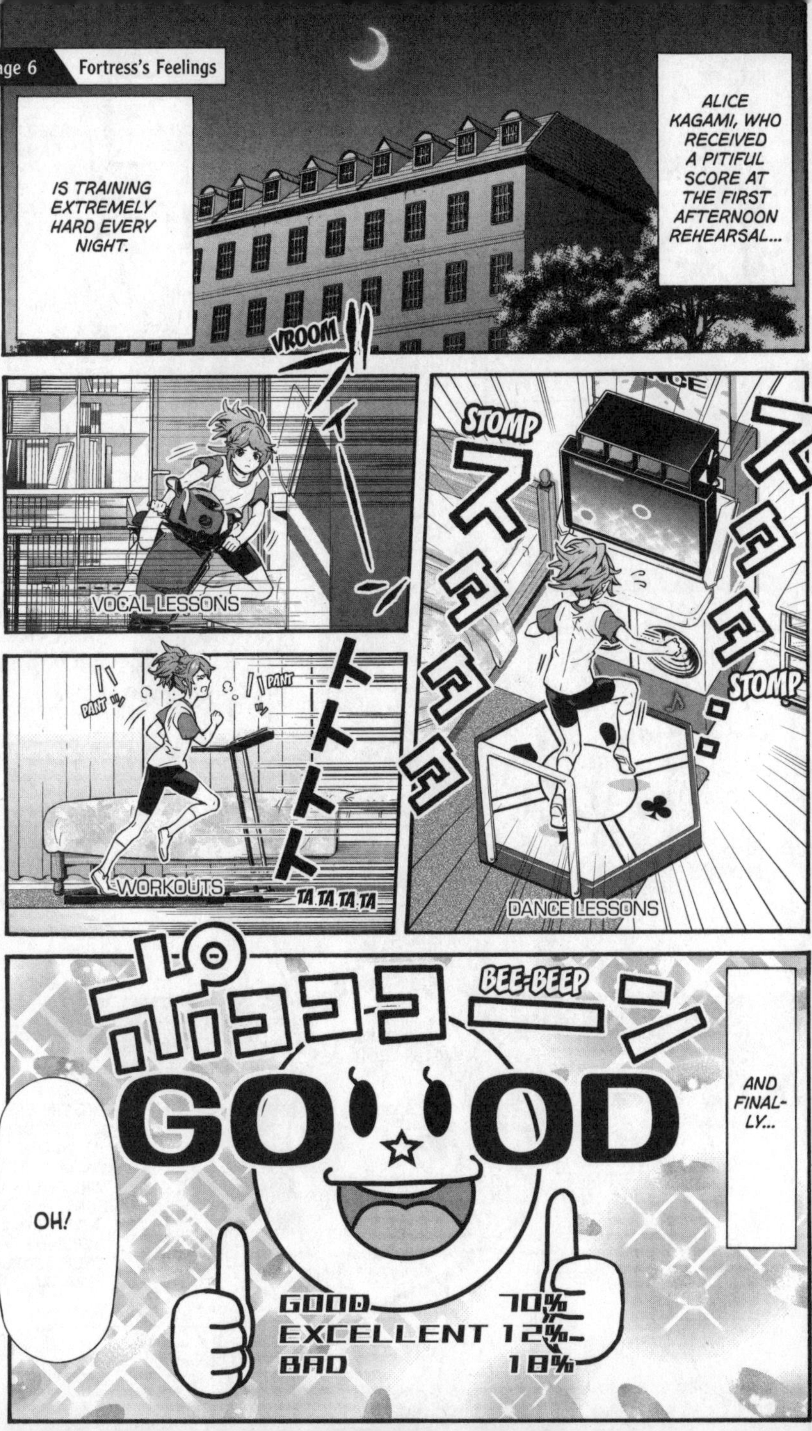

ALICE KAGAMI, WHO RECEIVED A PITIFUL SCORE AT THE FIRST AFTERNOON REHEARSAL...
IS TRAINING EXTREMELY HARD EVERY NIGHT.
VROOM
STOMP
STOMP
DANCE LESSONS
VOCAL LESSONS
PANT
PANT
TA TA TA TA
WORKOUTS
AND FINALLY...
BEE-BEEP
GOOD
GOOD 70%
EXCELLENT 12%
BAD 18%
OH!

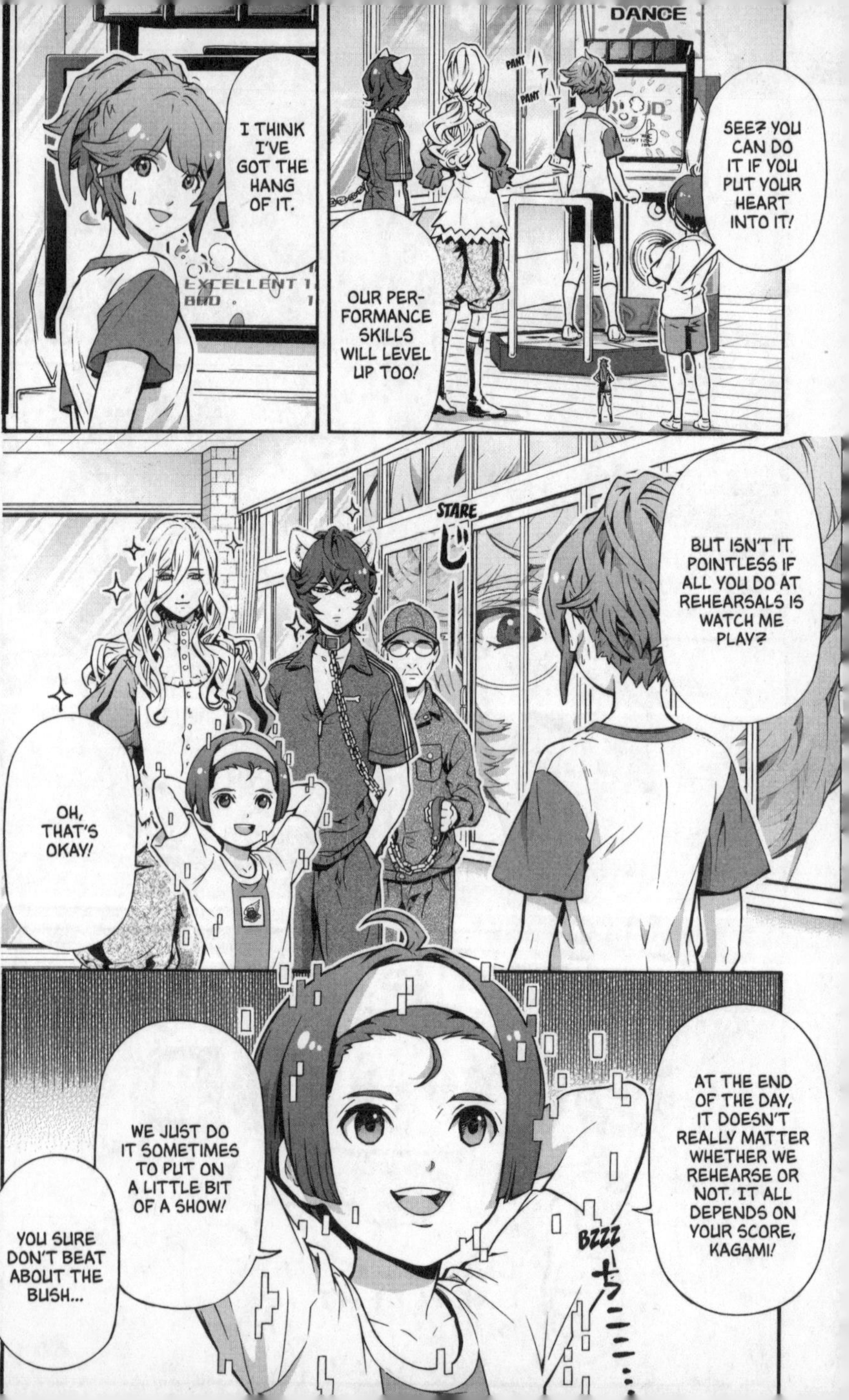
DANCE
PANT
PANT
SEE? YOU CAN DO IT IF YOU PUT YOUR HEART INTO IT!
OUR PER-FORMANCE SKILLS WILL LEVEL UP TOO!
I THINK I'VE GOT THE HANG OF IT.
EXCELLENT 1
BAD 1
BUT ISN'T IT POINTLESS IF ALL YOU DO AT REHEARSALS IS WATCH ME PLAY?
STARE
OH, THAT'S OKAY!
AT THE END OF THE DAY, IT DOESN'T REALLY MATTER WHETHER WE REHEARSE OR NOT. IT ALL DEPENDS ON YOUR SCORE, KAGAMI!
BZZZ
WE JUST DO IT SOMETIMES TO PUT ON A LITTLE BIT OF A SHOW!
YOU SURE DON'T BEAT ABOUT THE BUSH...

Stage 6

Fortress's Feelings

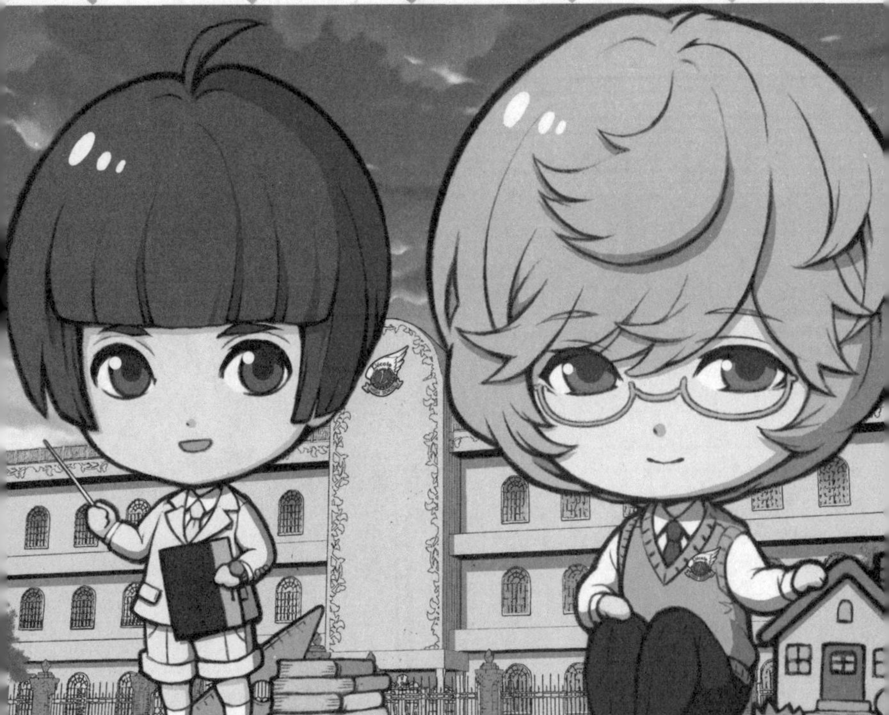

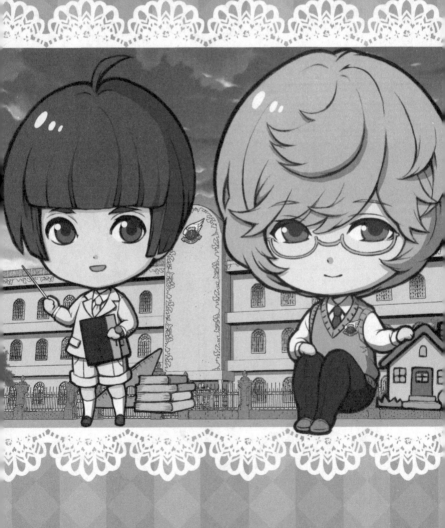

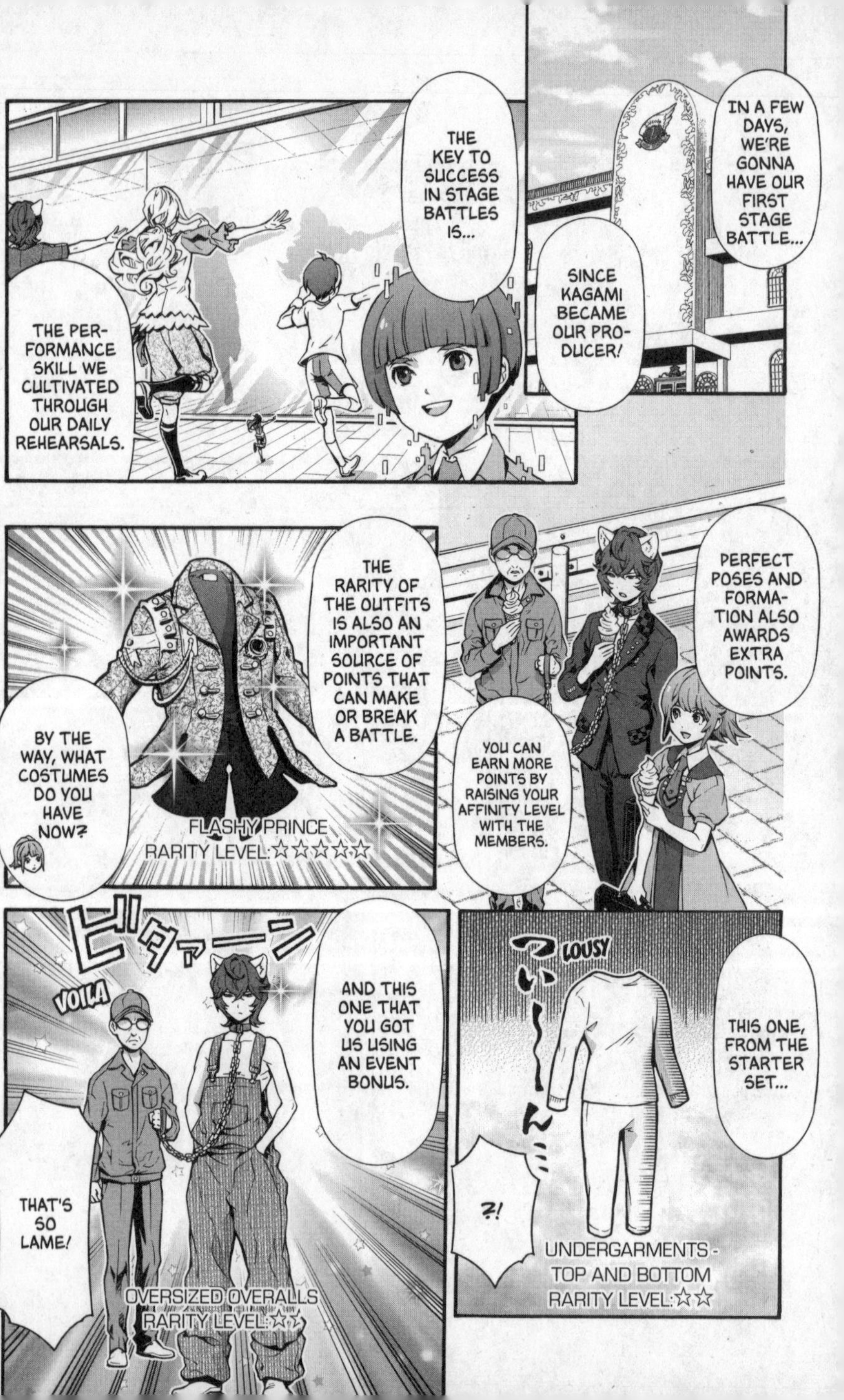

IN A FEW DAYS, WE'RE GONNA HAVE OUR FIRST STAGE BATTLE...
SINCE KAGAMI BECAME OUR PRODUCER!
THE KEY TO SUCCESS IN STAGE BATTLES IS...
THE PERFORMANCE SKILL WE CULTIVATED THROUGH OUR DAILY REHEARSALS.
PERFECT POSES AND FORMATION ALSO AWARDS EXTRA POINTS.
YOU CAN EARN MORE POINTS BY RAISING YOUR AFFINITY LEVEL WITH THE MEMBERS.
THE RARITY OF THE OUTFITS IS ALSO AN IMPORTANT SOURCE OF POINTS THAT CAN MAKE OR BREAK A BATTLE.
FLASHY PRINCE
RARITY LEVEL:☆☆☆☆☆
BY THE WAY, WHAT COSTUMES DO YOU HAVE NOW?
THIS ONE, FROM THE STARTER SET...
LOUSY
?!
UNDERGARMENTS - TOP AND BOTTOM
RARITY LEVEL:☆☆
VOILA
AND THIS ONE THAT YOU GOT US USING AN EVENT BONUS.
OVERSIZED OVERALLS
RARITY LEVEL:☆☆
THAT'S SO LAME!

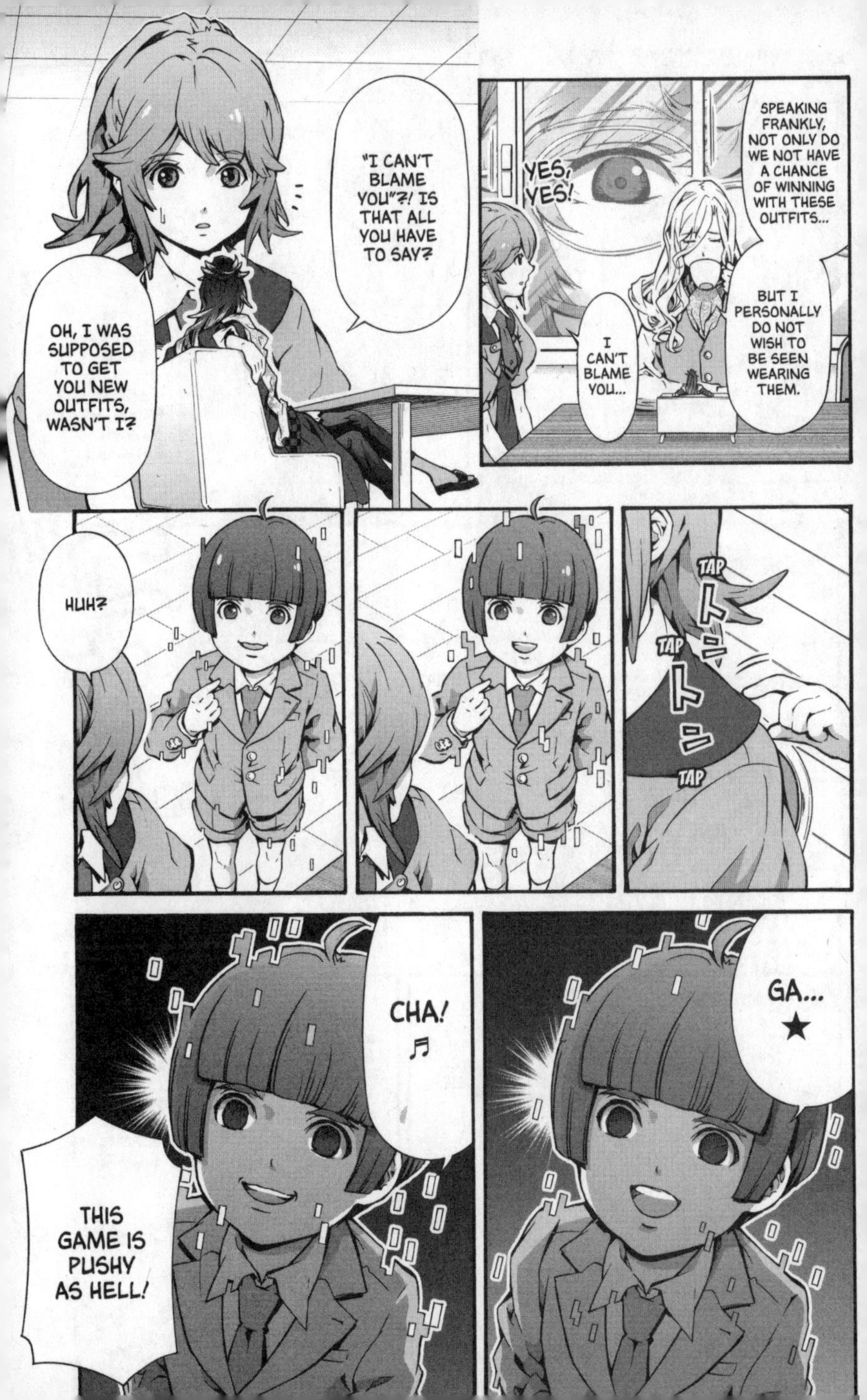
SPEAKING FRANKLY, NOT ONLY DO WE NOT HAVE A CHANCE OF WINNING WITH THESE OUTFITS...
BUT I PERSONALLY DO NOT WISH TO BE SEEN WEARING THEM.
YES, YES!
I CAN'T BLAME YOU...
"I CAN'T BLAME YOU"?! IS THAT ALL YOU HAVE TO SAY?
OH, I WAS SUPPOSED TO GET YOU NEW OUTFITS, WASN'T I?
TAP
TAP
TAP
HUH?
GA... ★
CHA! ♬
THIS GAME IS PUSHY AS HELL!

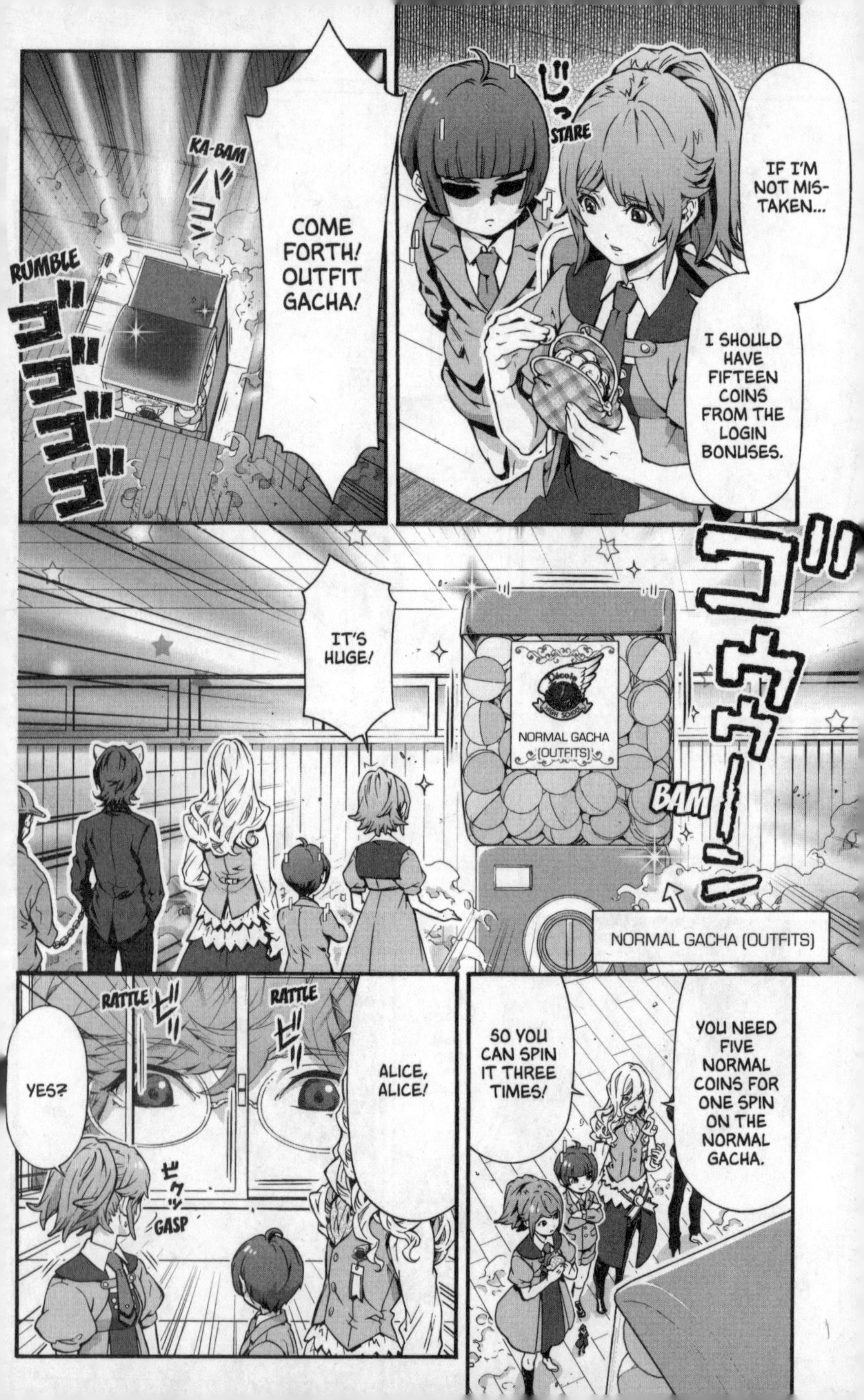
STARE
IF I'M NOT MIS-TAKEN...
I SHOULD HAVE FIFTEEN COINS FROM THE LOGIN BONUSES.
COME FORTH! OUTFIT GACHA!
KA-BAM
RUMBLE
BAM
NORMAL GACHA (OUTFITS)
IT'S HUGE!
NORMAL GACHA (OUTFITS)
YOU NEED FIVE NORMAL COINS FOR ONE SPIN ON THE NORMAL GACHA.
SO YOU CAN SPIN IT THREE TIMES!
RATTLE
RATTLE
ALICE, ALICE!
YES?
GASP

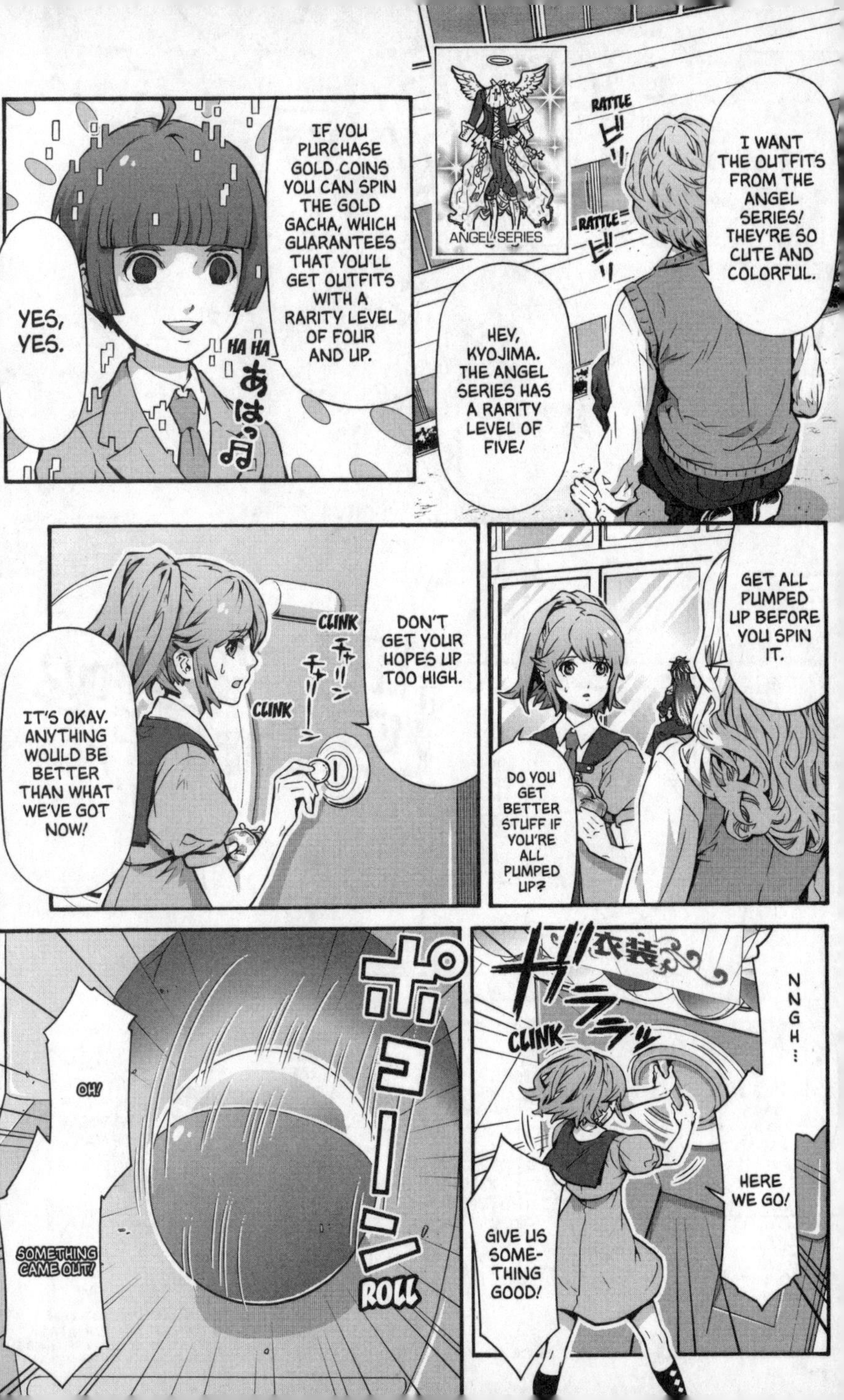
I WANT THE OUTFITS FROM THE ANGEL SERIES! THEY'RE SO CUTE AND COLORFUL.
RATTLE
ビッ
RATTLE
ビッ
ANGEL SERIES
HEY, KYOJIMA. THE ANGEL SERIES HAS A RARITY LEVEL OF FIVE!
IF YOU PURCHASE GOLD COINS YOU CAN SPIN THE GOLD GACHA, WHICH GUARANTEES THAT YOU'LL GET OUTFITS WITH A RARITY LEVEL OF FOUR AND UP.
HA HA
あはっ♫
YES, YES.
GET ALL PUMPED UP BEFORE YOU SPIN IT.
DO YOU GET BETTER STUFF IF YOU'RE ALL PUMPED UP?
DON'T GET YOUR HOPES UP TOO HIGH.
CLINK
チャリン
CLINK
チャリーン
IT'S OKAY. ANYTHING WOULD BE BETTER THAN WHAT WE'VE GOT NOW!
NNGH...
衣装
ガラララッ
CLINK
HERE WE GO!
GIVE US SOMETHING GOOD!
ポコーン
ROLL
OH!
SOMETHING CAME OUT!

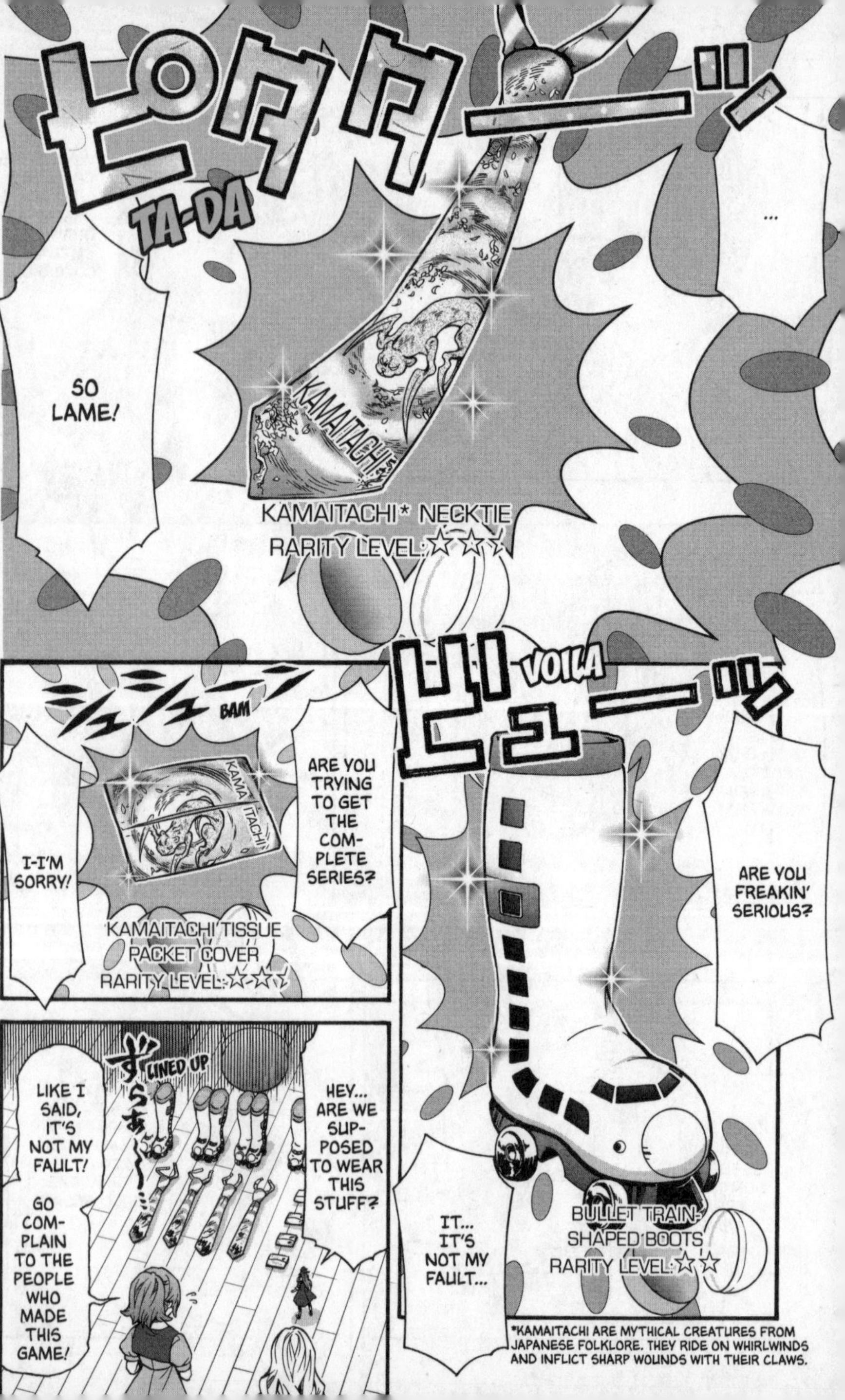
...
TA-DA
KAMAITACHI
KAMAITACHI* NECKTIE RARITY LEVEL:☆☆☆
SO LAME!
VOILA
ARE YOU FREAKIN' SERIOUS?
BULLET TRAIN-SHAPED BOOTS RARITY LEVEL:☆☆
IT... IT'S NOT MY FAULT...
BAM
KAMA ITACHI
ARE YOU TRYING TO GET THE COMPLETE SERIES?
KAMAITACHI TISSUE PACKET COVER RARITY LEVEL:☆☆☆
I-I'M SORRY!
LINED UP
HEY... ARE WE SUPPOSED TO WEAR THIS STUFF?
LIKE I SAID, IT'S NOT MY FAULT!
GO COMPLAIN TO THE PEOPLE WHO MADE THIS GAME!

*KAMAITACHI ARE MYTHICAL CREATURES FROM JAPANESE FOLKLORE. THEY RIDE ON WHIRLWINDS AND INFLICT SHARP WOUNDS WITH THEIR CLAWS.

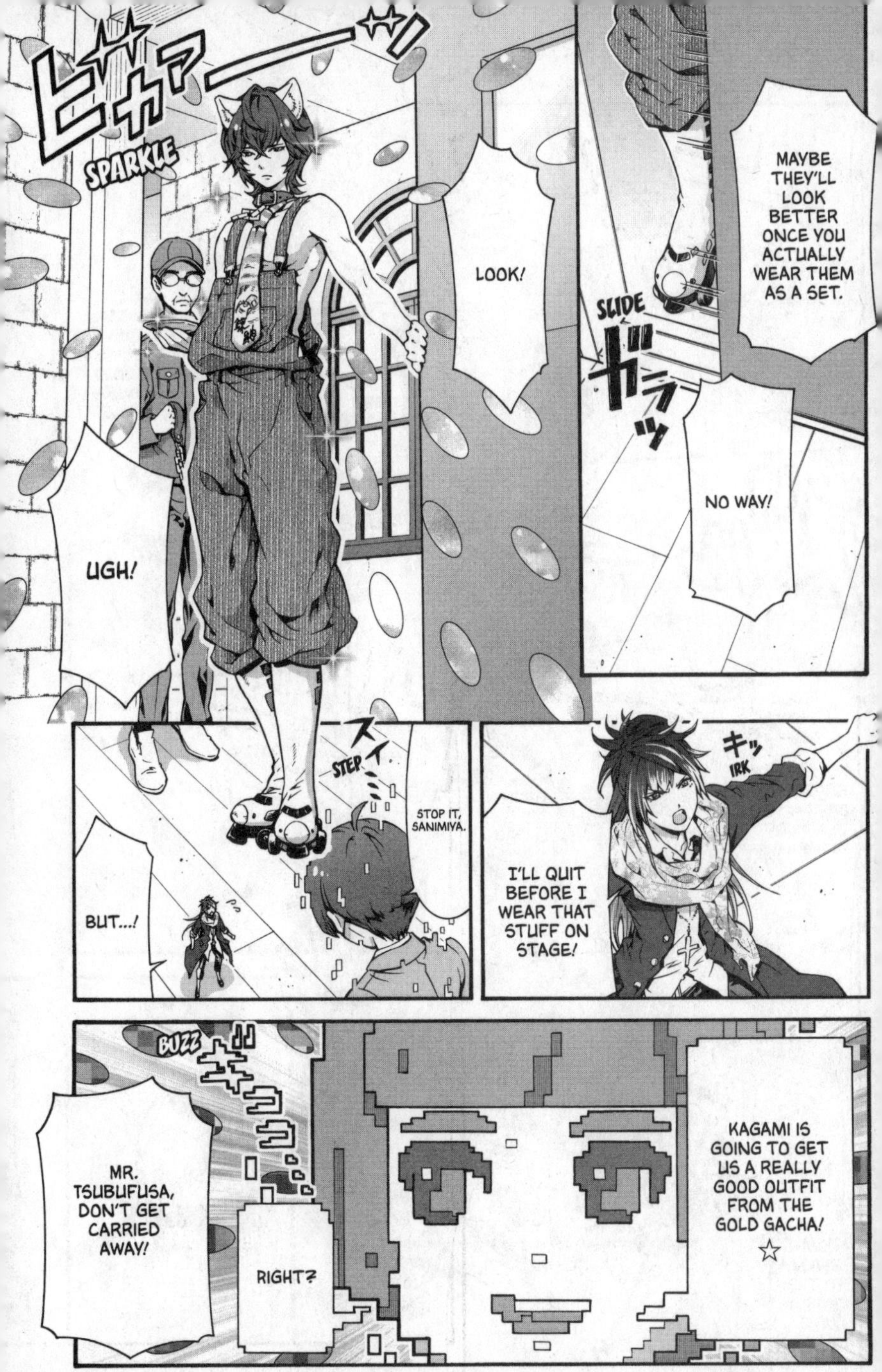
MAYBE THEY'LL LOOK BETTER ONCE YOU ACTUALLY WEAR THEM AS A SET.
SLIDE
NO WAY!
SPARKLE
LOOK!
UGH!
IRK
I'LL QUIT BEFORE I WEAR THAT STUFF ON STAGE!
STEP
STOP IT, SANIMIYA.
BUT...!
KAGAMI IS GOING TO GET US A REALLY GOOD OUTFIT FROM THE GOLD GACHA! ☆
RIGHT?
BUZZ
MR. TSUBUFUSA, DON'T GET CARRIED AWAY!

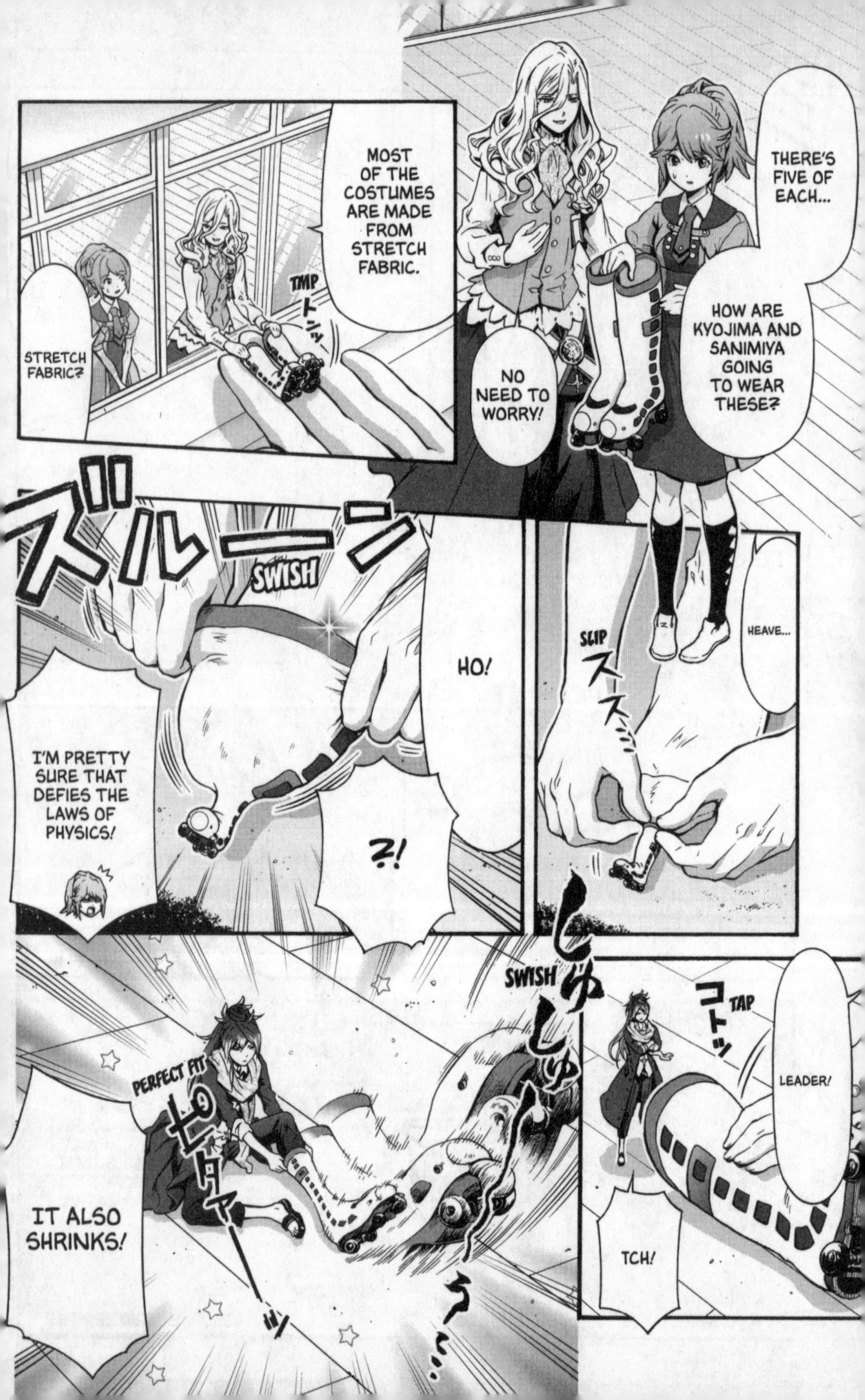
THERE'S FIVE OF EACH...
HOW ARE KYOJIMA AND SANIMIYA GOING TO WEAR THESE?
NO NEED TO WORRY!
MOST OF THE COSTUMES ARE MADE FROM STRETCH FABRIC.
TMP
STRETCH FABRIC?
HEAVE...
SLIP
HO!
?!
SWISH
I'M PRETTY SURE THAT DEFIES THE LAWS OF PHYSICS!
LEADER!
TAP
TCH!
SWISH
PERFECT FIT
IT ALSO SHRINKS!

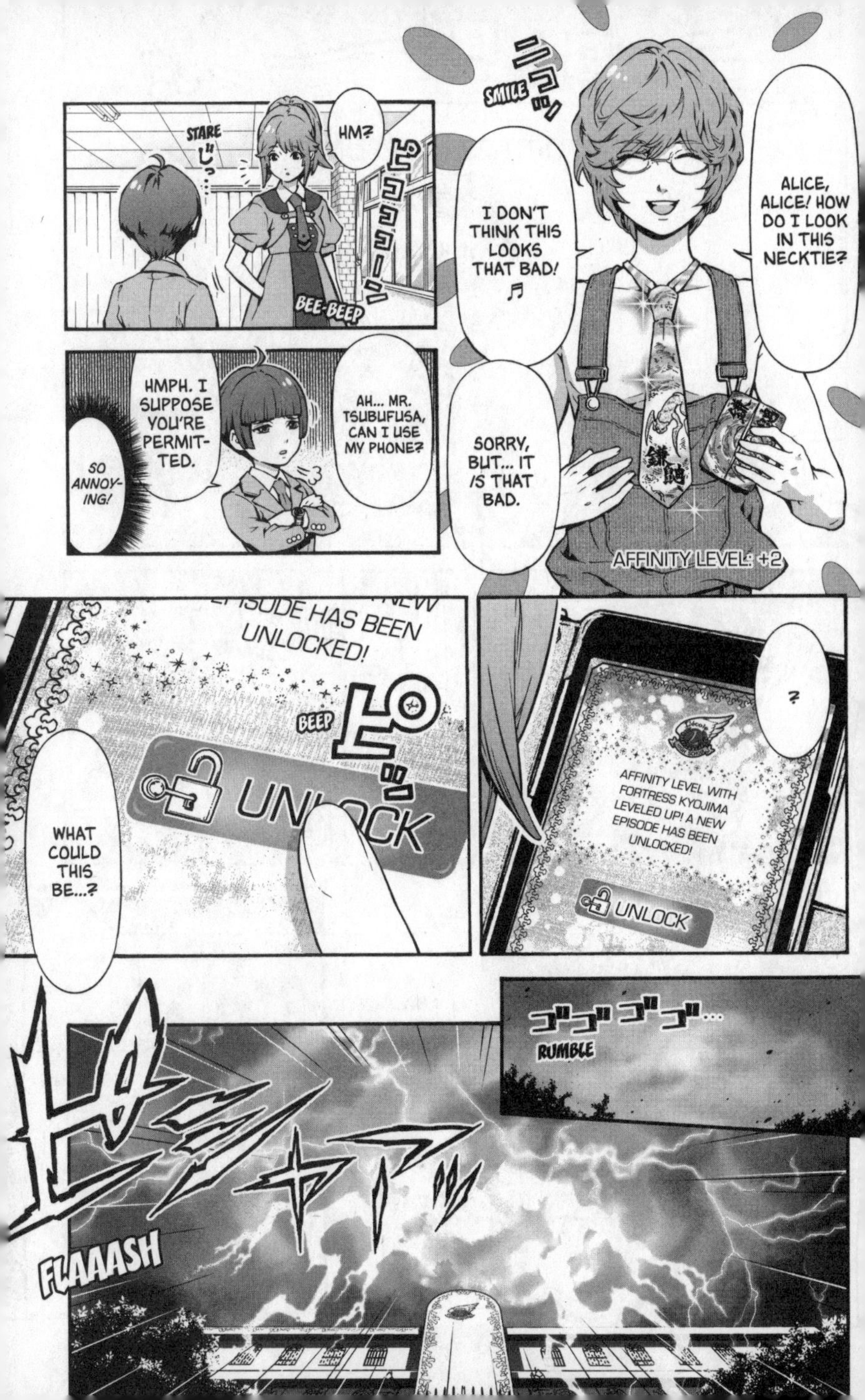
SMILE
ALICE, ALICE! HOW DO I LOOK IN THIS NECKTIE?
I DON'T THINK THIS LOOKS THAT BAD! ♫
SORRY, BUT... IT IS THAT BAD.
AFFINITY LEVEL: +2
BEE-BEEP
HM?
STARE
AH... MR. TSUBUFUSA, CAN I USE MY PHONE?
HMPH. I SUPPOSE YOU'RE PERMIT-TED.
SO ANNOY-ING!
?
AFFINITY LEVEL WITH FORTRESS KYOJIMA LEVELED UP! A NEW EPISODE HAS BEEN UNLOCKED!
UNLOCK
EPISODE HAS BEEN UNLOCKED!
BEEP
UNLOCK
WHAT COULD THIS BE...?
RUMBLE
FLAAASH

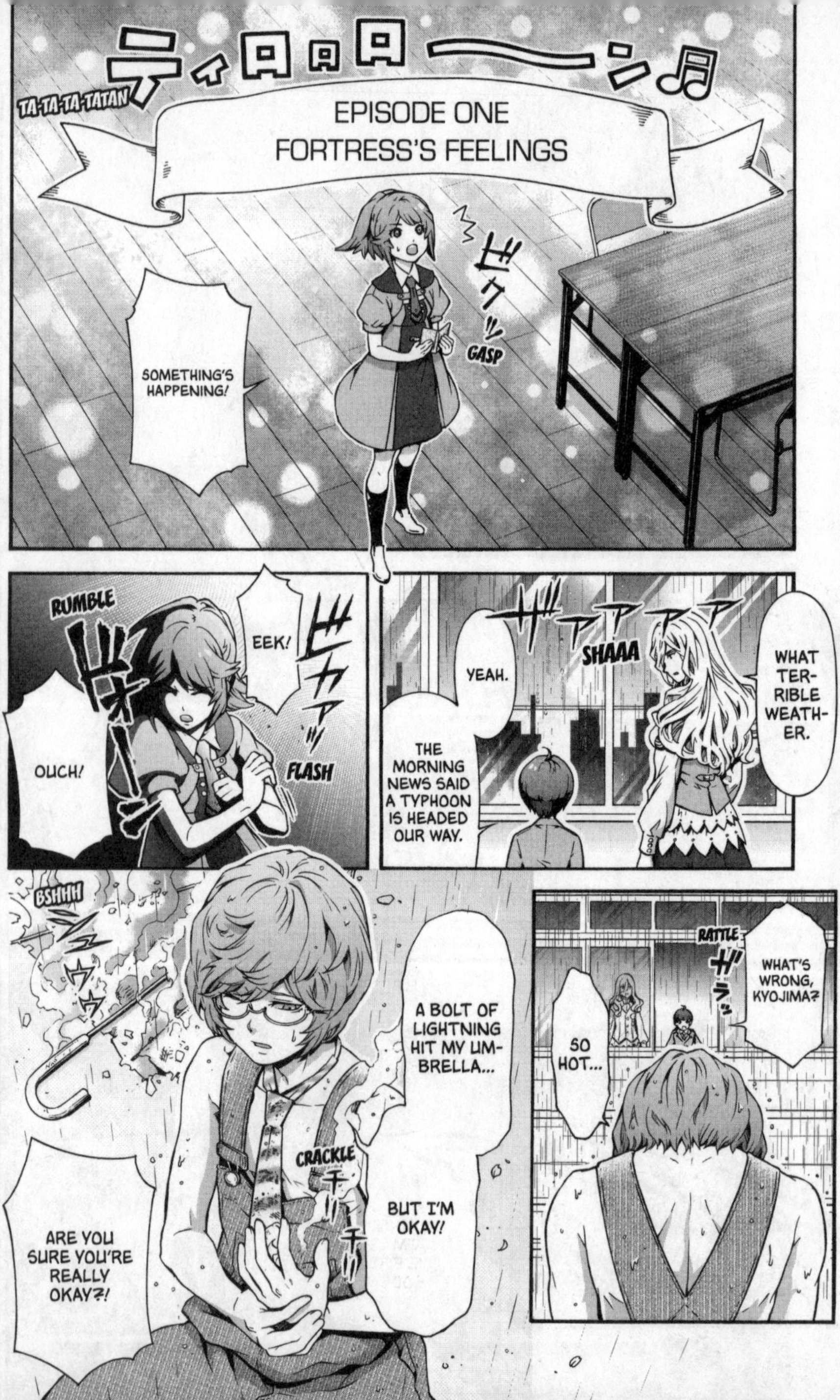
TA-TA-TA-TATAN
EPISODE ONE
FORTRESS'S FEELINGS
GASP
SOMETHING'S HAPPENING!
WHAT TERRIBLE WEATHER.
SHAAA
YEAH.
THE MORNING NEWS SAID A TYPHOON IS HEADED OUR WAY.
EEK!
FLASH
RUMBLE
OUCH!
RATTLE
WHAT'S WRONG, KYOJIMA?
SO HOT...
A BOLT OF LIGHTNING HIT MY UMBRELLA...
BUT I'M OKAY!
CRACKLE
BSHHH
ARE YOU SURE YOU'RE REALLY OKAY?!

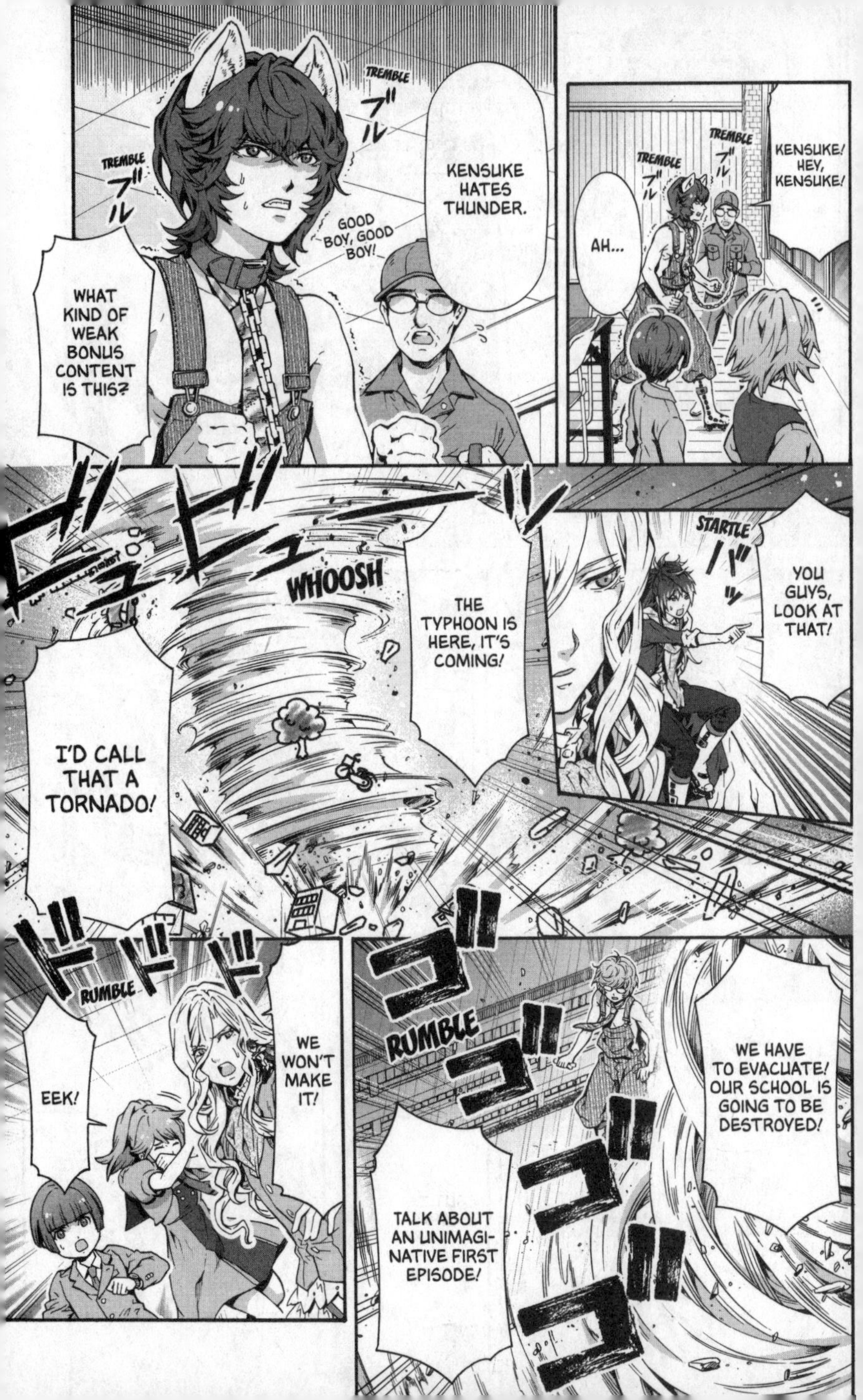
KENSUKE! HEY, KENSUKE!
TREMBLE
ブル
TREMBLE
ブル
AH...
KENSUKE HATES THUNDER.
TREMBLE
ブル
GOOD BOY, GOOD BOY!
TREMBLE
ブル
WHAT KIND OF WEAK BONUS CONTENT IS THIS?
STARTLE
バ
YOU GUYS, LOOK AT THAT!
WHOOSH
THE TYPHOON IS HERE, IT'S COMING!
I'D CALL THAT A TORNADO!
ゴゴゴゴ
RUMBLE
WE HAVE TO EVACUATE! OUR SCHOOL IS GOING TO BE DESTROYED!
TALK ABOUT AN UNIMAGINATIVE FIRST EPISODE!
ドドド
RUMBLE
WE WON'T MAKE IT!
EEK!

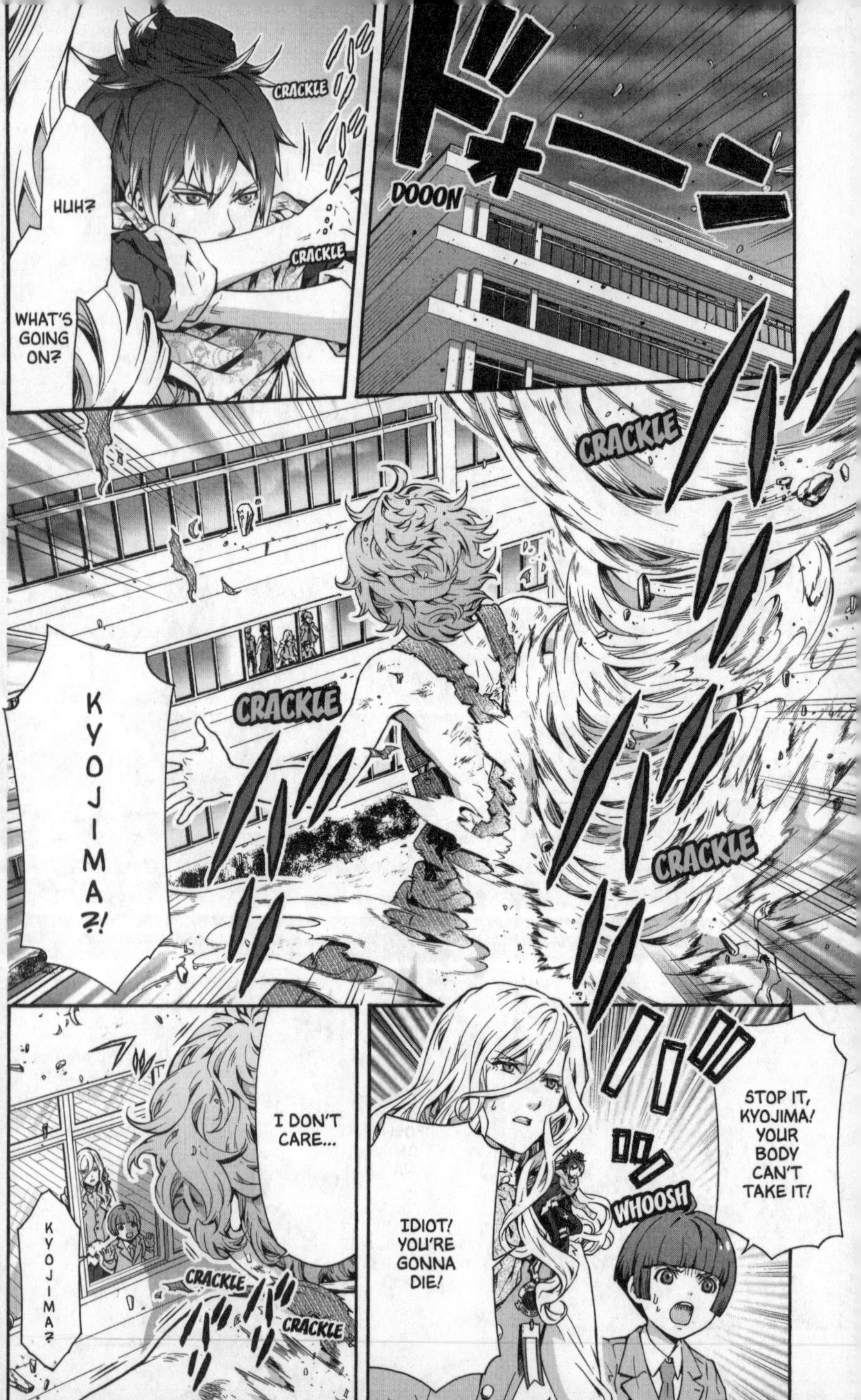
ドォーン
DOOON
CRACKLE
HUH?
CRACKLE
WHAT'S GOING ON?
CRACKLE
KYOJIMA?!
CRACKLE
CRACKLE
STOP IT, KYOJIMA! YOUR BODY CAN'T TAKE IT!
WHOOSH
IDIOT! YOU'RE GONNA DIE!
I DON'T CARE...
KYOJIMA?
CRACKLE
CRACKLE

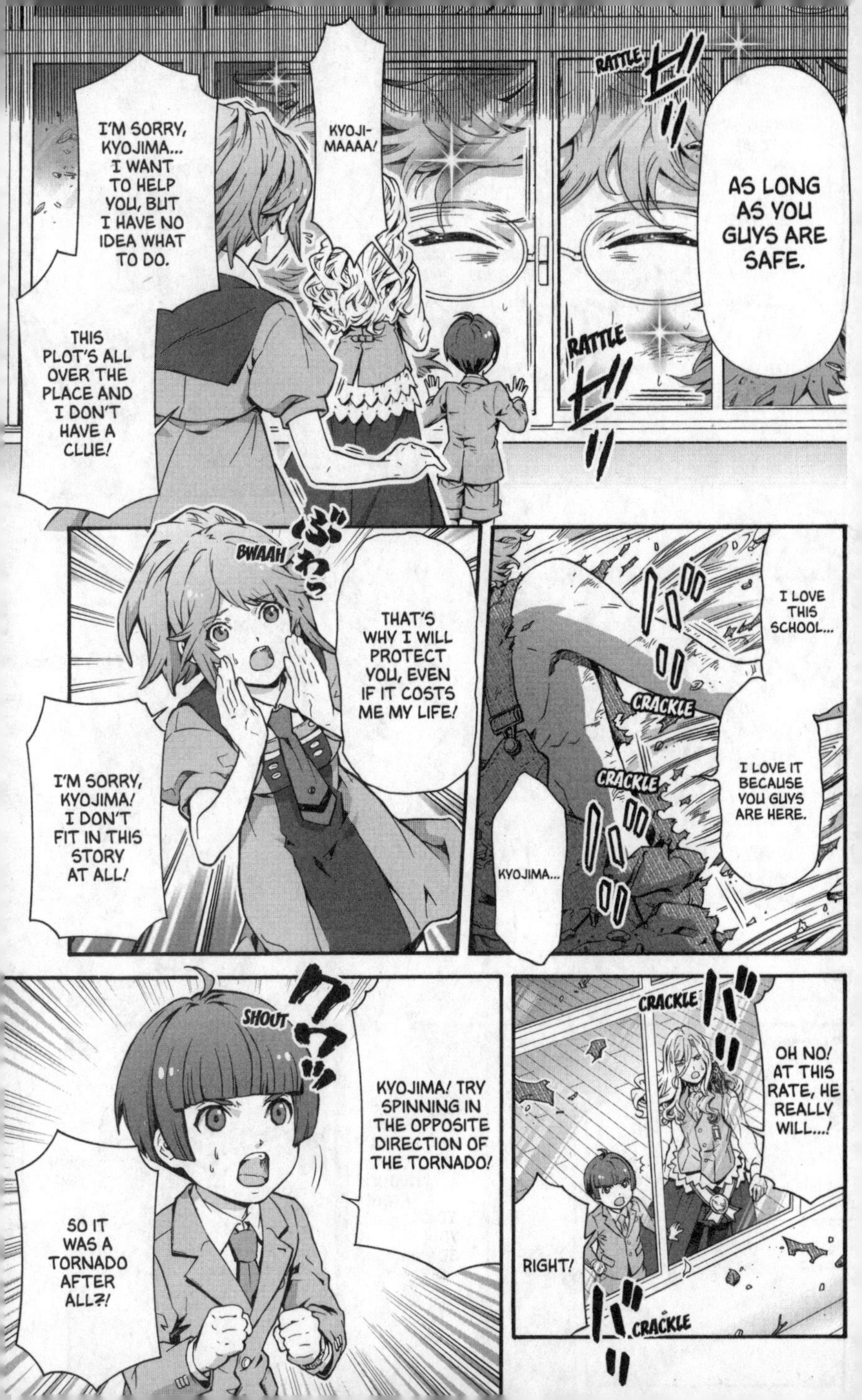
RATTLE
AS LONG AS YOU GUYS ARE SAFE.
RATTLE
KYOJI-MAAAA!
I'M SORRY, KYOJIMA... I WANT TO HELP YOU, BUT I HAVE NO IDEA WHAT TO DO.
THIS PLOT'S ALL OVER THE PLACE AND I DON'T HAVE A CLUE!
I LOVE THIS SCHOOL...
CRACKLE
CRACKLE
I LOVE IT BECAUSE YOU GUYS ARE HERE.
KYOJIMA...
BWAAH
THAT'S WHY I WILL PROTECT YOU, EVEN IF IT COSTS ME MY LIFE!
I'M SORRY, KYOJIMA! I DON'T FIT IN THIS STORY AT ALL!
CRACKLE
OH NO! AT THIS RATE, HE REALLY WILL...!
RIGHT!
CRACKLE
SHOUT
KYOJIMA! TRY SPINNING IN THE OPPOSITE DIRECTION OF THE TORNADO!
SO IT WAS A TORNADO AFTER ALL?!

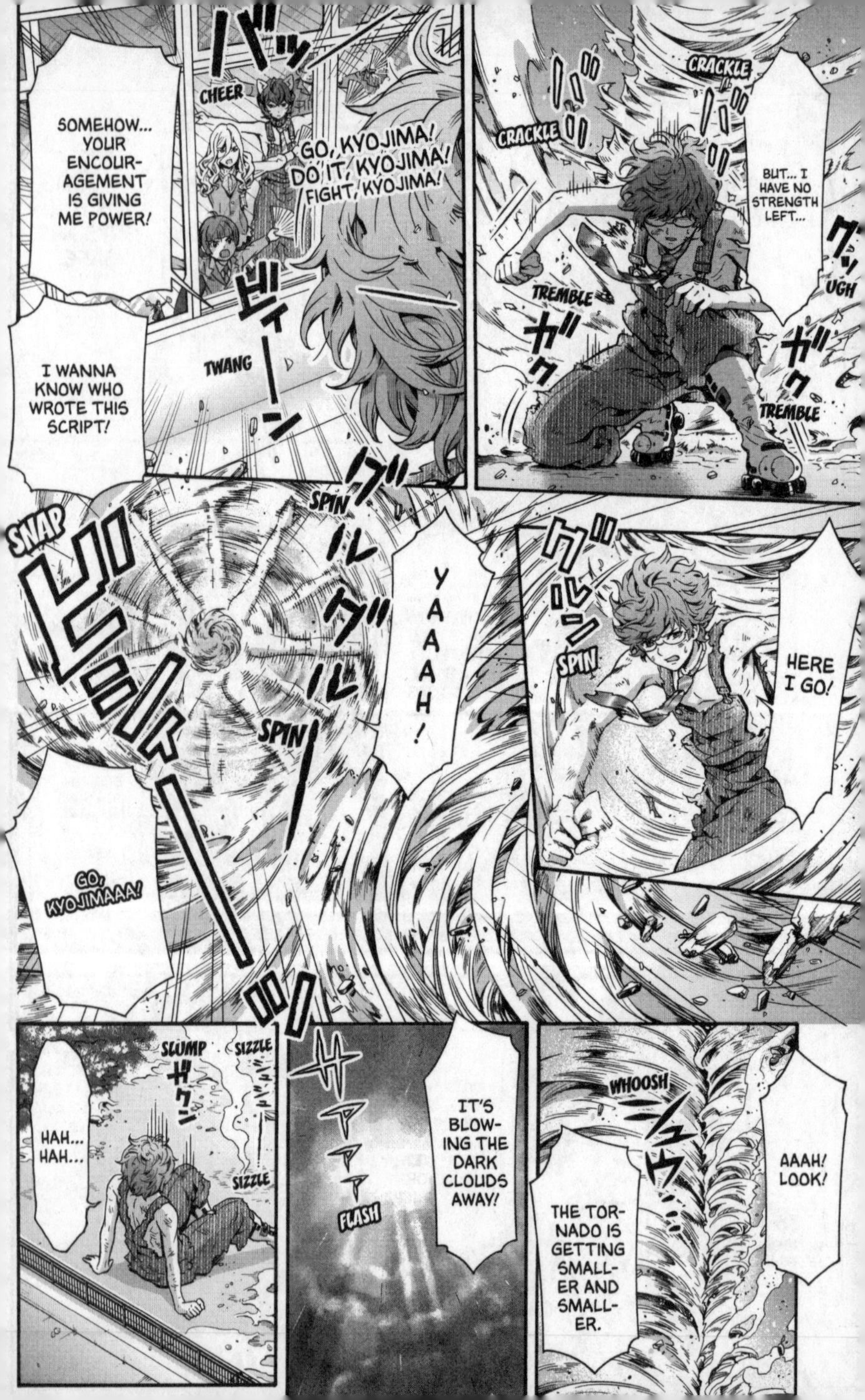
CRACKLE
CRACKLE
BUT... I HAVE NO STRENGTH LEFT...
UGH
TREMBLE
TREMBLE
CHEER
SOMEHOW... YOUR ENCOURAGEMENT IS GIVING ME POWER!
GO, KYOJIMA! DO IT, KYOJIMA! FIGHT, KYOJIMA!
I WANNA KNOW WHO WROTE THIS SCRIPT!
TWANG
SPIN
HERE I GO!
SPIN
YAAAAH!
SNAP
SPIN
GO, KYOJIMAAA!
AAAH! LOOK!
WHOOSH
THE TORNADO IS GETTING SMALLER AND SMALLER.
IT'S BLOWING THE DARK CLOUDS AWAY!
FLASH
SLUMP
SIZZLE
HAH... HAH...
SIZZLE

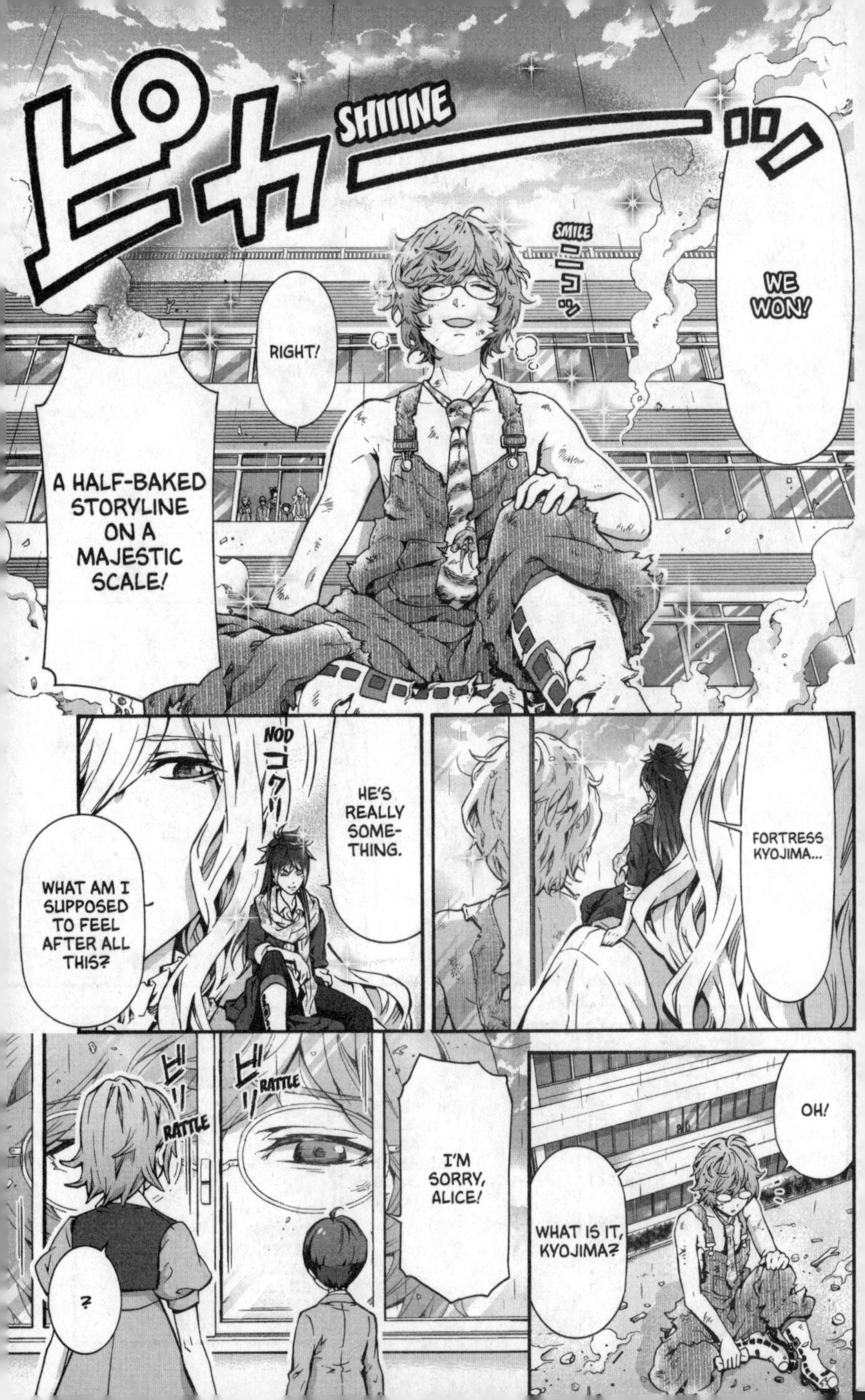
SHIIINE
WE WON!
SMILE
RIGHT!
A HALF-BAKED STORYLINE ON A MAJESTIC SCALE!
FORTRESS KYOJIMA...
NOD
HE'S REALLY SOMETHING.
WHAT AM I SUPPOSED TO FEEL AFTER ALL THIS?
OH!
WHAT IS IT, KYOJIMA?
RATTLE
I'M SORRY, ALICE!
RATTLE
?

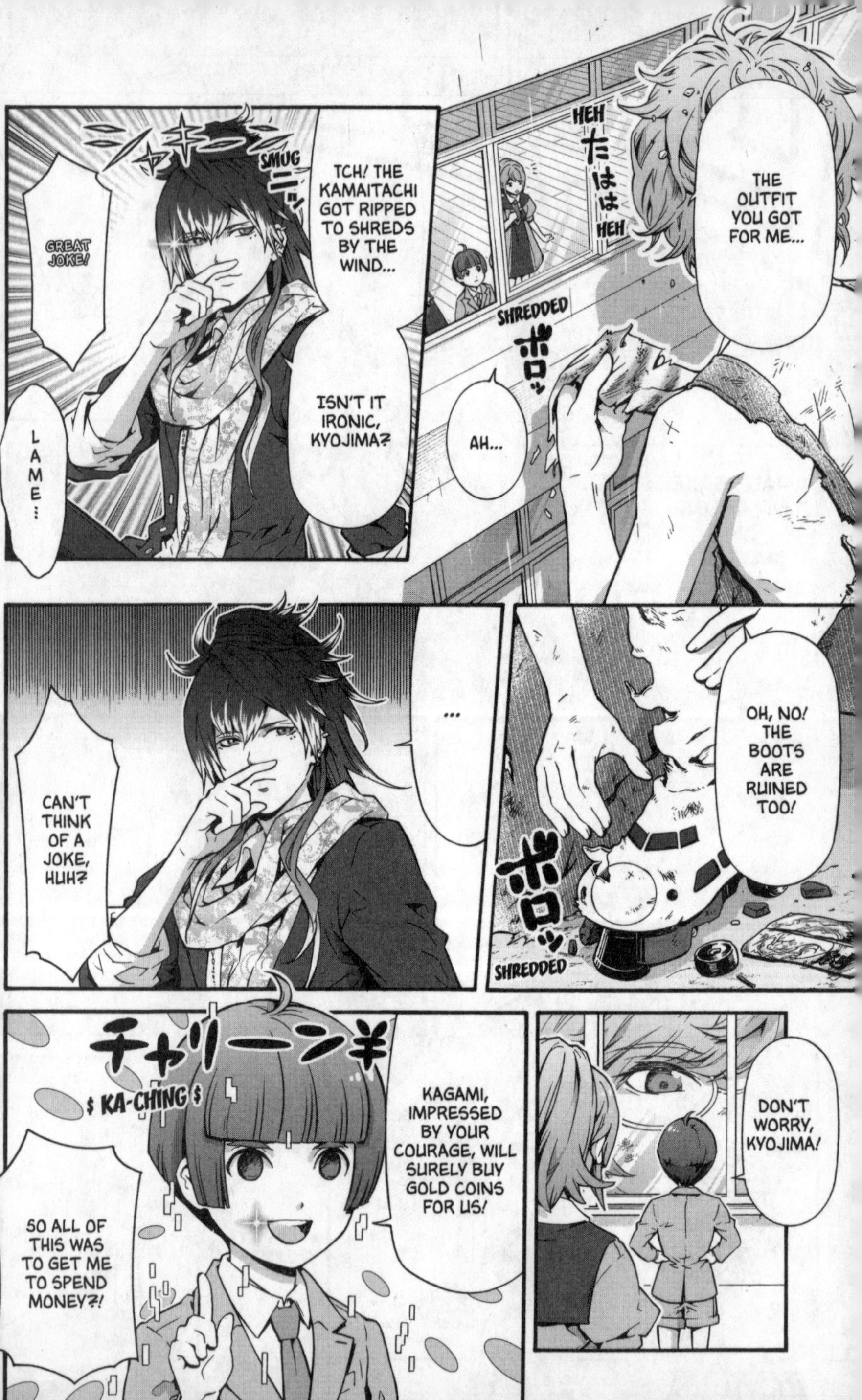
THE OUTFIT YOU GOT FOR ME...
HEH たはは HEH
SHREDDED ボロッ
AH...
TCH! THE KAMAITACHI GOT RIPPED TO SHREDS BY THE WIND...
SMUG ニヤッ
ISN'T IT IRONIC, KYOJIMA?
GREAT JOKE!
LAME...
OH, NO! THE BOOTS ARE RUINED TOO!
ボロッ SHREDDED
...
CAN'T THINK OF A JOKE, HUH?
DON'T WORRY, KYOJIMA!
チャリーン
$ KA-CHING $
KAGAMI, IMPRESSED BY YOUR COURAGE, WILL SURELY BUY GOLD COINS FOR US!
SO ALL OF THIS WAS TO GET ME TO SPEND MONEY?!

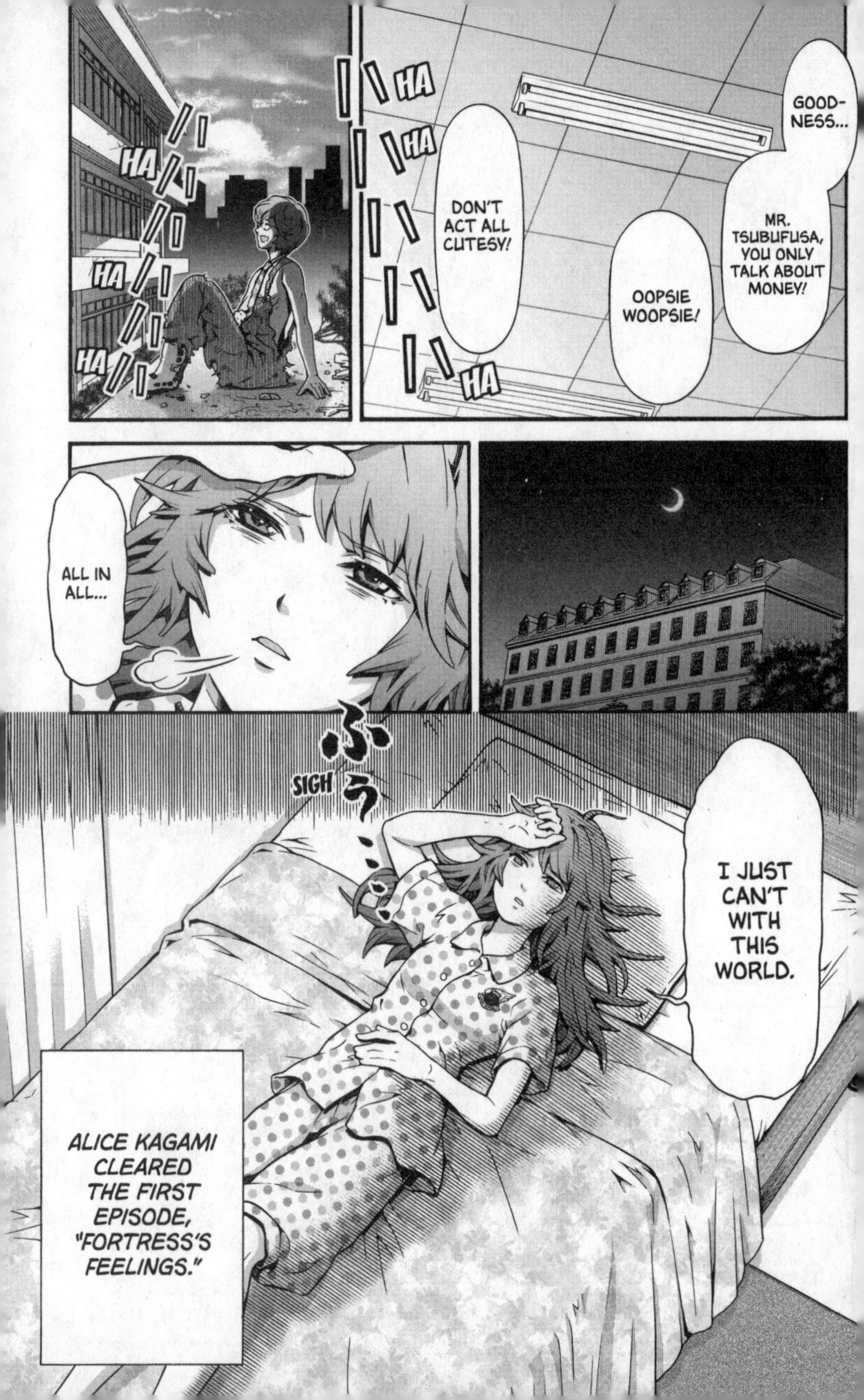
GOOD-NESS...
MR. TSUBUFUSA, YOU ONLY TALK ABOUT MONEY!
OOPSIE WOOPSIE!
DON'T ACT ALL CUTESY!
HA
HA
HA
HA
HA
HA
HA
ALL IN ALL...
I JUST CAN'T WITH THIS WORLD.
SIGH
ALICE KAGAMI CLEARED THE FIRST EPISODE, "FORTRESS'S FEELINGS."

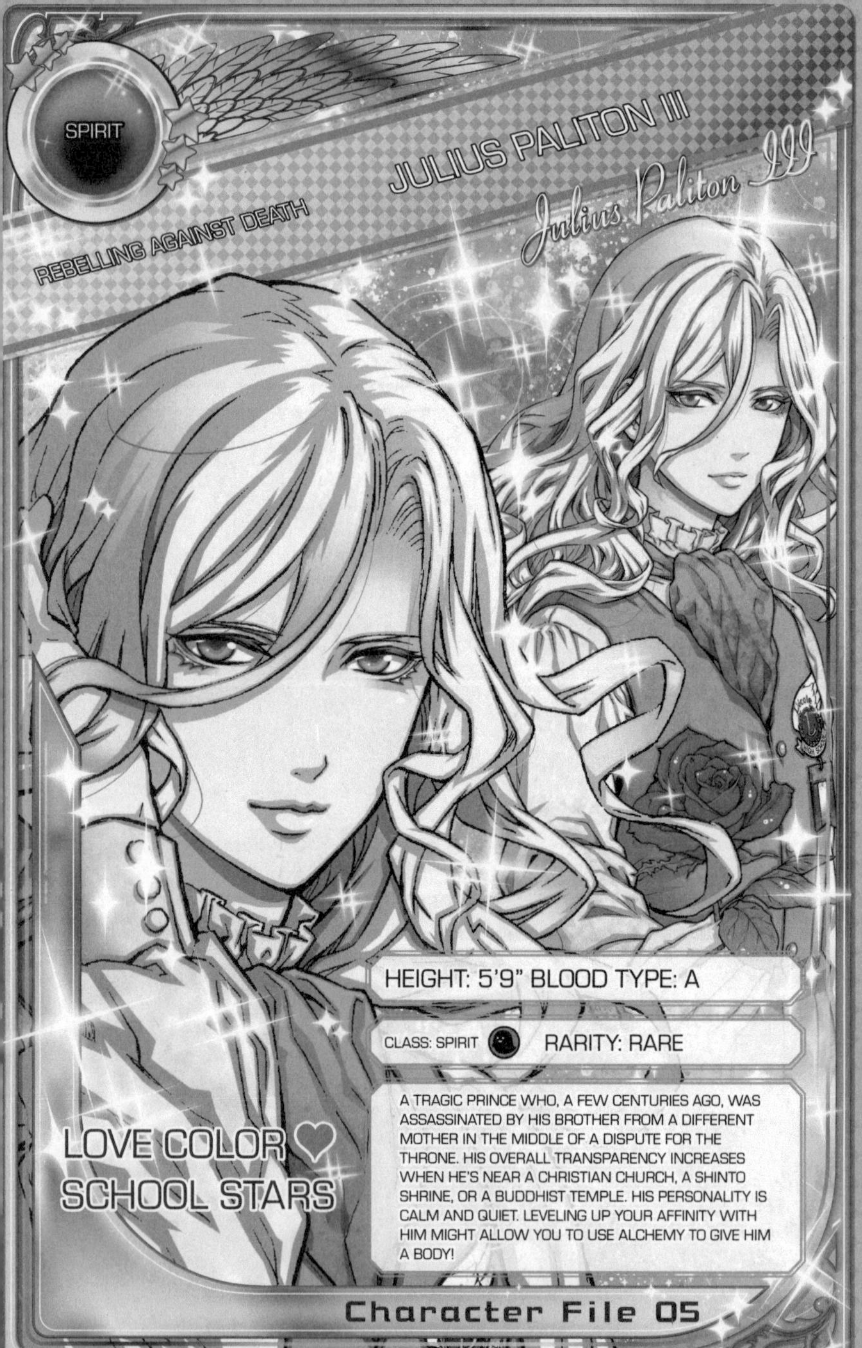
SPIRIT
JULIUS PALITON III
Julius Paliton III
REBELLING AGAINST DEATH
HEIGHT: 5'9" BLOOD TYPE: A
CLASS: SPIRIT
RARITY: RARE
A TRAGIC PRINCE WHO, A FEW CENTURIES AGO, WAS ASSASSINATED BY HIS BROTHER FROM A DIFFERENT MOTHER IN THE MIDDLE OF A DISPUTE FOR THE THRONE. HIS OVERALL TRANSPARENCY INCREASES WHEN HE'S NEAR A CHRISTIAN CHURCH, A SHINTO SHRINE, OR A BUDDHIST TEMPLE. HIS PERSONALITY IS CALM AND QUIET. LEVELING UP YOUR AFFINITY WITH HIM MIGHT ALLOW YOU TO USE ALCHEMY TO GIVE HIM A BODY!
LOVE COLOR ♡
SCHOOL STARS
Character File 05

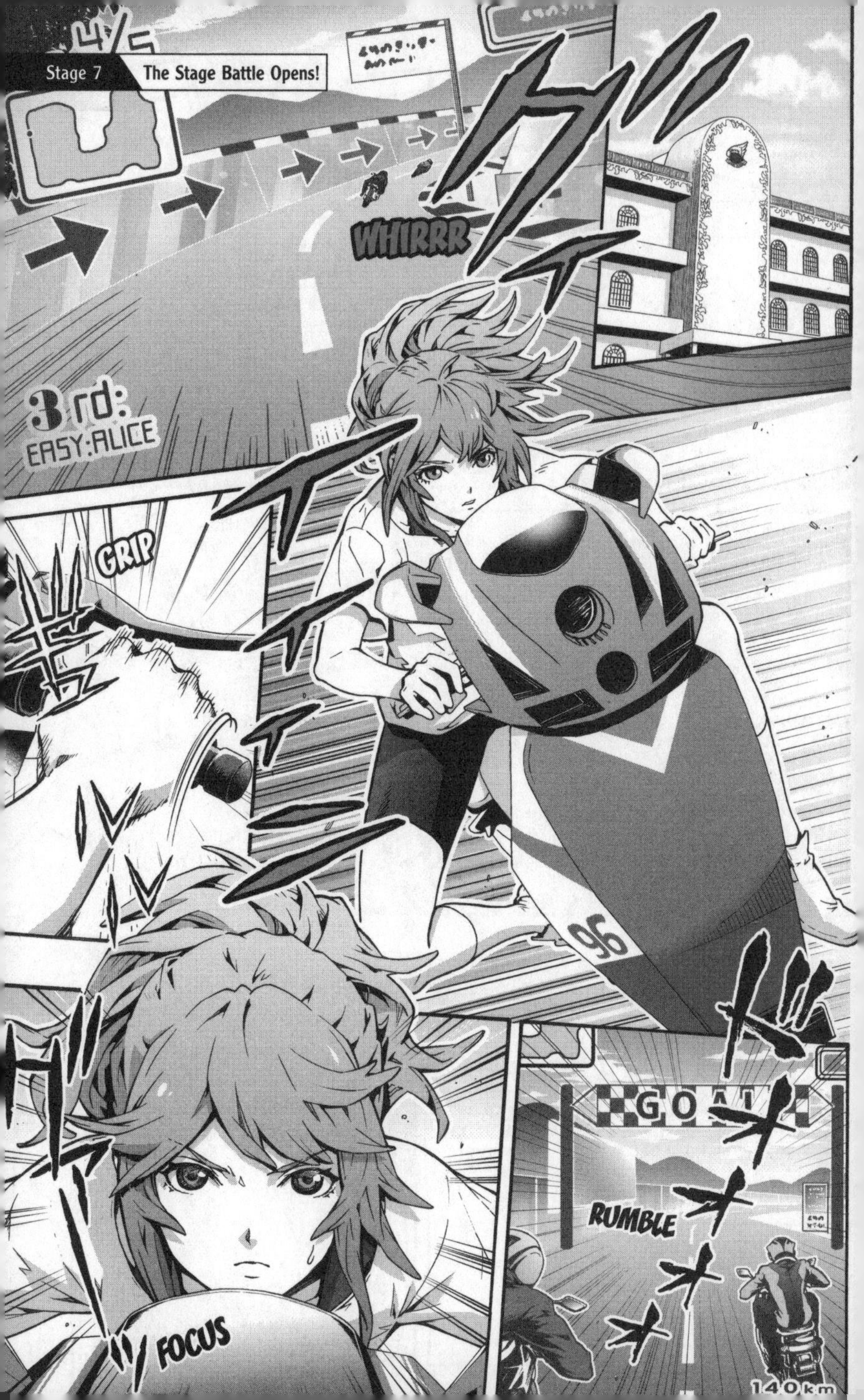
Stage 7
The Stage Battle Opens!
WHIRRR
3rd:
EASY:ALICE
GRIP
RUMBLE
140km
FOCUS

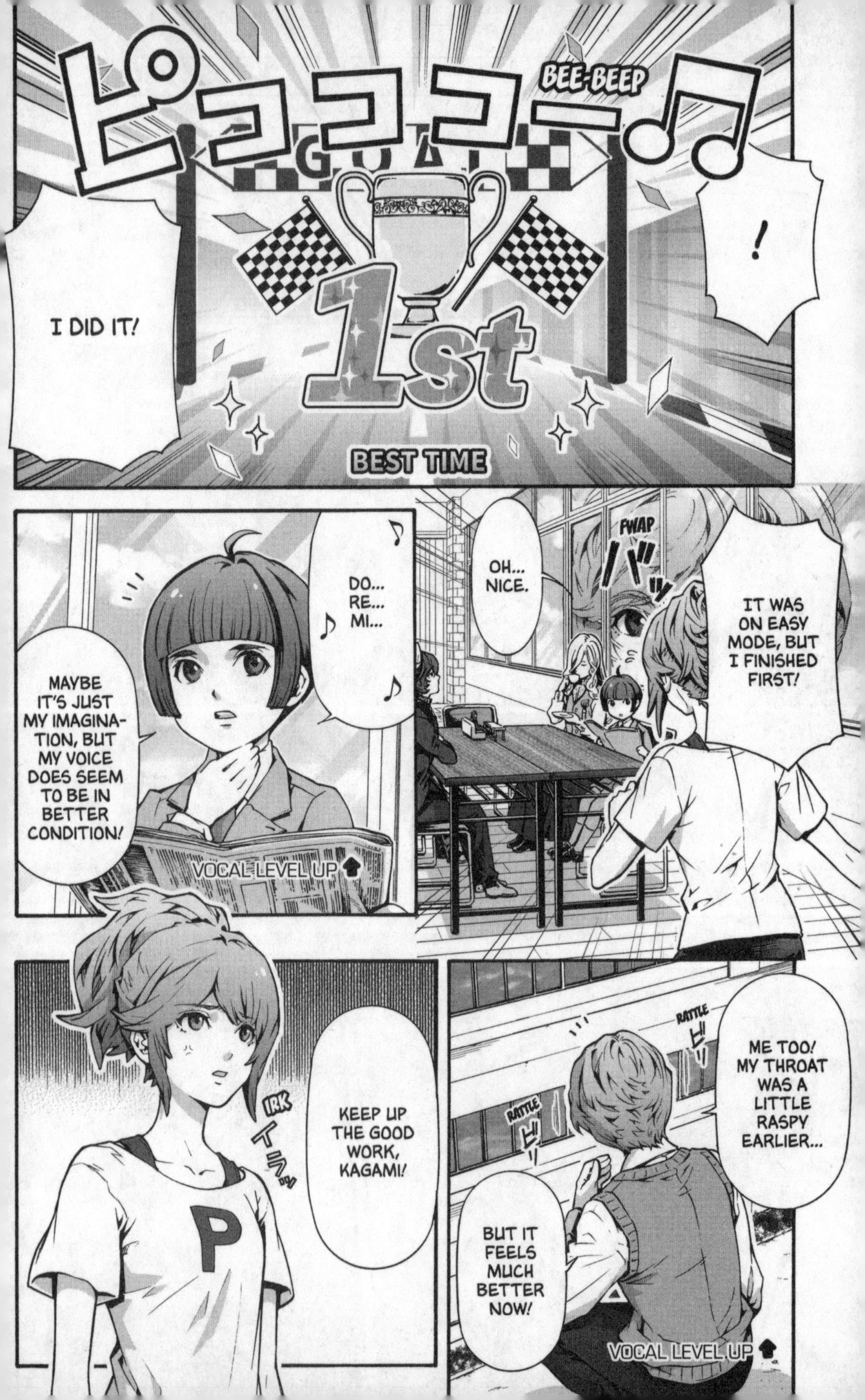
ピコココー♫
BEE-BEEP
!
I DID IT!
1st
BEST TIME
IT WAS ON EASY MODE, BUT I FINISHED FIRST!
PWAP
OH... NICE.
DO... RE... MI...
MAYBE IT'S JUST MY IMAGINATION, BUT MY VOICE DOES SEEM TO BE IN BETTER CONDITION!
VOCAL LEVEL UP
RATTLE
ME TOO! MY THROAT WAS A LITTLE RASPY EARLIER...
RATTLE
BUT IT FEELS MUCH BETTER NOW!
VOCAL LEVEL UP
KEEP UP THE GOOD WORK, KAGAMI!
IRK

Stage 7:

The Stage Battle Opens!

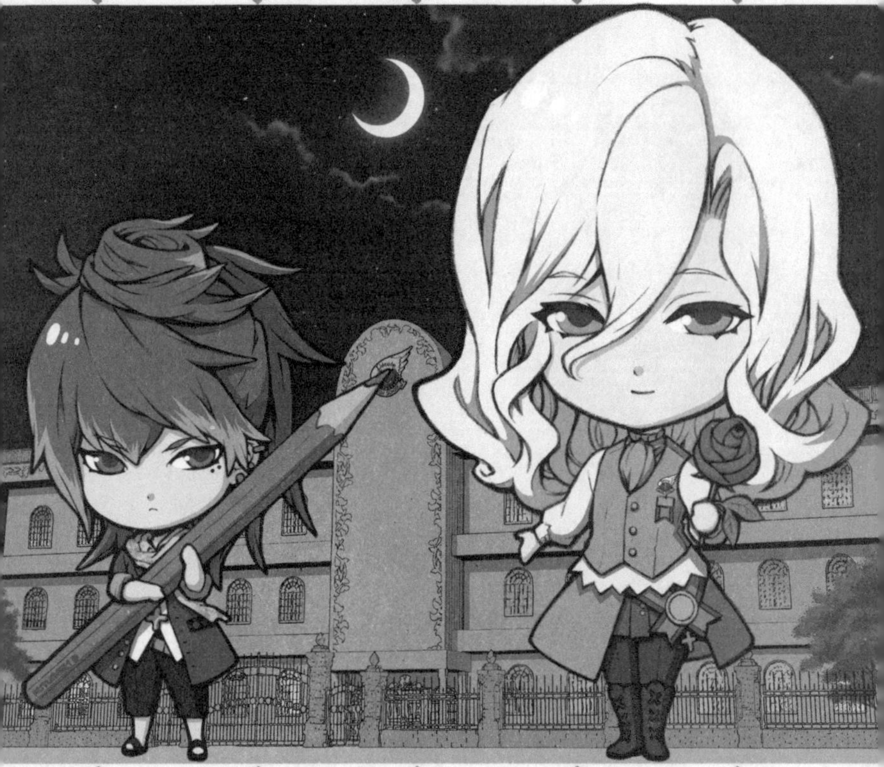

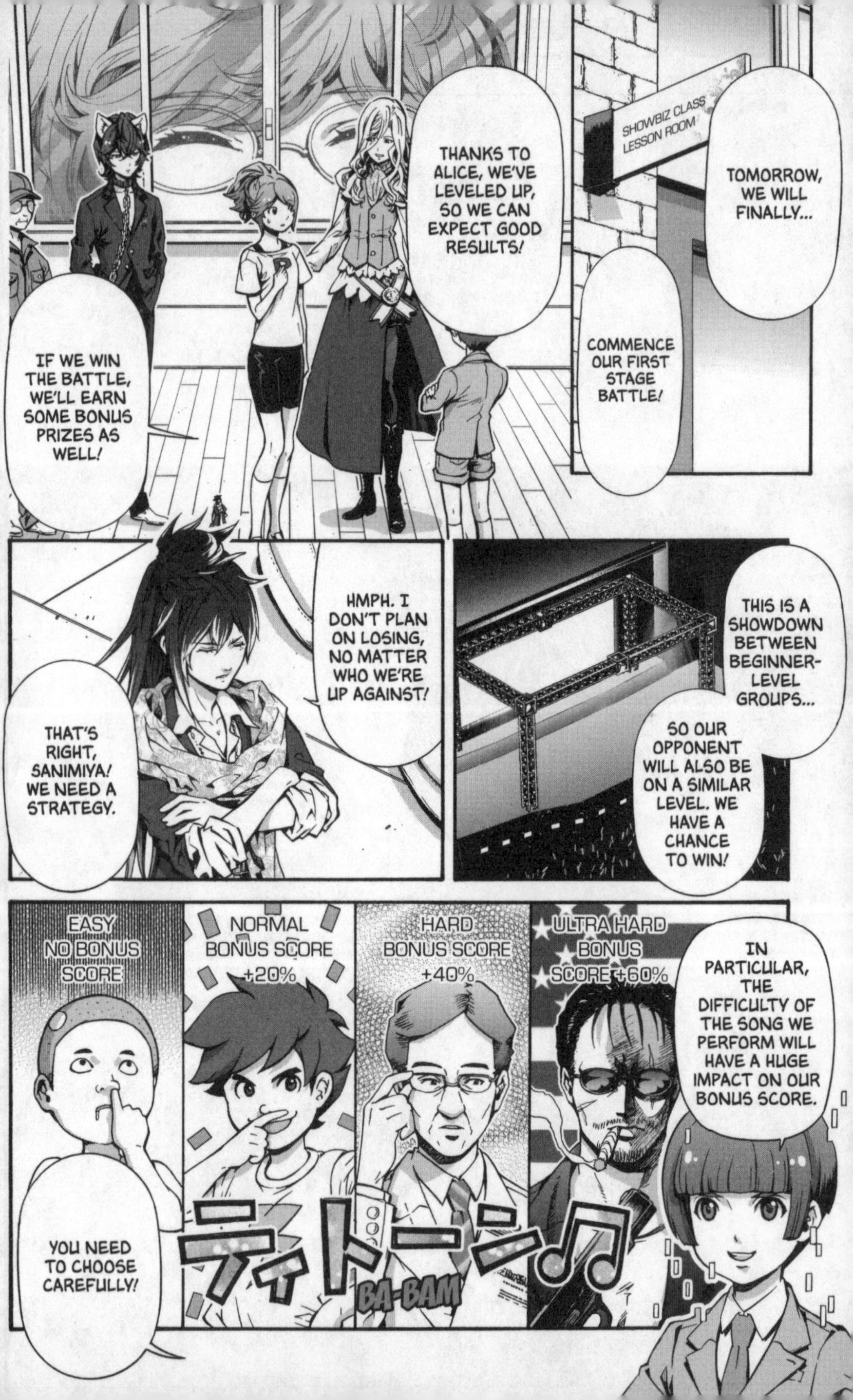
SHOWBIZ CLASS LESSON ROOM
TOMORROW, WE WILL FINALLY...
COMMENCE OUR FIRST STAGE BATTLE!
THANKS TO ALICE, WE'VE LEVELED UP, SO WE CAN EXPECT GOOD RESULTS!
IF WE WIN THE BATTLE, WE'LL EARN SOME BONUS PRIZES AS WELL!
THIS IS A SHOWDOWN BETWEEN BEGINNER-LEVEL GROUPS...
SO OUR OPPONENT WILL ALSO BE ON A SIMILAR LEVEL. WE HAVE A CHANCE TO WIN!
HMPH. I DON'T PLAN ON LOSING, NO MATTER WHO WE'RE UP AGAINST!
...
THAT'S RIGHT, SANIMIYA! WE NEED A STRATEGY.
IN PARTICULAR, THE DIFFICULTY OF THE SONG WE PERFORM WILL HAVE A HUGE IMPACT ON OUR BONUS SCORE.
ULTRA HARD BONUS SCORE +60%
HARD BONUS SCORE +40%
NORMAL BONUS SCORE +20%
EASY NO BONUS SCORE
ティトーン♫
BA-BAM
YOU NEED TO CHOOSE CAREFULLY!

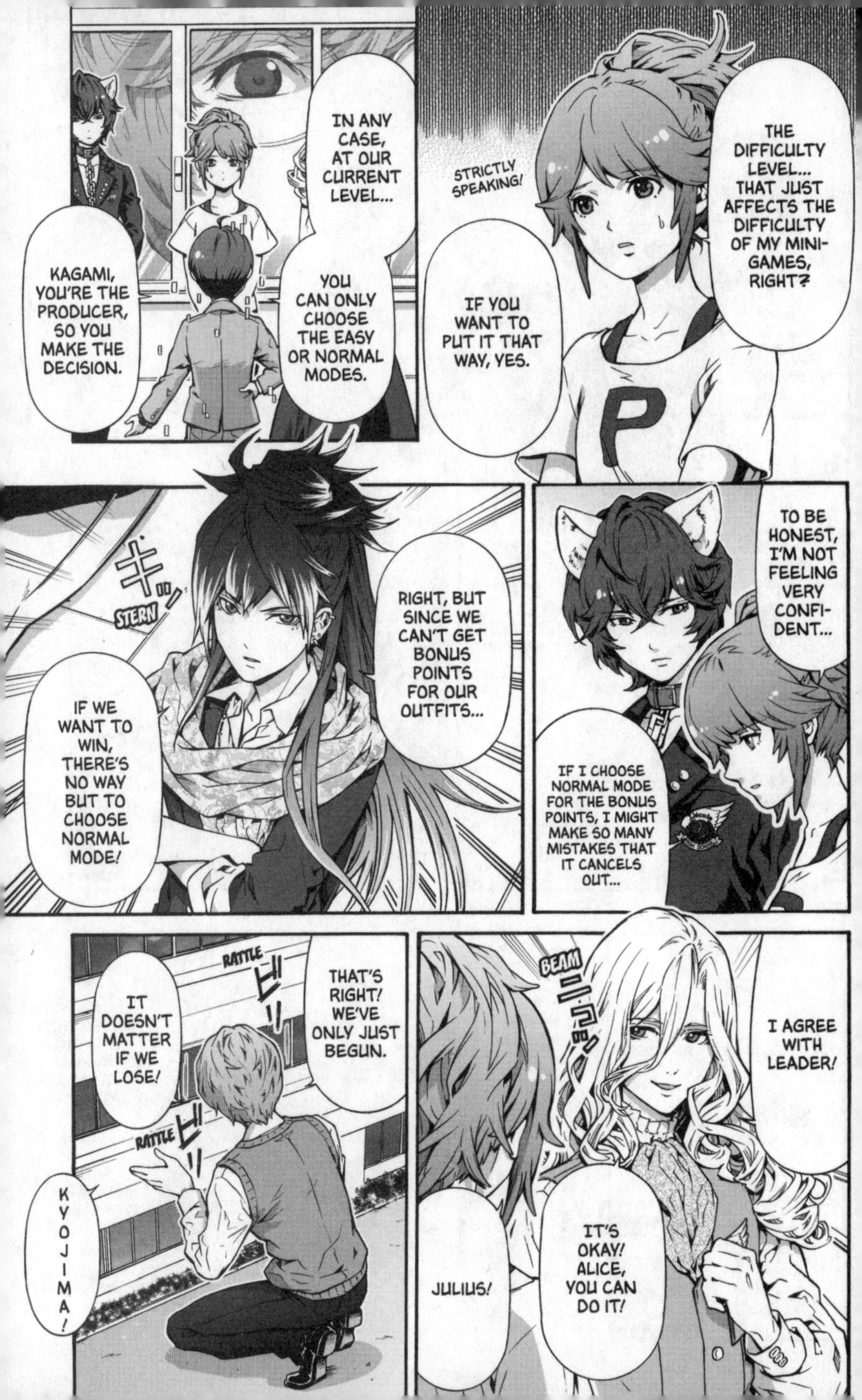
THE DIFFICULTY LEVEL... THAT JUST AFFECTS THE DIFFICULTY OF MY MINI-GAMES, RIGHT?
STRICTLY SPEAKING!
IF YOU WANT TO PUT IT THAT WAY, YES.
IN ANY CASE, AT OUR CURRENT LEVEL...
YOU CAN ONLY CHOOSE THE EASY OR NORMAL MODES.
KAGAMI, YOU'RE THE PRODUCER, SO YOU MAKE THE DECISION.
TO BE HONEST, I'M NOT FEELING VERY CONFI-DENT...
IF I CHOOSE NORMAL MODE FOR THE BONUS POINTS, I MIGHT MAKE SO MANY MISTAKES THAT IT CANCELS OUT...
STERN
RIGHT, BUT SINCE WE CAN'T GET BONUS POINTS FOR OUR OUTFITS...
IF WE WANT TO WIN, THERE'S NO WAY BUT TO CHOOSE NORMAL MODE!
BEAM
I AGREE WITH LEADER!
IT'S OKAY! ALICE, YOU CAN DO IT!
JULIUS!
RATTLE
THAT'S RIGHT! WE'VE ONLY JUST BEGUN.
IT DOESN'T MATTER IF WE LOSE!
RATTLE
KYOJIMA!

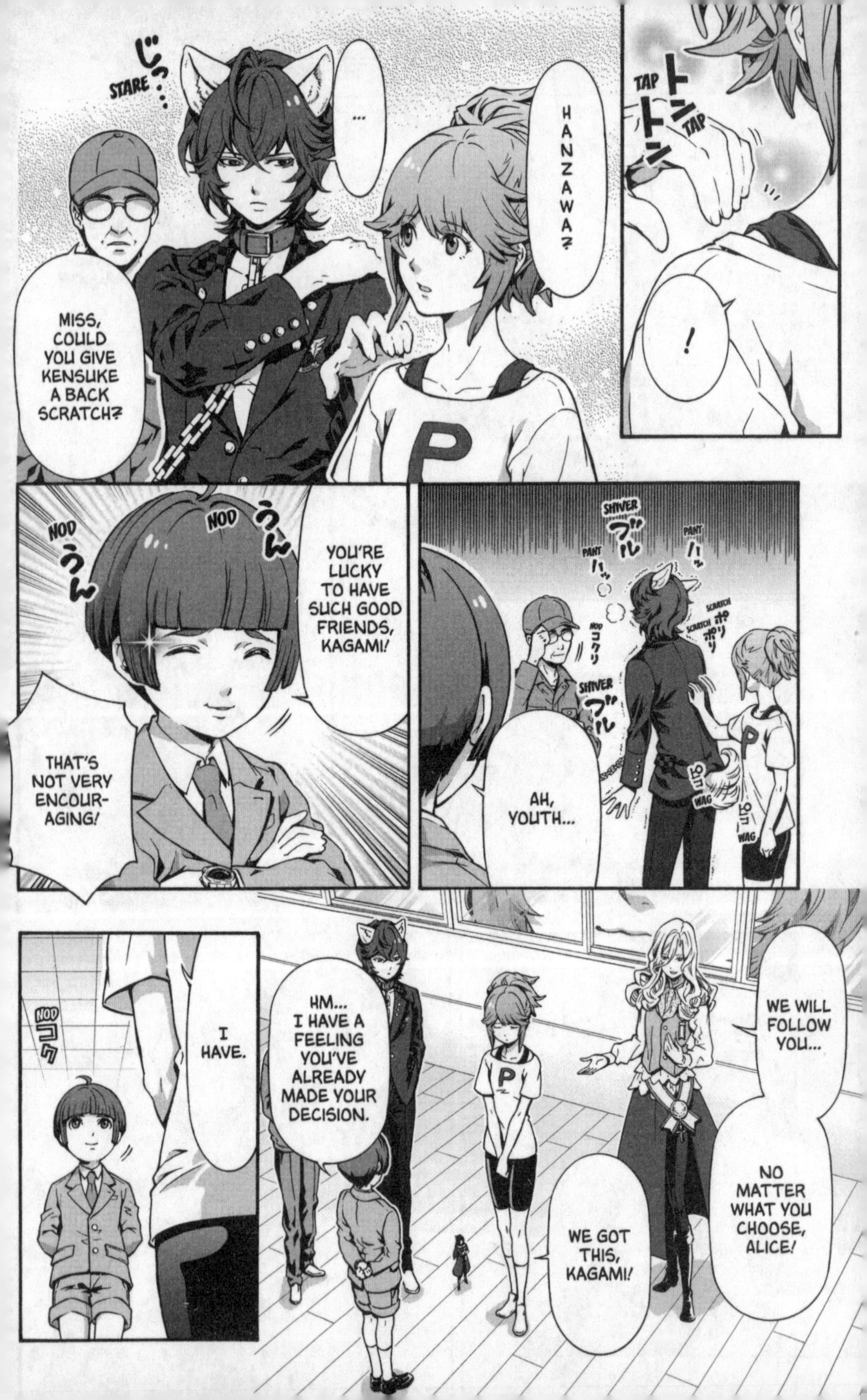

TAP トン
TAP トン
!
HANZAWA?
...
STARE じっ…
MISS, COULD YOU GIVE KENSUKE A BACK SCRATCH?
SHIVER ブル
PANT ハッ
PANT ハッ
SCRATCH ポリ
SCRATCH ポリ
NOD コクリ
SHIVER ブル
AH, YOUTH...
WAG
WAG
YOU'RE LUCKY TO HAVE SUCH GOOD FRIENDS, KAGAMI!
NOD うん
NOD うん
THAT'S NOT VERY ENCOUR-AGING!
WE WILL FOLLOW YOU...
NO MATTER WHAT YOU CHOOSE, ALICE!
WE GOT THIS, KAGAMI!
HM... I HAVE A FEELING YOU'VE ALREADY MADE YOUR DECISION.
I HAVE.
NOD コク

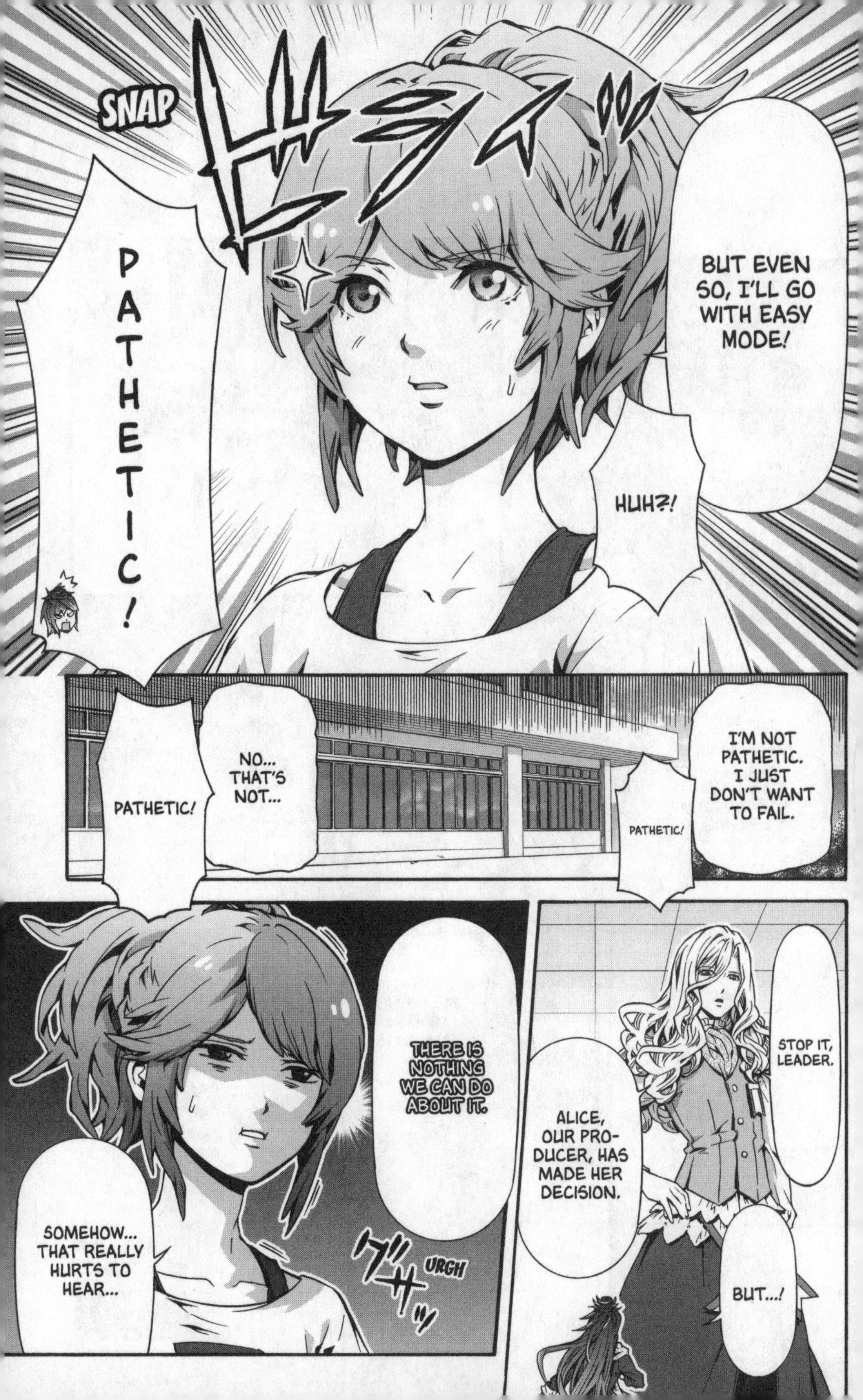
BUT EVEN SO, I'LL GO WITH EASY MODE!
SNAP
HUH?!
PATHETIC!
I'M NOT PATHETIC. I JUST DON'T WANT TO FAIL.
PATHETIC!
NO... THAT'S NOT...
PATHETIC!
STOP IT, LEADER.
ALICE, OUR PRO-DUCER, HAS MADE HER DECISION.
BUT...!
THERE IS NOTHING WE CAN DO ABOUT IT.
URGH
SOMEHOW... THAT REALLY HURTS TO HEAR...

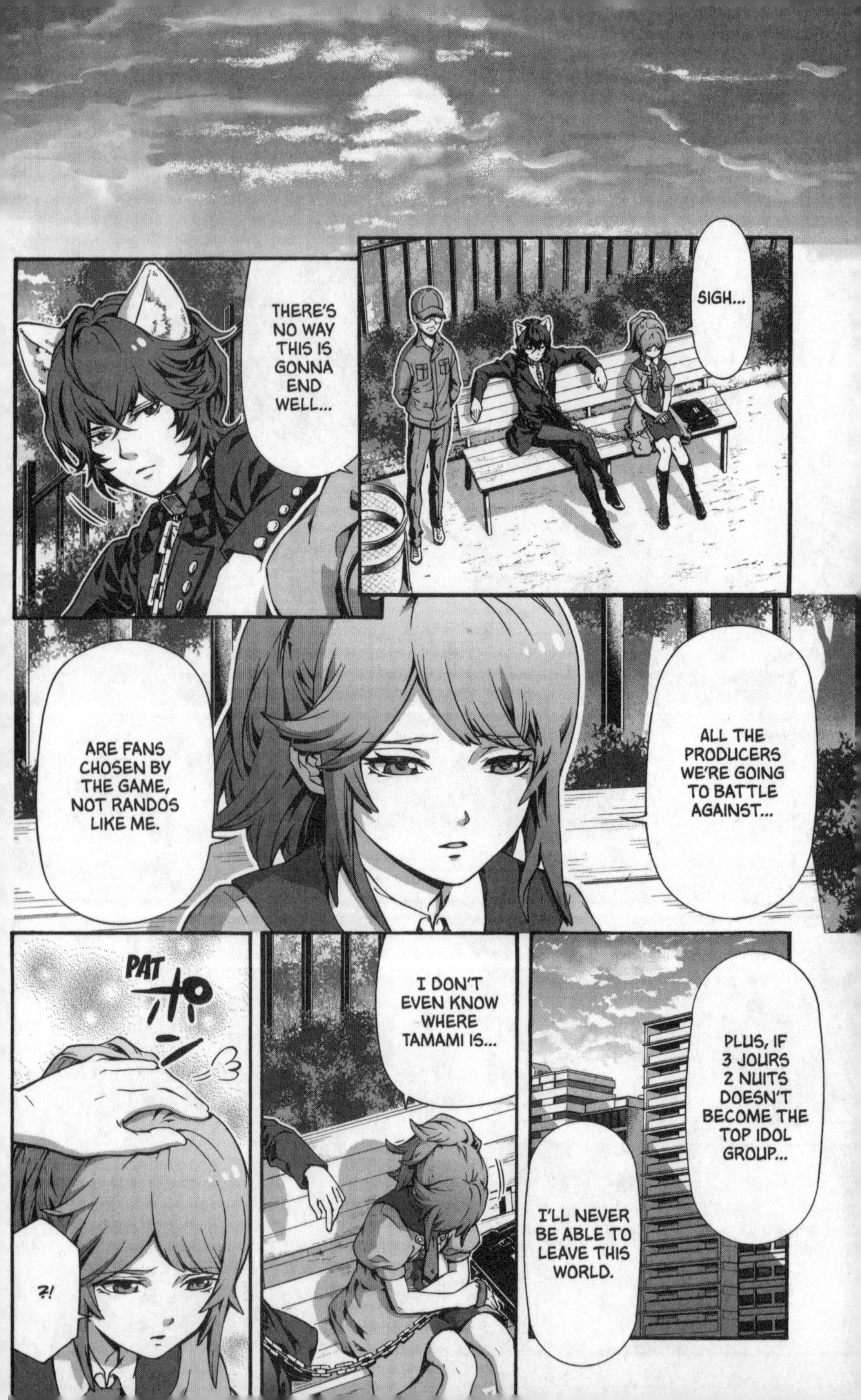
SIGH...
THERE'S NO WAY THIS IS GONNA END WELL...
ALL THE PRODUCERS WE'RE GOING TO BATTLE AGAINST...
ARE FANS CHOSEN BY THE GAME, NOT RANDOS LIKE ME.
PLUS, IF 3 JOURS 2 NUITS DOESN'T BECOME THE TOP IDOL GROUP...
I'LL NEVER BE ABLE TO LEAVE THIS WORLD.
I DON'T EVEN KNOW WHERE TAMAMI IS...
PAT
?!

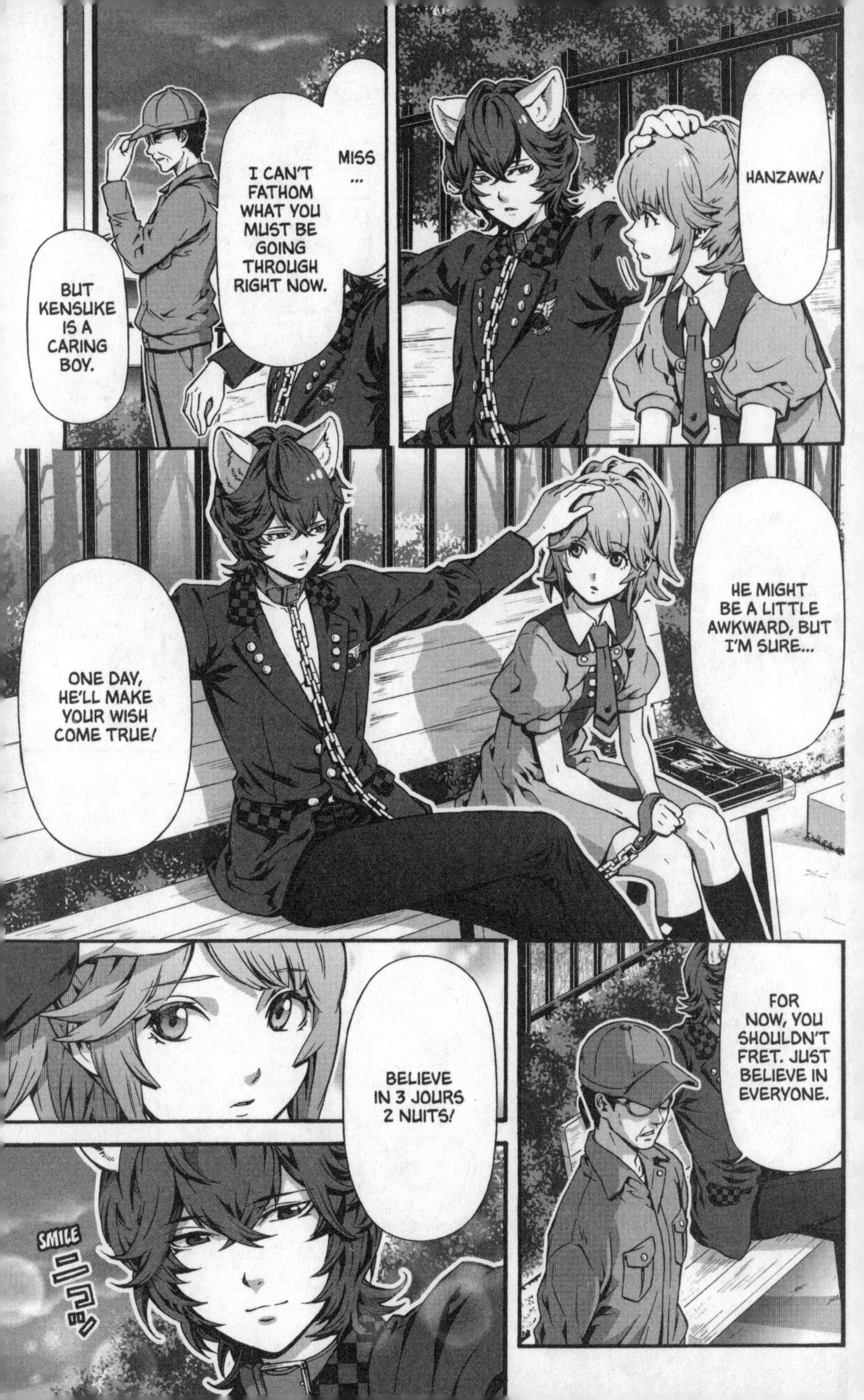
HANZAWA!
MISS ...
I CAN'T FATHOM WHAT YOU MUST BE GOING THROUGH RIGHT NOW.
BUT KENSUKE IS A CARING BOY.
HE MIGHT BE A LITTLE AWKWARD, BUT I'M SURE...
ONE DAY, HE'LL MAKE YOUR WISH COME TRUE!
FOR NOW, YOU SHOULDN'T FRET. JUST BELIEVE IN EVERYONE.
BELIEVE IN 3 JOURS 2 NUITS!
SMILE
ニコッ

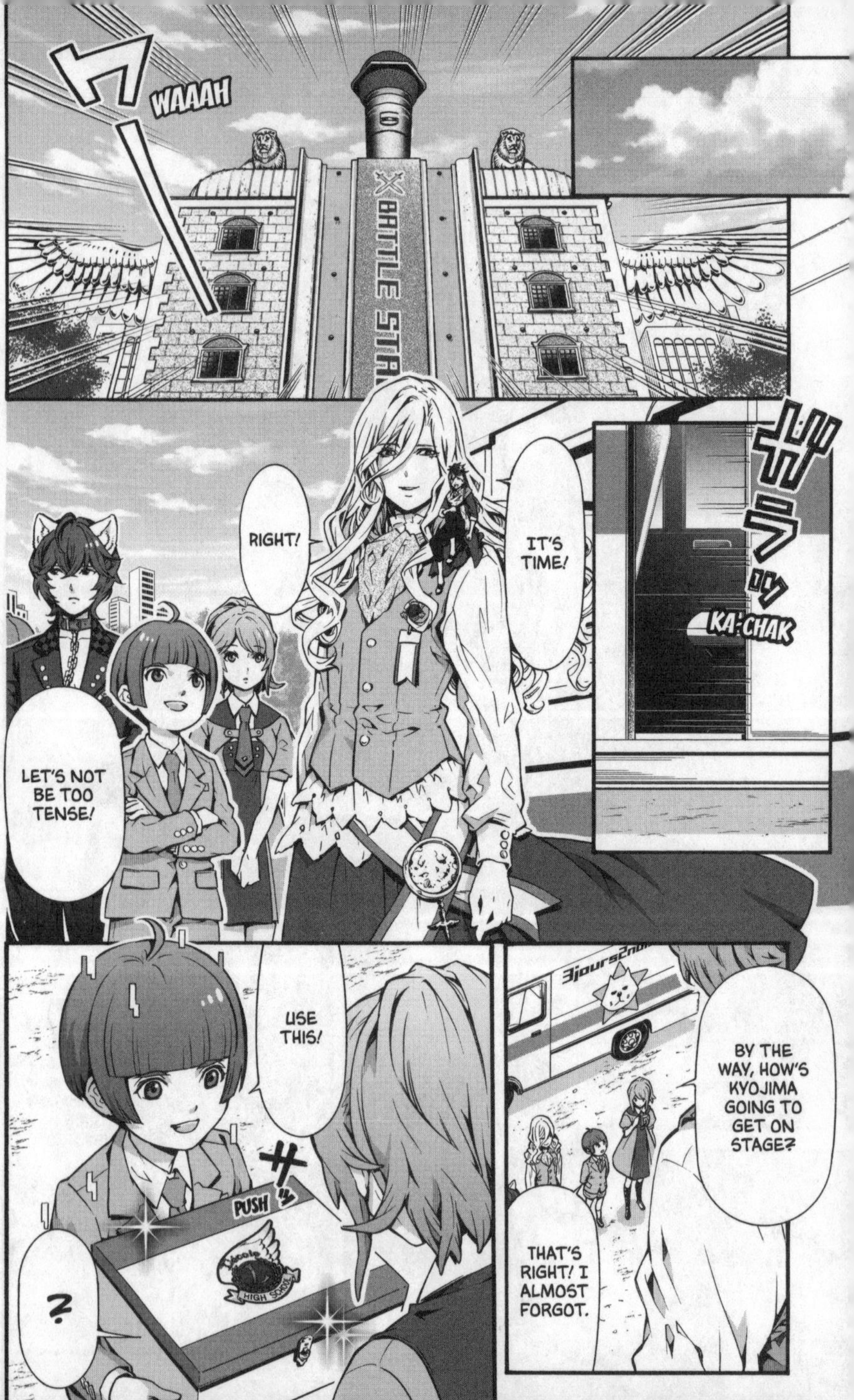
WAAAH
BATTLE STA
KA-CHAK
IT'S TIME!
RIGHT!
LET'S NOT BE TOO TENSE!
BY THE WAY, HOW'S KYOJIMA GOING TO GET ON STAGE?
THAT'S RIGHT! I ALMOST FORGOT.
USE THIS!
PUSH
HIGH SCHOOL
?

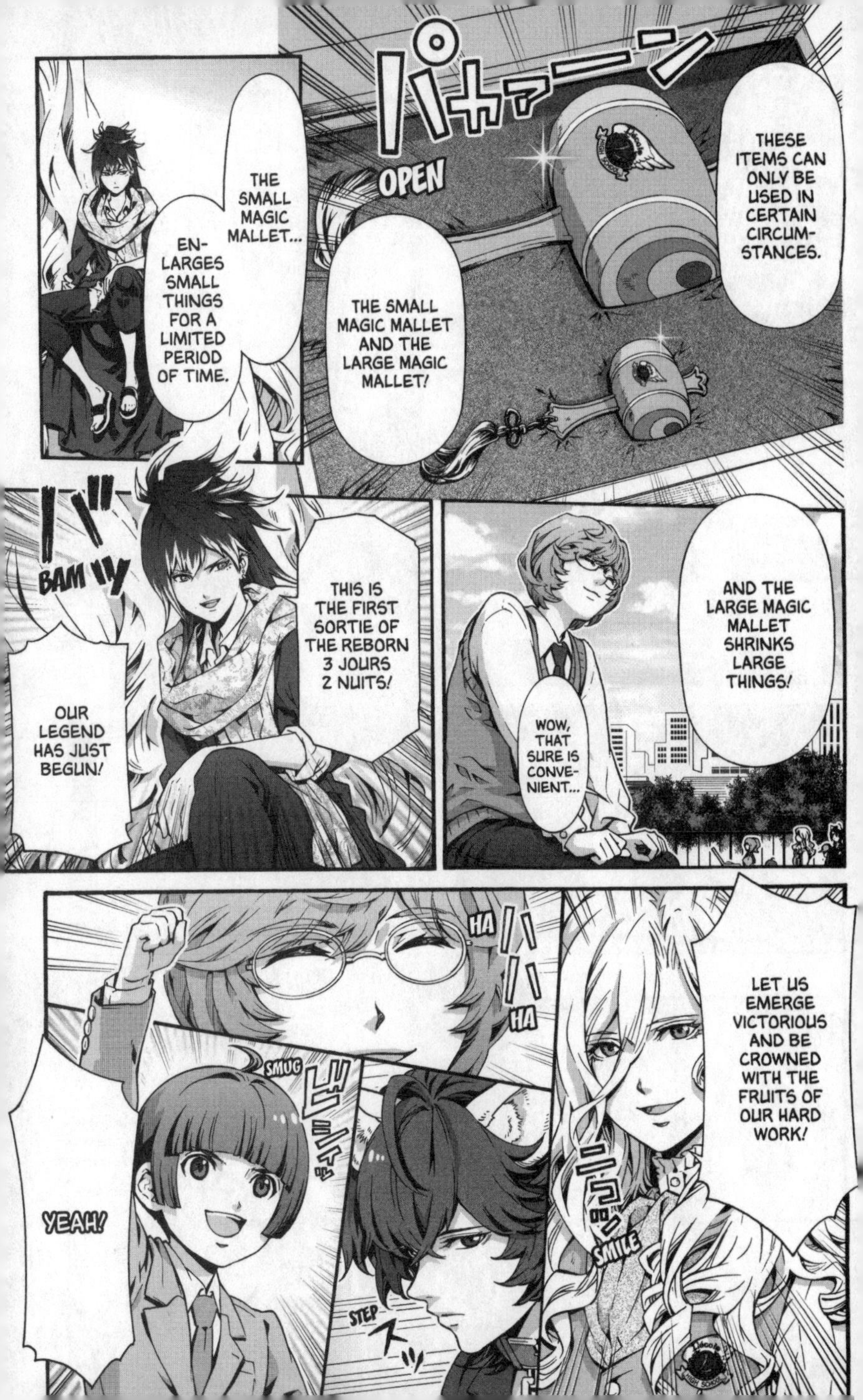
OPEN
THESE ITEMS CAN ONLY BE USED IN CERTAIN CIRCUM-STANCES.
THE SMALL MAGIC MALLET AND THE LARGE MAGIC MALLET!
THE SMALL MAGIC MALLET...
EN-LARGES SMALL THINGS FOR A LIMITED PERIOD OF TIME.
AND THE LARGE MAGIC MALLET SHRINKS LARGE THINGS!
WOW, THAT SURE IS CONVE-NIENT...
BAM
THIS IS THE FIRST SORTIE OF THE REBORN 3 JOURS 2 NUITS!
OUR LEGEND HAS JUST BEGUN!
LET US EMERGE VICTORIOUS AND BE CROWNED WITH THE FRUITS OF OUR HARD WORK!
SMILE
HA
HA
SMUG
STEP
YEAH!

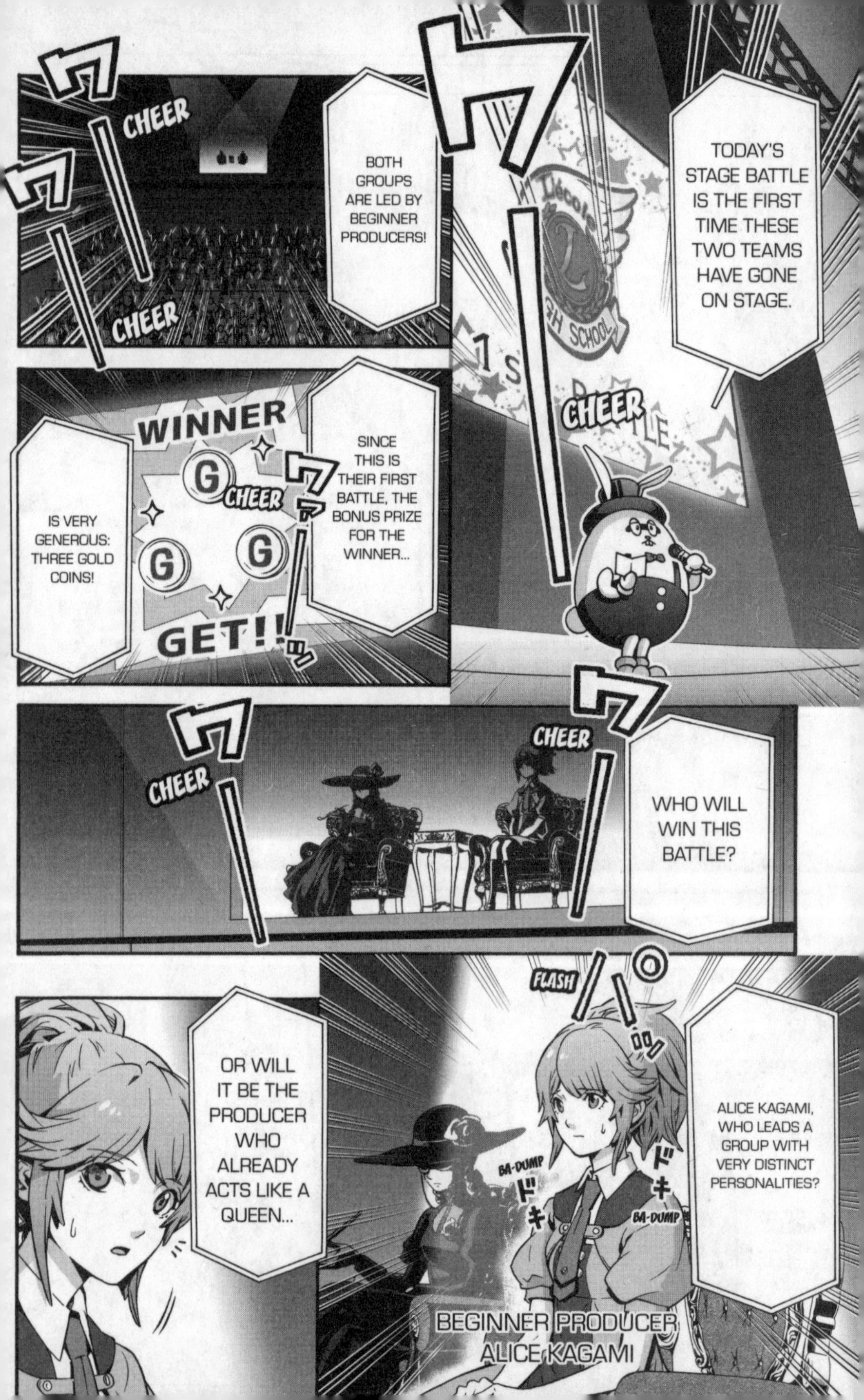
TODAY'S STAGE BATTLE IS THE FIRST TIME THESE TWO TEAMS HAVE GONE ON STAGE.
CHEER
BOTH GROUPS ARE LED BY BEGINNER PRODUCERS!
CHEER
CHEER
SINCE THIS IS THEIR FIRST BATTLE, THE BONUS PRIZE FOR THE WINNER...
WINNER
CHEER
GET!!
IS VERY GENEROUS: THREE GOLD COINS!
CHEER
WHO WILL WIN THIS BATTLE?
CHEER
ALICE KAGAMI, WHO LEADS A GROUP WITH VERY DISTINCT PERSONALITIES?
FLASH
BA-DUMP
BA-DUMP
BEGINNER PRODUCER ALICE KAGAMI
OR WILL IT BE THE PRODUCER WHO ALREADY ACTS LIKE A QUEEN...

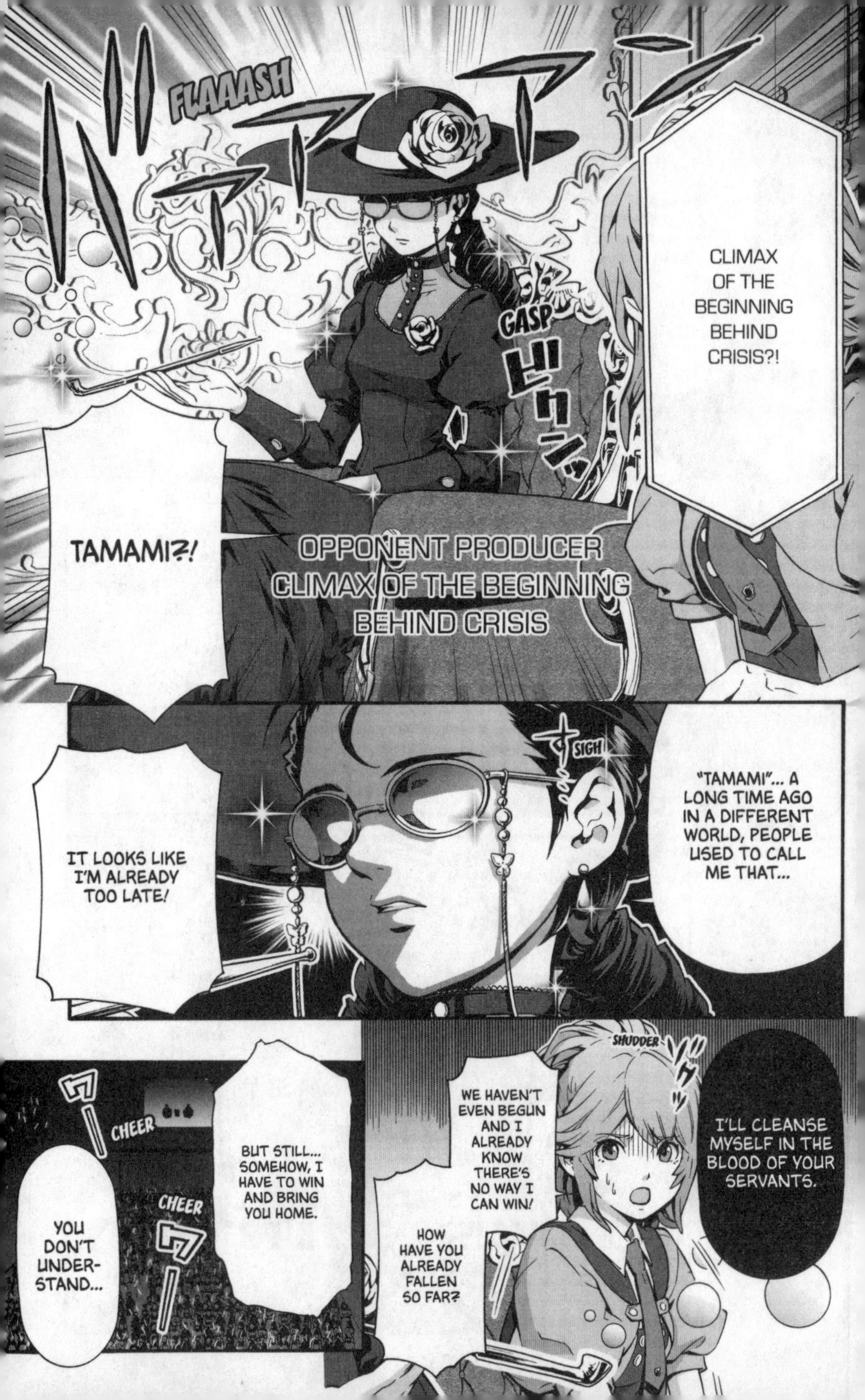
CLIMAX OF THE BEGINNING BEHIND CRISIS?!
FLAAASH
GASP
OPPONENT PRODUCER CLIMAX OF THE BEGINNING BEHIND CRISIS
TAMAMI?!
"TAMAMI"... A LONG TIME AGO IN A DIFFERENT WORLD, PEOPLE USED TO CALL ME THAT...
SIGH
IT LOOKS LIKE I'M ALREADY TOO LATE!
SHUDDER
I'LL CLEANSE MYSELF IN THE BLOOD OF YOUR SERVANTS.
WE HAVEN'T EVEN BEGUN AND I ALREADY KNOW THERE'S NO WAY I CAN WIN!
HOW HAVE YOU ALREADY FALLEN SO FAR?
BUT STILL... SOMEHOW, I HAVE TO WIN AND BRING YOU HOME.
CHEER
CHEER
YOU DON'T UNDER-STAND...

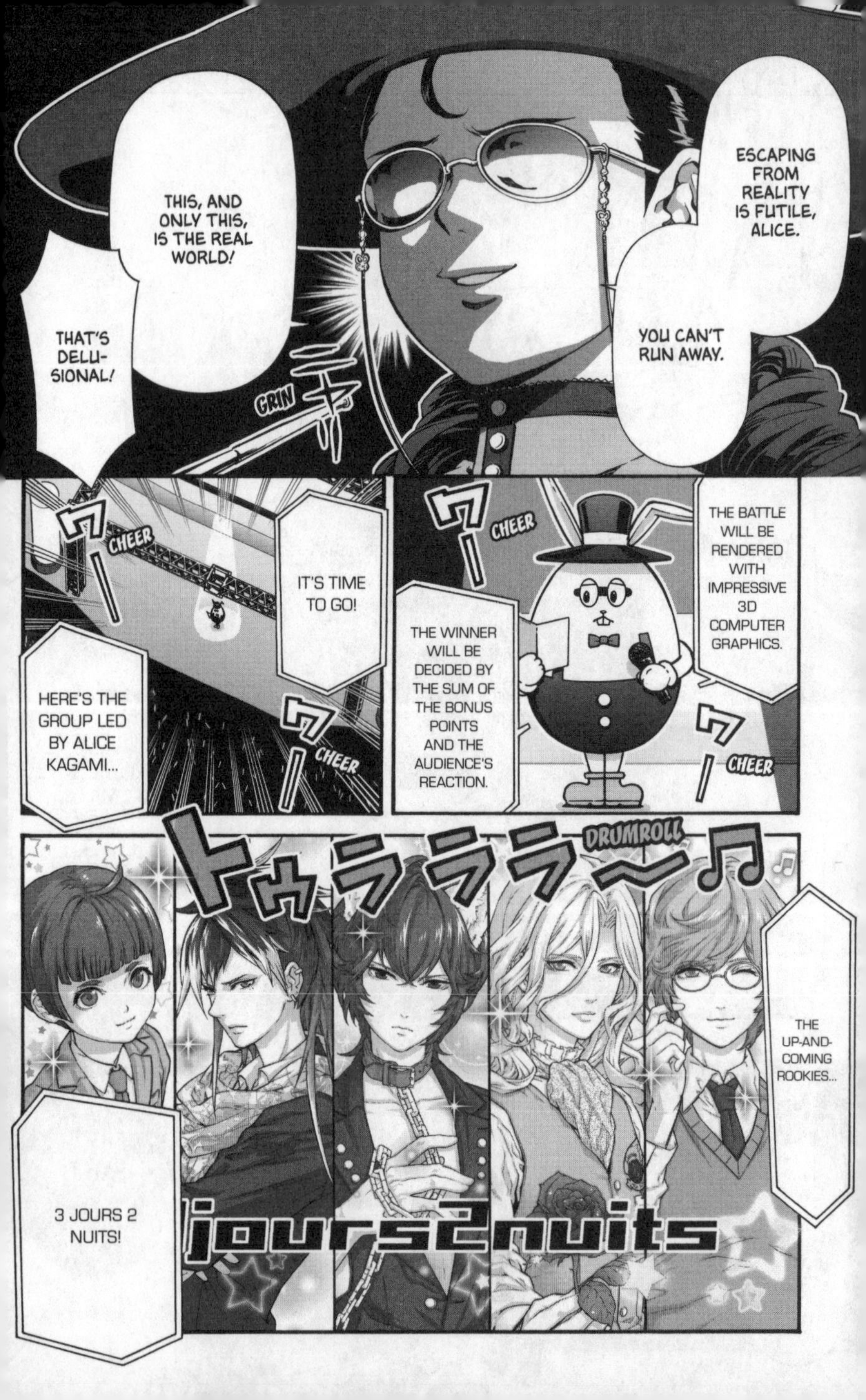
ESCAPING FROM REALITY IS FUTILE, ALICE.
YOU CAN'T RUN AWAY.
GRIN
THIS, AND ONLY THIS, IS THE REAL WORLD!
THAT'S DELU-SIONAL!
THE BATTLE WILL BE RENDERED WITH IMPRESSIVE 3D COMPUTER GRAPHICS.
CHEER
THE WINNER WILL BE DECIDED BY THE SUM OF THE BONUS POINTS AND THE AUDIENCE'S REACTION.
CHEER
CHEER
IT'S TIME TO GO!
CHEER
HERE'S THE GROUP LED BY ALICE KAGAMI...
トゥラララ〜♫
DRUMROLL
THE UP-AND-COMING ROOKIES...
jours2nuits
3 JOURS 2 NUITS!

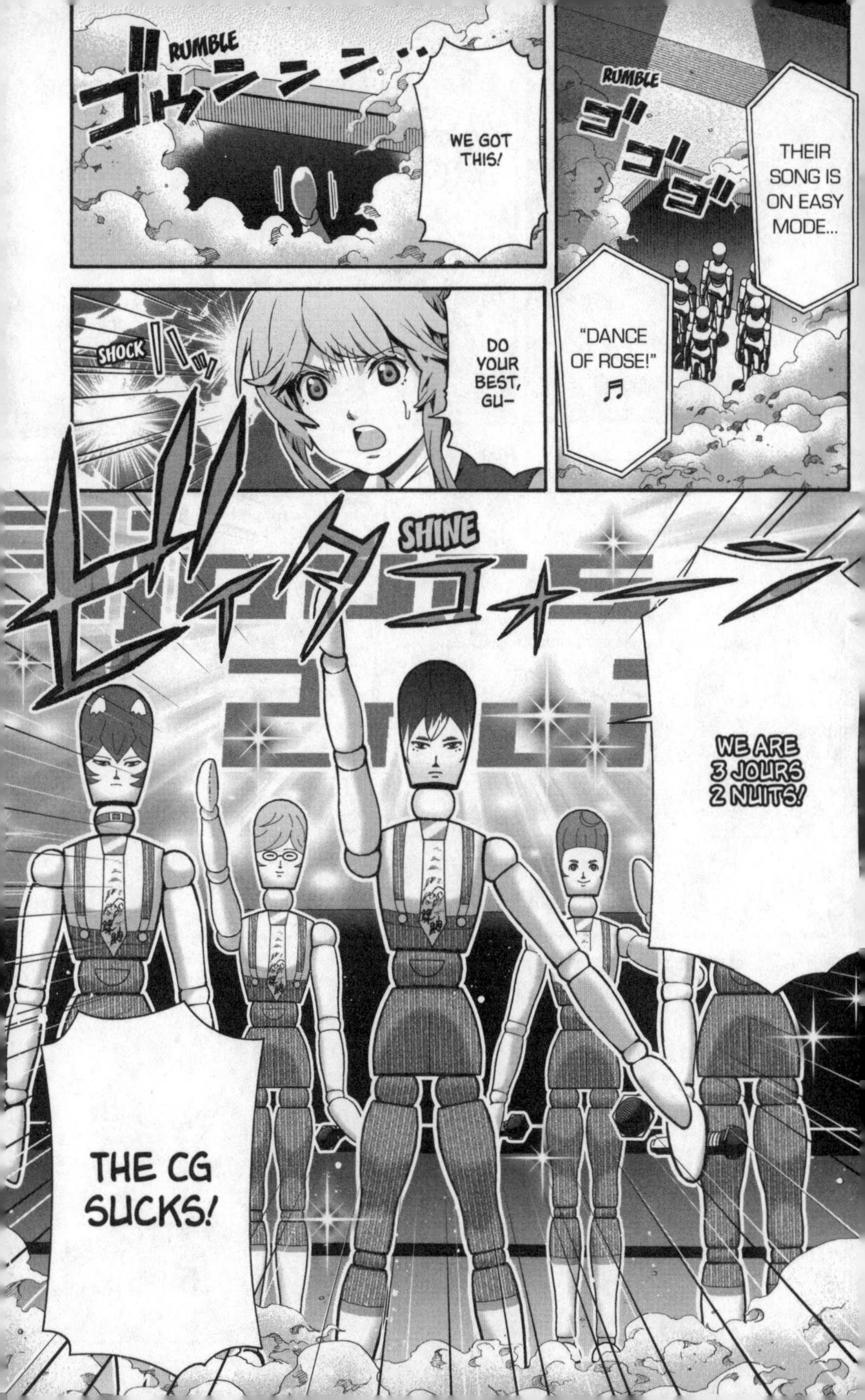
RUMBLE
THEIR SONG IS ON EASY MODE...
"DANCE OF ROSE!" ♪
RUMBLE
WE GOT THIS!
SHOCK
DO YOUR BEST, GU–
SHINE
WE ARE 3 JOURS 2 NUITS!
THE CG SUCKS!

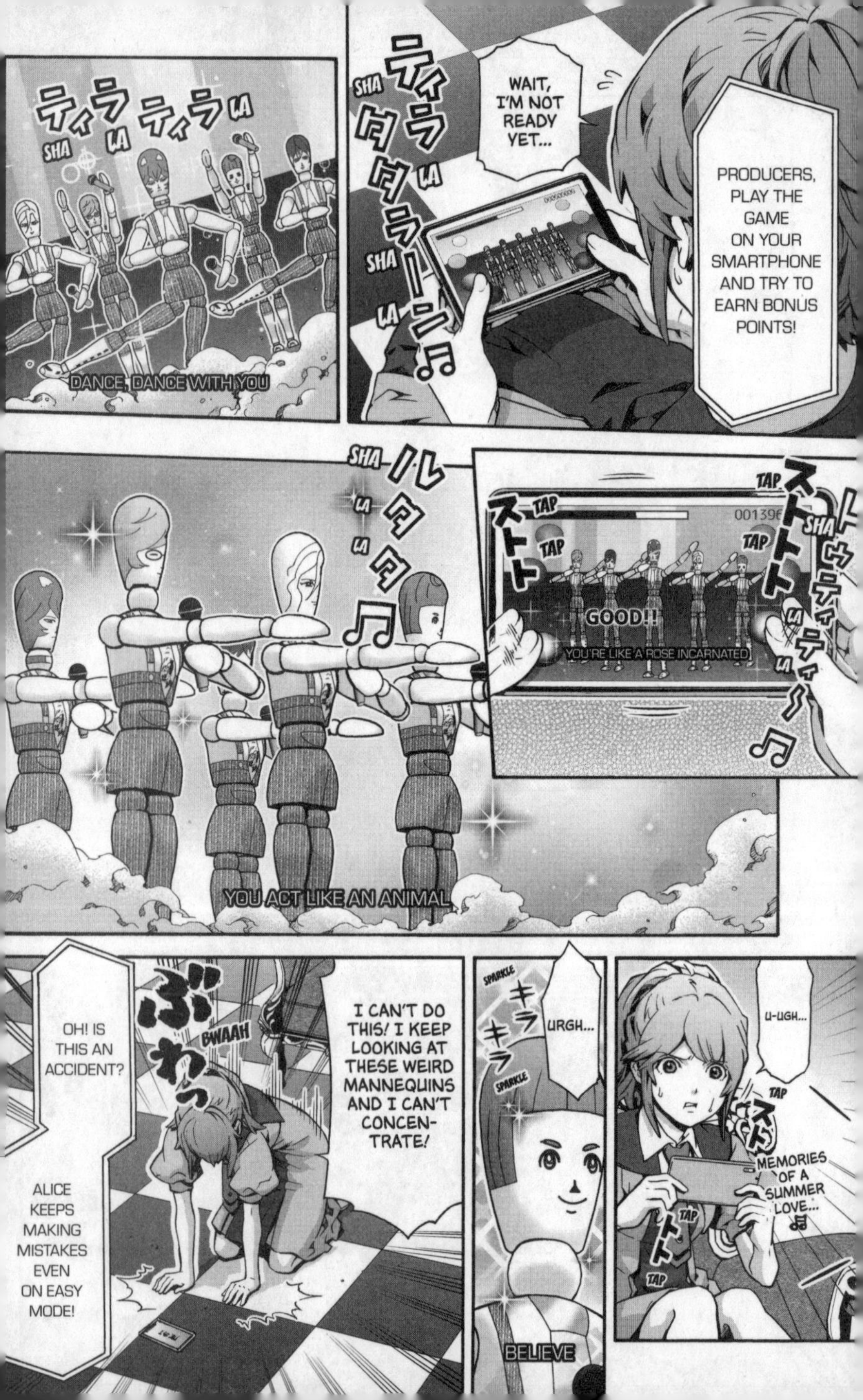

PRODUCERS, PLAY THE GAME ON YOUR SMARTPHONE AND TRY TO EARN BONUS POINTS!
WAIT, I'M NOT READY YET...
SHA ティラ LA タ LA タラーー♪ SHA LA
ティラ SHA LA ティラ LA
DANCE, DANCE WITH YOU
TAP TAP TAP TAP
001396
GOOD!!
YOU'RE LIKE A ROSE INCARNATED
SHA LA LA
SHA ル LA タ LA タ♪
YOU ACT LIKE AN ANIMAL
U-UGH...
TAP TAP TAP
MEMORIES OF A SUMMER LOVE...♬
URGH...
SPARKLE キラ キラ SPARKLE
BELIEVE
I CAN'T DO THIS! I KEEP LOOKING AT THESE WEIRD MANNEQUINS AND I CAN'T CONCEN-TRATE!
OH! IS THIS AN ACCIDENT?
BWAAH
ALICE KEEPS MAKING MISTAKES EVEN ON EASY MODE!

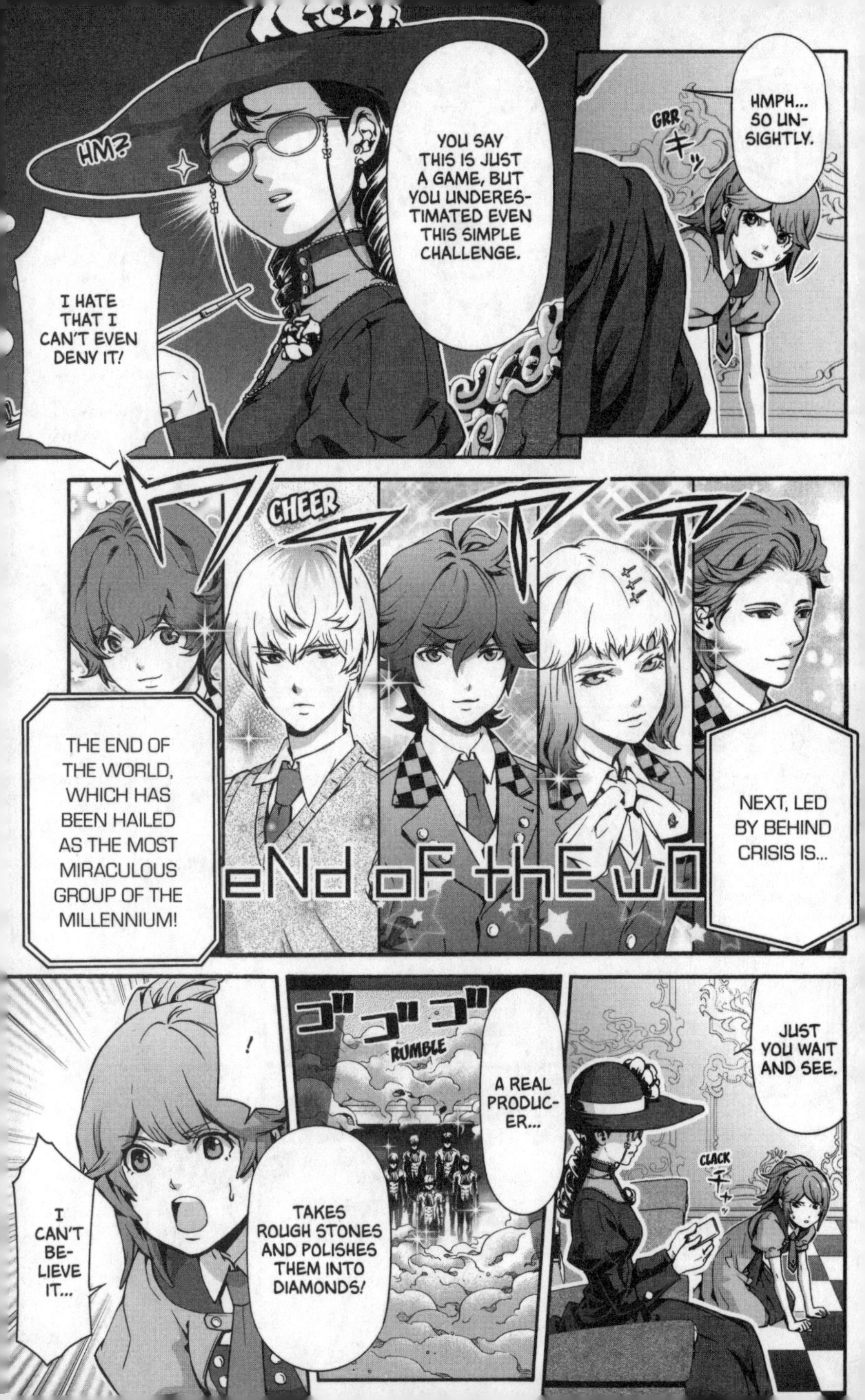
GRR
HMPH... SO UN-SIGHTLY.
YOU SAY THIS IS JUST A GAME, BUT YOU UNDERES-TIMATED EVEN THIS SIMPLE CHALLENGE.
HM?
I HATE THAT I CAN'T EVEN DENY IT!
NEXT, LED BY BEHIND CRISIS IS...
CHEER
THE END OF THE WORLD, WHICH HAS BEEN HAILED AS THE MOST MIRACULOUS GROUP OF THE MILLENNIUM!
eNd oF thE wO
JUST YOU WAIT AND SEE.
CLACK
A REAL PRODUC-ER...
RUMBLE
TAKES ROUGH STONES AND POLISHES THEM INTO DIAMONDS!
!
I CAN'T BE-LIEVE IT...

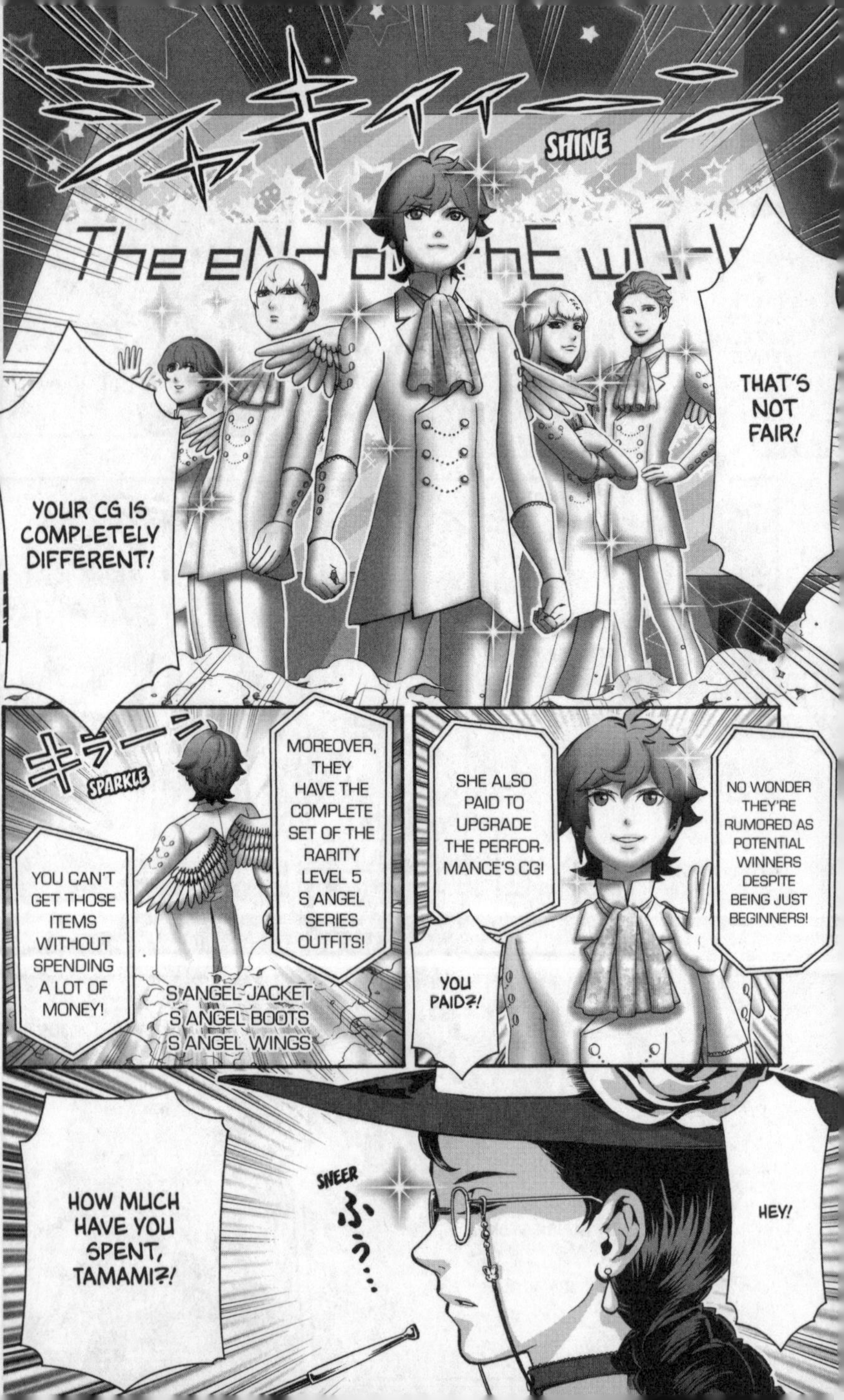
SHINE
THAT'S NOT FAIR!
YOUR CG IS COMPLETELY DIFFERENT!
NO WONDER THEY'RE RUMORED AS POTENTIAL WINNERS DESPITE BEING JUST BEGINNERS!
SHE ALSO PAID TO UPGRADE THE PERFORMANCE'S CG!
YOU PAID?!
MOREOVER, THEY HAVE THE COMPLETE SET OF THE RARITY LEVEL 5 S ANGEL SERIES OUTFITS!
キラーン
SPARKLE
YOU CAN'T GET THOSE ITEMS WITHOUT SPENDING A LOT OF MONEY!
S ANGEL JACKET
S ANGEL BOOTS
S ANGEL WINGS
HEY!
SNEER
ふぅ…
HOW MUCH HAVE YOU SPENT, TAMAMI?!

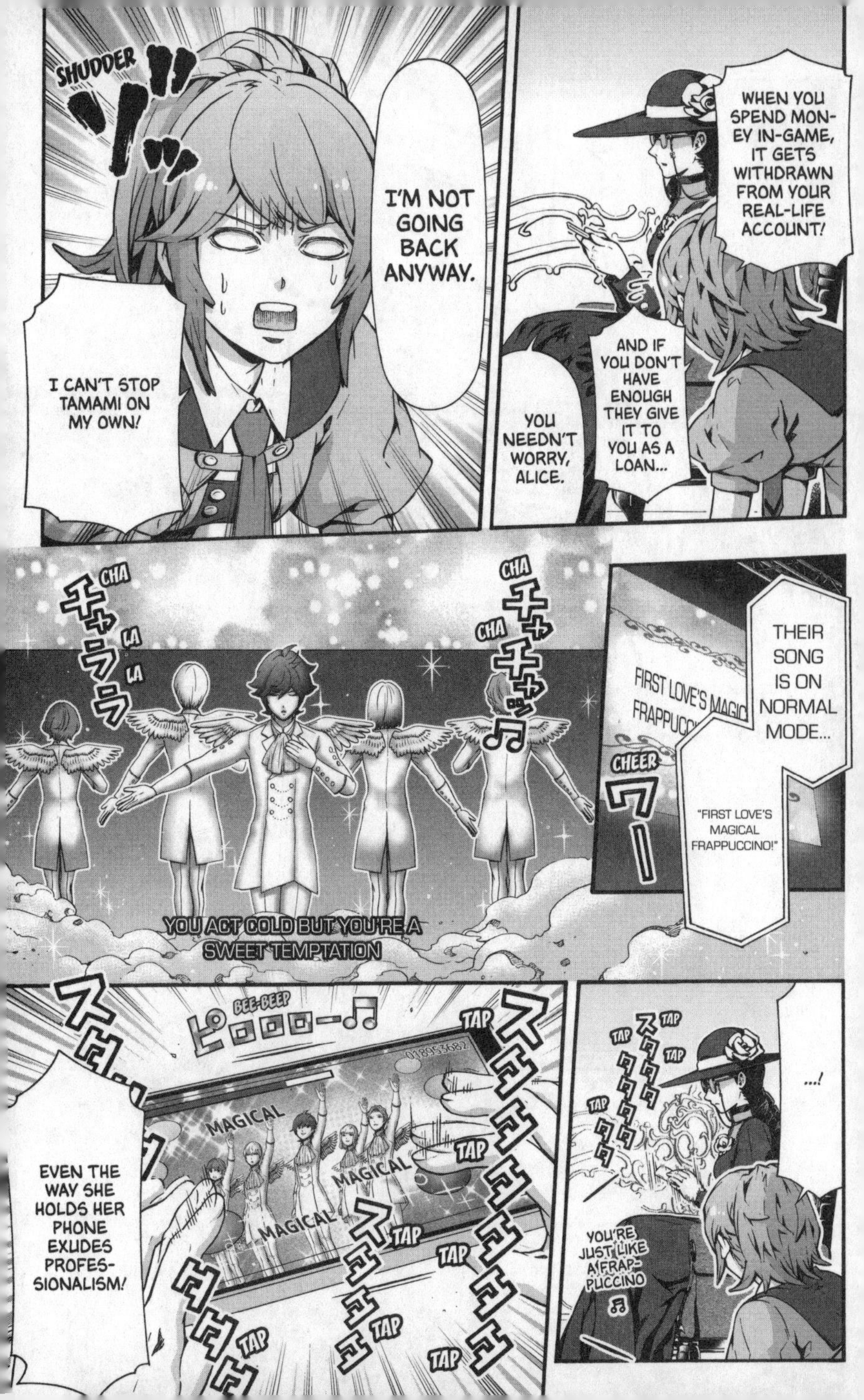

WHEN YOU SPEND MONEY IN-GAME, IT GETS WITHDRAWN FROM YOUR REAL-LIFE ACCOUNT!
AND IF YOU DON'T HAVE ENOUGH THEY GIVE IT TO YOU AS A LOAN...
YOU NEEDN'T WORRY, ALICE.
SHUDDER
I'M NOT GOING BACK ANYWAY.
I CAN'T STOP TAMAMI ON MY OWN!
THEIR SONG IS ON NORMAL MODE...
"FIRST LOVE'S MAGICAL FRAPPUCCINO!"
CHEER
CHA
CHA
CHA
LA
LA
YOU ACT COLD BUT YOU'RE A SWEET TEMPTATION
TAP
TAP
TAP
TAP
...!
YOU'RE JUST LIKE A FRAPPUCCINO ♫
BEE-BEEP
MAGICAL
MAGICAL
MAGICAL
TAP
TAP
TAP
TAP
TAP
TAP
EVEN THE WAY SHE HOLDS HER PHONE EXUDES PROFESSIONALISM!

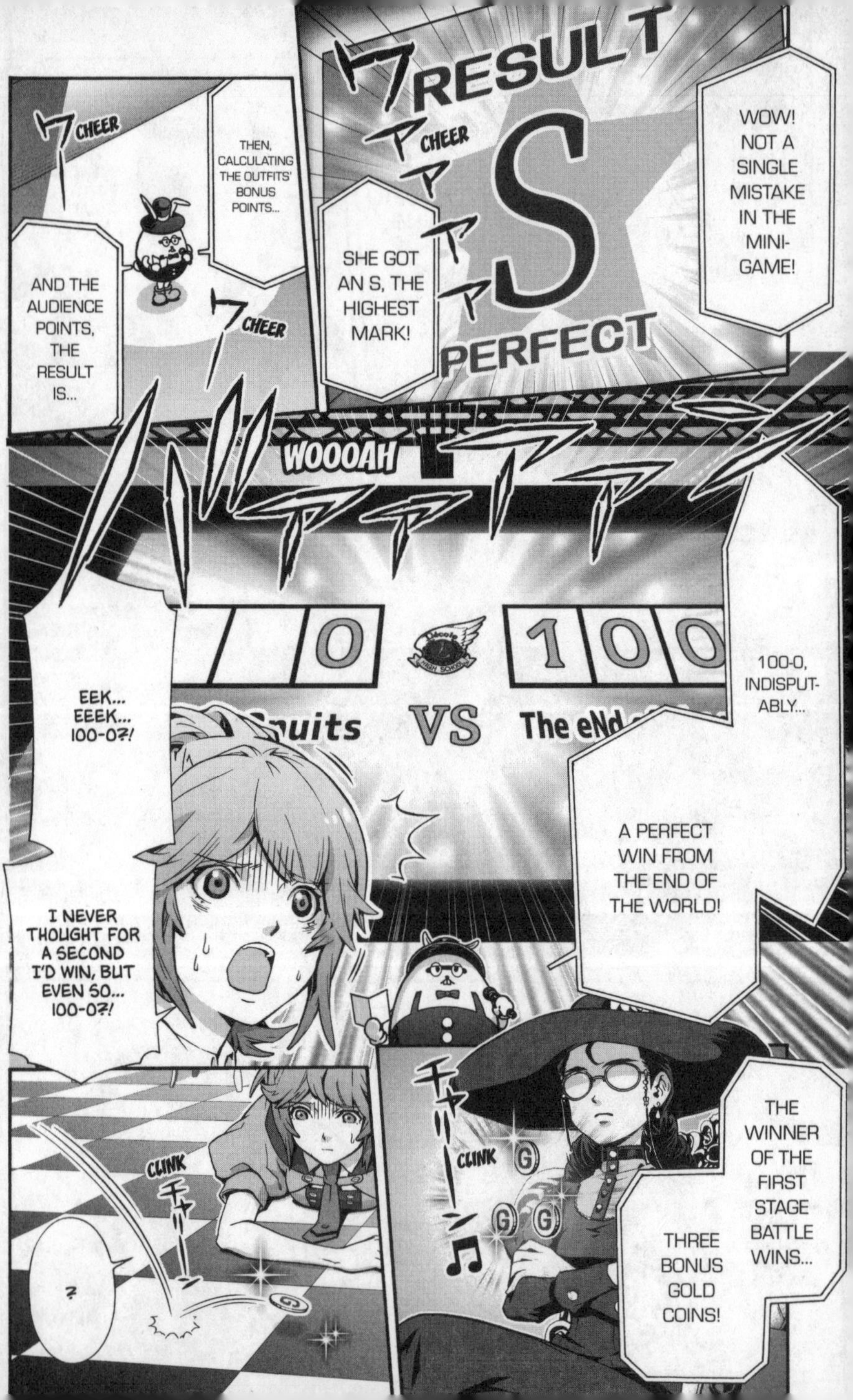
RESULT
CHEER
WOW! NOT A SINGLE MISTAKE IN THE MINI-GAME!
SHE GOT AN S, THE HIGHEST MARK!
S
PERFECT
CHEER
THEN, CALCULATING THE OUTFITS' BONUS POINTS...
AND THE AUDIENCE POINTS, THE RESULT IS...
CHEER
WOOOAH
100-0, INDISPUTABLY...
A PERFECT WIN FROM THE END OF THE WORLD!
0
100
VS
The eNd
EEK... EEEK... 100-0?!
I NEVER THOUGHT FOR A SECOND I'D WIN, BUT EVEN SO... 100-0?!
THE WINNER OF THE FIRST STAGE BATTLE WINS...
THREE BONUS GOLD COINS!
CLINK
CLINK
?

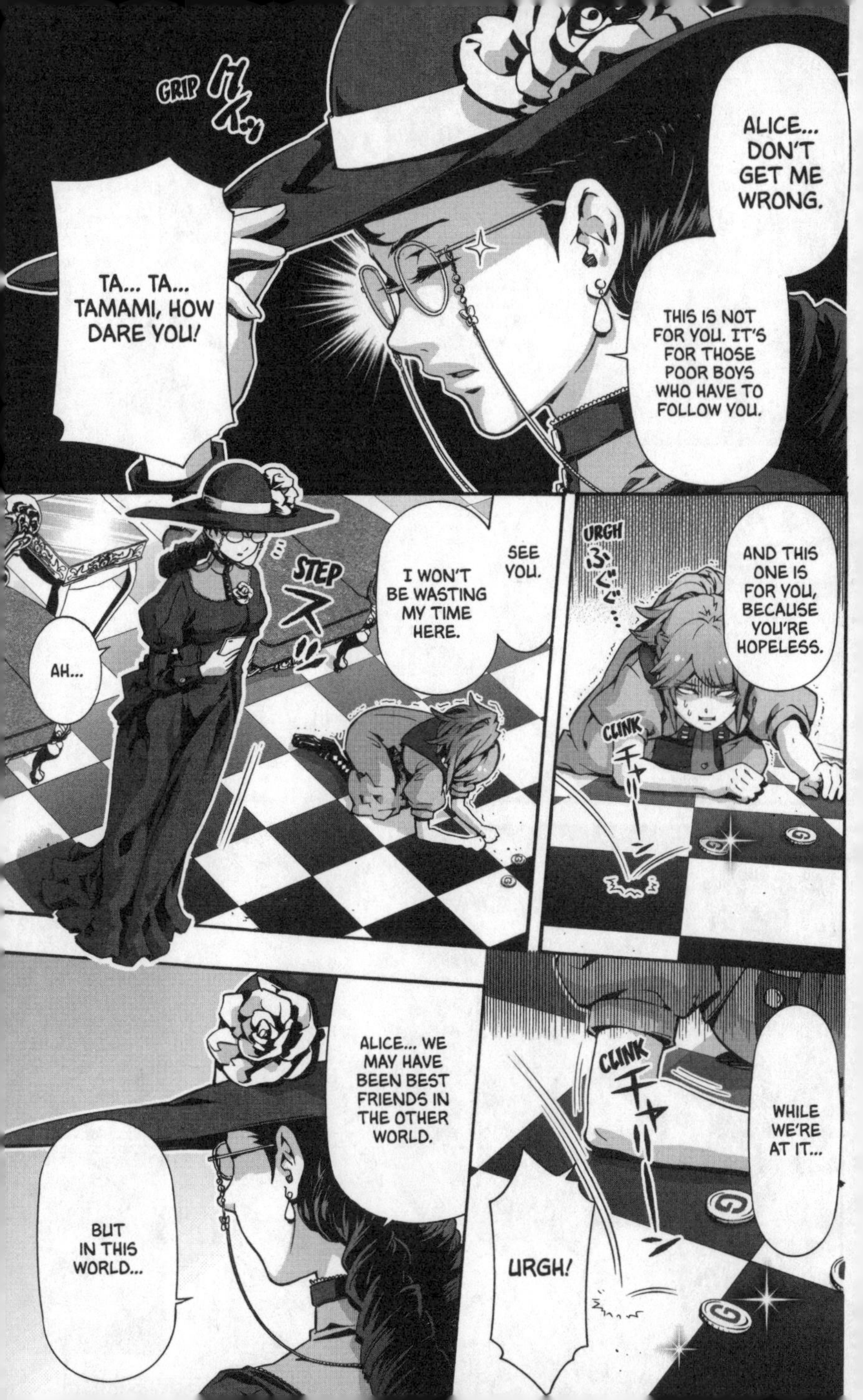
ALICE... DON'T GET ME WRONG.
THIS IS NOT FOR YOU. IT'S FOR THOSE POOR BOYS WHO HAVE TO FOLLOW YOU.
GRIP
TA... TA... TAMAMI, HOW DARE YOU!
URGH
AND THIS ONE IS FOR YOU, BECAUSE YOU'RE HOPELESS.
CLINK
SEE YOU.
I WON'T BE WASTING MY TIME HERE.
STEP
AH...
WHILE WE'RE AT IT...
CLINK
URGH!
ALICE... WE MAY HAVE BEEN BEST FRIENDS IN THE OTHER WORLD.
BUT IN THIS WORLD...

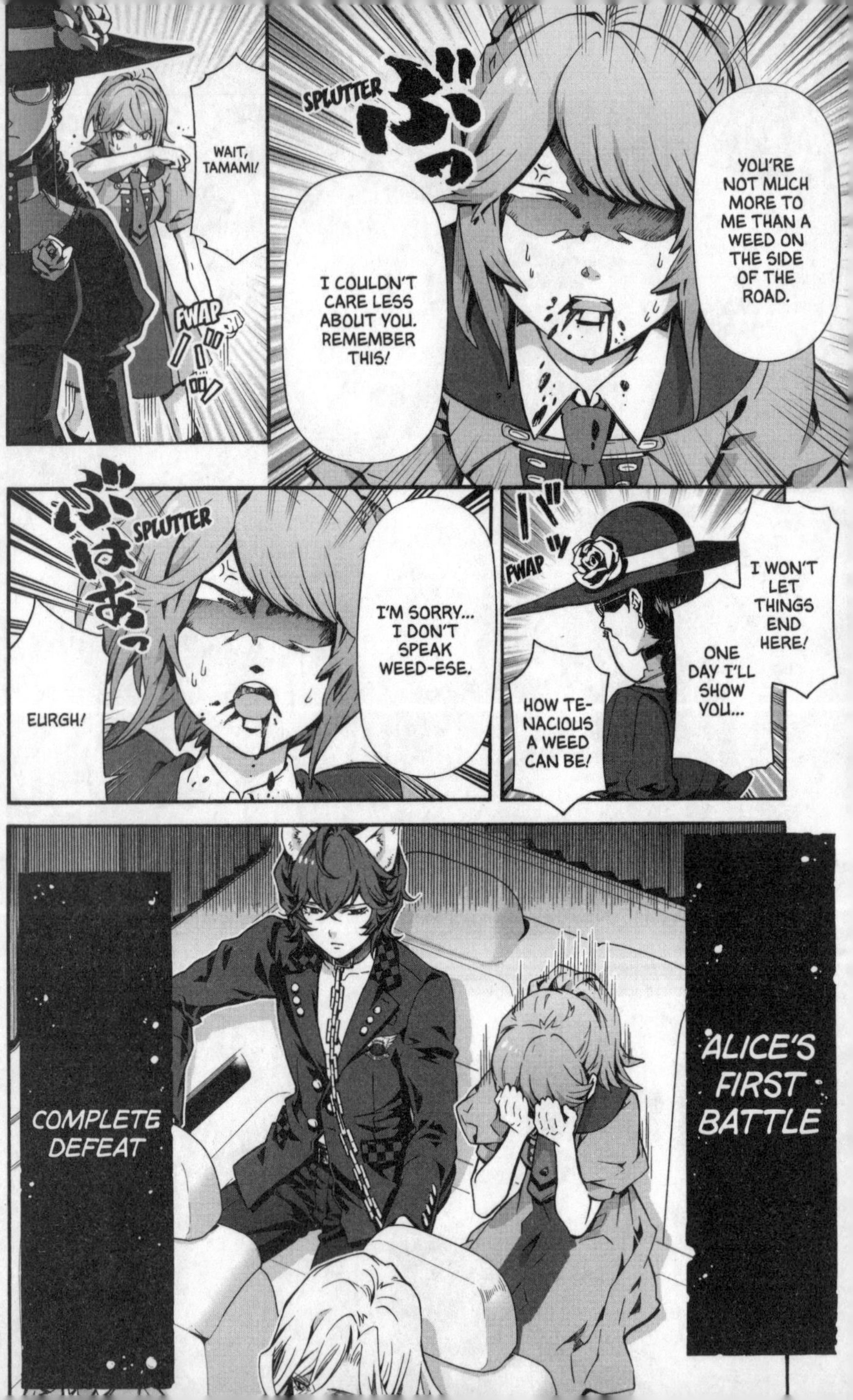
SPLUTTER
ぶっ
YOU'RE NOT MUCH MORE TO ME THAN A WEED ON THE SIDE OF THE ROAD.
I COULDN'T CARE LESS ABOUT YOU. REMEMBER THIS!
WAIT, TAMAMI!
FWAP
FWAP
I WON'T LET THINGS END HERE!
ONE DAY I'LL SHOW YOU...
HOW TE-NACIOUS A WEED CAN BE!
ぶはあっ
SPLUTTER
I'M SORRY... I DON'T SPEAK WEED-ESE.
EURGH!
ALICE'S FIRST BATTLE
COMPLETE DEFEAT

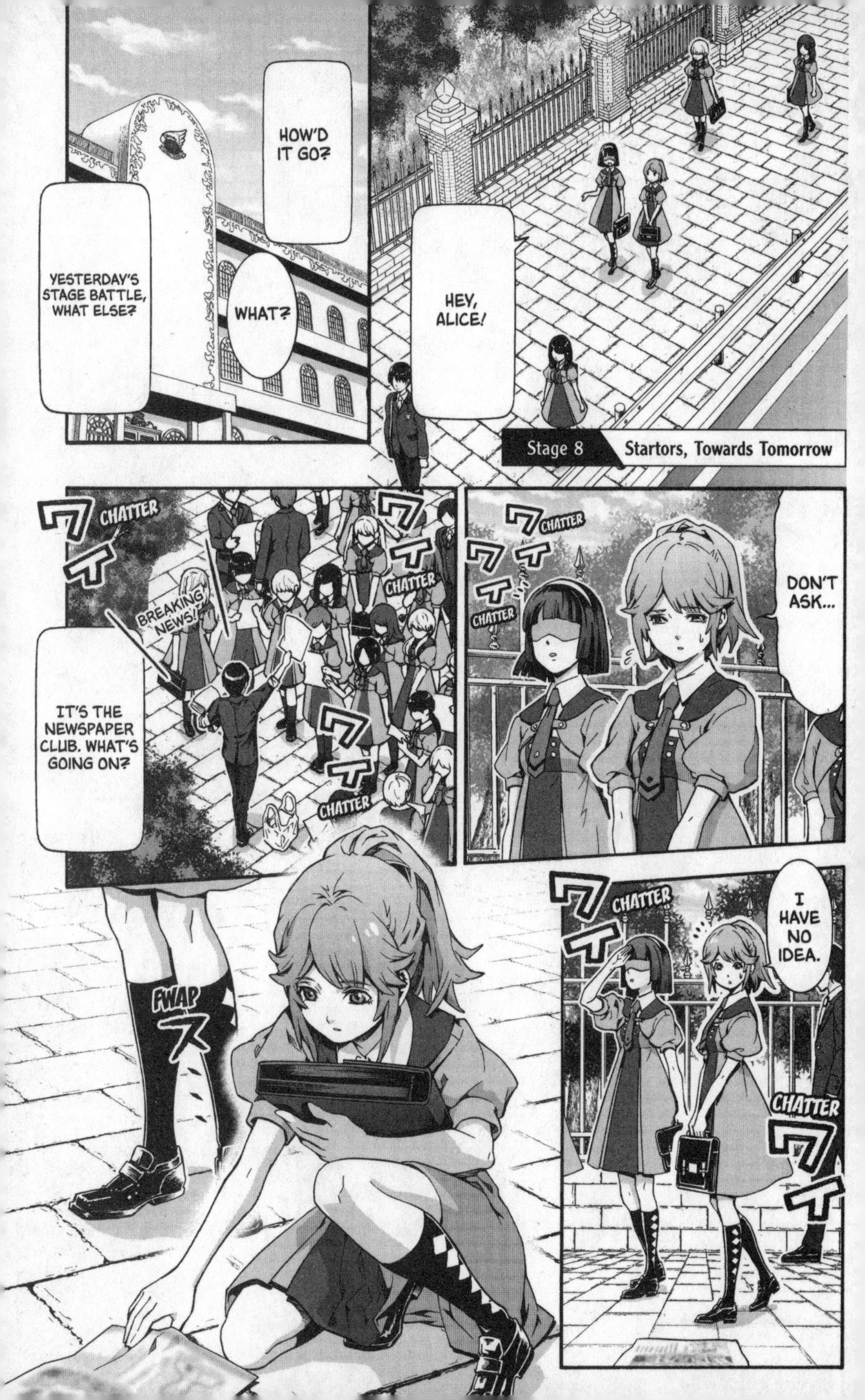
HEY, ALICE!
Stage 8 Startors, Towards Tomorrow
HOW'D IT GO?
WHAT?
YESTERDAY'S STAGE BATTLE, WHAT ELSE?
ワイ CHATTER
ワイ CHATTER
DON'T ASK...
ワイ CHATTER
ワイ CHATTER
BREAKING NEWS!
ワイ CHATTER
IT'S THE NEWSPAPER CLUB. WHAT'S GOING ON?
ワイ CHATTER
I HAVE NO IDEA.
ワイ CHATTER
ス FWAP

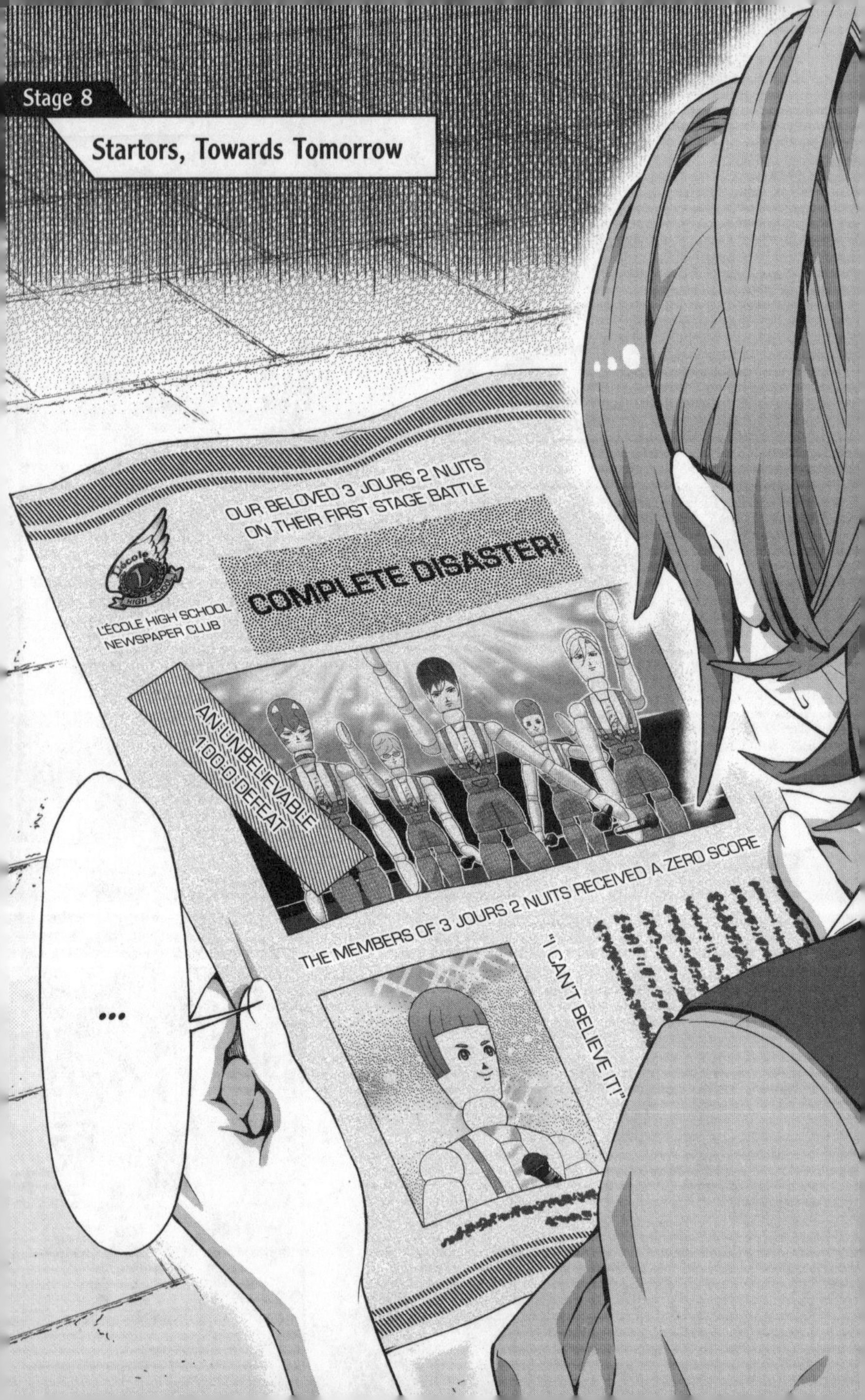
Stage 8
Startors, Towards Tomorrow
OUR BELOVED 3 JOURS 2 NUITS ON THEIR FIRST STAGE BATTLE
COMPLETE DISASTER!
L'ÉCOLE HIGH SCHOOL NEWSPAPER CLUB
AN UNBELIEVABLE 100-0 DEFEAT
THE MEMBERS OF 3 JOURS 2 NUITS RECEIVED A ZERO SCORE
"I CAN'T BELIEVE IT!"
...

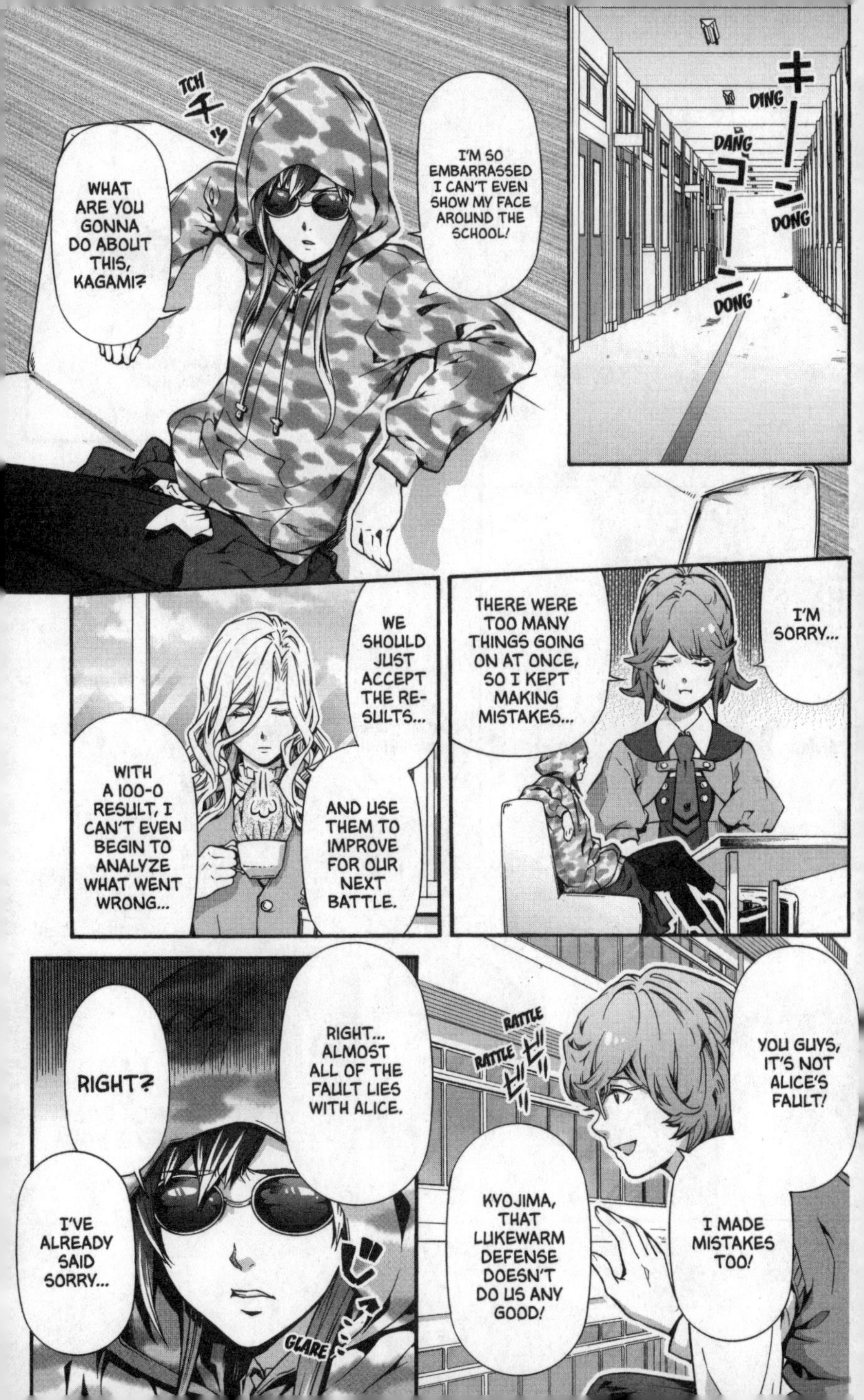
DING
DANG
DONG
DONG
I'M SO EMBARRASSED I CAN'T EVEN SHOW MY FACE AROUND THE SCHOOL!
TCH
WHAT ARE YOU GONNA DO ABOUT THIS, KAGAMI!?
I'M SORRY...
THERE WERE TOO MANY THINGS GOING ON AT ONCE, SO I KEPT MAKING MISTAKES...
WE SHOULD JUST ACCEPT THE RE-SULTS...
AND USE THEM TO IMPROVE FOR OUR NEXT BATTLE.
WITH A 100-0 RESULT, I CAN'T EVEN BEGIN TO ANALYZE WHAT WENT WRONG...
YOU GUYS, IT'S NOT ALICE'S FAULT!
I MADE MISTAKES TOO!
RATTLE
RATTLE
KYOJIMA, THAT LUKEWARM DEFENSE DOESN'T DO US ANY GOOD!
RIGHT... ALMOST ALL OF THE FAULT LIES WITH ALICE.
RIGHT!?
I'VE ALREADY SAID SORRY...
GLARE

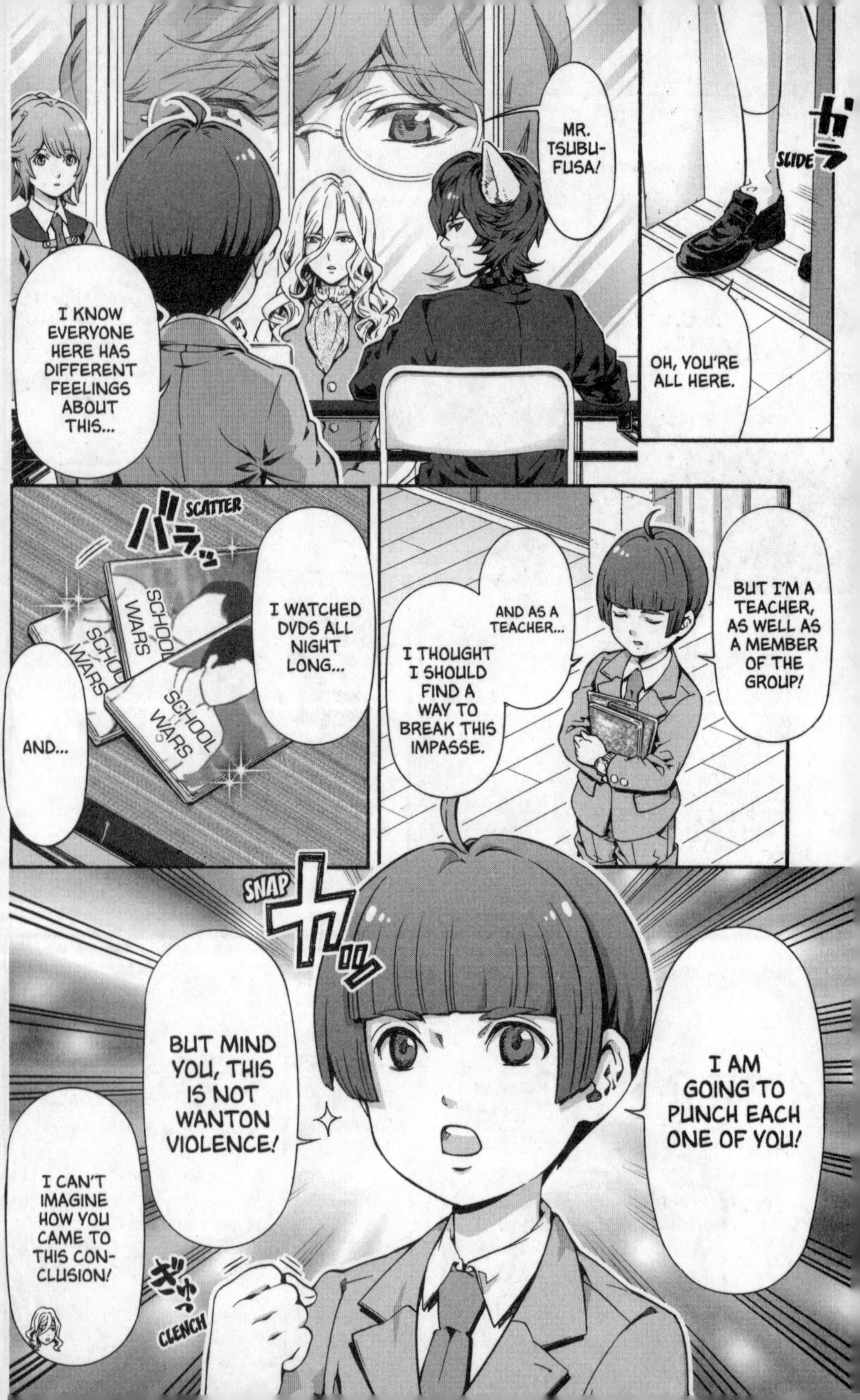
SLIDE
OH, YOU'RE ALL HERE.
MR. TSUBU-FUSA!
I KNOW EVERYONE HERE HAS DIFFERENT FEELINGS ABOUT THIS...
BUT I'M A TEACHER, AS WELL AS A MEMBER OF THE GROUP!
AND AS A TEACHER...
I THOUGHT I SHOULD FIND A WAY TO BREAK THIS IMPASSE.
SCATTER
I WATCHED DVDS ALL NIGHT LONG...
SCHOOL WARS
SCHOOL WARS
SCHOOL WARS
AND...
I AM GOING TO PUNCH EACH ONE OF YOU!
SNAP
BUT MIND YOU, THIS IS NOT WANTON VIOLENCE!
I CAN'T IMAGINE HOW YOU CAME TO THIS CON-CLUSION!
CLENCH

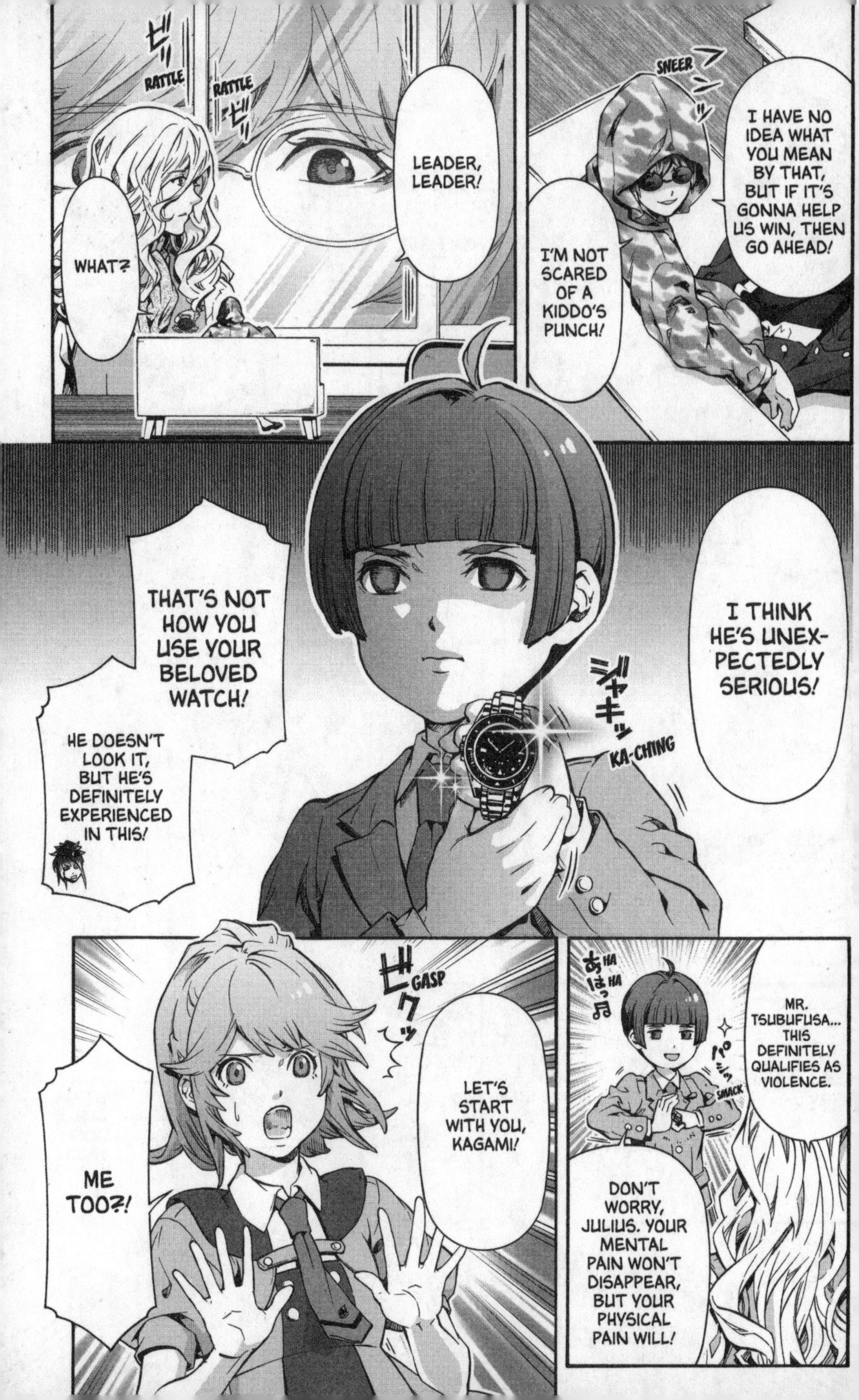
SNEER
I HAVE NO IDEA WHAT YOU MEAN BY THAT, BUT IF IT'S GONNA HELP US WIN, THEN GO AHEAD!
I'M NOT SCARED OF A KIDDO'S PUNCH!
RATTLE
RATTLE
LEADER, LEADER!
WHAT?
I THINK HE'S UNEX-PECTEDLY SERIOUS!
KA-CHING
THAT'S NOT HOW YOU USE YOUR BELOVED WATCH!
HE DOESN'T LOOK IT, BUT HE'S DEFINITELY EXPERIENCED IN THIS!
HA HA
MR. TSUBUFUSA... THIS DEFINITELY QUALIFIES AS VIOLENCE.
SMACK
DON'T WORRY, JULIUS. YOUR MENTAL PAIN WON'T DISAPPEAR, BUT YOUR PHYSICAL PAIN WILL!
GASP
LET'S START WITH YOU, KAGAMI!
ME TOO?!

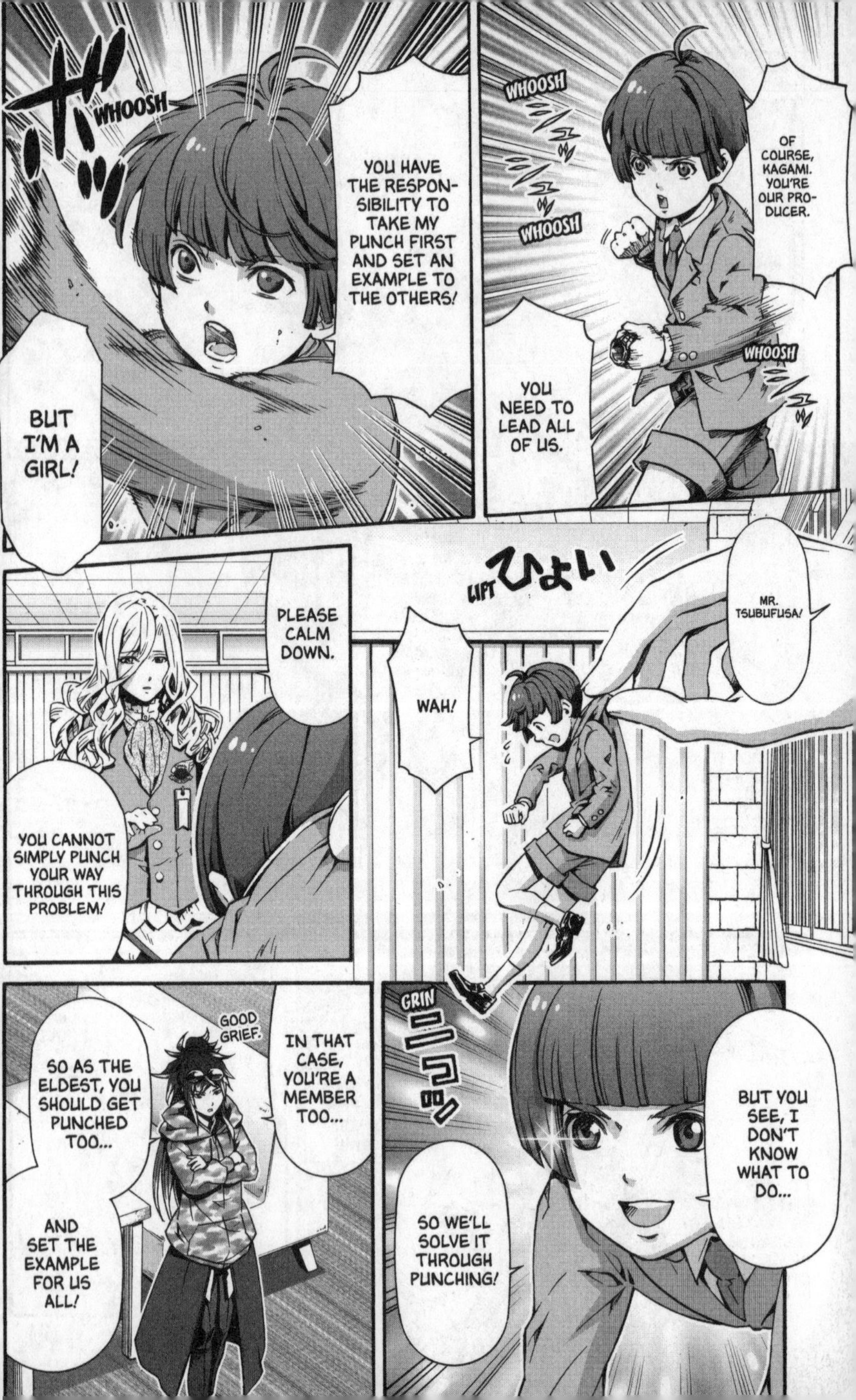
WHOOSH
OF COURSE, KAGAMI. YOU'RE OUR PRODUCER.
WHOOSH
YOU NEED TO LEAD ALL OF US.
WHOOSH
WHOOSH
YOU HAVE THE RESPONSIBILITY TO TAKE MY PUNCH FIRST AND SET AN EXAMPLE TO THE OTHERS!
BUT I'M A GIRL!
MR. TSUBUFUSA!
LIFT ひょい
WAH!
PLEASE CALM DOWN.
YOU CANNOT SIMPLY PUNCH YOUR WAY THROUGH THIS PROBLEM!
GRIN
BUT YOU SEE, I DON'T KNOW WHAT TO DO...
SO WE'LL SOLVE IT THROUGH PUNCHING!
IN THAT CASE, YOU'RE A MEMBER TOO...
GOOD GRIEF.
SO AS THE ELDEST, YOU SHOULD GET PUNCHED TOO...
AND SET THE EXAMPLE FOR US ALL!

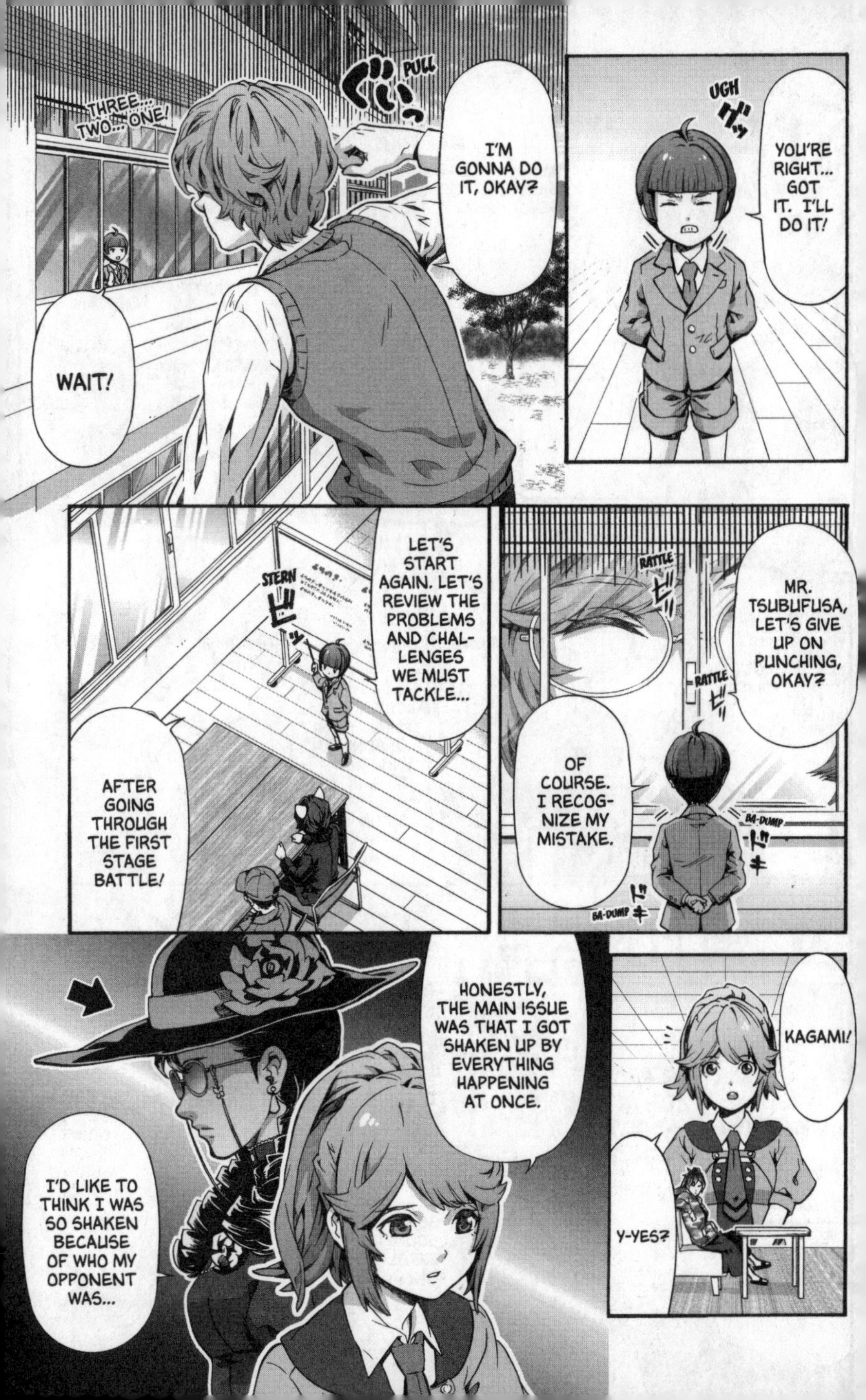
UGH
YOU'RE RIGHT... GOT IT. I'LL DO IT!
PULL
I'M GONNA DO IT, OKAY?
THREE... TWO... ONE!
WAIT!
RATTLE
RATTLE
MR. TSUBUFUSA, LET'S GIVE UP ON PUNCHING, OKAY?
OF COURSE. I RECOGNIZE MY MISTAKE.
BA-DUMP
BA-DUMP
LET'S START AGAIN. LET'S REVIEW THE PROBLEMS AND CHALLENGES WE MUST TACKLE...
STERN
AFTER GOING THROUGH THE FIRST STAGE BATTLE!
KAGAMI!
Y-YES?
HONESTLY, THE MAIN ISSUE WAS THAT I GOT SHAKEN UP BY EVERYTHING HAPPENING AT ONCE.
I'D LIKE TO THINK I WAS SO SHAKEN BECAUSE OF WHO MY OPPONENT WAS...

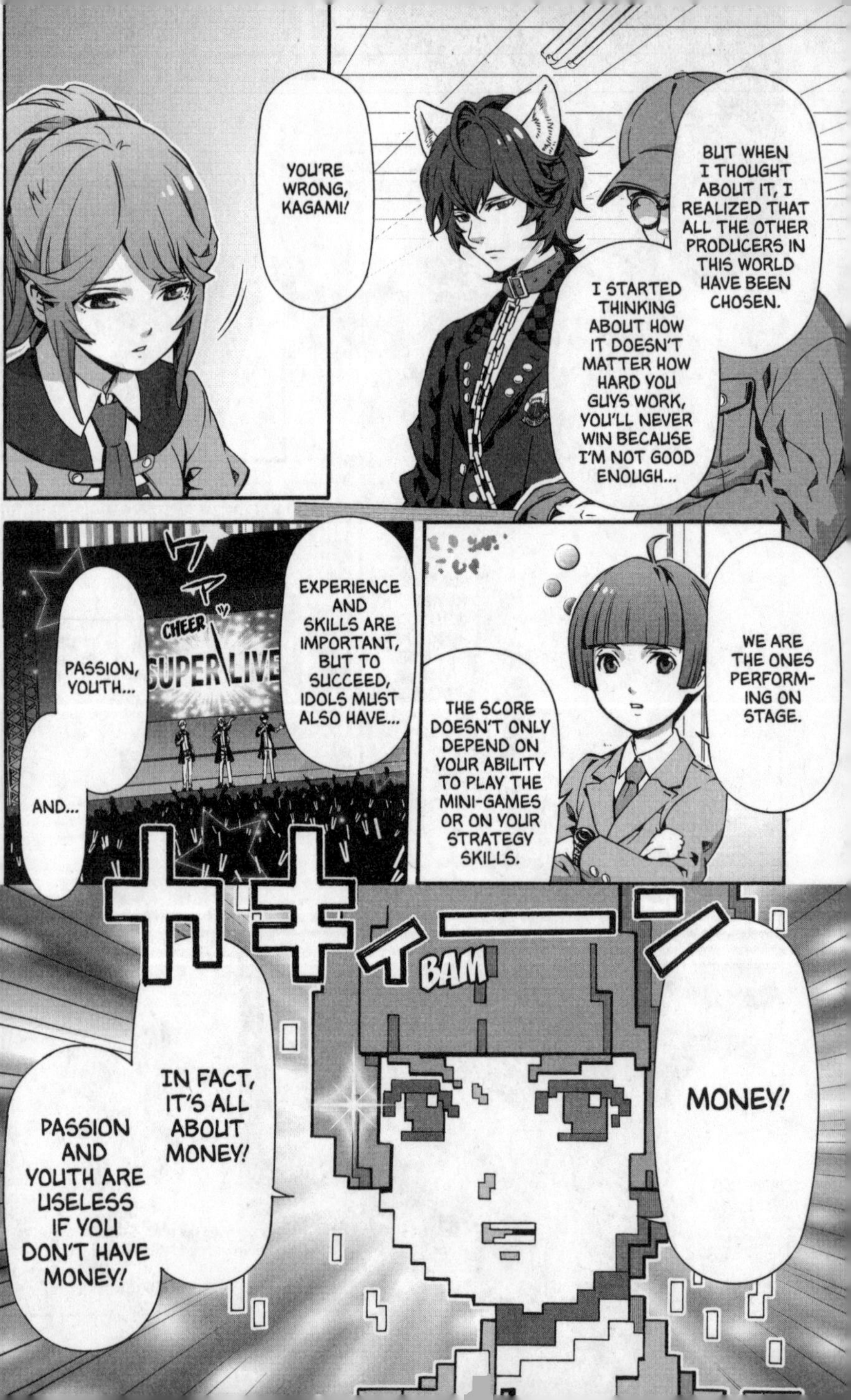
BUT WHEN I THOUGHT ABOUT IT, I REALIZED THAT ALL THE OTHER PRODUCERS IN THIS WORLD HAVE BEEN CHOSEN.
I STARTED THINKING ABOUT HOW IT DOESN'T MATTER HOW HARD YOU GUYS WORK, YOU'LL NEVER WIN BECAUSE I'M NOT GOOD ENOUGH...
YOU'RE WRONG, KAGAMI!
WE ARE THE ONES PERFORMING ON STAGE.
THE SCORE DOESN'T ONLY DEPEND ON YOUR ABILITY TO PLAY THE MINI-GAMES OR ON YOUR STRATEGY SKILLS.
EXPERIENCE AND SKILLS ARE IMPORTANT, BUT TO SUCCEED, IDOLS MUST ALSO HAVE...
ワァッ
CHEER
SUPER LIVE
PASSION, YOUTH...
AND...
カキィーン
BAM
MONEY!
IN FACT, IT'S ALL ABOUT MONEY!
PASSION AND YOUTH ARE USELESS IF YOU DON'T HAVE MONEY!

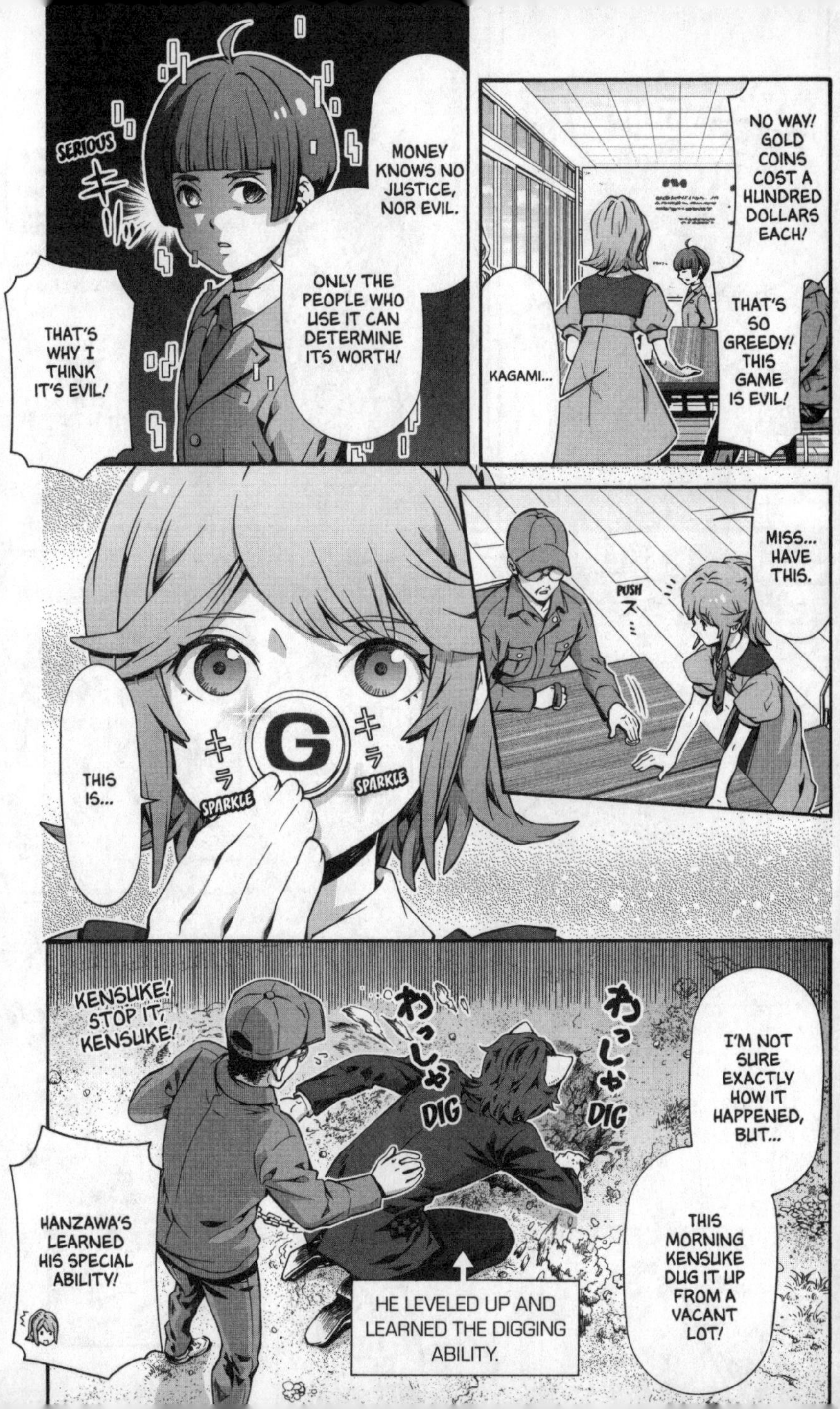
NO WAY! GOLD COINS COST A HUNDRED DOLLARS EACH!
THAT'S SO GREEDY! THIS GAME IS EVIL!
KAGAMI...
SERIOUS
MONEY KNOWS NO JUSTICE, NOR EVIL.
ONLY THE PEOPLE WHO USE IT CAN DETERMINE ITS WORTH!
THAT'S WHY I THINK IT'S EVIL!
MISS... HAVE THIS.
PUSH
SPARKLE
SPARKLE
THIS IS...
I'M NOT SURE EXACTLY HOW IT HAPPENED, BUT...
THIS MORNING KENSUKE DUG IT UP FROM A VACANT LOT!
DIG
DIG
KENSUKE! STOP IT, KENSUKE!
HANZAWA'S LEARNED HIS SPECIAL ABILITY!
HE LEVELED UP AND LEARNED THE DIGGING ABILITY.

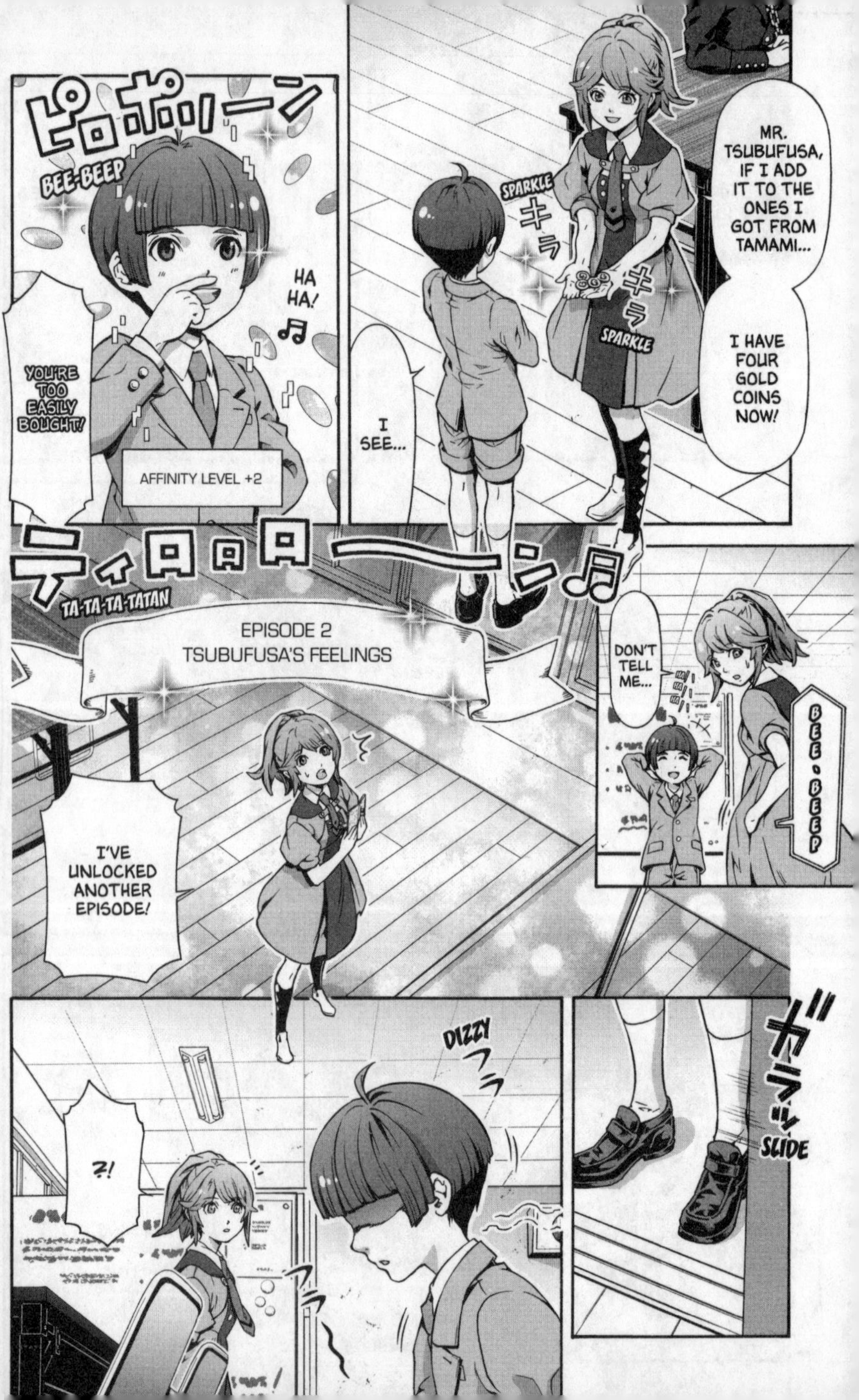
MR. TSUBUFUSA, IF I ADD IT TO THE ONES I GOT FROM TAMAMI...
SPARKLE
SPARKLE
I HAVE FOUR GOLD COINS NOW!
I SEE...
BEE-BEEP
HA HA!
YOU'RE TOO EASILY BOUGHT!
AFFINITY LEVEL +2
DON'T TELL ME...
BEE-BEEP
TA-TA-TA-TATAN
EPISODE 2
TSUBUFUSA'S FEELINGS
I'VE UNLOCKED ANOTHER EPISODE!
SLIDE
DIZZY
?!

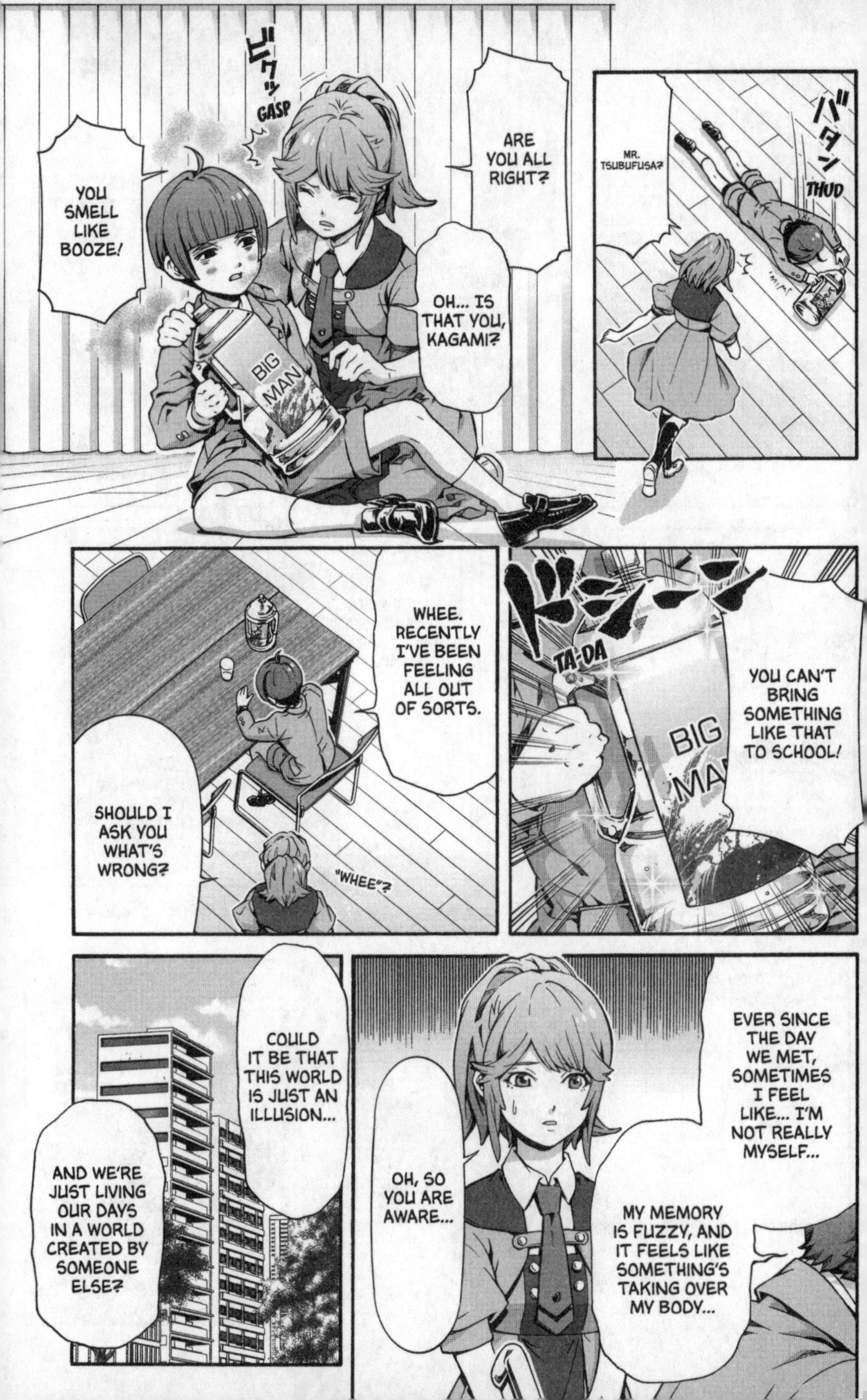

バタン
THUD
MR. TSUBUFUSA?
ARE YOU ALL RIGHT?
OH... IS THAT YOU, KAGAMI?
ビクッ
GASP
YOU SMELL LIKE BOOZE!
TA-DA
YOU CAN'T BRING SOMETHING LIKE THAT TO SCHOOL!
BIG MAN
WHEE. RECENTLY I'VE BEEN FEELING ALL OUT OF SORTS.
SHOULD I ASK YOU WHAT'S WRONG?
"WHEE"?
EVER SINCE THE DAY WE MET, SOMETIMES I FEEL LIKE... I'M NOT REALLY MYSELF...
MY MEMORY IS FUZZY, AND IT FEELS LIKE SOMETHING'S TAKING OVER MY BODY...
OH, SO YOU ARE AWARE...
COULD IT BE THAT THIS WORLD IS JUST AN ILLUSION...
AND WE'RE JUST LIVING OUR DAYS IN A WORLD CREATED BY SOMEONE ELSE?

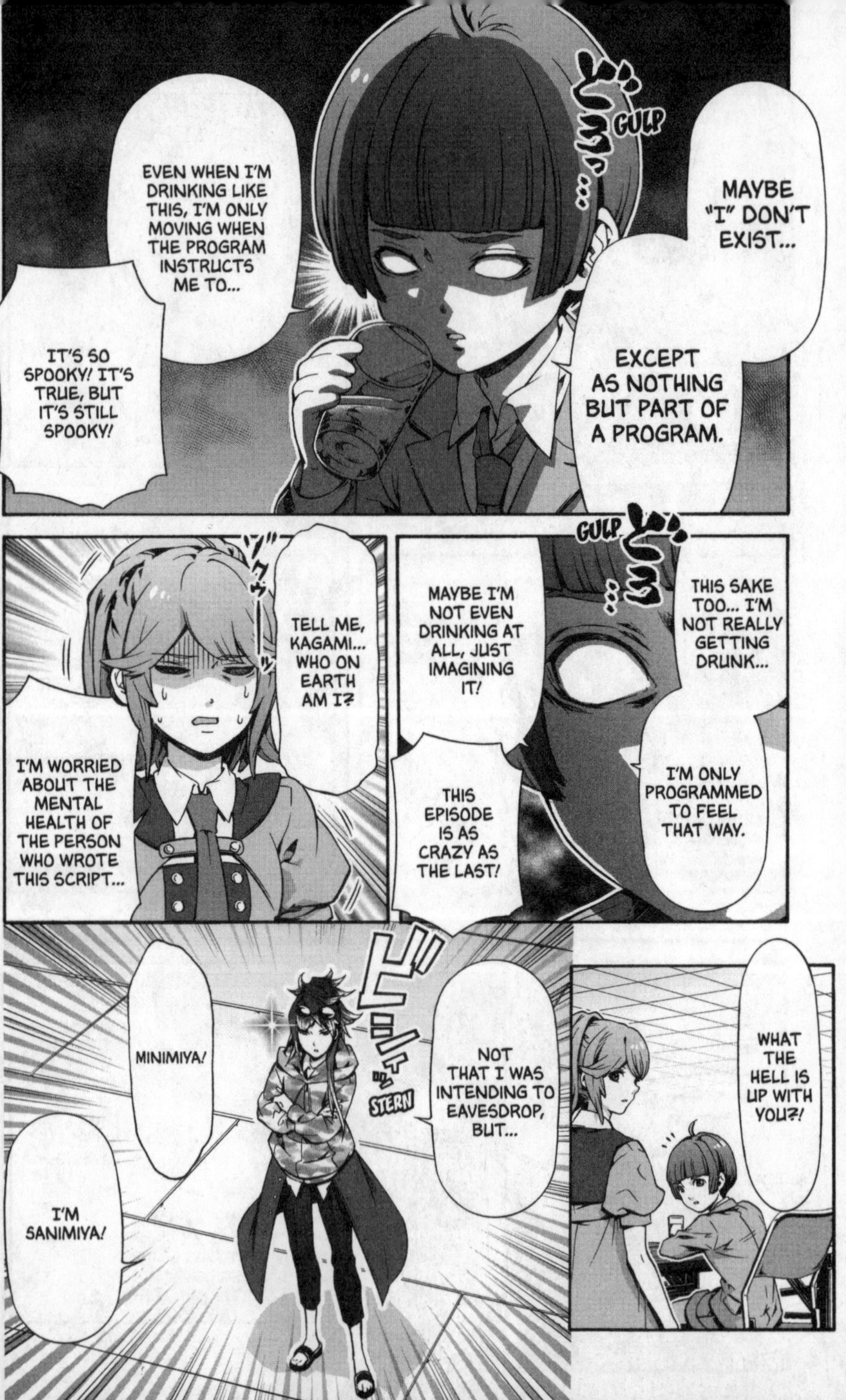
GULP
MAYBE "I" DON'T EXIST...
EXCEPT AS NOTHING BUT PART OF A PROGRAM.
EVEN WHEN I'M DRINKING LIKE THIS, I'M ONLY MOVING WHEN THE PROGRAM INSTRUCTS ME TO...
IT'S SO SPOOKY! IT'S TRUE, BUT IT'S STILL SPOOKY!
GULP
THIS SAKE TOO... I'M NOT REALLY GETTING DRUNK...
MAYBE I'M NOT EVEN DRINKING AT ALL, JUST IMAGINING IT!
I'M ONLY PROGRAMMED TO FEEL THAT WAY.
THIS EPISODE IS AS CRAZY AS THE LAST!
TELL ME, KAGAMI... WHO ON EARTH AM I?
I'M WORRIED ABOUT THE MENTAL HEALTH OF THE PERSON WHO WROTE THIS SCRIPT...
WHAT THE HELL IS UP WITH YOU?!
STERN
NOT THAT I WAS INTENDING TO EAVESDROP, BUT...
MINIMIYA!
I'M SANIMIYA!

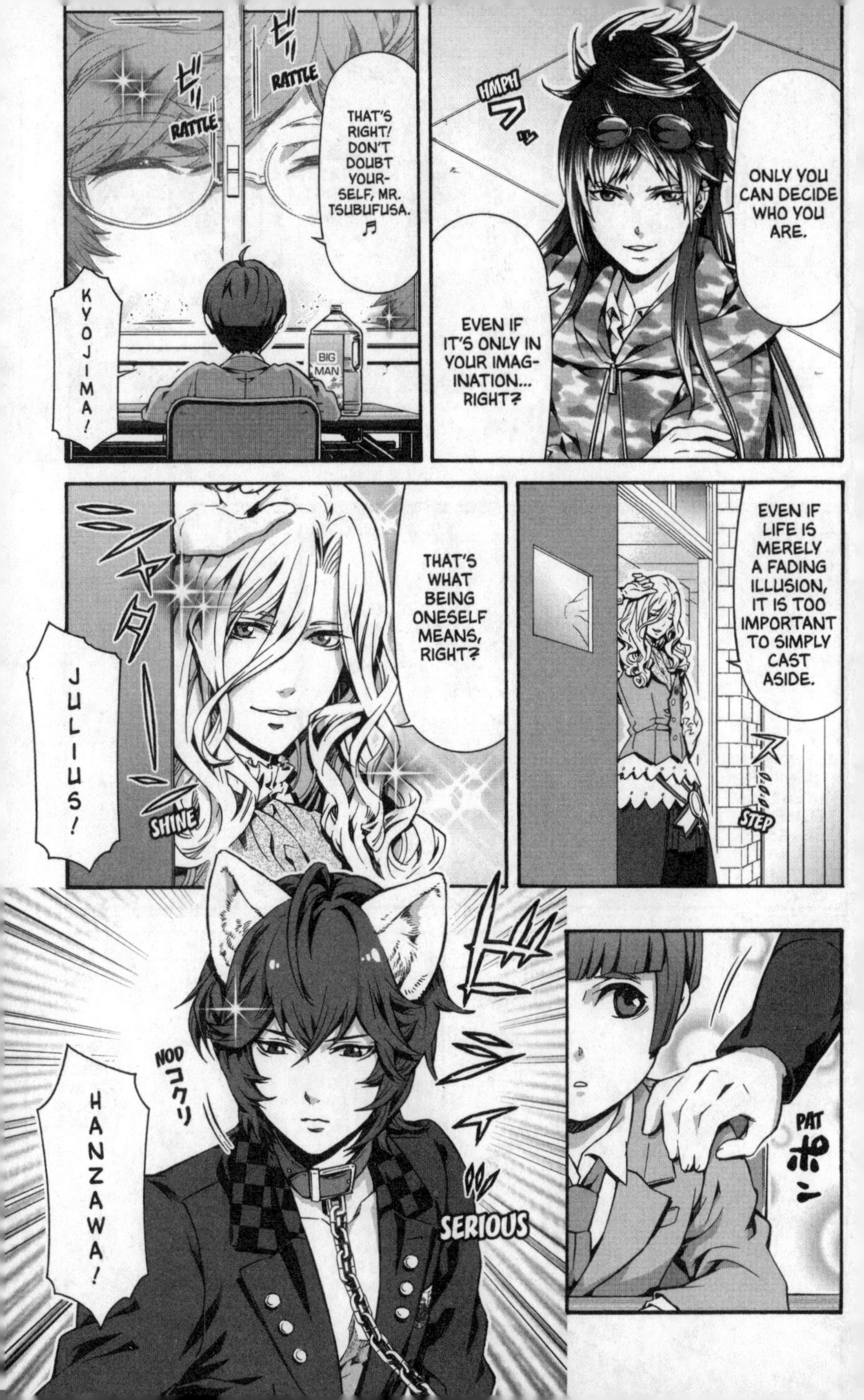
HMPH
ONLY YOU CAN DECIDE WHO YOU ARE.
EVEN IF IT'S ONLY IN YOUR IMAGINATION... RIGHT?
RATTLE
THAT'S RIGHT! DON'T DOUBT YOURSELF, MR. TSUBUFUSA. ♬
RATTLE
BIG MAN
KYOJIMA!
EVEN IF LIFE IS MERELY A FADING ILLUSION, IT IS TOO IMPORTANT TO SIMPLY CAST ASIDE.
STEP
THAT'S WHAT BEING ONESELF MEANS, RIGHT?
SHINE
JULIUS!
PAT
NOD
SERIOUS
HANZAWA!

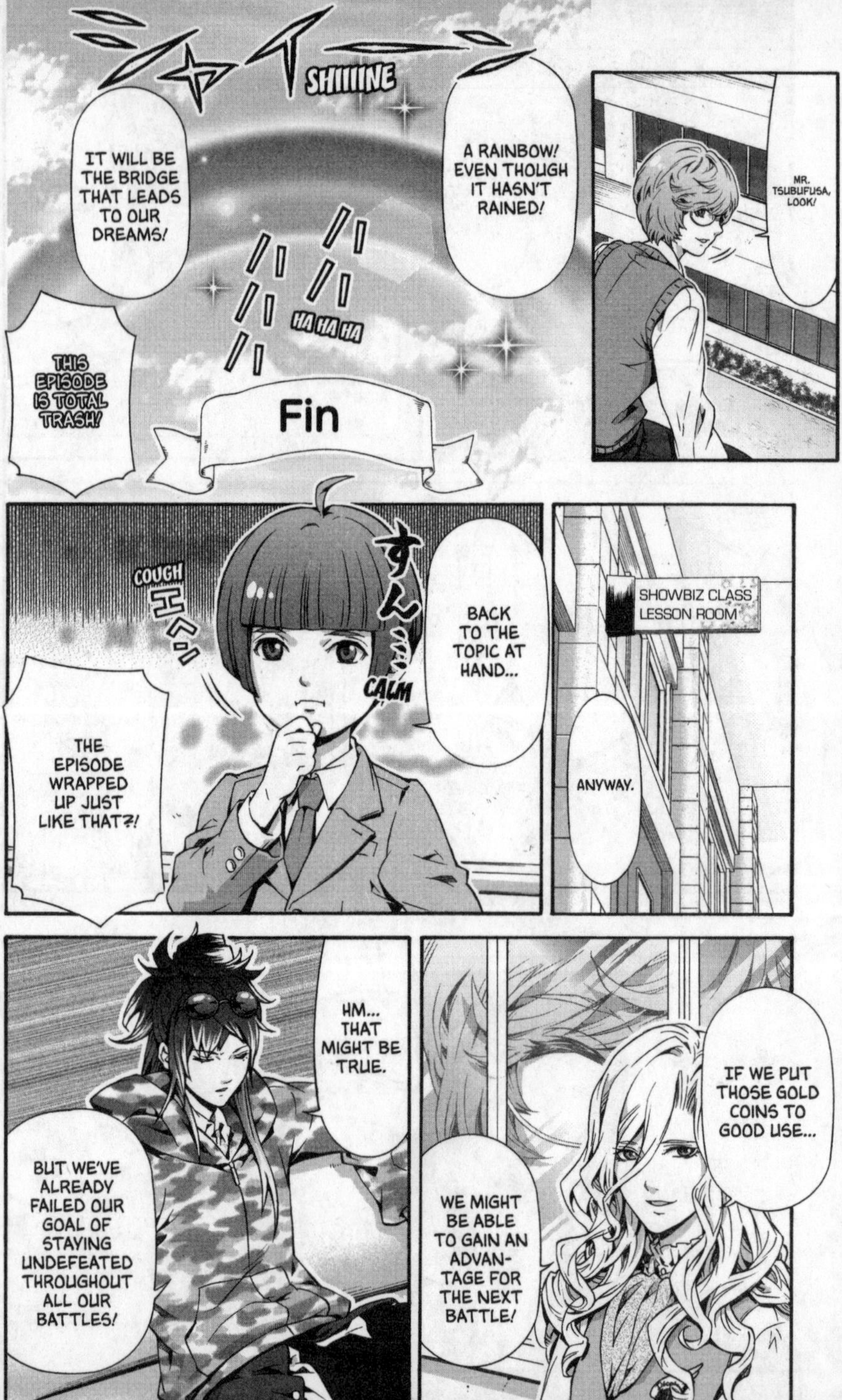
MR. TSUBUFUSA, LOOK!
A RAINBOW! EVEN THOUGH IT HASN'T RAINED!
SHIIIINE
IT WILL BE THE BRIDGE THAT LEADS TO OUR DREAMS!
HA HA HA
Fin
THIS EPISODE IS TOTAL TRASH!
SHOWBIZ CLASS LESSON ROOM
ANYWAY.
BACK TO THE TOPIC AT HAND...
CALM
COUGH
THE EPISODE WRAPPED UP JUST LIKE THAT?!
IF WE PUT THOSE GOLD COINS TO GOOD USE...
WE MIGHT BE ABLE TO GAIN AN ADVANTAGE FOR THE NEXT BATTLE!
HM... THAT MIGHT BE TRUE.
BUT WE'VE ALREADY FAILED OUR GOAL OF STAYING UNDEFEATED THROUGHOUT ALL OUR BATTLES!

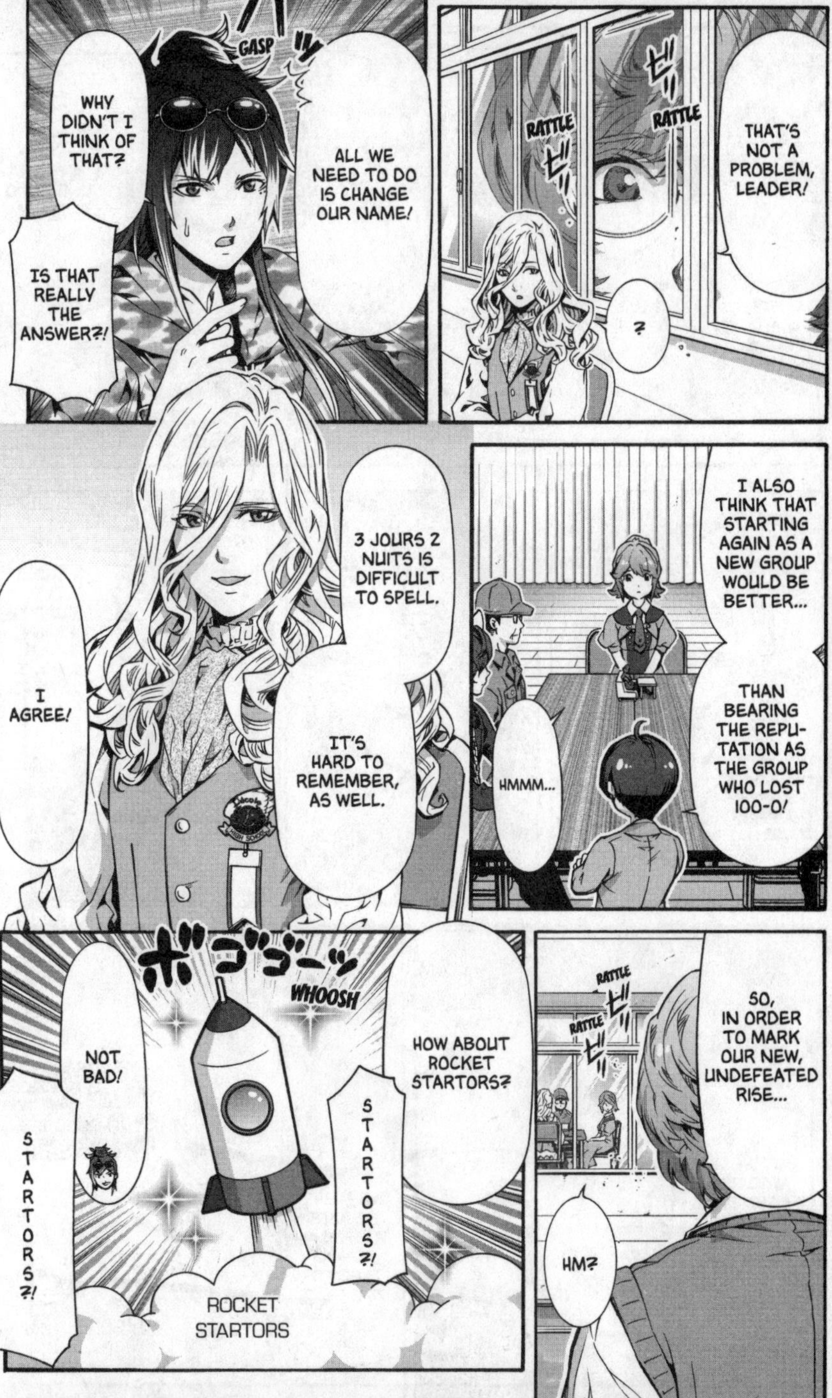
THAT'S NOT A PROBLEM, LEADER!
RATTLE
RATTLE
?
ALL WE NEED TO DO IS CHANGE OUR NAME!
GASP
WHY DIDN'T I THINK OF THAT?
IS THAT REALLY THE ANSWER?!
I ALSO THINK THAT STARTING AGAIN AS A NEW GROUP WOULD BE BETTER...
THAN BEARING THE REPUTATION AS THE GROUP WHO LOST 100-0!
HMMM...
3 JOURS 2 NUITS IS DIFFICULT TO SPELL.
IT'S HARD TO REMEMBER, AS WELL.
I AGREE!
RATTLE
RATTLE
SO, IN ORDER TO MARK OUR NEW, UNDEFEATED RISE...
HM?
HOW ABOUT ROCKET STARTORS?
WHOOSH
STARTORS?!
NOT BAD!
STARTORS?!
ROCKET STARTORS

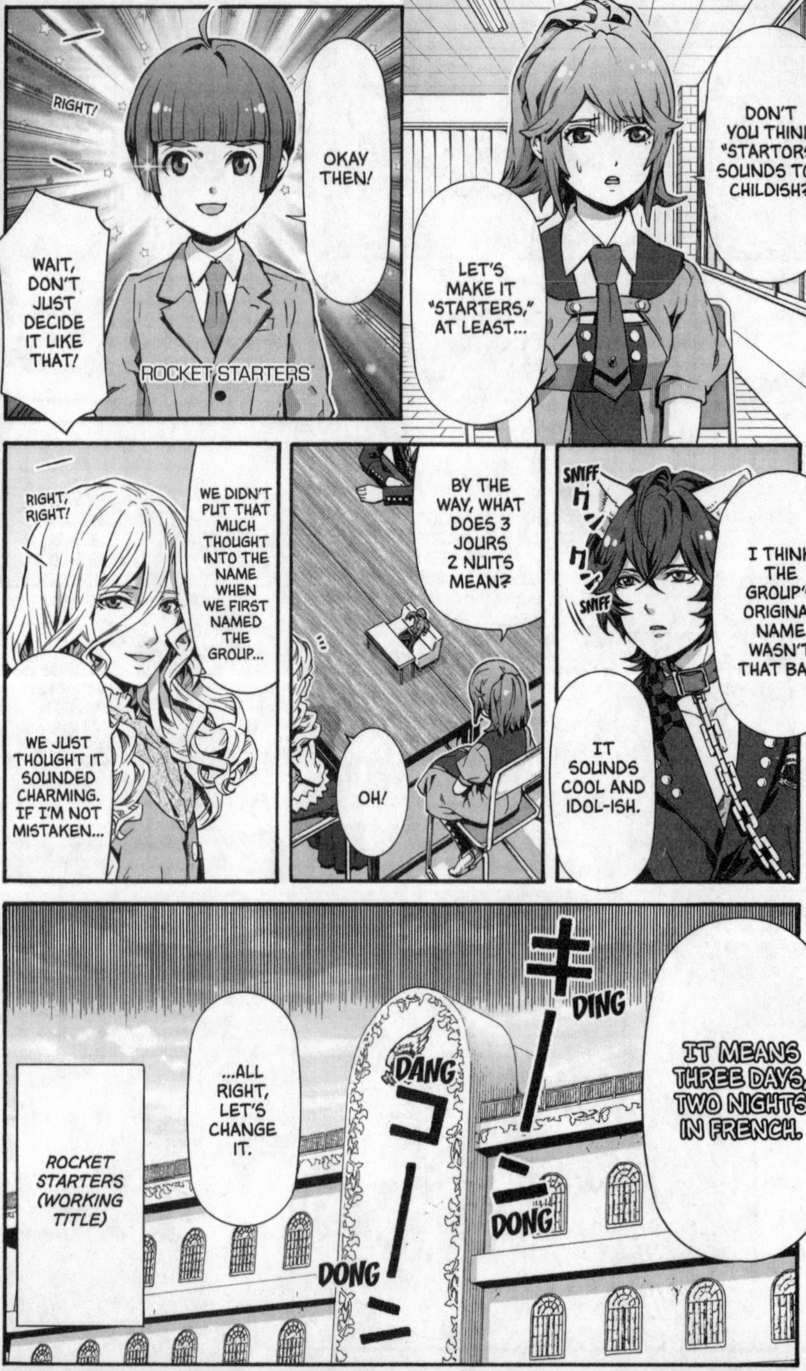
DON'T YOU THINK "STARTORS" SOUNDS TOO CHILDISH?
LET'S MAKE IT "STARTERS," AT LEAST...
OKAY THEN!
RIGHT!
ROCKET STARTERS
WAIT, DON'T JUST DECIDE IT LIKE THAT!
SNIFF
SNIFF
I THINK THE GROUP'S ORIGINAL NAME WASN'T THAT BAD.
IT SOUNDS COOL AND IDOL-ISH.
BY THE WAY, WHAT DOES 3 JOURS 2 NUITS MEAN?
OH!
WE DIDN'T PUT THAT MUCH THOUGHT INTO THE NAME WHEN WE FIRST NAMED THE GROUP...
RIGHT, RIGHT!
WE JUST THOUGHT IT SOUNDED CHARMING. IF I'M NOT MISTAKEN...
IT MEANS THREE DAYS, TWO NIGHTS IN FRENCH.
DING
DONG
DANG
...ALL RIGHT, LET'S CHANGE IT.
DONG
ROCKET STARTERS (WORKING TITLE)

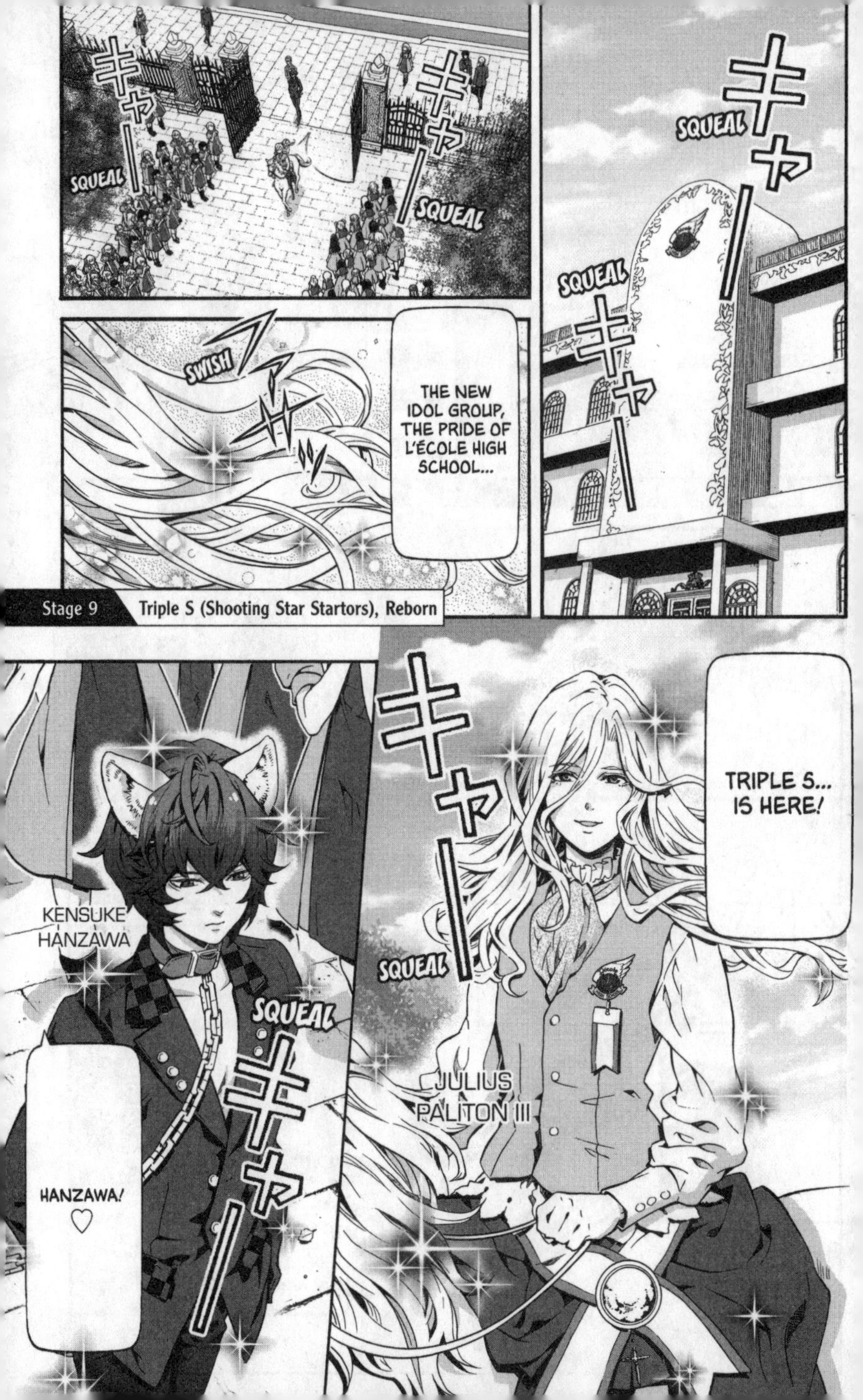
SQUEAL
キャー
SQUEAL
キャー
SQUEAL
キャー
SQUEAL
キャー
THE NEW IDOL GROUP, THE PRIDE OF L'ÉCOLE HIGH SCHOOL...
SWISH
Stage 9
Triple S (Shooting Star Startors), Reborn
TRIPLE S... IS HERE!
キャー
SQUEAL
JULIUS PALITON III
KENSUKE HANZAWA
SQUEAL
キャー
HANZAWA! ♡

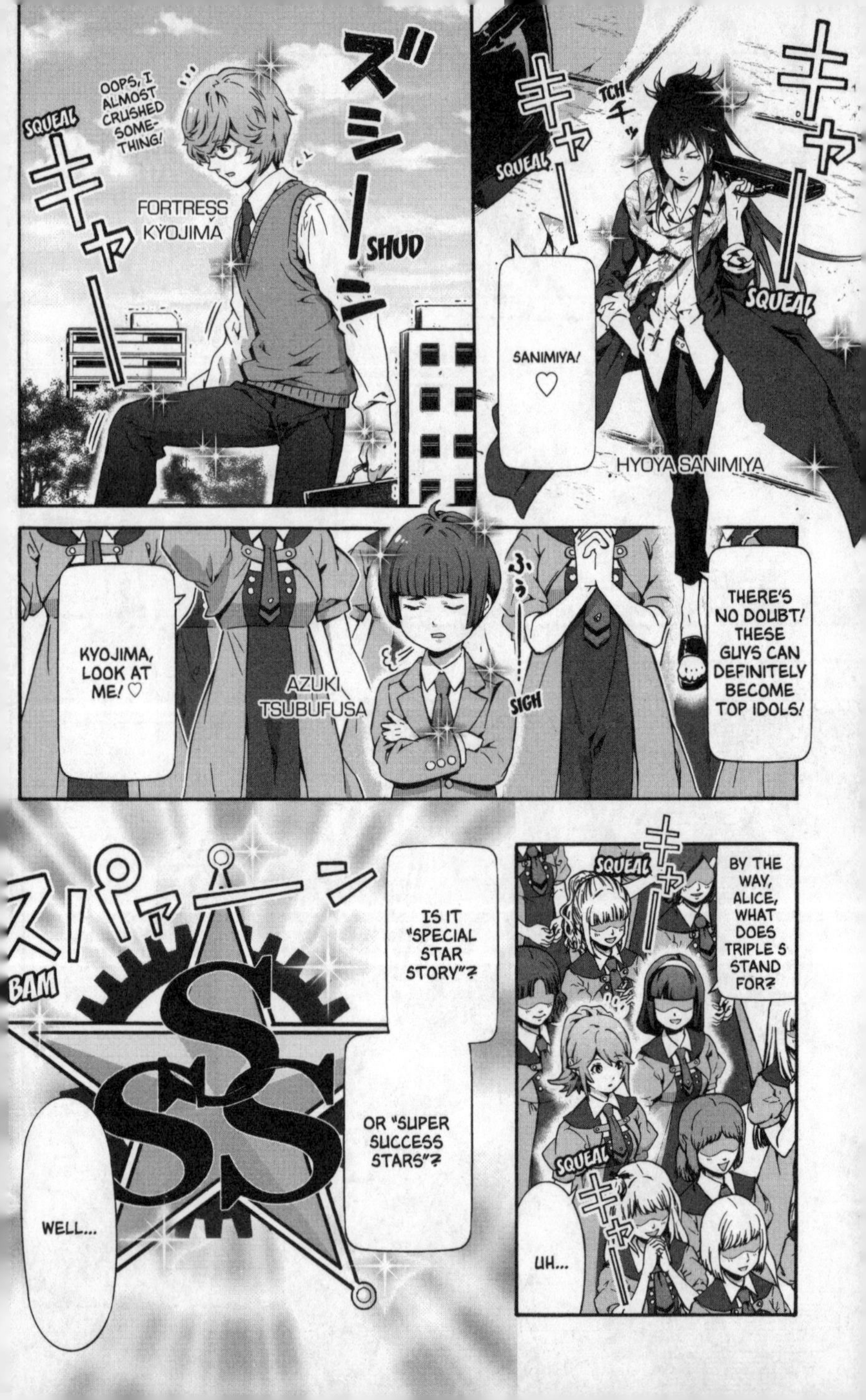
キャー
TCH チッ
SQUEAL キャー
SANIMIYA! ♡
HYOYA SANIMIYA
SQUEAL
ズシーン
SHUD
OOPS, I ALMOST CRUSHED SOME-THING!
FORTRESS KYOJIMA
SQUEAL キャー
THERE'S NO DOUBT! THESE GUYS CAN DEFINITELY BECOME TOP IDOLS!
SIGH ふぅ
AZUKI TSUBUFUSA
KYOJIMA, LOOK AT ME! ♡
BY THE WAY, ALICE, WHAT DOES TRIPLE S STAND FOR?
SQUEAL キャー
UH...
SQUEAL キャー
IS IT "SPECIAL STAR STORY"?
OR "SUPER SUCCESS STARS"?
BAM スパァーン
WELL...

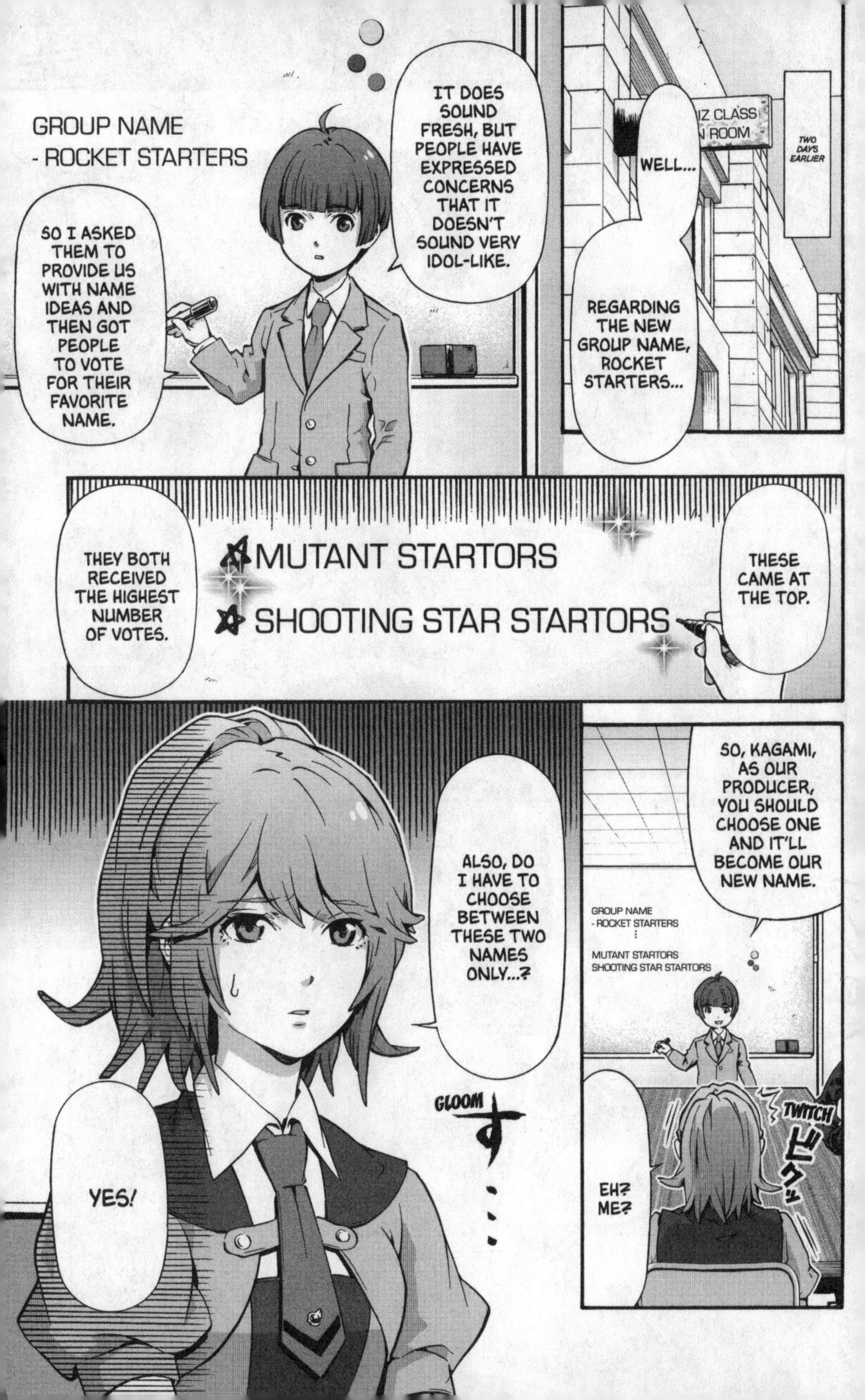
TWO DAYS EARLIER
WELL...
REGARDING THE NEW GROUP NAME, ROCKET STARTERS...
IT DOES SOUND FRESH, BUT PEOPLE HAVE EXPRESSED CONCERNS THAT IT DOESN'T SOUND VERY IDOL-LIKE.
GROUP NAME
- ROCKET STARTERS
SO I ASKED THEM TO PROVIDE US WITH NAME IDEAS AND THEN GOT PEOPLE TO VOTE FOR THEIR FAVORITE NAME.
THESE CAME AT THE TOP.
MUTANT STARTORS
SHOOTING STAR STARTORS
THEY BOTH RECEIVED THE HIGHEST NUMBER OF VOTES.
SO, KAGAMI, AS OUR PRODUCER, YOU SHOULD CHOOSE ONE AND IT'LL BECOME OUR NEW NAME.
GROUP NAME
- ROCKET STARTERS
MUTANT STARTORS
SHOOTING STAR STARTORS
TWITCH
ビクッ
EH? ME?
ALSO, DO I HAVE TO CHOOSE BETWEEN THESE TWO NAMES ONLY...?
GLOOM
す
YES!

Stage 9

Triple S (Shooting Star Startors), Reborn

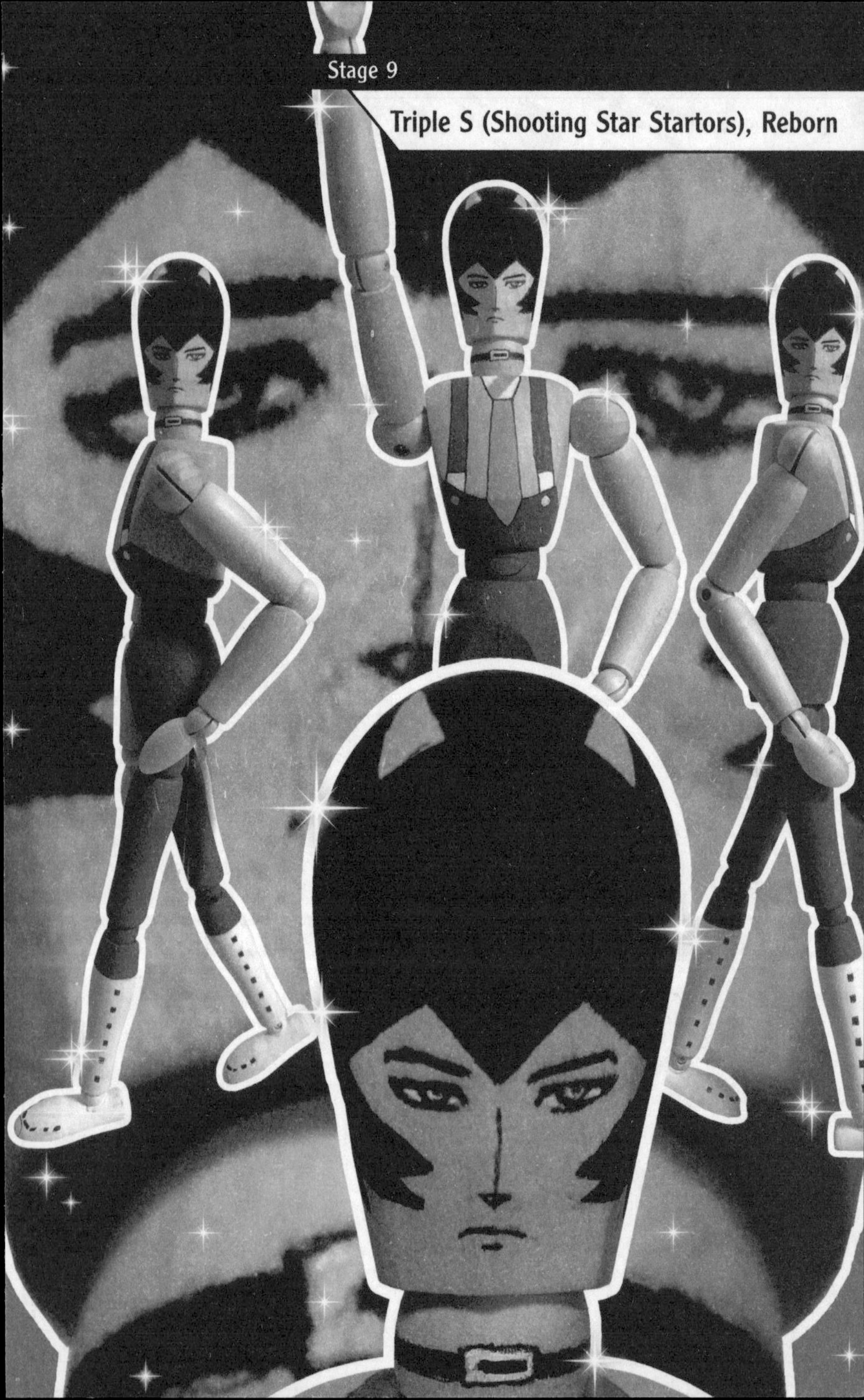

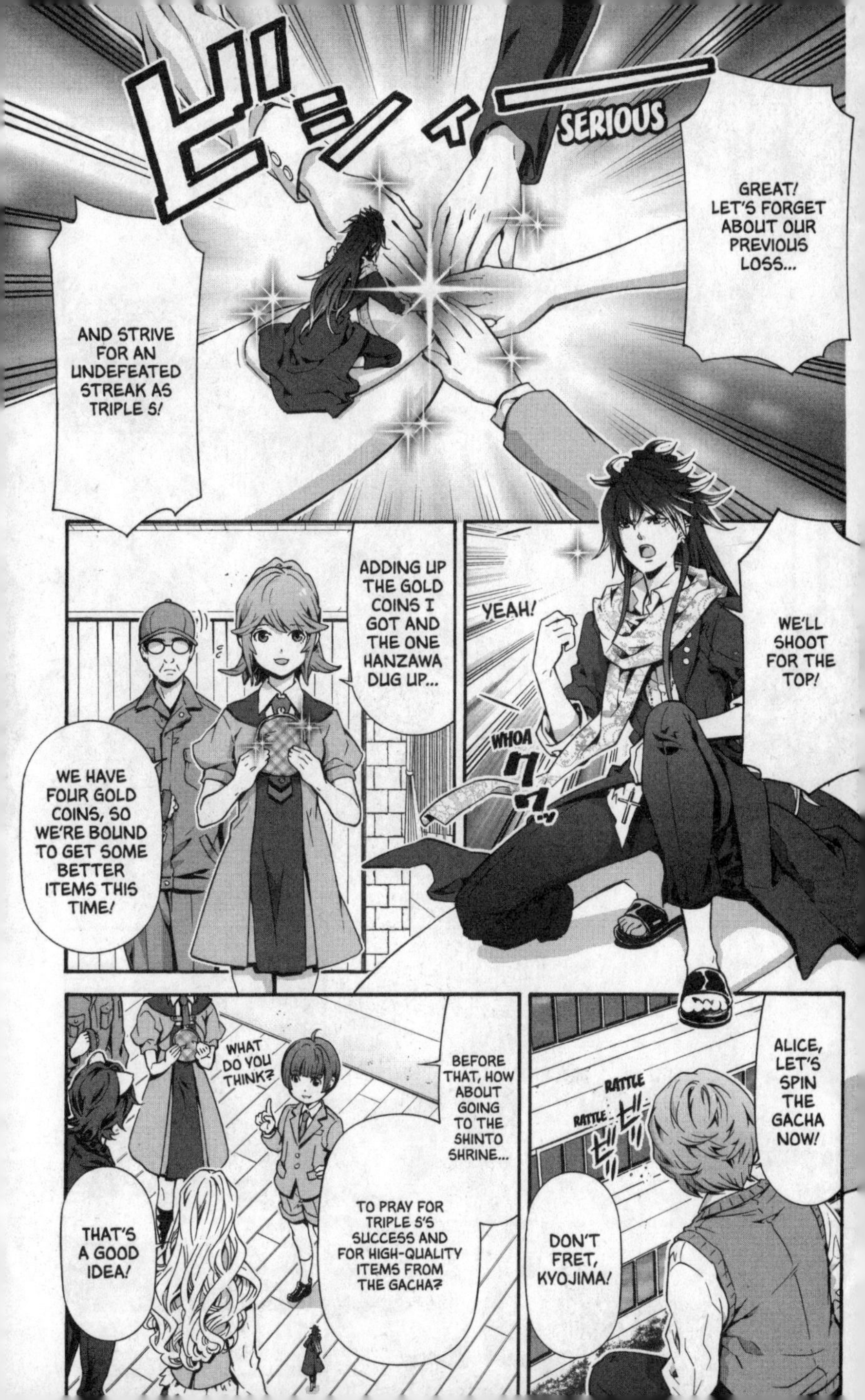
SERIOUS
GREAT! LET'S FORGET ABOUT OUR PREVIOUS LOSS...
AND STRIVE FOR AN UNDEFEATED STREAK AS TRIPLE S!
WE'LL SHOOT FOR THE TOP!
YEAH!
WHOA
ADDING UP THE GOLD COINS I GOT AND THE ONE HANZAWA DUG UP...
WE HAVE FOUR GOLD COINS, SO WE'RE BOUND TO GET SOME BETTER ITEMS THIS TIME!
ALICE, LET'S SPIN THE GACHA NOW!
RATTLE
RATTLE
DON'T FRET, KYOJIMA!
BEFORE THAT, HOW ABOUT GOING TO THE SHINTO SHRINE...
WHAT DO YOU THINK?
TO PRAY FOR TRIPLE S'S SUCCESS AND FOR HIGH-QUALITY ITEMS FROM THE GACHA?
THAT'S A GOOD IDEA!

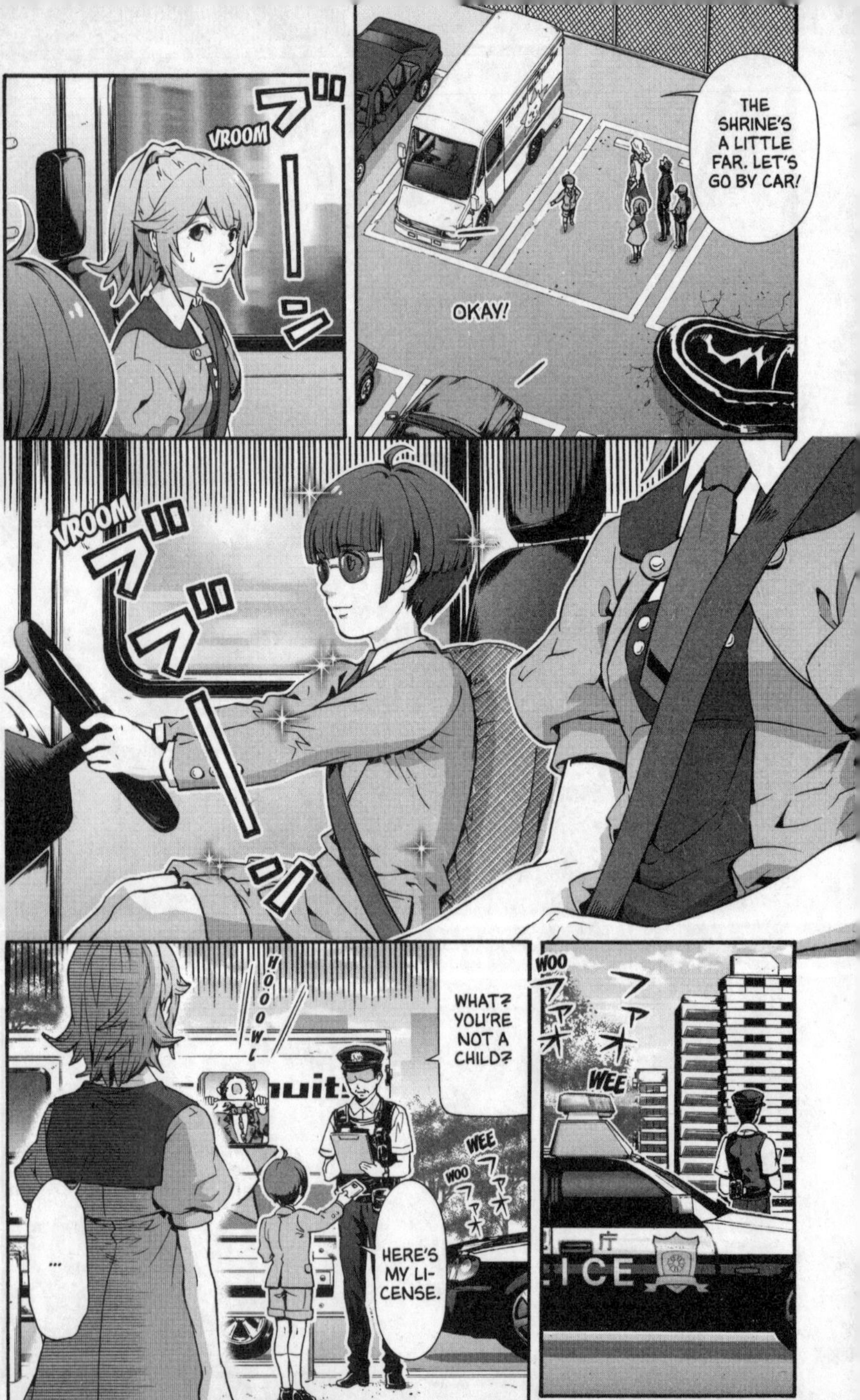
THE SHRINE'S A LITTLE FAR. LET'S GO BY CAR!
OKAY!
VROOM
ブローン
VROOM
ブブーン
WOO
ファオ
ファオ
WEE
WHAT? YOU'RE NOT A CHILD?
HOOOWL
WEE
WOO
ファオ
ファオ
HERE'S MY LICENSE.
...

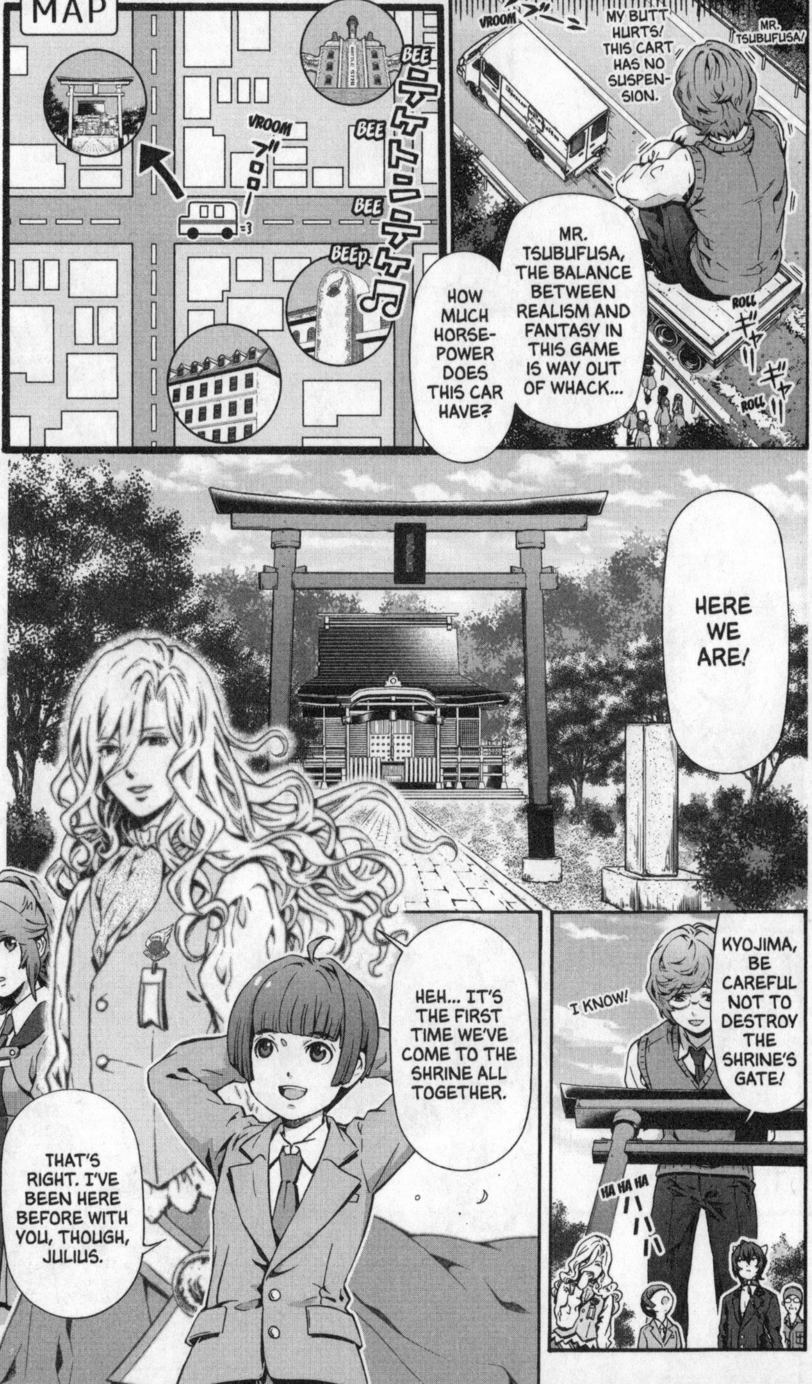
MR. TSUBUFUSA!
MY BUTT HURTS! THIS CART HAS NO SUSPENSION.
VROOM
MR. TSUBUFUSA, THE BALANCE BETWEEN REALISM AND FANTASY IN THIS GAME IS WAY OUT OF WHACK...
ROLL
ROLL
MAP
BEE
BEE
VROOM
BEE
BEEp
HOW MUCH HORSEPOWER DOES THIS CAR HAVE?
HERE WE ARE!
KYOJIMA, BE CAREFUL NOT TO DESTROY THE SHRINE'S GATE!
I KNOW!
HA HA HA
HEH... IT'S THE FIRST TIME WE'VE COME TO THE SHRINE ALL TOGETHER.
THAT'S RIGHT. I'VE BEEN HERE BEFORE WITH YOU, THOUGH, JULIUS.

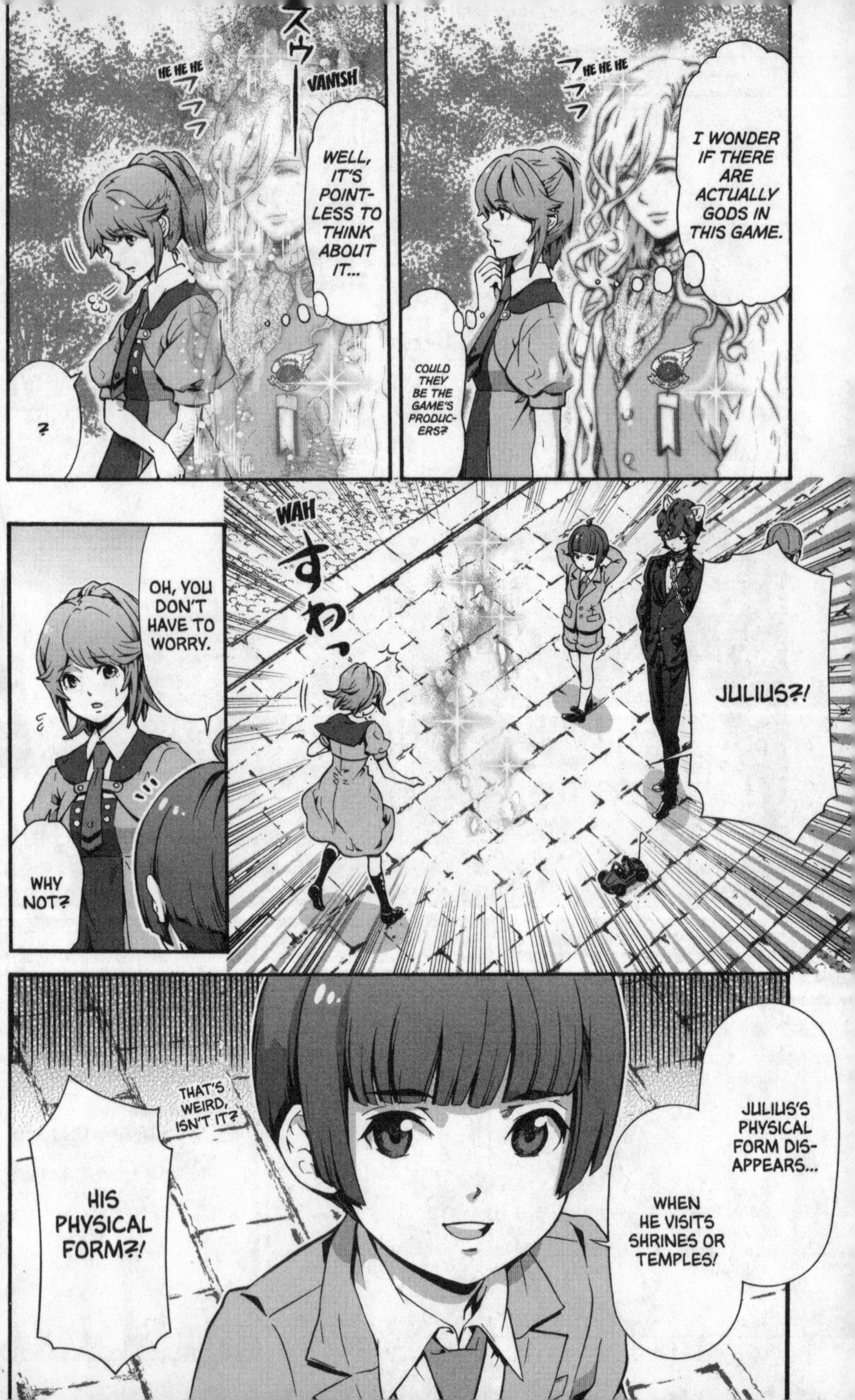

HE HE HE
I WONDER IF THERE ARE ACTUALLY GODS IN THIS GAME.
COULD THEY BE THE GAME'S PRODUCERS?
スウー
VANISH
HE HE HE
WELL, IT'S POINTLESS TO THINK ABOUT IT...
?
WAH
すわっ
JULIUS?!
OH, YOU DON'T HAVE TO WORRY.
WHY NOT?
JULIUS'S PHYSICAL FORM DISAPPEARS...
WHEN HE VISITS SHRINES OR TEMPLES!
THAT'S WEIRD, ISN'T IT?
HIS PHYSICAL FORM?!

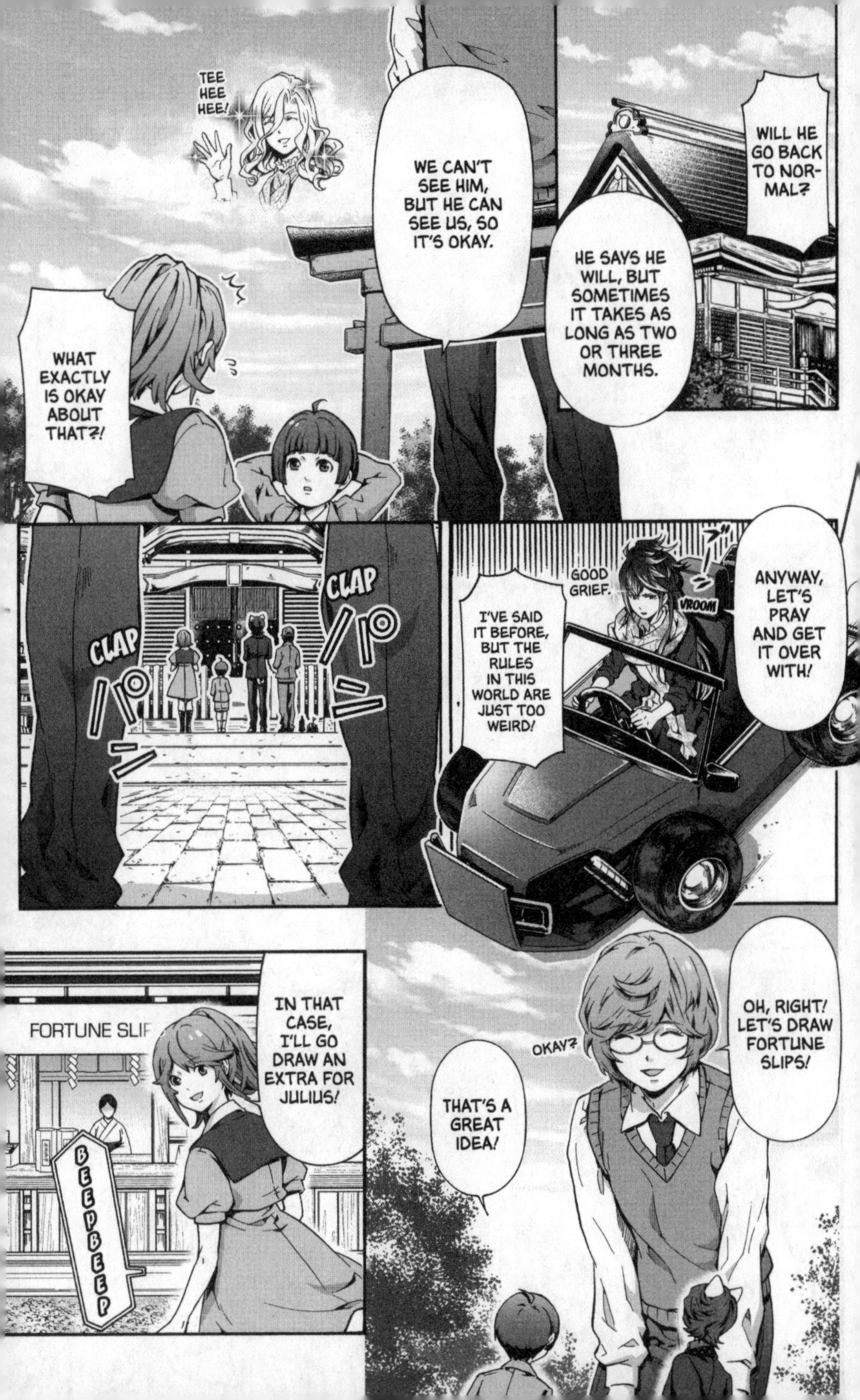
WILL HE GO BACK TO NOR-MAL?
HE SAYS HE WILL, BUT SOMETIMES IT TAKES AS LONG AS TWO OR THREE MONTHS.
TEE HEE HEE!
WE CAN'T SEE HIM, BUT HE CAN SEE US, SO IT'S OKAY.
WHAT EXACTLY IS OKAY ABOUT THAT?!
ANYWAY, LET'S PRAY AND GET IT OVER WITH!
VROOM
GOOD GRIEF.
I'VE SAID IT BEFORE, BUT THE RULES IN THIS WORLD ARE JUST TOO WEIRD!
CLAP
CLAP
OH, RIGHT! LET'S DRAW FORTUNE SLIPS!
OKAY?
THAT'S A GREAT IDEA!
IN THAT CASE, I'LL GO DRAW AN EXTRA FOR JULIUS!
FORTUNE SLIP
BEEPBEEP

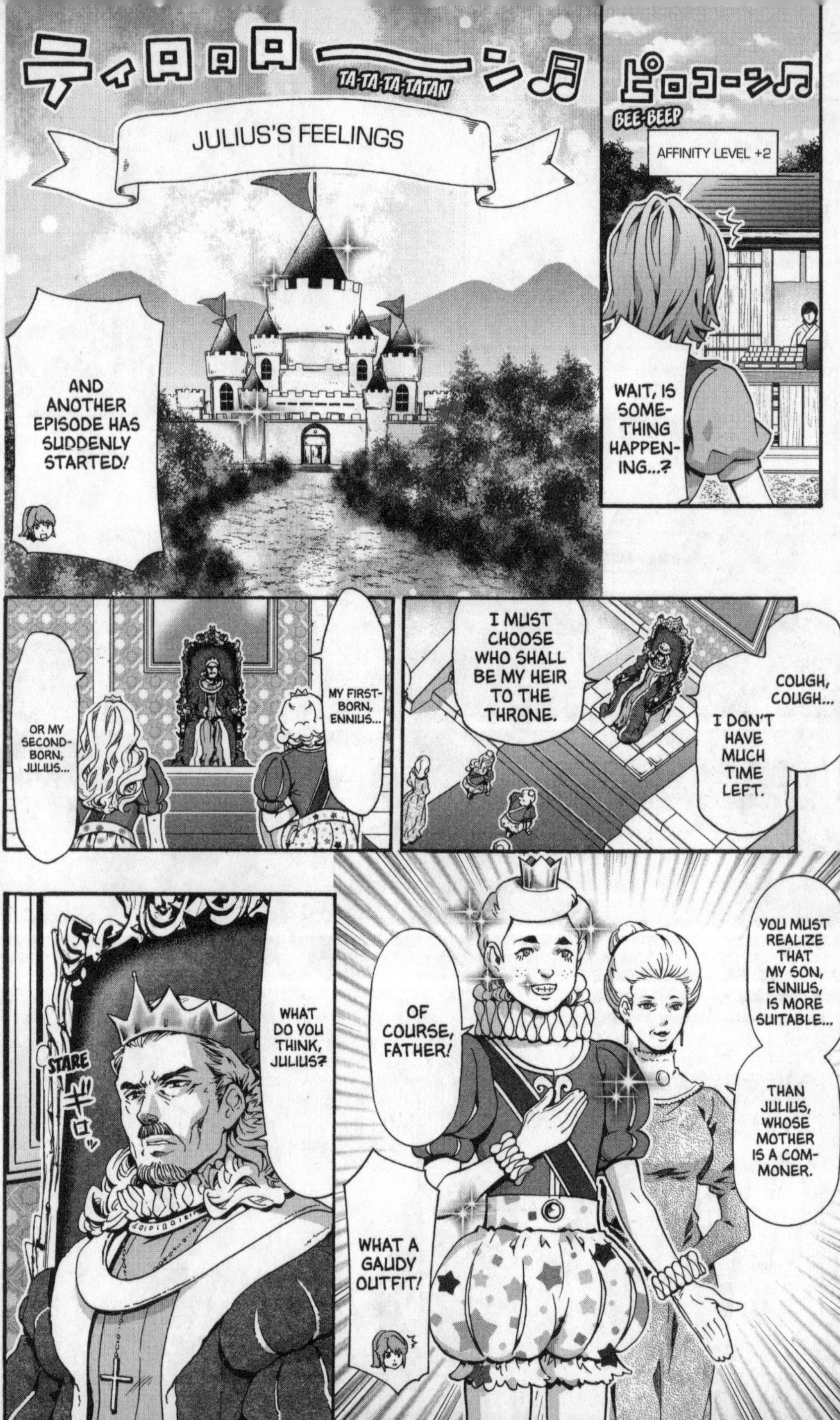

ピロコーン♫
BEE-BEEP
AFFINITY LEVEL +2
WAIT, IS SOME-THING HAPPEN-ING...?
ティロロロ——ン♫
TA-TA-TA-TATAN
JULIUS'S FEELINGS
AND ANOTHER EPISODE HAS SUDDENLY STARTED!
COUGH, COUGH...
I DON'T HAVE MUCH TIME LEFT.
I MUST CHOOSE WHO SHALL BE MY HEIR TO THE THRONE.
MY FIRST-BORN, ENNIUS...
OR MY SECOND-BORN, JULIUS...
YOU MUST REALIZE THAT MY SON, ENNIUS, IS MORE SUITABLE...
THAN JULIUS, WHOSE MOTHER IS A COM-MONER.
OF COURSE, FATHER!
WHAT A GAUDY OUTFIT!
WHAT DO YOU THINK, JULIUS?
STARE
ギロッ

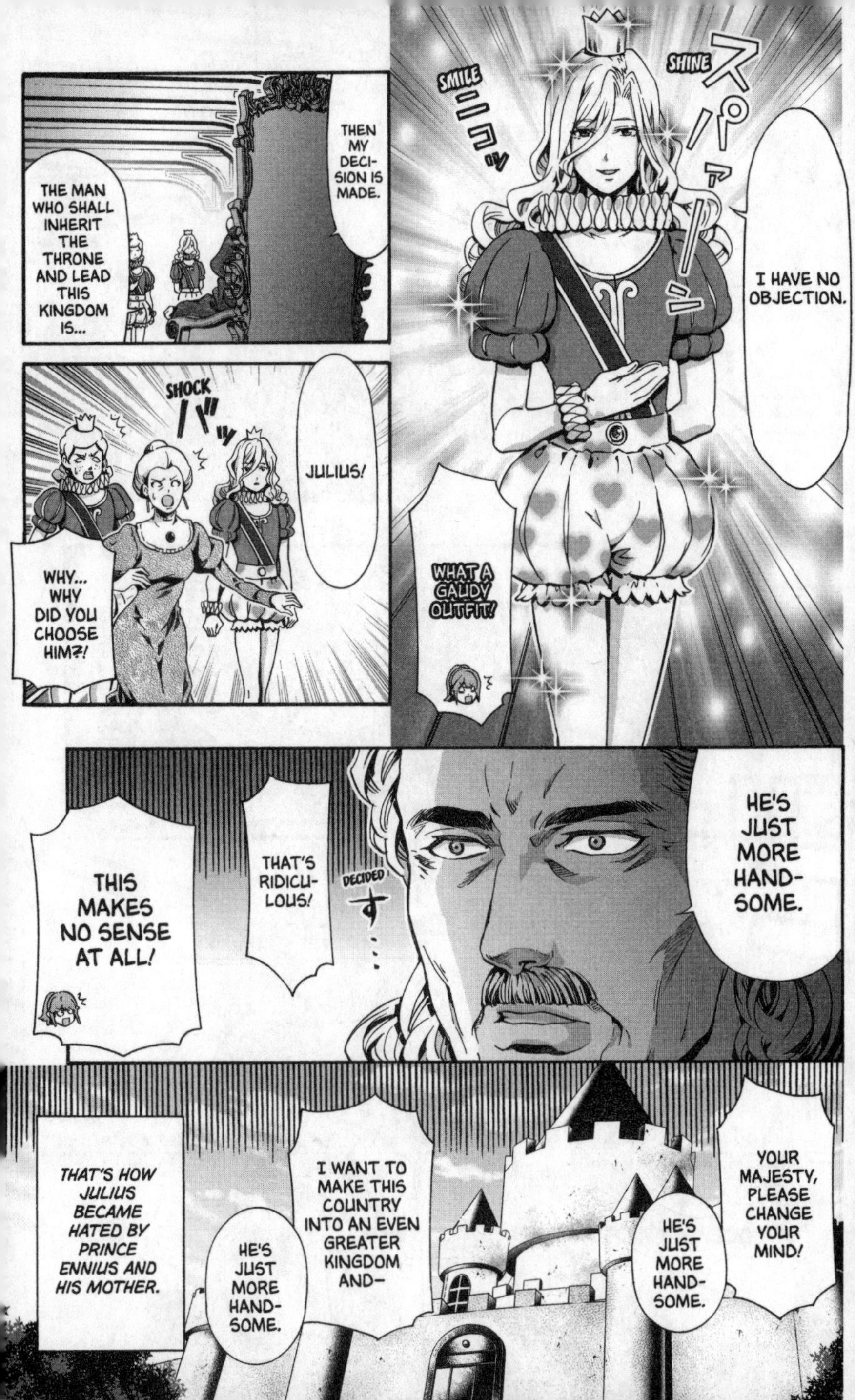
SHINE
SMILE
I HAVE NO OBJECTION.
WHAT A GAUDY OUTFIT!
THEN MY DECISION IS MADE.
THE MAN WHO SHALL INHERIT THE THRONE AND LEAD THIS KINGDOM IS...
JULIUS!
SHOCK
WHY... WHY DID YOU CHOOSE HIM?!
HE'S JUST MORE HANDSOME.
DECIDED
THAT'S RIDICULOUS!
THIS MAKES NO SENSE AT ALL!
YOUR MAJESTY, PLEASE CHANGE YOUR MIND!
HE'S JUST MORE HANDSOME.
I WANT TO MAKE THIS COUNTRY INTO AN EVEN GREATER KINGDOM AND–
HE'S JUST MORE HANDSOME.
THAT'S HOW JULIUS BECAME HATED BY PRINCE ENNIUS AND HIS MOTHER.

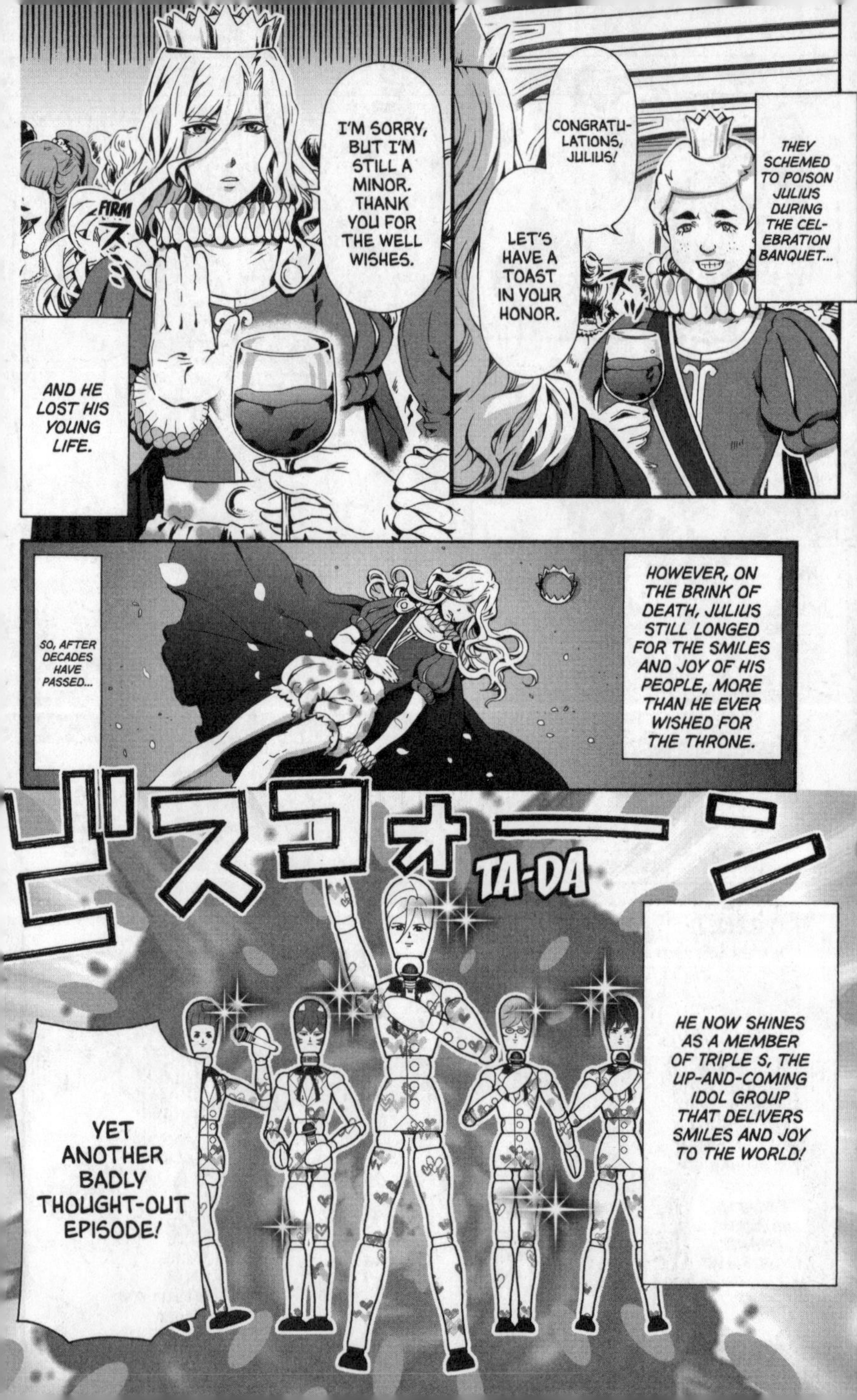
THEY SCHEMED TO POISON JULIUS DURING THE CELEBRATION BANQUET...
CONGRATULATIONS, JULIUS!
LET'S HAVE A TOAST IN YOUR HONOR.
I'M SORRY, BUT I'M STILL A MINOR. THANK YOU FOR THE WELL WISHES.
FIRM
AND HE LOST HIS YOUNG LIFE.
HOWEVER, ON THE BRINK OF DEATH, JULIUS STILL LONGED FOR THE SMILES AND JOY OF HIS PEOPLE, MORE THAN HE EVER WISHED FOR THE THRONE.
SO, AFTER DECADES HAVE PASSED...
ジスコオーーン
TA-DA
HE NOW SHINES AS A MEMBER OF TRIPLE S, THE UP-AND-COMING IDOL GROUP THAT DELIVERS SMILES AND JOY TO THE WORLD!
YET ANOTHER BADLY THOUGHT-OUT EPISODE!

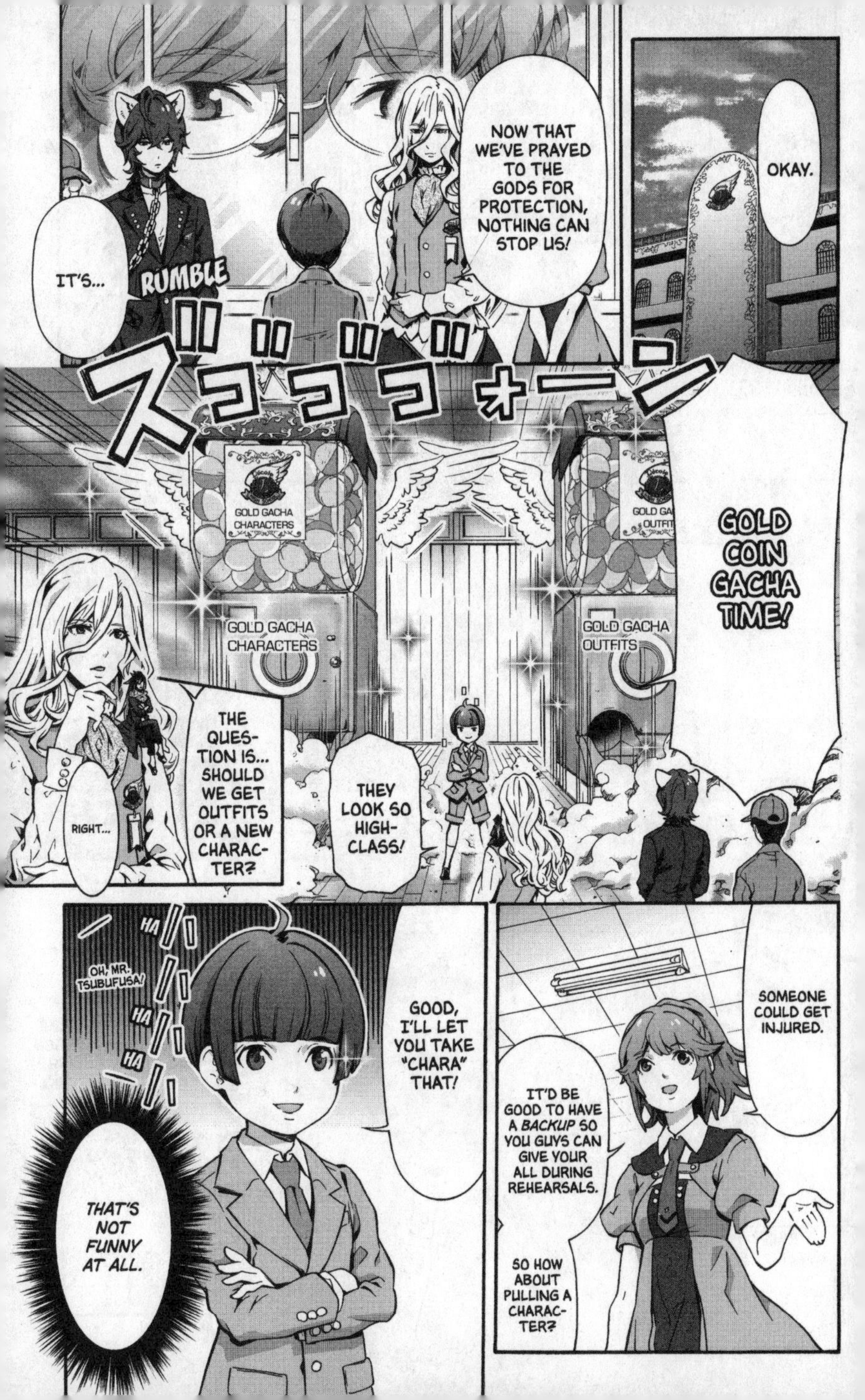
OKAY.
NOW THAT WE'VE PRAYED TO THE GODS FOR PROTECTION, NOTHING CAN STOP US!
RUMBLE
IT'S...
ズゴゴゴオーン
GOLD COIN GACHA TIME!
GOLD GACHA OUTFITS
GOLD GACHA CHARACTERS
GOLD GACHA OUTFITS
GOLD GACHA CHARACTERS
THEY LOOK SO HIGH-CLASS!
THE QUESTION IS... SHOULD WE GET OUTFITS OR A NEW CHARACTER?
RIGHT...
SOMEONE COULD GET INJURED.
IT'D BE GOOD TO HAVE A *BACKUP* SO YOU GUYS CAN GIVE YOUR ALL DURING REHEARSALS.
SO HOW ABOUT PULLING A CHARACTER?
GOOD, I'LL LET YOU TAKE "CHARA" THAT!
HA HA HA
OH, MR. TSUBUFUSA!
THAT'S NOT FUNNY AT ALL.

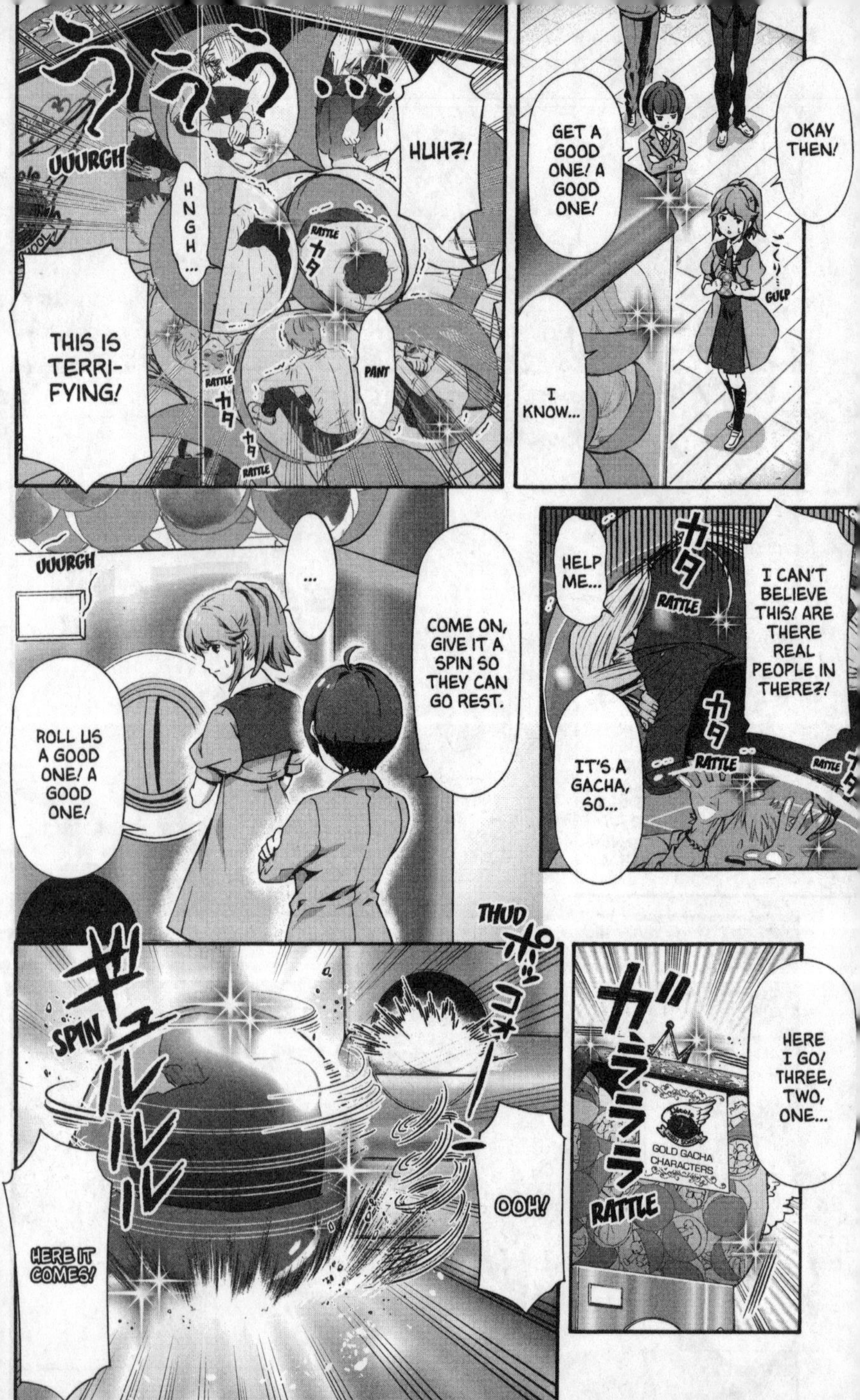
OKAY THEN!
GET A GOOD ONE! A GOOD ONE!
I KNOW...
ごくり…
GULP
HUH?!
HNGH...
UUURGH
RATTLE
カタ
THIS IS TERRI-FYING!
PANT
RATTLE
カタ
カタ
RATTLE
I CAN'T BELIEVE THIS! ARE THERE REAL PEOPLE IN THERE?!
HELP ME...
カタ
RATTLE
IT'S A GACHA, SO...
カタ
RATTLE
RATTLE
...
COME ON, GIVE IT A SPIN SO THEY CAN GO REST.
UUURGH
ROLL US A GOOD ONE! A GOOD ONE!
HERE I GO! THREE, TWO, ONE...
ガラララ
RATTLE
GOLD GACHA CHARACTERS
THUD
ポコォー
OOH!
ギュルルル
SPIN
HERE IT COMES!

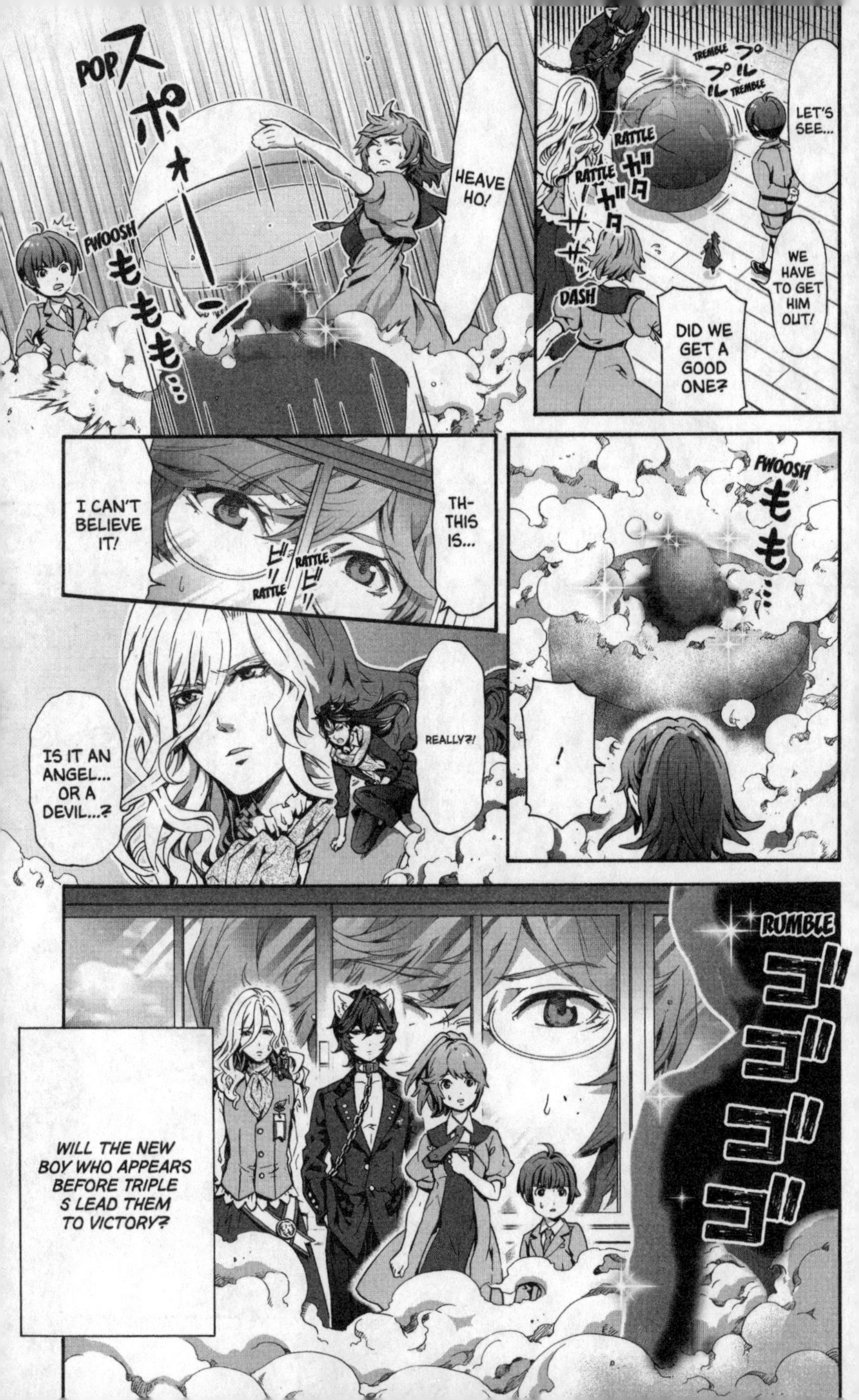
TREMBLE
TREMBLE
LET'S SEE...
RATTLE
RATTLE
ガタ
ガタ
WE HAVE TO GET HIM OUT!
DASH
DID WE GET A GOOD ONE?
POP
HEAVE HO!
FWOOSH
もももも...
FWOOSH
もも...
!
TH-THIS IS...
I CAN'T BELIEVE IT!
RATTLE
RATTLE
REALLY?!
IS IT AN ANGEL... OR A DEVIL...?
RUMBLE
WILL THE NEW BOY WHO APPEARS BEFORE TRIPLE S LEAD THEM TO VICTORY?

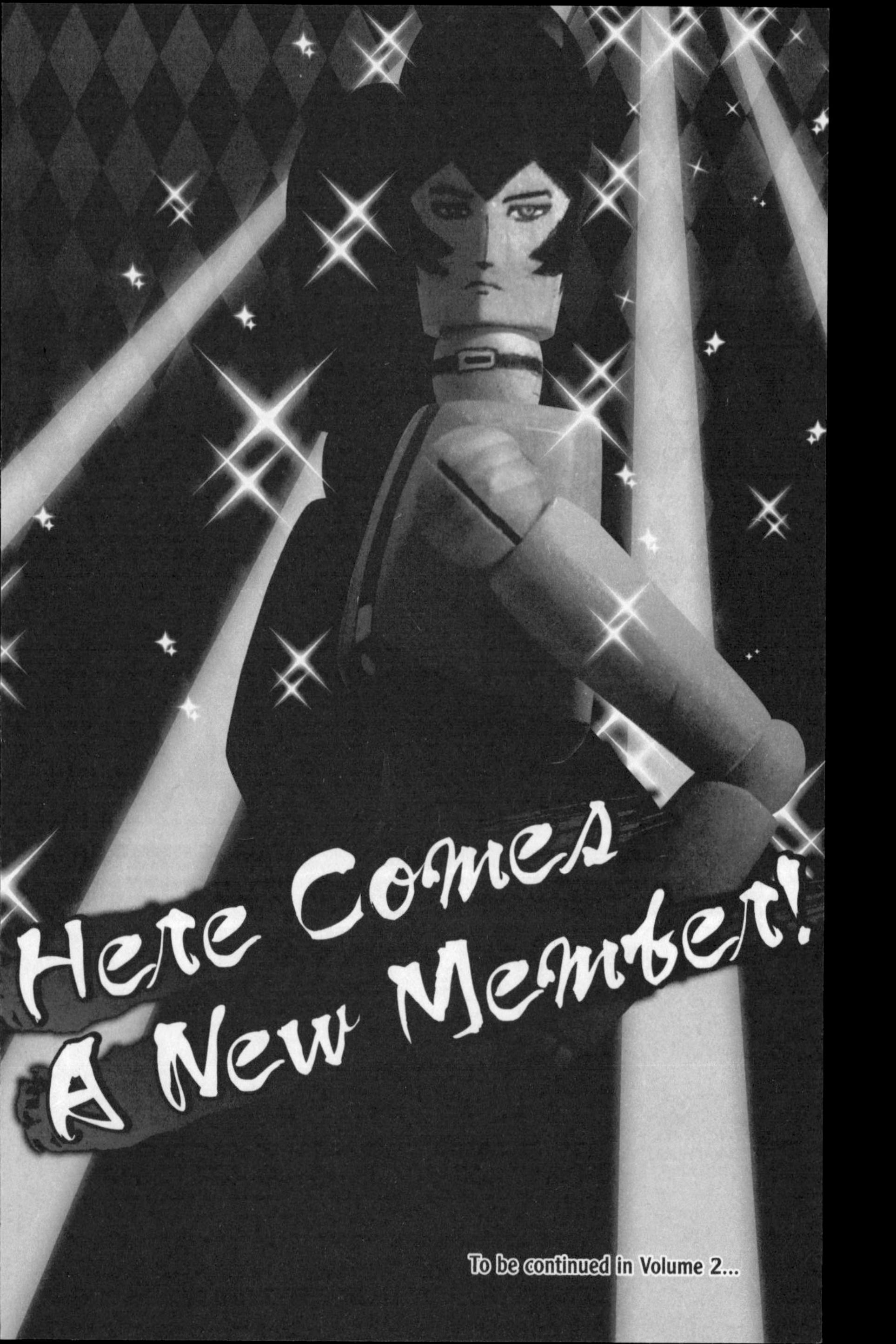
Here Comes
A New Member!
To be continued in Volume 2...

ALICE *in*
BISHOUNEN-LAND

LOVE x LOVE

TOKYOPOP believes all types of romances deserve to be celebrated. *LOVE x LOVE* was born from that idea and our commitment to representing a variety of stories and voices as diverse as our fans.

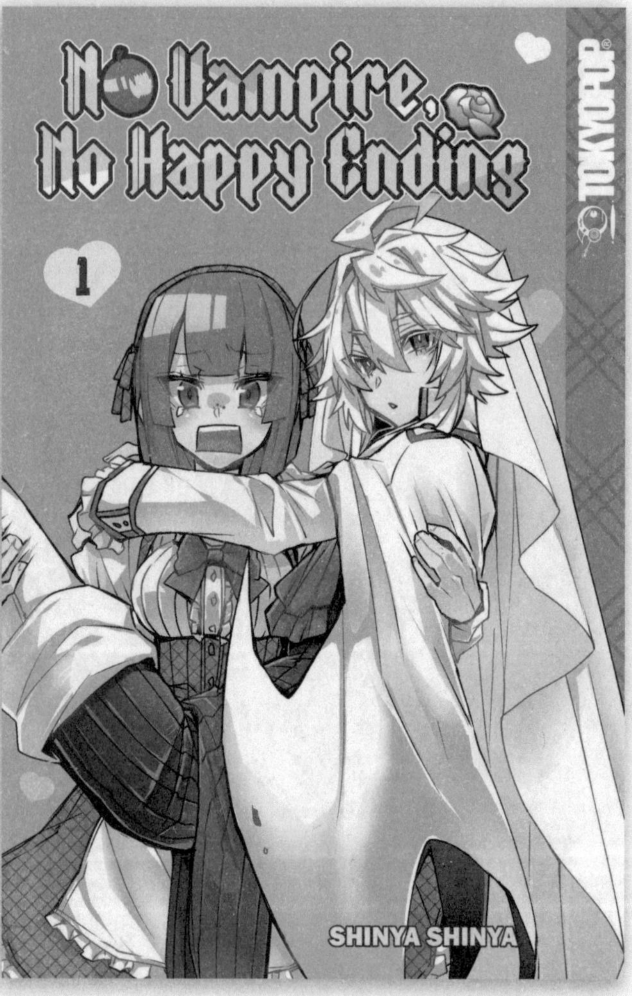
No Vampire, No Happy Ending
1
TOKYOPOP
SHINYA SHINYA

NO VAMPIRE, NO HAPPY ENDING, VOLUME 1

Shinya Shinya

LOVE-x-LOVE

Arika is what you could charitably call a vampire "enthusiast." When she stumbles across the beautiful and mysterious vampire Divo however, her excitement quickly turns to disappointment as she discovers he's not exactly like the seductive, manipulative villains in her stories. His looks win first place, but his head's a space case. Armed with her extensive knowledge of vampire lore, Arika downgrades Divo to a beta vampire and begins their long, long... long journey to educate him in the ways of the undead.

TOKYOPOP

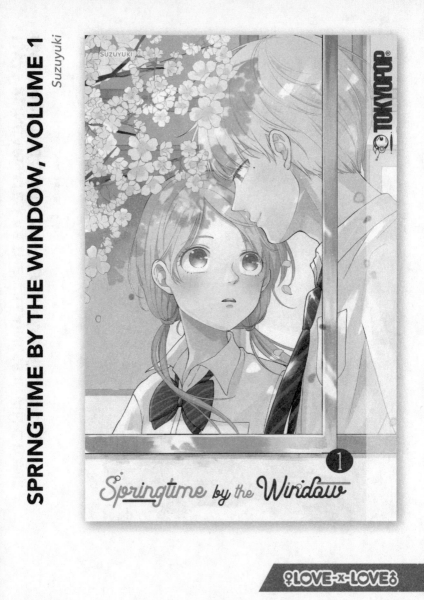

SPRINGTIME BY THE WINDOW, VOLUME 1

Suzuyuki

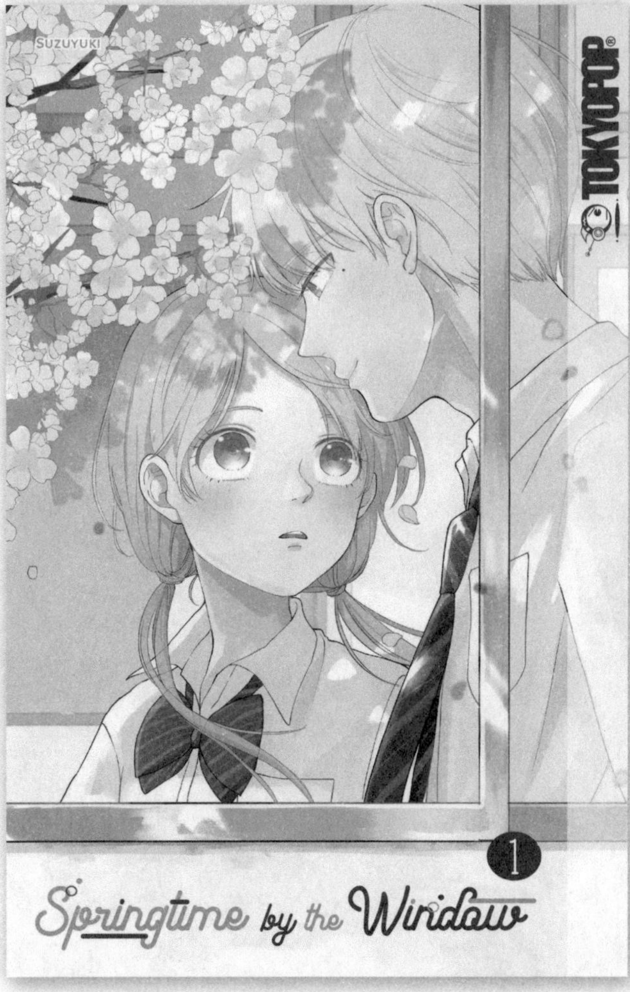
SUZUYUKI
TOKYOPOP
1
Springtime by the Window

LOVE x LOVE

TOKYOPOP

Cool and collected second-year Yamada is in love with his childhood friend, Seno. His classmates Akama and Toda are also starting to think about romance, though neither of them realizes yet that they might actually feel the same way about each other...

I WAS REINCARNATED AS THE VILLAINESS IN AN OTOME GAME BUT THE BOYS LOVE ME ANYWAY!, VOLUME 1

Ataka, Sou Inaida, Hachipisu Wan

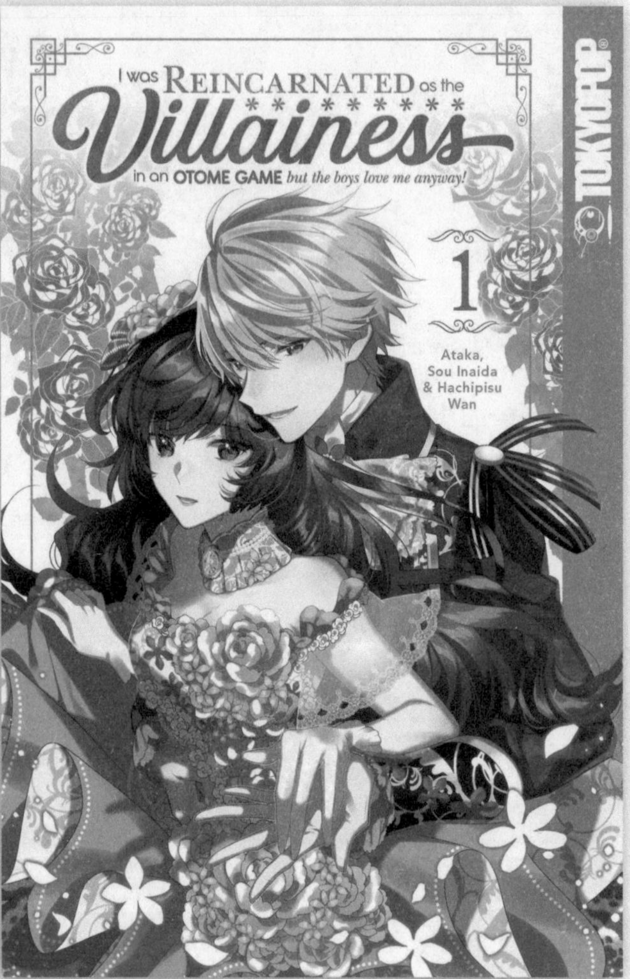
I was REINCARNATED as the
Villainess
in an OTOME GAME but the boys love me anyway!
TOKYOPOP
1
Ataka,
Sou Inaida
& Hachipisu
Wan

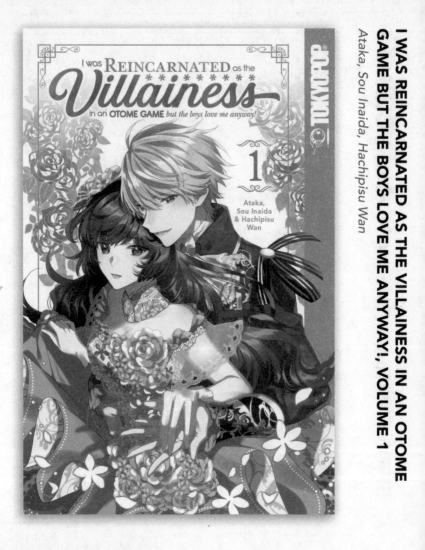

♀LOVE-x-LOVE♂

Mystia Aren is the daughter of a noble family, and she just started high school. She's surrounded by a group of adoring classmates and her charming fiancé. Everything seems perfect. Except that this world is actually a dating sim called Kyun-Love, and Mystia knows she's been reincarnated into the role of the main character's evil rival! Mystia is determined to do everything she can to avoid her fate, but it's not as easy as it sounds. Especially when all the boys keep falling in love with her!

TOKYOPOP

1

NEKO YOTSUBA,
KOU YATSUHASHI
& MITO NAGISHIRO

TOKYOPOP®

HER
Royal Highness
seems to be angry

ᛞLOVE-x-LOVEᛞ

Princess Leticiel is the most powerful sorceress of her kingdom, but as her land is ravaged by an endless war, she loses everything: her people, her family, and eventually, her own life. Until she opens her eyes and awakens in a place she's never seen before!

A thousand years have passed, and Leticiel finds herself reincarnated in the body of a duke's daughter named Drossell, a woman apparently despised by her own family and fiancé. There's a lot to be mad about, but first on the list: how on earth did future magic turn out so lame?

ALTER EGO

Ana C. Sánchez

♀LOVE-x-LOVE♀

Noel has always been in love with her best friend Elena, but she's never been able to find the courage to confess her feelings. Then, when her friend starts dating a boy, Noel's world collapses as she sees her chance at love slipping away. One night, in a moment of desperation, Noel ends up confessing her feelings for Elena to a complete stranger — but as fate would have it, this stranger turns out to be a girl named June, Elena's other best friend... and Noel's rival in love! Worst of all, now June knows Noel's secret. With everything suddenly going wrong, how can Noel ever win the girl of her dreams? The heart-pounding romantic drama by breakout Spanish artist Ana C. Sánchez!

THE TREASURE OF THE KING AND THE CAT

You Kajika

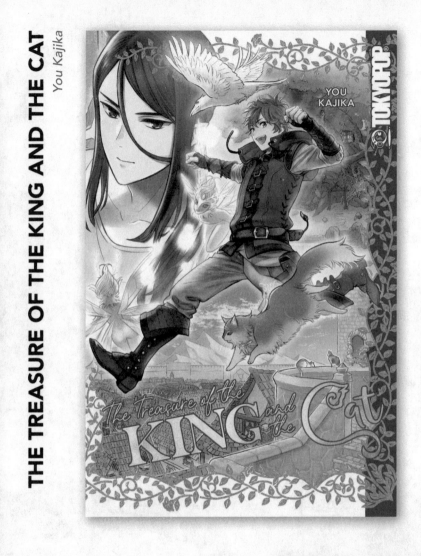

YOU KAJIKA

The Treasure of the KING and the Cat

♂LOVE-x-LOVE♂

One day, a large number of people suddenly disappeared in the royal capital. When young King Castio goes out to investigate this occurrence, he comes across the culprit... but the criminal puts a spell on him! To help him out, the king calls the wizard O'Feuille to his castle, along with Prince Volks and his loyal retainer Nios. Together, they're determined to solve this strange, fluffy mystery full of cats, swords and magic!

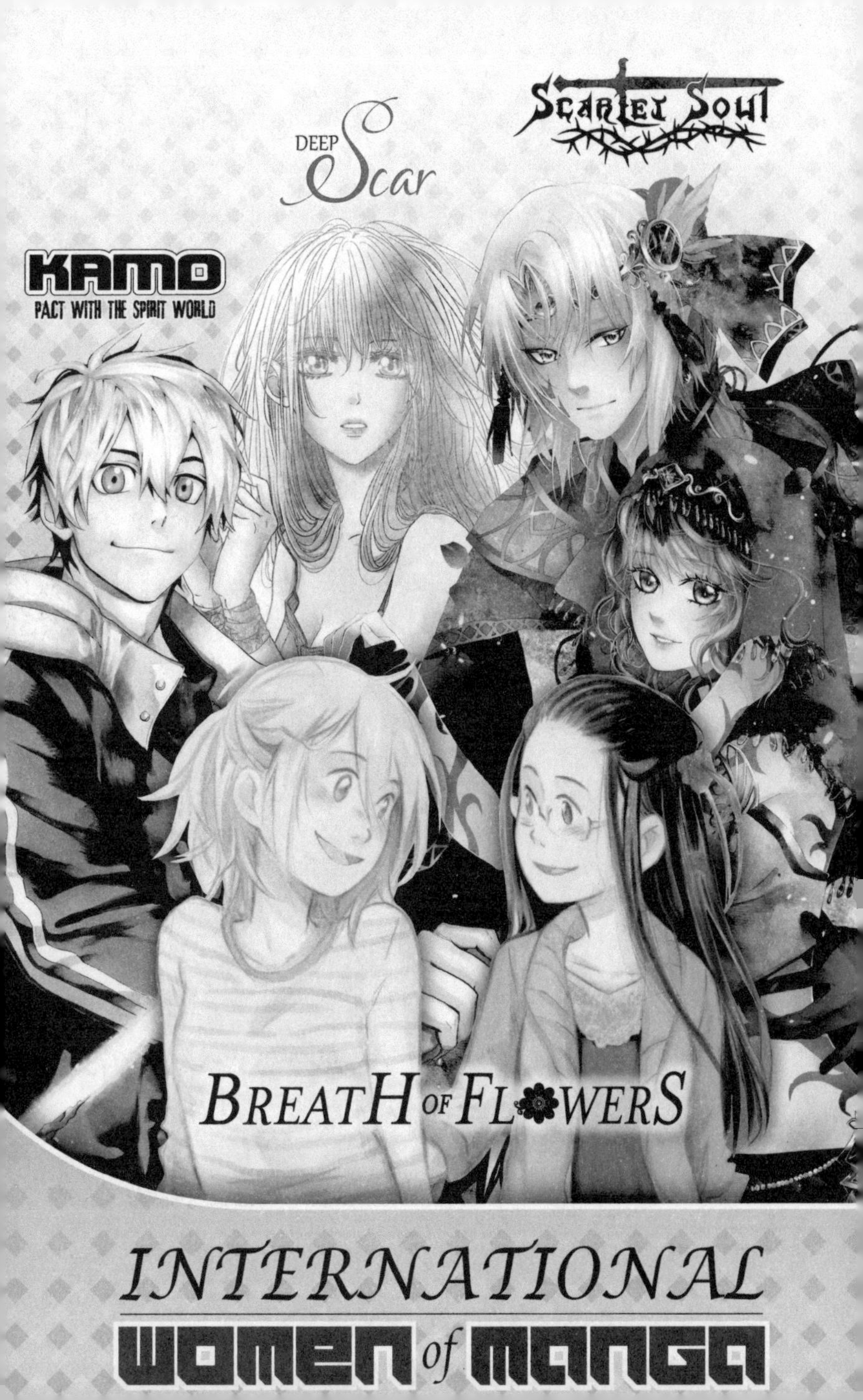

Scarlet Soul
DEEP Scar
KAMO
PACT WITH THE SPIRIT WORLD
BREATH OF FLOWERS
INTERNATIONAL
WOMEN of MANGA

SCARLET SOUL, VOLUME 1

Kira Yukishiro

The kingdom of Nohmur has been a peaceful land for humans since the exorcist Eron Shirano repelled the demons and sealed the way to the underworld of Ruhmon. Generations later, sisters Lys and Rin are the heirs of the illustrious Shirano family, the most powerful exorcist clan charged with watching over the barrier and maintaining balance between the two worlds with the aid of Hikaten, the Sword of a Hundred Souls. Until one day, for unknown reasons, demons begin slipping through once more... and suddenly, Lys vanishes without a trace, leaving the sacred sword behind for her little sister to take up. As the underworld threat grows, Rin sets out alongside her companion, the mysterious Aghyr, to find her missing sister and figure out how to fortify the weakening barrier between her world and that of the monstrous creatures that threaten her kingdom once again.

DEEP SCAR, VOLUME 1
Rossella Sergi

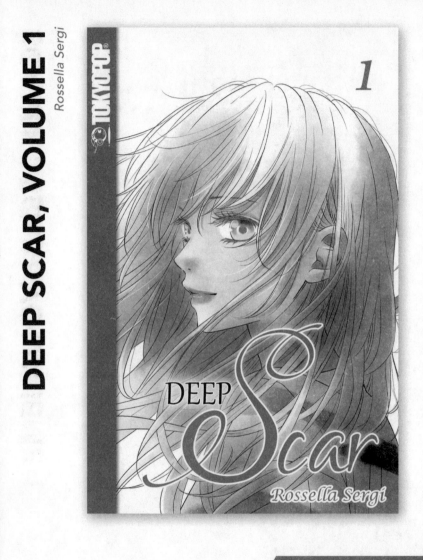

DEEP Scar

Rossella Sergi

♀LOVE-x-LOVE♂

Sofia is a quiet, shy young woman who's never been away from home for long. When she moves to Turin for school, it's her first time away from her family and her boyfriend Luca. But her new roommate, Veronica, leads a life very different from hers: she prefers evenings in the company of beautiful boys! Meanwhile, Luca dreads the influence of Veronica and her entourage on Sofia, and especially the presence of the enigmatic Lorenzo, who seems to be a little too interested in his girlfriend...

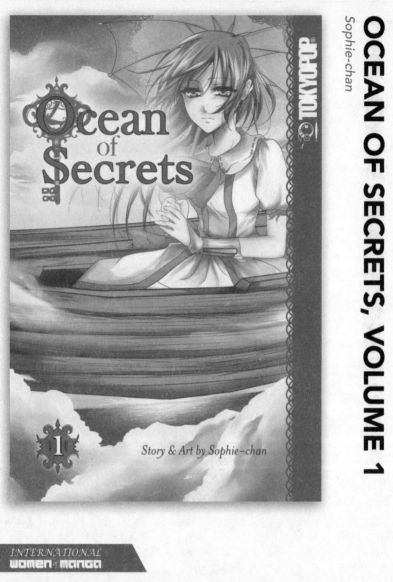

Lia, a 17-year old orphan living by the Atlantic is swept away by the ocean currents during a ruthless storm. She is then saved by Moria and Albert, a duo of illegal runaways on their magical ship! Her normal, mundane life suddenly becomes a supernatural adventure as she learns about the powers of their kind and their relations to the human world. But Lia soon discovers that there is a dark secret hidden in a mysterious kingdom. Join Lia as she unlocks the truth behind an Ocean of Secrets...

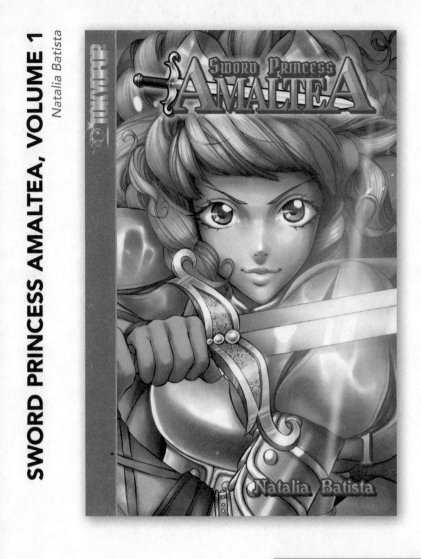

SWORD PRINCESS AMALTEA, VOLUME 1
Natalia Batista

We all know the way the story goes. The valiant prince goes on a perilous journey, kills a ferocious dragon, rescues a captive princess, earns his family's honor. But what if this time the prince... was a princess? In a fairytale world where Queens rule and magic is power, Princess Amaltea is sent on the biggest quest of her life — to rescue a prince in need and fulfill her duties as a princess. Spoiled, prejudiced and sheltered from the world at large, Amaltea reluctantly sets out on her journey and finds her "lad in distress"... only to find out he's not so willing to join her.

Alice in Bishounen-Land, Volume 1

Story: Yushi Kawata
Art: Yukito

Editor - Lena Atanassova
Translator - Claudia Takizawa
Quality Check - Shingo Nemoto
Copy Editor - Tina Tseng
Proofreader - Katie Kimura
Graphic Designer - Sol DeLeo
Marketing Associate - Kae Winters
Editorial Associate - Janae Young
Retouching and Lettering - Vibrraant Publishing Studio
Licensing Specialist - Arika Yanaka
Editor-in-Chief & Publisher - Stu Levy

A 🔵 **TOKYOPOP**® Manga

TOKYOPOP and 🔵 are trademarks or registered trademarks of TOKYOPOP Inc.

TOKYOPOP Inc.
5200 W. Century Blvd. Suite 705
Los Angeles, 90045

E-mail: info@TOKYOPOP.com
Come visit us online at www.TOKYOPOP.com

f www.facebook.com/TOKYOPOP
🐦 www.twitter.com/TOKYOPOP
📷 www.instagram.com/TOKYOPOP

©Yushi Kawata 2020 ©Yukito 2020 /
HERO'S INC.

Originally published by HERO'S INC.

ISBN: 978-1-4278-6908-1
First TOKYOPOP Printing: December 2021
Printed in CANADA

STOP

THIS IS THE BACK OF THE BOOK!

How do you read manga-style? It's simple!
Let's practice -- just start in the top right panel and follow the numbers below!

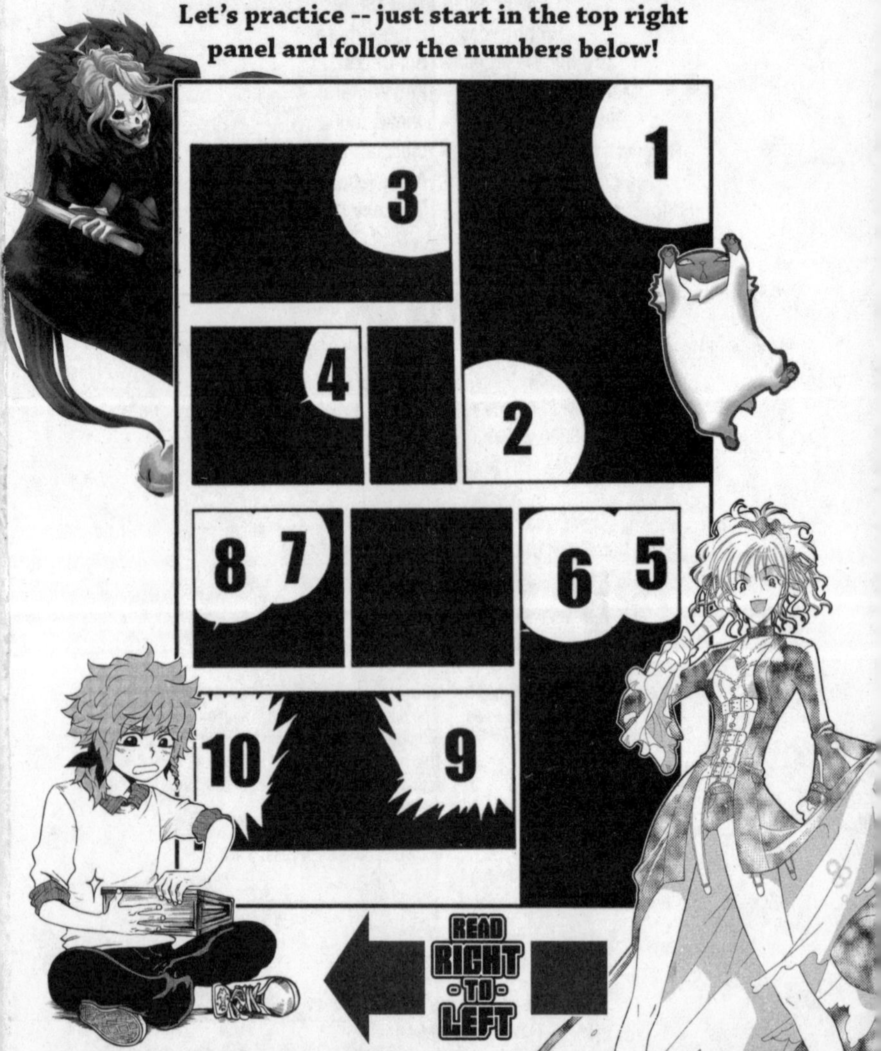

1
2
3
4
5
6
7
8
9
10
READ
RIGHT
-TO-
LEFT

Crimson from ***Kamo*** / Fairy Cat from ***Grimms Manga Tales***
Morrey from ***Goldfisch*** / Princess Ai from ***Princess Ai***